P9-DGU-578

Underage & Overweight

America's Childhood Obesity Crisis— What Every Family Needs to Know

Underage & Overweight

America's Childhood Obesity Crisis— What Every Family Needs to Know

Frances M. Berg, MS, LN

A HEALTHY LIVING BOOK

HATHERLEIGH PRESS

New York

Underage and Overweight
America's Childhood Obesity Crisis—What Every Family Needs to Know

Frances M. Berg

Hatherleigh Press
5-22 46th Avenue
Long Island City, NY 11101
1-800-528-2550

www.hatherleighpress.com

Library of Congress Cataloging-in-Publication Data available upon request

ISBN 1-57826-120-1

All Hatherleigh Press titles are available for special promotions and premiums. For more information, please contact the manager of our Special Sales department.

Cover design by Lisa Fyfe

Printed in Canada on acid-free paper

10 9 8 7 6 5 4 3 2

Contents

PREFACE

> "For the first time in the history of this country, young people are less healthy and less prepared to take their places in society than were their parents."
>
> —*National Commission on Role of School and Community in Improving Adolescent Health, CDC, 1990*

Fifteen percent of American children are overweight—three times as many as only 30 years ago—and another 15 percent are at risk for overweight. They are at risk for obesity and its associated health problems, as well as for related weight and eating problems including eating disorders and dysfunctional eating, hazardous weight loss, size prejudice, body hatred, and severe nutrient deficiencies.

How did we get here? The problem is extraordinarily complex. We need to step back and consider the root causes of this epidemic and question the prevailing wisdom. In the study of weight, many scientists have set out to prove their own certainties and failed to turn an objective eye on the results. Policy makers, healthcare providers, and the media have followed their lead, victimizing the very people who need their help.

Underage and Overweight untangles this multifaceted issue, exploring the roots of the problem and why past solutions have not worked. The book advocates an approach that embraces the whole family in sound physical, mental, and emotional health. Parents are assured that both smaller and larger children are a normal part of the human spectrum, and they can be healthy at their natural sizes.

Underage and Overweight brings parents a seven-step plan that helps them realign priorities and establish healthy non-diet lifestyles in their children's lives. It's a flexible plan that provides a sound foundation for the child's long-term healthy weight.

With this approach your child enjoys activity, eats normally without fear, builds self respect, and learns assertiveness and healthy coping skills. Creating a nurturing environment in which children feel good about themselves and others is one of a parent's most important tasks. All children deserve this.

PART I

♦ ♦ ❖ ♦ ♦ ❖ ♦ ♦ ❖ ♦ ♦ ❖ ♦ ♦ ❖ ♦ ♦ ❖ ♦ ♦

Battle for Our Children's Health

Chapter 1

♦ ♦ ❖ ♦ ♦ ❖ ♦ ♦ ❖ ♦ ♦ ❖ ♦ ♦ ❖ ♦ ♦ ❖ ♦ ♦

America's Childhood Obesity Crisis

"More American Children and Teens are Overweight"
—*Centers for Disease Control and Prevention Press Release March 12, 2001*

"Growing Up Too Fat, Kids Suffer Adult Ailments"
—*San Francisco Chronicle, May 12, 2002*

"Hospital Tab for Obese Kids: $127M a Year"
—*USA Today, April 30, 2002*

One can hardly pick up a newspaper or turn on the television without hearing the disturbing news that overweight is on the rise—for children as well as adults. It's front page news, the topic of television documentaries and talk show interviews with alarmed heart specialists.

And it's true. The prevalence of overweight has increased sharply since the early 1980s. Solid evidence for the increase comes from the National Health and Nutrition Examination Studies (NHANES), the nation's most comprehensive look at our health and nutrition. In this series of multiyear studies, beginning in the mid 1960s, large, representative samples of Americans were interviewed, weighed, measured, and clinically tested in mobile clinical centers. Our newest statistics, based on the 1999-2000 NHANES, provide the following findings for childhood overweight (that is, children whose weight falls at or above the 95th percentile):[1]

- ★ 15 percent of children age six to 19 are overweight.
- ★ 10 percent of children age two to five are overweight.

What alarms public health officials is that overweight rates for children have been steadily increasing since the 1960s and 1970s, when they had remained fairly stable, at about 5 to 6 percent. A comparison of the above statistics with those of previous years clearly illustrates the increasing prevalence of overweight for children and adolescents aged six to nineteen:

- ★ 5 percent were overweight in 1963 to 1970.
- ★ 6 percent were overweight in 1971 to 1980.
- ★ 11 percent were overweight in 1988 to 1994.
- ★ 13 percent were overweight in 1999.
- ★ 15 percent were overweight in 1999 to 2000.

Overweight rates doubled in the 1980s, and have now tripled. The studies also found that not only are more American youngsters overweight today, but they are more severely overweight than ever before.[2] The sobering statistics for overweight teenagers are of particular concern because the older they are, the more likely it is they will become overweight adults.

The target set for *Healthy People 2010,* the ten-year health goals for the nation from the U.S. Department of Health and Human Services, is to reduce the percentages to a more normal 5 percent.[3] Unfortunately, this is not likely to happen.

The Big Picture

Though statistics on the prevalence of overweight in children are staggering, it is important to consider them in their proper context—not all kids are gaining weight. However, there are more overweight children now than there were in the past.

A few decades ago there was perhaps one large child in a class of twenty students—now there are two or three. In areas with low income or high minority populations as many as half of the students may be overweight.

Nonetheless, if you go to a school and look around you'll see that most children and teenagers are quite slender. They are representative of that other 85 percent of children, whose body types range from tall and rail thin to short with soft curves, and everything in between. In this 85 percent you will see the signs of children moving through natural stages of puberty, rapid growth, and emerging maturity. It is important to remember that the weights of children, other than the 15 percent who are overweight, have remained steady over the past three decades.[4]

Yet if we use current adult rates of overweight to project the future for our typical class of twenty, six students will become obese and six will become overweight as they reach adulthood.[5] And as percentages of childhood overweight continue to rise, so do risks for a new generation of adults susceptible to weight-related health conditions.

A similar pattern of increasing weight for children can be seen worldwide. Western European countries have generally had lower overweight rates than the U.S. But in Germany a recent survey found that in the past twenty years rates rose from 5 percent to 8 percent for boys and from 5 percent to 10 percent for girls. The peak increase came during the last decade.[6]

Some of the highest rates of obesity in the world are found in Polynesia, as people move from rural areas to the cities, changing both their activity levels and nutrition practices. About 77 percent of women in American Samoa and 63 percent of native Hawaiian women have a body mass index (BMI) of 27 or more. One study in Hawaii found an average BMI of 31 for both men and women.

Obesity is less common in Africa and Asia, but is becoming more prevalent in urban areas and is growing as people move into larger cities.[7] And there is every reason to expect that obesity and its associated health risks will extend globally in the future as developing countries modernize. Thus, prevention is of critical concern throughout the world.

What is BMI?

Body mass index is determined as follows:

★ BMI (Metric formula) = Weight in kilograms divided by height in meters, squared, or wt/ht^2

★ BMI (American formula) = Weight in pounds divided by height in inches, squared, times 703

BMI is used to measure and track children's weight through the CDC growth charts. For children, overweight is defined as BMI-for-age at or above the 95th percentile. (BMI Charts are available at www.cdc.gov/growthcharts.)

Higher Rates for Minorities

In the United States, children of African-American, Hispanic, and Native-American descent as well as those from low-income families are most susceptible to weight gain. The 1999–2000 NHANES study that found 15 percent of all teenagers to be overweight indicated that the rates were higher for minority populations—23 percent of Mexican-Americans aged twelve to nineteen and 24 percent of African-Americans were overweight compared to 13 percent of Caucasians.

This same study indicated that younger children (ages six to eleven) were slightly less overweight than teens. Among Mexican-American children, 24 percent were overweight at ages six to eleven and 20 percent of African-American children compared to 12 percent of Caucasian. Ethnic differences were slight at age two to five: 11 percent of Mexican-American children, 8 percent of African-American children, and 10 percent of Caucasian children were overweight.

African-American children tend to be taller, heavier, and mature earlier than their Caucasian counterparts. This was readily apparent in the results of a Harlem study that found ten year old African-American girls to be 11 pounds heavier, an inch and a half taller, and higher body fat percentage than Caucasian girls of the same age, and also reached puberty at an earlier age.[8]

The prevalence of overweight is also high for Native-American children.[9] A Zuni study found more than half of girls and one-third of boys overweight. Among Cherokee teens, half of boys and one-fourth of girls were overweight.[10] Among Pima Indians, who suffer extremely high rates of type 2 diabetes associated with obesity, about half of children exceeded the 95th percentile.[11]

A high incidence of overweight can also be seen among minority preschoolers from low-income families. In 1998 among preschoolers in the low-income Women, Infants and Children supplemental nutrition program, Native-American children had the highest rates of overweight at 19 percent, while Hispanic children were close at 16 percent.

TABLE 1.1 **Prevalence of Overweight or at Risk for Overweight in Children by Sex and Age Group (NHANES 1999-2000)**[a]

Sex	Age	Overweight or at Risk[a]	Overweight[b]
	(years)	(percent)	(percent)
Both sexes	2-5	21	10
	6-11	30	15
	12-19	30	16
Male	2-5	30	10
	6-11	33	16
	12-19	31	16
Female	2-5	20	11
	6-11	28	15
	12-19	30	16

[a] Body mass index for age in the 85th percentile or higher.
[b] Body mass index for age in the 95th percentile or higher.

Defining Overweight and Risk

Body Mass Index value, a measure of weight to height, is used to define obesity and overweight in adults, as follows:

- ⋆ *Overweight:* BMI of 25 to 29.9
- ⋆ *Obesity:* BMI of 30 or more

These cut-off points are being used to help establish a relationship between weight and risk factors for chronic disease and premature death in adults.[12]

For children, BMI is plotted on growth charts that are carefully calibrated for age and gender, which helps parents and health professionals trace the pattern of a child's growth from ages two to twenty as compared with averages compiled from large groups of children.[13]

Educators and children's specialists have emphatically warned against labeling children obese. The Guidelines for Childhood Obesity Prevention programs, developed by nutrition experts in the Weight Realities Division of the Society for Nutrition Education, advise against emphasizing obesity and its risks, warning, "This can contribute to fear, shame, disturbed eating, social discrimination, and size harassment. Special thought should be given to assessments so that stigmatization and humiliation are avoided." Mindful of potential criticism, health authorities have established categories for children that roughly correspond to the adult definitions of Overweight and Obesity:

* *Overweight:* 95th percentile and above
* *At risk:* 85th to 95th percentile

Based on the current standard, 15 percent of children are overweight and 15 percent of children are "at risk" for overweight.[14]

The 95th percentile is used as the cut-off point for defining childhood overweight because it is less likely to include children who are muscular, or in the midst of puberty fat changes and growth spurts. It is important to remember that even at the 95th percentile, weight is only one of many factors used to gauge potential health risks for children. A thoughtful determination of overweight is not made based on weight alone. Other factors considered when defining childhood overweight include: percent body fat, fat distribution on the body, stage of maturity, physical activity, family history, and genetic influences. For example, though the weight of a growing athlete may fall above the 95th percentile he would not be considered overweight because of his high muscle-to-fat ratio. The weights of early-maturing youngsters also tend to fall above the 95th percentile.

Thus, the designated cut-off points should be used as reference guides only within the context of other factors in each child's overall health, maturity level and family history. As federal health advisors point out, the risks associated with overweight are part of a continuum for each individual and do not conform to rigid cut-off points.[15]

Problems with a Definition Based on Weight

Using weight as the sole criterion to identify potential health risks is problematic because studies suggest that excess body fat and its location—not weight—is associated with increased health risks.[16] A Swedish research study that followed 735 men over a lifetime found that in all weight categories the men who had the lowest percentage of body fat and highest percent of muscle mass lived longer. The researchers concluded that BMI did not accurately predict risk for individuals because it did not provide an accurate measurement of body fat percentage.[17] The *Healthy People 2010* report agreed, "Simple, health-oriented definitions of overweight and obesity should be based on the amount of excess body fat at which health risks to individuals begin to increase."

Unfortunately, no such definitions exist. Body fat is not easy to measure accurately, so the assumption is made that higher weight equals higher percentage of body fat, which in turn equals higher health risk.

Therefore, health policy makers have accepted the weight cut-off points as indicators for potential health risks. This system works for large groups and comparisons between these groups, because on average those with higher BMIs have the higher body fat associated with health risks. But it doesn't work well for individuals. Too many children and adults fall outside those average levels of body fat percentages. Within each weight group body fat percentages vary greatly.

Children in particular grow and develop in widely different ways. At the same age, especially around puberty, kids represent vastly different sizes and build—just ask any sixth grade teacher. A recent nutrition study of 979 children ages three to eighteen at the U.S. Department of Agriculture drew attention to the extent of this error. One-fourth of the children labeled as "at risk" for overweight turned out to have normal body fat percentages. There were further errors for children with high body fat who weighed in at much lower levels. One of every six children with a normal weight had a high percentage of body fat that ranged from 10 to 40 percent. Mislabeling so many children is a major concern, USDA researchers warn.[18]

Apple, Pear, or In Between?

The location of fat on the body can foreshadow health problems for overweight children and adults. Excess fat concentrated in the upper body or abdomen, in a centralized pattern, is referred to as an *apple shaped* body type, and has been linked to risk factors for chronic diseases. When excess fat accumulates in the lower body, thighs and hips, it is referred to as a *pear shaped* body type, and indicates diminished health risk.[19]

Genetic factors largely determine where excess fat will be deposited. African-American and Mexican-American children tend to have more upper body fat (apple shape) than Caucasian children. This accumulation of upper body fat increases with age, particularly for boys. People with apple-shaped bodies have larger waist measurements than their pear-shaped counterparts, so waist circumference is used as another way of assessing potential health risks.[20]

Another factor considered when assessing health risks is whether excess abdominal fat is visceral (located internally) or subcutaneous (just under the skin). Adults with more visceral fat tend to have higher risk for obesity-related health problems, such as heart disease. It can be measured by the height of the abdomen while the individual is lying on his or her back. In contrast, subcutaneous fat tends to fall to the side and the abdomen to compress.[21]

Shifting Fat Patterns

Body fat shifts over the years as children grow and develop. Infants have an extremely high percentage of body fat, needed to fuel rapid growth in early months. The percentage of body fat decreases between ages two and five as toddlers stretch out and grow taller. Between the ages of five and seven children undergo a normal fat rebound, which may be a sign they will soon experience a growth spurt.

In plotting growth on charts, a child may fall around the 50th percentile, which is average, or at either the thin or heavy end of the spectrum. Some shorter or lighter children will consistently follow the 5th percentile curve over a period of years. Other taller or heavier children will consistently follow the 95th percentile curve. This is considered normal, according to Ellyn Satter, a recognized authority on feeding children. Major deviations in the child's usual curve may be of concern, suggesting a disruption of growth that may need to be monitored.[22]

Before puberty and during adolescence boys lose some of their fat as they grow taller and more muscular. Conversely, girls continue putting on fat through puberty as their bodies mature and accumulate the fat needed later in life for successful pregnancies.[23]

How—and Why?

So why did it happen? Why this big increase in weight from 5 percent of children in the 1960s to 15 percent in 2003? Is it our sedentary lifestyle? Do kids just eat too much or eat too much of the wrong foods? Has restrictive dieting backfired? Is overweight related to genetic vulnerability? Infection? Or is due to our biggest population increases occurring in the very groups most vulnerable to obesity?

Fifteen years ago obesity researchers examined their data on child and adult weight gains, and shook their heads, "We haven't seen anything yet," they said, "just wait until these kids grow up."

The time to wait and see is over. The time to act is now.

Chapter 2

♦ ♦ ❖ ♦ ♦ ❖ ♦ ♦ ❖ ♦ ♦ ❖ ♦ ♦ ❖ ♦ ♦ ❖ ♦ ♦

The Dangers of Childhood Obesity

Ten-year-old Shirleisa Rogers gives herself a shot of insulin three times a day—in the fat on the back of her right arm, in the back of her left arm, and in her stomach.[24] *One might think Shirleisa is too young to give herself shots—and certainly too young to have type 2 diabetes, a disease so rare in children that it was known earlier as "adult onset" diabetes.*

Only a few years ago, that would have been true. Pediatricians seldom saw the disease in children and teens, except as type 1 (then called "juvenile" diabetes). But Shirleisa weighs over 200 pounds. Now at Children's Hospital in Oakland, where she and other severely obese children from northern California go for treatment, specialists see two to five youngsters a day with this disease.

"I'm looking nine-year-olds in the eye and talking to them about their bodies as if they are fifty- or sixty-year-olds," said Barbara King-Hooper, a nurse educator at the Oakland hospital.

She and other health care providers see teenage boys with hip bones forced from their sockets. They treat girls with hormonal changes so altered they are growing beards. They prescribe high blood pressure pills for twelve-year-olds and warn patients of potential heart attacks or strokes. Neck, elbows and joints might develop thick, velvety skin folds that become dark with pigment, a consequence of insulin resistance associated with obesity.[25] Type 2 diabetes is closely linked to overweight and obesity. And like others around the country, California's kids are the fattest they've ever been.

How can we as a nation turn this around? How do we reduce the effects of weight-related illness for these kids? How can we prevent this crisis from recurring for the next generation of children?

It can be done, and needs to begin right now. Prevention will take a concerted national effort that must go forward in a way that does no harm, that heals and promotes health and well-being for every child, no matter what their size or weight. Our children deserve no less.

Kids' Health Risks

Type 2 diabetes has been rising steadily in children, according to reports from clinics around the country. African-American, Hispanic and Native-American kids, who have the highest rates of obesity, are especially vulnerable.

During the 1990s, cases of diagnosed diabetes for all ages rose 33 percent nationwide, with a 38 percent increase among Hispanics. There are no national figures for minority children, but studies in Cincinnati, Charleston, Los Angeles, San Antonio, and other large inner city areas show that newly diagnosed diabetes cases have risen from less than 5 percent of children in 1994 to 30 to 50 percent.[26]

Diabetes is the seventh leading cause of death in this country and a major contributor to such health problems as heart disease, stroke, blindness, high blood pressure, kidney disease, and amputations.[27] Experts warn that the strongest impact of the obesity upsurge on increased diabetes rates may be felt some years from now, because of the delay between its onset and the subsequent development of diabetes.

While the increase in diabetes is causing the most immediate concerns, a rise in other troubling conditions parallels the rise in overweight. Risk factors for heart disease, such as high cholesterol and high blood pressure, occur with increased frequency in overweight children and adolescents.[28]

> *Billy, age 12, weighs 210 pounds. He can't play outside after school, because he's a latch-key kid—his mom tells him to get off the bus, come straight inside, lock the door, then call her so she knows he's home. Heart disease runs in the family, and Billy's blood pressure sometimes runs high—but his mom is too busy to take him to the park or on a walk. Gym class isn't much fun for him and he participates as little as possible. His mom and dad watch a lot of TV and are tired when they get home at night, so Billy sits in front of the TV most of the evening.*
>
> *Billy eats a good breakfast and lunch, but also eats almsot continuously once he gets home from school. About three or four times a week the family eats out—often at a fast food place or at an all-you-can-eat buffet, with plenty of crisp, deep-fat fried foods.*

Health risks related specifically to adolescent overweight, as defined by Pauline Powers, MD, at the NIH Strategy Development Workshop for Public Education on Weight and Obesity are:

* Increased blood pressure (hypertension)
* Increased total cholesterol and lipid abnormalities
* Insulin resistance (hyperinsulineamia)[29]

Hypertension

Hypertension, or high blood pressure, means increased pressure against the walls of blood vessels. It occurs when passages are narrowed, stiff or constricted. It causes the heart to work harder and may damage the heart, brain and kidneys. Blood pressure is measured by two readings: systolic pressure refers to the pressure when blood is pumped out to the arteries; diastolic pressure is the pressure on the arteries between heartbeats. An optimal reading is 120 (systolic) over 80 (diastolic). A high reading is 130-139 over 85-89.

High blood pressure is a complex problem. While its causes are not clearly understood, they appear to be genetic and lifestyle, such as inactivity, excess body fat, smoking, alcohol, and possibly stress. It is managed by a combination of medication, diet, and lifestyle changes.[30]

Cholesterol

Blood or serum cholesterol circulates in the bloodstream. HDL, or high-density lipoprotein, cholesterol is known as the "good" cholesterol and is associated with lower risk of heart disease. LDL or low-density lipoprotein cholesterol ("bad" cholesterol) forms deposits on the walls of arteries and other blood vessels, and is associated with increased risk for heart disease. The ratio of these lipids—levels of HDL to LDL—suggests the risk level. (Note: this is a different type of cholesterol than dietary cholesterol, which comes from food.)[31]

Hyperinsulinemia (IR)

Insulin resistance, or hyperinsulinemia, is a condition in which the cells resist the action of insulin so glucose cannot pass through. More insulin is produced, resulting in higher levels of glucose in the blood. Insulin resistance puts people at high risk for developing Type 2 diabetes, and is believed to be the key factor in the metabolic syndrome, a cluster of risk factors for chronic disease. About half the cases of insulin resistance are probably inherited. Lifestyle plays a role in whether a person who is genetically susceptible will develop insulin resistance or diabetes. Obesity may cause insulin resistance and the metabolic syndrome, because they are often found together. A relatively new question is whether insulin resistance may in fact *promote* obesity and abdominal obesity. Hyperinsulinemia creates a metabolic situation that promotes fat gain—the more insulin in the bloodstream, the greater the likelihood the body will store fat.[32]

Obstructive Sleep Apnea

Sleep apnea is a chronic disorder in which breathing is briefly suspended repeatedly during sleep. It is measured by the number of suspensions or apneas per hour of sleep, and is often associated with obesity. Patients with sleep apnea have reduced upper-airway size; impaired reflex compensation in reaction to airway closure during sleep; and chronic airway vibration. Symptoms include heavy snoring and excessive daytime sleepiness, which can lead to impaired work performance and increased driving accidents. Treatment includes nasal continuous positive airway pressure devices and upper airway surgery.[33]

In the Bogalusa Heart Study of children, a clustering of these three risk factors are highly correlated with overweight. This is especially true when children also have an apple shape or centralized location of fat (fat located on upper body and stomach rather than on thighs and legs).

Obstructive sleep apnea is another severe complication showing up more often in overweight children. It can cause hypoventilation and sudden death in severe cases.[34] Excess weight for growing children can cause bowed legs, joint problems and back pain.[35]

As obesity and its associated risks have risen, so has the resulting economic health care burden. Annual hospital costs for treatment of obesity-related diseases in 6- to 17-year-olds more than tripled from 1979 to 1999, rising from $35 million to $127 million. The primary diagnoses were diabetes, obesity, sleep apnea, and gallbladder disease.

Young people not only had increased disease rates, but also stayed in the hospital longer. Their average length of stay increased from 6.4 days in 1979-1981 to 13.5 days in 1997-1999 (HHS urges community partnerships to improve physical activity: a CDC study finds medical costs among obese young people are increasing significantly.[36]

Early Puberty

Early puberty is another unfortunate result of overweight and inactivity. Though largely unrecognized as a risk factor, early puberty is related to higher rates of reproductive cancers later in life, and is a factor in the high rates of preteen pregnancy in the United States. Inactivity and high body fat can trigger these hormonal changes at an early age, pushing today's young children into early puberty and sexual maturity.

> *By age six, and a chubby 135 pounds, Tabithia was already showing signs of puberty. Her breasts began to develop. Her periods started at age nine; she was already sexually mature and able to bear a child. By then she was a big girl, tall, and rounded. Older boys began to notice, to tease and flirt. She liked the attention, which had never come easily to her before.*

The age of puberty for both Americans and Europeans has dropped steadily during the past hundred years. Instead of reaching menarche at age fifteen or sixteen and their adult height at twenty to twenty-one years as they did one hundred years ago, American girls now reach menarche at an average of 12.8 years and complete growth by age sixteen to eighteen. Girls and boys both are maturing earlier today because of generally sedentary lifestyles and higher body fat.[37]

For African-American girls, puberty comes even earlier. On average they reach menarche by age 12.2. One-half are developing sexually by age eight, compared with only 15 percent of Caucasian girls.[38] Excess fat can make the body produce excess estrogen, which can lead to early puberty in girls.[39]

Active living makes a big difference. Girls who are on sports teams usually have lower body fat, and average 15.5 years at menarche, about the same as a century ago. Often it is delayed much longer. In one study cited by Frisch, young women athletes in college who began training before menarche, started their periods about three years later than those who began after menarche.[40]

Polycystic Ovary Syndrome—The Hidden Epidemic

Polycystic ovary syndrome (PCOS) is a complex hormonal disturbance that affects the entire body and has numerous implications for general health and well being. An inherited syndrome, it affects an estimated 5 percent of women and most don't know they have it.

Symptoms include weight gain or obesity, hirsutism (excess hair) or scalp hair loss, acne, irregular or absent periods, infertility, insulin resistance, and enlarged ovaries containing many small cysts. However, symptoms can be very different from one woman to the next. PCOS is probably the single most common cause of menstrual cycle disturbance and infertility due to lack of ovulation. Women with PCOS may have migraines and depression, and are at risk for developing diabetes, hypertension, gallbladder disease, and heart problems. Early diagnosis and intervention are the key for a woman to maintain her long-term health and fertility, but for too long PCOS has been under-diagnosed and under-treated.[41]

Being overweight as a child may influence adult health as well. Tufts University researchers found that men who were twenty pounds or more overweight as teenagers were twice as likely to have died or developed heart disease by age seventy. They were also more likely to suffer colon and rectal cancer and gout (a painful joint condition). Women who had been overweight as teens had double the risk of arthritis and eight times as much difficulty in walking a quarter of a mile, climbing stairs and lifting heavy objects. Men who had been overweight as teens but not as adults had lower risk. The study looked at health records of students and tracked their weights and health for fifty-five years.[42]

Dangerous Weight Loss

Injury and death from weight loss attempts and treatments contribute to the risks of being overweight. Children and teens often use dangerous methods in their struggles to lose weight, since the social stigma of being overweight is so strong. (For more information on high-risk weight-loss methods, refer to Chapter 9.)

Deadly Diet Teas

When her boyfriend left her for a slimmer girl, Rosalita, age sixteen, looked for an easy way to lose weight. The answer came in a colorful ad in the Sunday newspaper supplement—a "safe, all natural" herbal tea that guaranteed she'd "lose 10-20-30 pounds fast, without dieting or exercise." It didn't mention that the active ingredients, senna, cascara, and buckthorn, come together to make a strong laxative. Rosalita sent off for the tea, used it once or twice, but it didn't seem to have much effect. One night she tripled the strength and felt stomach pains—it was working! The next night she dropped four tea bags into a cup of boiling water and let it steep an hour before drinking. She heated it up in the microwave again before removing the tea bags, then drank it. She went to bed with severe stomach cramps. Rosalita's younger sister found her dead in bed in the morning. The intensified laxative effect coupled with lack of food apparently triggered a heart attack.

Liposuction, for example, seems harmless in the advertisements, but, known as a pulmonary embolism, a blood clot in the lung is one of those rare but dangerous side effects of this invasive medicine. In liposuction, blood clots are the single worst culprit in fatal complications, accounting for a quarter of surgery-related deaths, according to a recent study.

> *Tiffany Hall, a young San Francisco woman, walked into the California Pacific Medical Center's Davies Hospital early one morning for what she expected would be a simple little liposuction surgery. The next morning, she was dead. Blood clots had migrated from her right calf into her lungs, one of the rare but troubling fatal complications of the fat-reduction surgery—one of America's most popular cosmetic surgery procedures.*

Mental Risks of Overweight

> *As a preschooler, Matthew had a happy childhood. He was bigger than most kids and his parents took pride in this, gave him lots of attention, and rewarded him often with food. "Eat your beans, and you can have three cookies for dessert," his mother would say. When he'd hurt his finger, Mom would give it a kiss and offer candy.*
>
> *But when Matthew entered first grade, things began to change. He was the biggest kid in class, and shy. The playground bully knew a vulnerable target for cruel taunts and jokes when he saw it, "Fatty, fatty, two by four..." "Hey, Fatso!" Others took up the teasing, and his former friends edged away and no longer played with him. Gradually he withdrew into himself, lonely and hurt at the rejection. At recess when classmates choose sides, Matthew stands off by himself, knowing he won't be chosen, knowing they don't want him to play.*

Overweight can be a severe social handicap. Children who are teased, labeled, and stigmatized may have long-term damage to self-esteem and body concept. Some experts suggest their greatest problems are probably not health risks, but emotional and psychological damage.[43]

Yet others point out that while cultural stigma against overweight is powerful, it is not a reason to change the child, but rather to change the culture. Large children would be much happier in an accepting atmosphere. Girls, especially, experience severe censure.

Metabolic Syndrome

Many of the most severe health risks associated with obesity—diabetes, cardiovascular disease and stroke—are closely related to a cluster of abnormalities often found together. Increasingly, the entire cluster, called *metabolic syndrome or syndrome X,* is showing up in children. It includes hypertension, insulin resistance (abnormal glucose tolerance), and lipid abnormality (elevated triglycerides and low HDL cholesterol). However, it's not yet clear how all these fit together and link with obesity, nor how they develop over time.

The entire cluster does not usually come together in children, but severely overweight children often have glucose intolerance or insulin resistance, as reported recently in the *New England Journal of Medicine.*

Adult Risks Related to Obesity

Overweight children and adolescents are more likely to become overweight and obese adults, therefore at increased risk for developing chronic disease and other health problems.

In December 2001, Surgeon General David Satcher sent out a national call to action to prevent and decrease overweight and obesity.[44] He listed the following risks:

Premature death. Risk of death rises with increasing weight.

Heart disease. The incidence of heart disease (heart attack, congestive heart failure, sudden cardiac death, angina or chest pain, and abnormal heart rhythm) is increased.

Diabetes. Over 80 percent of people with type 2 diabetes are overweight or obese. A weight gain of 11 to 18 pounds increases a person's risk of developing type 2 diabetes to twice that of individuals who have not gained weight.

Cancer. Risk is increased for some types of cancer including endometrial (cancer of the lining of the uterus), colon, gall bladder, prostate, kidney, and postmenopausal breast cancer.

Hypertension. High blood pressure is twice as common in obese adults.

Lipid abnormality. Obesity is associated with elevated triglycerides (blood fat) and decreased HDL cholesterol (the "good" cholesterol).

Breathing problems. Sleep apnea (interrupted breathing while sleeping) and asthma are more common in obese persons.

Reproductive complications. Obesity is associated with irregular menstrual cycles and infertility. Complications of pregnancy include increased risk of high blood pressure for the mother, gestational diabetes, problems with labor and delivery, and high birth weight infants leading to higher rate of Cesarean delivery and low blood sugar.

Other. Increased risk of arthritis, gall bladder disease, incontinence, increased surgical risk, and depression are linked to obesity.

Quality of life. Mobility may be limited and physical endurance decreased, and social, academic, and job discrimination increased.

Tracking Overweight Into Adulthood

Three major factors predict whether overweight will track into adulthood: severity of fatness, age of the child, and whether one or both parents are overweight.

Severe overweight at any age is more likely to continue. The older the child, the more likely it will track. In a University of Iowa study, over half of children and teens in the highest of five weight categories remained in the highest category as adults. Yet nearly one-third dropped down into the lowest three quintiles.[45] Perhaps the strongest predictor is the parents' size and shape, revealing the strength of genetics.

Julianne was a 10-pound baby, happy and contented, with a big appetite. She was large through infancy, and didn't walk until nearly fifteen months. Her arms and legs were wrapped in large, soft rolls of fat. Her mom worried that she'd gain too much fat, but was wise enough to let her regulate her own eating, and didn't interfere. Then at age three Julianne began stretching up. She grew into her fat, and eventually became tall and slender, without any hint of a weight problem.

The following data, compiled from four studies, suggests the likelihood of overweight tracking into adulthood, as the child grows older:[46]

TABLE 2.1 **Tracking Overweight into Adulthood**[b]

Age of overweight child	Percent who become obese adults
0-6 months	14
6 months-5.5 years	20
7 years	41
10-12 years	70

NHLBI 1992

About 80 percent of overweight five-year-olds and 60 percent of seven-year-olds will not be obese as adults. A 22-year follow-up of 151 overweight youngsters in Japan, ages six to fourteen, found two-thirds were no longer overweight by the age of twenty.[47] Thus, it is important for parents not to overreact. Interfering with natural growth can distort a child's development.

Overweight that begins in adolescence tends to be more severe than adult-onset. Most severely obese adults were overweight as teens, one review finds. It suggests this is especially true for women. About one-third of all obesity in women began in adolescence, and obesity is more likely to continue for women than men.[48]

Refrain From Exaggeration

Despite concerns over the risks of obesity, it is a mistake to exaggerate those risks. Overemphasizing health risks increases fear, shame, disturbed eating, social discrimination, and size harassment, and this will not help a child lose weight. Fears of a child's being too heavy can cause that child or parents to take drastic action causing injury or stunted growth. When researchers in New York looked at 200 short or delayed-puberty children, they found 7 percent were suffering from malnutrition because of fear of fat.[49] Most of the families were preoccupied with slim figures, and the children were eating as little as one-third of recommended calories.

> *Joe is scared and depressed. At age fourteen, he weighs 300 pounds, and is reminded by his physical education coach nearly every day that he needs to lose weight. Just the other day the teacher wrote a long list of health risks on the chalkboard, and looked right at Joe when he said that overweight kids risk early death.*
>
> *His classmates repeat the mantra, telling him he has to lose weight or die. It doesn't help that he's the only Native-American in his class, or that his big brother is a basketball star—Joe seems to have the family genes for fatness. His brother said, "If you just diet you'll lose weight!" Joe tried it. He tried the steroids his brother gave him, but they didn't help either.*
>
> *His mom is scared, too—because his father and grandmother have diabetes. His dad lost a foot and his grandma is going blind. His mom took him to the health clinic where the doctor put him on a 700-calorie liquid diet. He worked hard at it and was excited that he lost a lot of weight over the first three months. But then it all came back in a rush—a terrible experience. Now he's more depressed than ever. The window of opportunity closed for him, the time when he was eager, hopeful and willing to work hard to change his lifestyle. Now, with adults and peers predicting his demise, it all seems useless and hopeless.*

In truth, a higher weight in the moderate range, while associated with health problems in some areas, is protective against others. Developing strong bones is important, especially for girls, whose frequent dieting and weight loss fosters bone loss. Heavier people have stronger and heavier bones, while those who are thinner have weaker, less dense bones and are more subject to stress fractures. Obese women have a much lower risk of osteoporosis than do thinner women.[50]

Breast cancer rates are lower for obese young women than for other women of the same age. The National Institutes of Health reports that this breast cancer "premenopausal benefit" of obesity holds for ten or more years past menopause. Then the shift goes the other way, and larger women are at more risk.[51]

Heavier weight also is protective against infectious diseases, chronic obstructive pulmonary disease, mitral valve prolapse, intermittent claudication, renovascular hypertension, eclampsia, premature birth, anemia, type 1 diabetes, peptic ulcer, scoliosis, suicide, and cancer, reports Paul Ernsberger, PhD, a hypertension specialist at Case Western Reserve University School of Medicine in Cleveland. He notes heavy weight also improves survival rates for several disease conditions, including hypertension, type 2 diabetes, and high cholesterol.[52]

HIV-positive people who are overweight are slower to develop AIDS. When AIDS develops, the disease progresses more slowly, and they have lower viral counts than thinner people. Gaining even a few pounds helps delay disease progression and viral replication.[53]

Further, it should never be assumed that an increase in risks means that all or even most obese people will develop those risk factors. Some health risks are important in public health terms, and reach statistical significance because of the large population surveyed, yet carry only a slight risk to the individual. Others are so slight they threaten to shorten one's life span by only a few weeks—meaningless in the real world. Other risks mainly affect the relatively few people with severe obesity, but when research groups them with people of moderate obesity, all appear to share equally the increased risk.

Indeed, most children and adults classified as overweight or obese are in good health. The idea that large individuals are unhealthy, and thin ones healthy is untrue and a distortion of general facts.

For example, hypertension is one of the health risks most closely associated with overweight. Those with a BMI of 30 or over are twice as likely to have high blood pressure as thinner people with a BMI under 25. Yet the majority of obese persons, 62 percent of men and 68 percent of women, check out with normal blood pressure and *do not* have hypertension. At the same time, a considerable number of lean people *do have* hypertension—18 percent of men and 16 percent of women.[54]

The Mystery Figure

When experts report the risks of obesity they often warn of 300,000 deaths a year. Frequently they say that obesity causes these 300,000 deaths. This "fact" has been repeated in more than 1,000 news stories over the past three years alone, according to a Lexis database search.[55] Other times these deaths are laid to poor diet and inactivity. This confusion needs to be cleared up, each one leads to different solutions.

In 1993, J. Michael McGinnis, Deputy Assistant Secretary for Health, and William Foege, former Director of the Centers for Disease Control and Prevention, reviewed available studies on the leading nongenetic causes of death in the U.S.[56]

Here are ways their conclusions are being translated:

- ★ 2001 Surgeon General's Call to Action: *An estimated 300,000 deaths per year may be attributable to obesity.*[57]
- ★ Sen. Bill Frist, R-Tenn., a physician, quoted in Hearst Newspapers, 2002: *Health problems stemming from being overweight or obese are responsible for 300,000 deaths a year, putting weight problems right behind tobacco smoking as leading factors in causing death.* [58]
- ★ Centers for Disease Control and Prevention: *Diet and physical activity patterns together account for at least 300,000 deaths among adults in the United States each year; only tobacco use contributes to more deaths.*[59]

What McGinnis and Foege actually said is: *Dietary factors and activity patterns that are too sedentary are together accountable for at least 300,000 deaths each year.*

They list the top causes of death:

Cause	Deaths (1990)	Percent of deaths
Tobacco	400,000	19
Diet/activity patterns	300,000	14
Alcohol	100,000	5
Microbial agents	90,000	4
Toxic agents	60,000	3
Firearms	35,000	2

They go on to link poor diet and inactivity *combined* to 22 to 30 percent of cardiovascular deaths, 20 to 60 percent of fatal cancers, and 30 percent of diabetes deaths. While they mention obesity, as well as other conditions, they do not make the leap of suggesting it *causes* any of these deaths. Presumably, their figures on deaths from poor diet also include those from anorexia nervosa, malnutrition, and nutritional deficiencies.

Thus, while the research defining the same 300,000 deaths has often been given a creative spin to argue for various health agendas, correctly stated, it refers only to diet and inactivity combined.

Some policy makers go even farther and omit diet, suggesting the problem lies with inactivity. *"Nationally, lack of physical activity contributes to an estimated 300,000 preventable deaths each year from diseases such as heart disease, stroke and diabetes,"* says a recent federal news release encouraging families to walk on Mother's Day.[60] This could be placing the blame where it belongs. A large and growing body of evidence suggests inactivity may be at the root of obesity and its health risks, while evidence pointing the finger at poor diet is less conclusive.

Is A Third Factor To Blame?

If obesity does cause the metabolic syndrome and related diseases, such as diabetes and heart disease, then what is the source of this risk? Is it weight? Or is it excess fat? Or does a third factor cause both obesity and its related risks?

Most traditional obesity experts say that weight is not the real problem, instead, they blame excessive fat and fat location. Obesity has been defined as excessive storage of energy in the form of fat. The Surgeon General explains that BMI (a measure of weight to height) is used as a proxy for fat.[61] Body fat is more closely linked to disease risk than is weight, but whether it causes the risk is by no means established.

In fact, new studies challenge the risks traditionally blamed on obesity. A statement from the editors of the *New England Journal of Medicine* expressed dismay with the usual diagnosis, "Given the enormous social pressure to lose weight, one might suppose there is clear and overwhelming evidence of the risks of obesity and the benefits of weight loss. Unfortunately, the data linking overweight and death, as well as the data showing the beneficial effects of weight loss, are limited, fragmentary, and often ambiguous ... Although some claim that every year 300,000 deaths in the United States are caused by obesity, that figure ... is derived from weak or incomplete data."[62]

Increasingly, scientists are questioning whether the risks may actually stem from a third factor. Just because A is linked to B, they point out, it doesn't necessarily follow that A causes B. Another factor, C, may be causing both. They point the finger at inactivity and sedentary lifestyles as the most likely candidate, or possibly a combination of diet and inactivity.

Stress is another possibility. Research with monkeys suggests that stress can increase abdominal obesity and the internal fat deposits known as visceral obesity. Monkeys in a defeated, uncontrollable situation develop the metabolic syndrome (insulin resistance, decreased glucose tolerance, hyperlipidemia, hypertension), and other features of humans with visceral obesity, explains Per Bjorntorp, a Swedish researcher at the University of Goteborg.

Visceral obesity is likely an integral part of the metabolic syndrome, says Bjorntorp, and the entire syndrome can develop through stress alone in monkeys. He suggests these same responses may affect persons who have trouble coping with stress in modern life, who feel they are cornered and cannot control their lives. They secrete excess amounts of cortisol. Smoking and excess alcohol add to cortisol release, and are linked to visceral obesity. Increased cortisol may be the real key to risk, he suggests, along with an increase in certain hormones and circulatory factors. Visceral obesity may be a marker for risk factors, rather than a risk in itself.

The traditional approach is to treat risks related to obesity with weight reduction. Weight loss is recommended for hypertension, type 2 diabetes, and heart disease. But if these health risks stem primarily from a third factor, such as inactivity, then losing weight may not be the answer. Improvement in type 2 diabetes comes with short-term weight loss, but a review of controlled trials of weight reduction with follow-up of six to eighteen months shows a deterioration back to starting values even when weight loss is maintained.[63]

Weight loss is also the most common non-drug treatment for hypertension, though it provides only short-term improvement. Unfortunately, long-term results are disappointing, with results of maintained weight loss on par with starting values over time. NHLBI guidelines report that weight loss without increased physical activity fails to improve cardio-respiratory fitness.[64]

Weight Cycling Risks

The potential risks of repeated bouts of losing and regaining weight, known as weight cycling, or yo-yo dieting, cannot be ignored by health care providers. An impressive body of evidence shows weight cycling is associated with higher mortality.

The Harvard Alumni studies reported by Steven N. Blair, an epidemiologist at the Cooper Institute for Aerobics Research in Dallas, show that men risk heart disease, hypertension and diabetes by "always dieting." The more often these men dieted, the higher their rates of disease. This was basically unchanged by physical activity, smoking, or alcohol intake.[65]

Weight cycling can predispose lab animals to diabetes, according to a study that tested 64 female rats over a period of one year.[66]

Kelly Brownell, PhD, obesity specialist at Yale University, concludes that the harmful effects of weight cycling are similar to those associated with obesity. He finds weight fluctuation increases risk about 1.25 to 2.00 times, similar to the risk attributed to obesity.[67]

A growing body of evidence suggests that when weight continuously fluctuates and leads to weight cycling, the person may be worse off than before. The Framingham Heart Study examined the effects of weight cycling and weight fluctuations in 3,130 men and women over a 32-year period. Subjects who had high weight variability, multiple weight changes, or extreme fluctuations in weight were 25 to 100 percent more likely to suffer from heart disease and premature death than those who maintained stable weights. Subjects with fluctuating weights also had a higher mortality and morbidity due to coronary disease.[68]

Yet, sixty to 80 million people in the United States are trying to lose weight. They lose weight and almost invariably regain it rapidly. In one study, 80 percent of college women had dieted, about half were currently dieting, and one-third had dieted six or more times. Some two-thirds of teenage girls and one-fourth of teen boys are trying to lose weight, though many are not overweight.

Girls who begin dieting before junior high, and perhaps boys who cut weight each week for wrestling competitions, may be setting a lifetime course of weight cycling and increasing their health risks.

Numerous health risks are associated with over weight and obesity. However, the key word is "associated." They are often found together, but we don't know that obesity causes related risks such as the metabolic syndrome, diabetes or heart disease. A growing body of evidence suggests that other factors may be causal to both.

For children, risk factors for chronic disease, including high blood pressure, total cholesterol and lipid abnormalities, and insulin resistance are on the increase, along with the increasing prevalence of overweight. Type 2 diabetes is also increasing among children. Treating and preventing these risks in ways that effectively address true causes is an urgent health concern.

PART II

♦ ♦ ❖ ♦ ♦ ❖ ♦ ♦ ❖ ♦ ♦ ❖ ♦ ♦ ❖ ♦ ♦ ❖ ♦ ♦

Root Causes

Chapter 3

♦ ♦ ❖ ♦ ♦ ❖ ♦ ♦ ❖ ♦ ♦ ❖ ♦ ♦ ❖ ♦ ♦ ❖ ♦ ♦

Childhood Obesity: Nature Versus Nurture

Fifteen percent of American kids are overweight, that's triple the number from thirty years ago. What is happening here?

An easy answer is that our steepest population increases have come in the very groups most vulnerable to obesity—minority groups, low-income families, and people whose parents have limited education. About twenty to twenty-four percent of African-American and Hispanic children are overweight. "Thrifty genes" may share the blame, along with other factors.

Yet increases have come across the board, in every ethnic, racial and economic group, for boys and girls of all ages. One logical and likely explanation for this increase is that children today are much more sedentary than children have ever been before. This is clearly part of the equation.

Once it was believed that obesity was mainly an overeating problem—simply too many calories. This is less certain today. Or maybe, as many believe, it's the wrong foods, too high in fat and sugars, and too low in fiber. But again, the answers are unclear. Over-consumption of rich foods may well be part of the problem, but perhaps only when combined with inactivity and sedentary living.

Other factors in the equation are even more complex: bigger babies, excess weight gain in pregnancy, babies semi-starved in the womb by dieting moms, multiple pregnancies for teenage moms, stress, disruption of normal eating, dieting, smoking cessation, medications, and possibly even infection. The interplay of these influences, along with the effects of culture and psychological factors all have an effect on metabolism, regulation of appetite and satiety, and how calories are used and stored as fat. What's more, the interplay of these relationships differs for individuals and various subgroups.

Obesity is a complex condition that baffles scientists at nearly every turn.

Vulnerable Periods Through a Lifespan

The most vulnerable times in life for the development of obesity have been identified by the World Health Organization as follows:

- ⋆ *Prenatal.* Nutrition during fetal life may affect development of size, shape, body composition and the way the body handles nutrients.
- ⋆ *Adiposity rebound.* Early pre-school years are a time of lower body fat, followed by a rapid rebound in fat.
- ⋆ *Adolescence.* Body changes at puberty promote increased fat deposition, especially for girls. This may also be a time of increasing inactivity and irregular eating.
- ⋆ *Early adulthood.* There may be marked reduction in physical activity and often weight gain.
- ⋆ *Pregnancy.* Weight gain for mothers averages about one pound with each child, but with wide variation. The more pregnancies, the higher the risk of big weight gains.
- ⋆ *Menopause.* Typically women experience a metabolic slowdown along with possibly reduced activity that results in weight gain at mid-life.[1]

Of these six periods, five affect children and teens. Childhood is indeed a vulnerable time.

Genetic Factors

Family genetics make a big difference when it comes to size, shape and weight. The strongest predictor of a child's weight is the weight of his or her parents. A child with two overweight parents has an 80 percent chance of becoming overweight, compared with 14 percent for the child of two average weight parents.[2]

The tendency to gain excessive fat varies from one person to another, even in the same family, and even when food intake, physical activity and lifestyle are similar. Just as one child in a family has blue eyes and another brown, one may have genes for fatness while another does not.

Metabolism

Basal metabolism is the amount of energy used to sustain life at rest. The chemical and physical processes that are continuously going on in our bodies, even when we sleep, use about 60 percent of the calories we take in. Our "inner clock" is always working, controlling heart beat, blood circulation, breathing, heat generation, digestion, cell repair and elimination. It also fights infection and produces and transports the many chemical compounds used daily throughout the body, and sends messages to and from the brain.

All this requires a great deal of energy, but the process can be readily adjusted or even nearly shut down at many points to burn fewer calories when fewer are available. For example, dieting slows down metabolism. The teenager who fasts and skips meals may have a lower metabolic rate, along with slowed heart rate, cold hands and feet, difficulty concentrating, and low resistance to colds. Metabolism speeds up during physical activity.

Genetic factors affect metabolic rate, thermogenesis, endocrine function, fat storage, appetite and satiety signals, and other functions. It is likely they are responsible for routing more fat into storage for some people, giving them an extraordinary ability to protect that stored fat in dieting or starvation, and restoring fat to depleted cells. In other words, certain bodies put on fat easily and resist fat loss. A different gene may be responsible for abdominal obesity, according to the National Heart, Lung, and Blood Institute Family Heart Study (NHLBI-FHS).[3]

Thermogenesis

Diet-induced thermogenesis is the heat generated by our bodies during and just after we eat. When food is taken in, heat is produced, muscles move the food through the digestive tract, and specialized cells secrete juices for digesting, absorbing and metabolizing the food. This uses about 10 percent of the day's calories, adjusted to how much energy is available. With an unusually large meal, more heat is generated and more calories are "wasted" as they burn off and dissipate. This is why eating a big holiday dinner of 7,000 calories usually does not add pounds.

Still, Claude Bouchard, PhD, a professor of exercise physiology at Laval University, Quebec, who has done extensive research comparing weight in twins, adoptees, and nine types of relatives, cautions against putting too much blame on genetics. Many complex factors are involved, he says, and "There is a lot of chaos in the body system we're working with...We are seeing big increases in obesity worldwide. This has to be the result of environmental factors."[4]

Thrifty Genes

The "thrifty gene" theory brings genetics and environment together in a complex interplay. It helps explain why obesity rates are so high for children of African, American Indian, Hispanic and Pacific Island descent. These kids are not "fated to be fat." But their genetic vulnerability makes it a real risk under modern conditions, unless they maintain healthy lifestyles. Having "thrifty genes" helped primitive people survive even in starvation conditions. They got a lot of mileage from small amounts of food, and stored away fat whenever possible.

Environmental Factors

It's a simple equation: Calories in = calories out.

If a person takes in more calories than are used in physical activity that person gains weight. Right?

Do the math. You eat a cookie, you need to walk an hour to burn it off—240 calories in equals 240 calories out. In this thinking, since 3,500 calories equal a pound, if you eat 1,000 calories less each day, in four days you'll lose more than a pound. But wait just a minute. It doesn't really work this way. The problem is, there are at least two big unknowns on the right side of the equation. We know about how many calories are used in physical activity, but adjustments are continually being made in the number used for metabolism and thermogenesis. To confuse the issue even more, the storage and release of body fat takes place outside the above equation. There's a strong genetic component in how easily fat is stored and how well it is defended. If a child has lean genes (inefficient), then excess calories are more likely to be burned off during the course of a day, not stored as fat. But for the child with fat-producing genes, an efficient system is ever seeking to tuck away stray bits of fat and calories for hard times to come, and to defend those fat cells from releasing any fat until on the brink of starvation. Only those hard times don't come much in America today, except in dieting, and fat continues to pile up.

Calories Out

Three factors result in calorie output:

⋆ *Physical activity*: Moving the body around may use about 30 percent of calories taken in, but that percent varies greatly depending how active or sedentary a person is. Regular physical activity is critical to the smooth balancing of the calorie equation.

⋆ *Heat Generated from Food:* Diet-induced thermogenesis is the heat generated when we eat. The more calories we consume, the more calories are burned. This may use about 10 percent of calories, but there's lots of room for adjustment and readjustment, "wasting" heat or conserving it for fat storage.

★ *Our inner clock:* Basal metabolism is the everyday running of our inner clock: heart beat, blood circulation, breathing, generating heat, digestion, cell repair, elimination, fighting infection, producing and transporting the many chemical compounds used daily throughout the body, and sending messages to and from the brain.

The marvelous machines that are our bodies, are continually testing, signaling, readjusting, and working to bring us back to our normal state—whether it is correct body temperature, or our usual weight and body fat level. But there's also opportunity for things to go wrong, especially when the system is overwhelmed by sedentary living and swamped by high-calorie food.

Body Weight is Defended

A kind of control system is surely operating. It slips into gear to call back fat that is lost, and to prevent the accumulation of fat in lean persons. This makes perfect sense. Throughout the body we have finely tuned regulators that maintain specific balances. For instance, sodium concentration in the blood is maintained despite salty diets, dehydration, or perspiration. Body temperature changes little even when weather is extremely cold or excess heat is generated through exercise. We should not be surprised if body weight and body fat are programmed and defended at a particular level for each individual.

So, no matter what the calorie input, the output strives to keep in balance. Only constant high input causes it to get off kilter. When calorie intake is high, or intermittently high, the body does lots of adjusting. Likewise, attempts to lose weight by eating fewer calories are sabotaged when the body adjusts by decreasing calorie output.

All these processes are probably influenced by genetics, too. Genetics help burn off the excess for lean people, and makes it more likely there will be calories left over for kids prone to obesity.

Calories In

Whether people eating more calories is part of the obesity equation is a matter of dispute. American adults may have increased their calorie intake slightly in recent years, according to NHANES III. It's clear that overeating is being promoted in our culture today—in all-you-can eat buffets, extra large servings, jumbo sizes, and in advertising. Customers expect larger portion sizes today, and restaurants are responding by giving them more food. People are eating more meals outside the home.[5]

Still, the average intake of women age nineteen to fifty is slightly below 1,800 calories, considerably less than the recommended 2,200 calories per day. Men average about 2,700 calories, somewhat less than the 2,900 calories recommended.[6]

Calories, also called energy, are the necessary fuel for living. They keep us alive and moving and keep kids growing in appropriate ways. But when calorie intake is too high, and the above adjustments are not able to balance out the equation, excess calories are stored as fat, and we gain weight.

Protein, Carbohydrate and Fat

Protein. Protein supplies amino acids, the building blocks that build, repair and maintain body tissues. A complete protein contains all nine essential amino acids. A high-quality protein is an easily digestible, complete protein with amino acids that precisely fit the pattern needed by humans. Foods of animal origin provide high-quality protein. However, a carefully planned vegetarian diet can also be complete in the essential amino acids. Good protein sources are lean meat, poultry, fish, eggs, milk, cheese, beans, tofu, nuts and peanut butter. Cereal, bread and vegetables also contain some protein.

Carbohydrate. The body's main source of energy or calories, carbohydrates include starches (complex) and sugars (simple). The body converts both starches and sugars to glucose and carries it to all body cells through the bloodstream. A certain level of blood glucose concentration is needed for a feeling of well-being. When it falls below normal, we may feel tired, hungry, and dispirited. Another carbohydrate important to health is fiber, but it is not digested or absorbed into the body, and not considered a nutrient. Our main sources of carbs are cereals, vegetables and fruits, although milk also contains simple sugar as lactose.

Fat. Fat is important for carrying fat-soluble vitamins and hormones into and out of the cells, and is an essential part of every cell. Fat is a concentrated energy source, and is stored to provide a continuous fuel supply to the body. It is made up of differing amounts of fatty acids, including monounsaturated, polyunsaturated, saturated, and trans fatty acids. Fat makes food more pleasurable: it carries flavor and aroma, and provides a smooth, creamy texture. Some fat on the body is beneficial, because it cushions and protects organs, and forms an insulating fat layer under the skin that helps us stay warm on a cold day. However, having too much stored fat is associated with health problems. Dietary sources are animal products and the seeds of oil producing plants. Recommendations are to eat moderate amounts of total fat, and to moderate our intake of saturated and trans fats.

Calories are provided to our bodies by the energy nutrients—protein, carbohydrates and fat. In addition, alcohol adds calories, though not considered a nutrient. Protein and carbs supply 4 calories per gram. Fat supplies 9 calories per gram, and alcohol, 7.

Some experts say: just add it up. "A calorie is a calorie is a calorie." "It's the calories, stupid." The more calories we eat, the more likely we'll gain excess weight, and it doesn't matter what kind of calories they are.

But diet composition can make a difference, too. At least it makes a difference in rat and mice experiments.

In regard to fat storage, here's what research shows:

- ⋆ Protein is not stored as fat. Even with excess calories, it's not stored.
- ⋆ Carbs are stored as fat when calorie intake is too high. However, there is considerable wastage in the conversion; almost one-fourth of calories are lost.
- ⋆ Fat is stored as fat. Fat enters the fat cells, easily and quickly, using up almost no calories in the process.
- ⋆ Alcohol stores as easily as fat and should be figured as fat. Nearly all foods contain mixtures of the three energy nutrients, although they may be classified as mainly one or another. Thus a carbohydrate-rich food like corn also contains fat and protein. Meat, rich in protein, also contains fat.

Using up Calories: Thermogenesis

Burning off excess calories seems to be an important way the body regulates and keeps weight stable. The thermic effect of food, or diet-induced thermogenesis, is an extra heating up of the body every time we eat. Thermogenesis is influenced by meal size and composition, timing of eating, how good the food tastes, and the person's genetics, age, fitness and sensitivity to insulin. It has been investigated as an explanation of obesity—one theory has been that obese persons have less thermic effect. Now this is considered unlikely.[7]

A review of research shows that an unbalanced diet, either high or low in protein, results in higher thermic effect. It has been proposed that diet-induced thermogenesis may have evolved as a way of enriching protein-poor diets by disposing of excess energy. This wasting, once fat is restored, would have helped prevent obesity, a hazard to survival in the wild.[8]

Metabolism

Basal metabolism increases as body size goes up, and for a given size can vary as much as 20 percent. It correlates best with fat free mass, so the more muscle a kid has, the faster his or her inner clock runs.[9]

It is known that metabolism drops with weight loss, that people burn fewer calories after losing weight. But does it drop below what would be expected to compensate for decreased lean mass? Two articles in the June 1999 issue of the *American Journal of Clinical Nutrition* debated this issue of whether formerly obese people must live with a lower metabolism than normal.[10,11]

A meta-analysis of twelve published studies reviewed by Arne Astrup and colleagues in Denmark found a three to five percent lower resting metabolic rate for reduced-obese persons. On the other hand, a study compared 40 obese persons who had lost weight from the National Weight Control Registry with 46 weight-matched controls, and found their drop in resting metabolic rate was not more than expected to compensate for reduced lean mass. However, this study found some indication of a higher fasting respiratory quotient for the formerly obese subjects, which is consistent with research that shows they may have a reduced capacity for fat oxidation.[12]

Thus, it is possible that after weight loss some people have both a lower metabolism and increased defense of stored fat, promoting easier weight gain and obesity.

Speeding up metabolism with drugs might sound like a good idea as a way to burn off more calories faster. In the 1920's, dintrophenol was used to increase metabolic rate. It caused blindness and death of thousands, was condemned by the AMA, but continued to be offered by mail order until into the 1930's. Thyroid hormone speeds up metabolism and was heavily used for decades for weight loss and is still used by some "diet doctors." The side effects can be horrific. A double blind study in the 1970's looked at the thyroid as a way of lowering cholesterol. They found that even though cholesterol fell, mortality was up in the treated group, and they terminated the trial prematurely.[13]

In the animal, world a faster metabolism is related to a shorter life span. A mouse has a very high metabolism and a short lifespan, compared to an elephant with lower metabolism and longer life. So what happens to human health and longevity if—with the next diet pill (such as the beta3-agonists now under development for weight loss)—metabolism is artificially speeded up to burn more calories? We might be concerned that these and other stimulants potentially reduce life expectancy. We don't know, and one-year safety data on those pills will not tell us. (see Chapter 8 for more on diet drugs under development.)

Physical Activity

The proven way to improve metabolism is with physical activity, which increases metabolic rate dramatically, and also increases longevity.

And in the controversy over which is more important in causing obesity, inactivity or overeating, inactivity usually wins. Yet if nearly everyone agrees, why is weight loss emphasis nearly always about cutting calories?

The percent body fat that preschool children carry is not related to food or diet, an Australian study finds. Instead, it is children's level of physical activity that links to body fat at this young age.[14] (See Chapters 4 and 14 for information on the sedentary lifestyles of children and teens.)

Food Intake

Calorie intake has been the focus of most research into the causes of overweight. Yet, though it has been studied intensively, there is no clear evidence that overweight is related to a higher intake of calories in children, or that overweight children eat more. It has even been reported that fatter children consume fewer calories than thinner children.

Further, there appears to be no increase in calorie intake for children over the last thirty years, during which time weight has increased steeply. Calorie increases, if any, appear to be small. Granted, food intake is difficult to measure accurately. Children and adults often underreport foods and serving sizes, and scientists have attempted to control for this in various ways, perhaps not always successfully.

Common sense tells us that children with more body fat *must* consume more calories and fat. Yet an extensive 1999 review of the available research, reported that most studies found neither calories nor fat intake was related to obesity later in childhood or during adulthood.[15] The Bogalusa Heart Study, an extensive long-term study of children in Bogalusa, La., reports a steady increase in obesity for kids over the years, but no increase in calorie intake.[16]

Is it the Fat?

Eating fat was thought to be a major culprit in obesity and its rising rates. But maybe not. Many scientists, pediatricians, and nutritionists are rethinking lowfat advice.

At first it seemed simple, back when those first studies came in showing rats and mice gained more weight and more fat when fed high-fat diets. It became clear that dietary fat is easily stored in the body. And research showed it is not regulated, with more being burned when more is available, as happens with protein and carbohydrate.

Americans responded by dropping their dietary fat intake from a high of about 44 percent of total calories in 1965 to 33 percent in 1996—and health gurus urged a still lower drop to 30 or 20 percent. Now we have the dangerous situation in which college women strive to eat no fat at all. Some of their diets have been analyzed at only 4 percent fat. Health-anxious, thin-obsessed parents wean their babies on skim milk, stunting the growth of some. Many teenage girls, already the most poorly nourished of any group in America, no longer drink milk or eat meat in their extreme fear of consuming fat.[17] At the same time, obesity rates have skyrocketed. The same thing happened in Europe and Australia, where obesity went up as fat intake dropped.

Today, kids are eating more deep-fat-fried meals at fast food restaurants, and more snack foods like cookies, crackers, chips, desserts and candy. In one large study, African-American girls ages nine and ten ate more calories and fat and tended to be heavier than Caucasian girls. Eating more high-fat foods was associated with overweight for both groups.[18]

Many youngsters have high-fat diets. Yet on average, children as well as adults are eating less fat today than a decade ago. Fat consumption has dropped from 36 to 33 percent of total calories in the last decade, according to USDA nutrient intake surveys.[19]

The surprising interaction between exercise and diet on lab rats has been extensively studied by Wayne C. Miller, PhD, an exercise physiology professor, George Washington University in Washington, DC. Laboratory rats were divided into three diet and exercise groups: (1) low-fat and low-sugar diet with no exercise; (2) high-fat and high-sugar diet, exercised by swimming two hours a day; and (3) high-fat and high-sugar with no exercise. For 20 weeks the rats ate freely as much as they liked. Groups 2 and 3 both consumed diets high in fat and sugar, but only group 3–with no exercise–became obese. As long as the rats were active, the calorie-dense diet did not make them fat. The rats in group 1 on the low-fat, low-sugar diet didn't fatten either, even though they were inactive. It was when the two came together, a calorie-dense diet combined with sedentary lifestyle that did it.

Not only were the "high-fat, high-sugar, no exercise" rats the fattest, but they ate the fewest total calories and the fewest per gram of body weight. The rats in group 2, "high-fat, high-sugar, exercise," ate the largest amount of calories and the most calories per gram of weight gained, yet because they were swimmers, they were only slightly heavier than the rats in group 1 who ate the low-fat, low-sugar diet and fewer total calories.[20]

In another study Miller and colleagues found that without exercise either high-fat or high-sugar diets independently caused severe obesity.[21] Miller suggests that when inactivity is combined with diets high in fat and/or sugar, as in the lifestyles of many kids today, there is increased risk of obesity. But neither alone is sufficient cause.

Rethinking Low-Fat Advice

Many experts are rethinking low-fat advice. "Diets high in fat are not the primary cause of the high prevalence of excess body fat in our society, nor are reductions in dietary fat a solution," concludes Walter Willett, of the Harvard School of Public Health.

In mixed meals it doesn't seem to make much difference whether people eat much or little fat as long as they do not overeat, according to research by Andrew Prentice, of the MRC Dunn Clinical Nutrition Centre, Cambridge, England. Unless calorie intake is high, he reports, there's little difference in fat storage, even when diets range from 10 percent to 80 percent fat. Only when people eat more than their bodies can use are more of the excess calories from high fat diets than low fat diets stored as fat.[22]

Lowering fat intake by itself has not been a successful weight loss method. For instance, women lost weight the first year when reducing their fat intake from 38 percent of the diet to an extremely low 20 percent in the Women's Health Trial, a treatment study of women with breast cancer. However, by the end of the second year, these highly-motivated women had regained it all and weighed about the same as the control group, even though they had carefully followed the low-fat diet.[23]

Another problem with low-fat diets is that they are not necessarily low in calories. Many low-fat processed foods are high in sugar and calories, including the fat-free cookies, cakes, chips and candies that now crowd supermarket shelves. As an example, adding chocolate powder to a glass of milk can double the calories but reduce the *percent* of fat so that it counts as a low-fat food, even though it is high in calories.

Eating Patterns

Children are snacking more today than they did twenty-five years ago. Researchers at the University of North Carolina compared information from three national surveys 1977 through 1996, and found that, while the average size of snacks and calories per snack remain relatively constant, the number of times kids eat between meals has increased. The snacks provided less calcium than regular meals and were higher in both calories and fat. Thus the "energy density" of what children eat over the course of a day has risen significantly, from 1.35 to 1.54 calories per gram. Children today take in about 25 percent of their calories in snacks (600 calories), compared with about 18 percent (450 calories) in the late 1970's.[24]

Children are also skipping breakfast, and more often eating at fast-food restaurants where increasingly larger quantities are being served, often of high-fat, calorie-dense foods. Some research shows eating breakfast is linked to less fat intake and less snacking during the day, and that kids who don't eat breakfast are more likely to be overweight.[25]

Alcohol

Alcohol consumption is often forgotten when experts talk about calorie intake, yet it accounts for 6 percent of calories in the average American diet and as much as 10 percent for regular adult drinkers. It is a significant factor for many teenagers. Because it doesn't promote growth, maintenance, or repair in the body, alcohol is not called a nutrient, but it does provides plenty of calories, nearly double that of protein and carbohydrates. It also seems that alcohol promotes fat storage in a special way, by allowing more of the calories from fat to be stored as fat.[26] Alcohol consumption is also associated with increased risk of abdominal fat, the proverbial "beer belly."[27]

Family Control

What you do, what you say and how you eat in a family counts. Simple things, like urging a child to clean her plate may have a direct effect on overweight.

FIGURE 3.1 **Average Number of Parental Food Prompts per Meal**[c]

	Normal Weight Child	Overweight Child
Encouragements to eat	4	16
Food presentations	11	20
Offers of food	3	7
Total food prompts	18	35

KLESGES 1983

Fourteen families with young children ages one to three were observed several times at meals in a study at North Dakota State University in Fargo. The researchers found that the overweight toddlers were urged both verbally and nonverbally to eat twice as often as the normal weight children, an average of 43 prompts per meal. All children usually ate more when urged to do so. When they refused, parents almost always encouraged them to eat more, and 70 percent of the time they did. The researchers concluded that many parents encourage overeating in their very young children in ways that override satiety signals and may lead to excess weight gain.[28] On the other hand, being underfed and encouraged to eat less than satisfies the child's needs can also promote overeating, binge eating, secret eating and excessive weight gain.[29]

Parents who try to control how much and what foods their children eat may find their efforts backfiring. Their children tend to eat more when not hungry, to choose the very foods being restricted, and to feel intense guilt about eating. Leann Birch, PhD, of

Pennsylvania State University, and colleagues studied 197 parents and daughters age four to seven. After eating a standard lunch, the girls—who were not hungry—were offered free access to snack foods. They ate from 0 to 436 calories. The more restrictive the parents were in feeding practices, the more the girls ate and the stronger were their negative feelings, either about eating too much or their mother or father finding out. Feelings of eating "too much" were not affected by how much they ate, but rather by whether they felt a food was "not allowed."[30]

Ellyn Satter, a dietitian and an internationally-known expert on childhood feeding, says young children can regulate their own food intake if allowed to do so. When parents focus too much on what to eat, when to eat, or how much food is left on the plate, their children don't learn to respond to natural hunger and satiety signals.

Poor family communication can also contribute to overweight. If children are isolated in a disinterested or disengaged family, they may be at a higher risk of overweight, reports Laurel Mellin, MA, RD, San Francisco. Her study of 254 obese adolescents found that four factors accounted for most of the weight differences: family cohesion, adolescent communication, age of obesity onset, and the mother's weight. Surprisingly, the major environmental factors were not diet or exercise. Instead, as families were less engaged and children less involved with family, their weight tended to be higher.[31]

Dieting and Disruptive Eating

Several studies suggest that dieting and weight loss efforts can themselves lead to higher weight gain. In a northern California study, for example, 692 ninth-grade girls from three high schools were studied over a period of three years. At every weight, girls who tried to lose were associated with greater risk for obesity. Their initial weight made no difference—thin girls were just as susceptible to weight gain if they dieted as girls who were overweight or average at baseline.

Restricting food made the difference. The risk for obesity was more than three times as great for dieters as for those who lived diet-free. Girls who reported the more strenuous dieting, exercise for weight control, and radical weight loss efforts such as use of laxatives, diet pills, vomiting and fasting gained even more weight over time. They also binged more. The researchers concluded that weight loss efforts can lead to "dysregulation of the normal appetite system," so that natural signals of satiety were disrupted.[32]

A Harvard study followed 5,865 girls and 4,322 boys, ages nine to fourteen years from 1996 to 1998. It found that regardless of their intake of calories, fat or carbohydrate or their physical activity or inactivity, the frequent dieters were significantly more likely to become overweight than those who never dieted.[33]

Other studies report this same "dieter's nightmare" for adults. In a large Finnish study, 36 percent of dieting younger men had gained more than 22.5 pounds, compared with 29 percent of nondieters. Twenty-four percent of dieting younger women gained over 20 pounds, versus only 13 percent of nondieters. Initial weight made no difference; neither did other confounders including smoking, alcohol, education, or marital status.[34]

Yo-Yoing Ratchets Up Weight

When weight loss programs are unsuccessful, as they typically are, the chronic dieter experiences the well-known yo-yoing of weight down and up, or weight cycling. But instead of regaining up to the initial level, her weight often ratchets up higher and higher each time.

> *Bonnie, age eighteen, has been struggling with her weight since she was thirteen. Now in college she is "always on a diet, planning a diet, or just blew a diet." She loses 10 pounds and gains back 12; she loses 20 pounds and gains back 28; or in a particularly serious effort she loses 40 pounds and gains 55. Some of her diets last only three days, some extend for weeks or even months. Like many chronic dieters, Bonnie doesn't know her weight because it is always shifting, always in flux, but she understands that it's going up. She frantically launches new diets—gleaned from her favorite magazines, through diet groups, in the doctor's office—but inexplicably the gain continues. Over the last*

five years this ratcheting has added over 80 pounds, and she blames herself. The more she loses, the more she gains.

Sally Smith, former executive director of the National Association to Advance Fat Acceptance, says there are many 450-pound women in NAAFA who were once 250-pound women. But because they tried so hard to reach 150 pounds, through an endless series of diet programs, hundreds of pounds lost and even more hundreds regained, their weight ratcheted up that extra 200 pounds. They are convinced that dieting and the weight loss treatments they suffered are to blame.

"Repeated dieting may result in a higher setpoint, as the body adjusts to this modern form of 'famine' by storing more fat," warns Esther Rothblum in *Feminist Perspectives on Eating Disorders.*[35]

A poll of obesity experts listed weight cycling as one of the key causes of obesity.[36] They believe it, their patients believe it, and maybe it's time the public starts believing, too.

Puberty

Three high risk times for excessive weight gain for females are all related to fertility, according to several studies presented at the 2001 annual meeting of the North American Association for the Study of Obesity in Long Beach, California. It's natural for girls to put on more body fat and develop a more curvaceous figure at puberty, while boys tend to develop more lean muscle at this time. Early puberty is more likely for both girls and boys who are inactive and have more body fat. Being taller at a younger age is also related to earlier maturity, which in turn is related to obesity.[37] Early puberty may be a pathway to obesity for girls, according to studies at Tufts University in Boston. It may further contribute to increased risk of later obesity. The researchers suggest targeting girls with early menarche for obesity prevention.[38]

Pregnancy

Just being female puts a girl at risk for weight gain, and pregnancy adds to that risk, especially for minority girls already at risk. Women have long recognized that gaining too much weight during pregnancy can trigger obesity. Unfortunately, this problem has been largely ignored by the medical and health community. Many doctors shrug off concerns, assuring pregnant women that any excess weight can be taken off later.

In 1989, U.S. Public Health directives called on pregnant teens and women to produce larger babies (averaging about 8 pounds), by gaining 25 to 35 pounds during their pregnancy, 3 to 8 pounds more than recommended in the past.[39]

The aim was to reduce the number of tiny premature babies born to many young growing teen and preteen girls, who are often already malnourished from dieting, and don't gain enough to support both their own healthy growth and that of the infant. But how increasing the average size of babies might do this is not clear. Low infant weights are influenced by many factors other than mother's weight gain, including substance abuse and mothers who are very young, of low socioeconomic level, with low pre-pregnancy weight. Smoking alone is blamed for an estimated 29 to 42 percent of low birth weight babies.

Thus the policy may be ill advised. It clearly increases the risk of obesity, especially among African-Americans and others who are already at risk.

More than half of mothers do not lose all the weight they gain during pregnancy, and nearly one-third of these retain over 11 pounds, according to the Swedish research.[40] Weight retention after pregnancy appears to be an even greater risk for African American women.[41]

Research is urgently needed to determine the optimal weight gain in pregnancy in different ethnic groups for both mother and child. Women need help now. The effects of unnecessary weight gain in pregnancy need to be taken seriously by the health community.

Prenatal

How well a mother eats while pregnant affects the developing fetus. Female babies whose mothers suffer from nutrient deficiencies while pregnant may be more likely to become obese in later life, according to a Dutch famine study.

Scientists could not account for the differences by food intake, smoking, alcohol or socioeconomic factors. They suggest that nutritional deprivation before birth may trigger an adaptive change, programming the individual to eat more and produce more body fat through life.[42]

In another twist, adult obesity has been linked to cold weather births. In a study of 1,750 men and women born in Hertfordshire, England, between 1920 and 1930, climate at time of birth had a significant effect for men. Birth weight was higher for men born in the first half of the year, from January to June, than for men born between July and December, and this was associated with more adult obesity.[43]

Bigger Babies

American babies are heavier at birth today than in the past. Weight has increased since 1989, when policy makers began urging women to have larger babies by gaining more weight in pregnancy. Some studies suggest heavier babies will continue heavier. Others show the mother's weight is the primary influence, and birth weight has little effect.

Ray Yip, MD, MPH, Centers for Disease Control, reports that CDC surveillance programs show birth weight influences later growth, that heavy babies are four times as likely to become heavy five-year-olds.[44] Another federal analysis of height and weight at age 6 to 11 showed similar results: children with higher birth weights were heavier and taller.[45]

From birth, babies born to obese mothers seem at highest risk of overweight. Studies of British and Canadian children show that even if the babies of larger women are average weight at birth, by six months they are heavier and growing faster than other infants.

The weight a child will attain is closely linked to the mother's pre-pregnancy weight. But during the first two years of life, a comprehensive University of Pennsylvania study of 78 infants found no differences between weight, weight for length, or skin-fold thicknesses for babies at high risk for obesity because of the mother's weight.

There is some evidence for a link between low birthweight and increased abdominal fat later in life, perhaps related to undernutrition in pregnancy, which is common for dieting pregnant teens.[46]

Quitting Smoking

Smoking cigarettes induces an acute rise in metabolic rate, a possible longer-term rise, and tends to reduce food intake, so there is some weight loss when kids begin smoking.[47] Then, if they quit, as nearly all say they intend to, they "catch up" with others who did not smoke.

Recently, Williamson studied a national sample of adults and found that on average the men gained six pounds and women eight pounds when they quit smoking. (This is about the same amount that smoking keeps off.) Younger people and heavier smokers, however, tended to have higher weight gain when they quit, up to 28 pounds.[48]

Inflammation Links to Obesity

Recently, inflammation—the pain, swelling and redness that occur after an injury or infection—has been implicated in some of the nation's leading killers: heart disease, diabetes, Alzheimer's and possibly even cancer.[49]

It is also being implicated in weight gain. University of Minnesota researchers measured the presence of fibrinogen and other markers of inflammation and infection over a three-year period in 13,017 middle-age men and women (age forty-five to sixty-four). They found those in the highest quartile of fibrinogen gained a half pound more each year than those in the lowest one-fourth. The researchers concluded that inflammation may stimulate weight gain, and this in turn may play a role in the development of the metabolic syndrome and cardiovascular disease.

Is Obesity Contagious?

Can obesity, or some part of it, be caused by a virus? Don't rule it out. University of Wisconsin scientists have found an intriguing virus—called *avian adenovirus*—that fattens chickens, and a related virus that causes them to develop an unusual amount of visceral or internal fat.

Previously it was not thought that these viruses could infect across species, but in four separate experiments they inoculated chickens and mice with a human adenovirus, and found that visceral fat, total body fat and body weight were significantly greater, compared with control groups. When they tested 154 obese and 45 average-weight men and women, they found that 15 percent of the obese adults carried antibodies for this virus, while none of the average-weight controls did. They also report that canine distemper virus can produce obesity in mice.[50]

Other Pathways to Obesity

Many essential medications promote weight gain. This is especially true of anti-depressants. Some patients have complained these drugs cause food cravings. But one study suggests the cause of weight gain with anti-depressants is a metabolic slowdown, not increased food intake.

Depression itself can lead to weight gain. Traditionally, concern has focused on the weight loss effects of depression, but more than one third of depressed patients gained weight in a University of Pennsylvania study.[51]

Stress may be another pathway to obesity. Many children and teens are feeling highly stressed today. They are awash in the information age, and are faced with a mind-boggling array of choices in every facet of their lives. Swedish research has linked stress to increased abdominal fat and the metabolic syndrome.

Prader-Willi Syndrome

Prader-Willi syndrome is a serious genetic disorder, usually non-hereditary. It is characterized by obesity, insatiable eating, and behavior problems related to food. Prader-Willi presents a double challenge for parents because of the need to restrict food and manage often-difficult behavior. Considered relatively common, it affects about one child in 15,000, both boys and girls, and is found in all countries and races. Physical activity levels are usually low, with small muscles, and low muscle tone. Abnormal-eating starts as early as age one, with an intense interest in food and eating. Daily intake, if unrestricted, was found in one study to be 4,600 to 5,600 calories. This leads to obesity at an early age, if not managed skillfully. Rapid weight gain and related problems can drastically shorten the life-span.[52]

Chapter 4

♦ ♦ ❖ ♦ ♦ ❖ ♦ ♦ ❖ ♦ ♦ ❖ ♦ ♦ ❖ ♦ ♦ ❖ ♦ ♦

The Consequences of Sedentary Living

"The burden of cardiovascular disease rests most heavily on the least active."
—The Surgeon General's Report

These are sedentary times. It's all too easy to shift into "couch potato" mode. And the less people move, the less they seem to want to move. Parents are often too busy, steering a stress-filled course from a peek at the morning television news to auto to office elevator to computer and back to exhaustion in front of the TV. *Sedentary death syndrome* is a new term coined by obesity researchers to describe what happens to people who sit around too much and get little physical activity.

Adults with sedentary lifestyles are prime targets for an array of ailments and chronic diseases. Children who are driven wherever they go and sit before screens at recess and after school instead of engaging in active play, fail to develop the muscles and strong cardiovascular system they need for a lifetime of good health.

"We are engaged in a major war against a silent enemy: the sedentary death syndrome," said Frank W. Booth, PhD, and Manu V.

Chakravarthy, MD, PhD, in a March 2002 article in the *President's Council on Physical Fitness and Sports Research Digest.*[53]

They warn that ultimately this syndrome results in increased death rates from modern chronic diseases, including type 2 diabetes, coronary heart disease, hypertension, osteoporosis, colon cancer, anxiety, and depression. In children we see the immediate effects of sedentary living in increasing rates of type 2 diabetes. Inactivity may be a factor in the high rates of childhood anxiety and depression as well.

250,000 Premature Deaths

Booth and Chakravarthy charge that 70 percent of the U.S. population is insufficiently active to achieve health benefits. Twenty-eight percent undertake no leisure-time physical activity, and 42 percent get less than thirty minutes of physical activity each day. In work, physical exertion has declined markedly in recent decades, a trend likely to continue.[54]

They calculate that about fifteen percent of 1.6 million deaths from four major chronic health conditions are due to sedentary lifestyle alone, exceeding all deaths from firearms, illicit usage of drugs, sexually transmitted diseases, and motor vehicle accidents.

Today the early stages of the sedentary death syndrome often begin in childhood with weak skeletal muscles, low bone density, low physical endurance, insulin resistance, high blood pressure, elevated cholesterol levels, low serum HDL, and excessive levels of body fat. Undetected changes slowly and inevitably build on each other and worsen over time.

His parents first noticed that Peter, age seven, an inactive child, was gaining weight. His mom felt a nagging worry, but she was busy with two jobs, and there was no time to make adjustments to the family's eating habits. Too much junk food, she thought, and was glad he was content to stay home watching television instead of going out on the streets. Besides, he seemed happy enough, day to day. When he was ten, the doctor diagnosed insulin resistance and warned that Peter could be pre-diabetic, and cautioned his mom on what to watch for. By age eleven, the signs were too obvious to ignore, and he was diagnosed with type 2 diabetes.

Children who are already leading sedentary lives are most likely to continue these habits and to swell the ranks of sedentary adults.[55] Sedentary children may have some of the precursors of cardiovascular and other chronic diseases. These precursors are clustered in the metabolic syndrome, or syndrome X, a condition defined as having three or more of the following risk factors: insulin resistance, high blood pressure, high triglyceride levels, low HDL, and abdominal obesity. As mentioned in Chapter 2, the entire cluster of symptoms does not usually develop in children, although severely overweight children often have glucose intolerance or insulin resistance and perhaps high blood pressure. And increasingly, there are cases of type 2 diabetes developing in children.[56]

Inactive Children: Why?

Today, many families have changed their lifestyles in response to fears that their communities are not safe. Parents who work long hours may feel too tired or too busy to supervise. In our high-tech world parents are often less physically active themselves, and more conveniences and remote controls mean a child need not even make the effort to open the garage door for Mom.

Inside, there are more television channels, more computer and video games, more movies and more hours Internet surfing than ever before—and a wide array of tempting snack foods too. Superheated and air-conditioned homes are fine, but may tempt full-time cocooning.

No wonder today's children and teenagers are the most sedentary generation in history. Although it doesn't necessarily show up on surveys, most experts agree there has been a continuous decline in physical activity over the last thirty years that closely parallels the steep rise in childhood obesity.

Sedentary living appears to be a major factor in the accumulation of excess body fat, particularly for genetically vulnerable youth. Even for preschoolers, a recent study shows the amount of their body fat is directly linked to how active they are, rather than food or any other factor.[57]

Children Don't Walk or Bike to School

Did you walk or ride a bike to school as a child? Thirty years ago more than 66 percent of children did. Today only 10 percent of America's children walk or bike to school, according to National Transportation Board statistics.[58] For recreation and other trips, too, children walk and ride their bikes 40 percent less than in 1977. And as walking declines, riding in cars increases. Children who are driven to school miss the opportunity to get out in the fresh air and arrive at school alert, refreshed, and ready to start their day.

Not so long ago, children were the major bikers in any community. But they have jumped off their bikes today, in part because of unsafe neighborhoods, heavy traffic, and a de-emphasis on the benefits of physical activity. American children biked 15 percent less in 1998 than eight years before, according to the League of American Bicyclists, which promotes bicycle-friendly communities.[59]

School Sports: All or Nothing

One solution is more physical education (PE) and after-school sports. Parents may expect that children are active during school hours. Unfortunately, in a time of budget cuts, many schools have cut physical education. There's been a drop in daily PE class from 42 percent of high school students enrolled in 1991 to only 29 percent in 1999.[60] Fewer than half of high school students take PE at all. As of this writing, only the state of Illinois requires daily PE for students in kindergarten through 12th grade.

What's more, the quality of physical education has declined significantly in recent years. The system leaves out a lot of students, students who need activity the most.[61]

Activity Drops with Age

Young children are the most active and physically fit of all Americans (except for athletes). These children are active because it's fun—not because it's good for them. On average, they spend an hour or two each day in moderate and vigorous physical activity.

But they're less active than their parents were, and many are developing habits that can turn them into inactive, unhealthy, overweight adults. Today, even infants spend more time restrained in baby seats and less time on a blanket on the floor where they can move freely, reach, and explore, child experts say. The less active children are, even at age three or four, the less active they will be later on. With each year they grow older, most youth become more sedentary.

This striking decline in physical activity is especially evident among girls. Many already lead almost totally sedentary lives by age fifteen. The percentage of girls who are active drops steeply between their freshman and senior years of high school—from 67 percent who are vigorously active at least three days a week as freshmen to only 45 percent who are this active as seniors, according to the Youth Risk Behavior Survey (YRBS), conducted by the Centers for Disease Control and Prevention to measure high-risk behaviors of the nation's high school students. About 28 percent of all girls are not active enough for good health as freshmen, and this

FIGURE 4.1. **Decline in Activity with Aged**

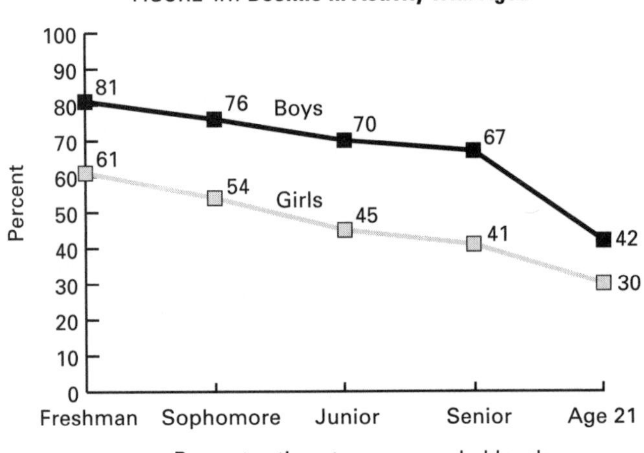

rises to 48 percent by their senior year, when 12 percent are almost completely sedentary. Boys mark a lower rate of decline—from 20 percent as freshmen to 30 percent who are not active enough by their senior year.[62]

Youth Risk Behavior Survey (YRBS) Statistics

According to the 2001 Youth Risk Behavior Survey (YRBS), two-thirds of high school students are *vigorously active* (defined as activities that make them sweat and breathe hard) for twenty minutes three or more days a week:

Boys: Caucasian	74
African-American	72
Hispanic	69
Girls: Caucasian	60
African-American	48
Hispanic	52

Lower income students tend to be less active in each ethnic and racial group. More than a third of young people in grades 9-12 do not regularly engage in vigorous physical activity.[63] One-fourth of high school students are *moderately active* (defined as activities that did not make them breathe hard or sweat) for at least thirty minutes on five or more days a week. Goals are to increase both kinds of activity in the next decade. The National Heart, Lung, and Blood Institute (NHLBI) study finds dramatic decline in physical activity among African-American and Caucasian girls.[64]

The YRBS also says that 12 percent of girls and 8 percent of boys reported no activity at all. These figures were higher for African-American and Hispanic boys and girls. Highest were African-American girls—17 percent reported no activity. The total physical activity of an individual throughout the day is difficult to measure. Many of these children are almost totally sedentary; others may be less so.

Girls Still Missing Out

Boys are more active than girls, and the gap widens through high school and college, according to researcher James Sallis, PhD.[65] Their generally sedentary lifestyles may put girls at high risk for inactivity-related health problems, he warns. Many girls who stay active focus only on weight loss, as if burning calories is their sole reason for movement, their only reason for being in sports.

In Mississippi, the least active state, over 20 percent of girls report no activity at all, and 52 percent are insufficiently active. In many large cities the situation is even worse. In the District of Columbia, the figure reaches 29 percent of all girls with no activity (62 percent get insufficient activity), and in the cities of Detroit, Milwaukee and New Orleans, that number tops 22 percent. At the other end of the spectrum, in Utah only 3 percent of girls report no activity. Yet even there one-third are insufficiently active, according to the YRBS survey.

A recent study at the National Heart, Lung, and Blood Institute found that pregnancy was a big factor for some African American girls' rapid decline in leisure-time physical activity, particularly the extraordinary amount of time it takes to care for one or more infants.[66] More Caucasian girls smoked, and for them, smoking meant a big decline in activity.

Television and Screen Time

Over one-third of children now watch more than five hours of television a day. Watching television is often used as a marker for sedentary living and increased from a median of two hours a day among adolescents in 1970 to nearly five hours in 1990.[67] Healthy People 2010 has set the goal of reducing time spent watching television to two hours or less per day for children and adolescents. In some homes and child care settings the television is "always on.

Mary goes to a large play school where one group of children is sitting on the floor listening to an aide reading a story. In another area kids are making roads in a sand table filled with rice. Others play with toys across the room. But from high on a shelf, where it can be seen by all the children, a television set runs continuous cartoons. Whatever their other activity, children's eyes stray back and forth to the cartoons. Some stop in their play to gaze at it.

One day Mary's mom took time to visit. She had stopped television at home because Mary seemed anxious, nervous, and easily upset, and it helped. She withdrew her daughter from daycare and explained why, "I just think it's too much television for Mary."

Watching television, playing video games, listening to music, and surfing the Internet has become the choice activity of the average American child, according to a new study by the Kaiser Family Foundation. The study shows an average child age two to eighteen spends nearly six hours, seven days a week, this way. Most is in isolation—in bedrooms fully media-equipped, with no parental supervision. The study found 65 percent of children age eight and older have television in their rooms, and that most parents have no rules at all about television watching. These children had computers, but spent less time using them than watching television. They were still reading—82 percent read for fun each day and spent about forty-five minutes on non-homework reading.[68]

In the 2001 YRBS study, 38 percent of high school students watch television more than three hours on school days. There's wide variation, from 69 percent of African-American youth, to 48 percent of Hispanic, to 31 percent of Caucasian children. High school freshmen are more likely to spend time in front of the television, than sophomores, juniors or seniors (45, 39, 35, and 31 percent, respectively). Boys are slightly more likely to watch television than girls (42 percent vs 35 percent).[69]

In many, but not all studies, the more time spent watching television, the higher children's risk for becoming overweight, no matter what their race. They may be less active, they watch more ads for high calorie snack foods, and they snack more in front of the screen. It may also mean that television itself may lower metabolism by having a lulling effect, as some evidence suggests.

Physical Education Programs Need to Change

When senior Rachel Willis thinks back on her career at Oakland's Fremont High School, gym time won't be among her memories.

> *That's because like most California high school students, she didn't have much of it.*
>
> *"I did PE when I was a freshman, and the only thing they made us do was run a mile," she said. "Other than that, it was like free time. They gave us some basketballs and footballs to play with, but about 20 percent of the time we just hung out on the benches and talked."*

California has required just two years of high school PE since the late '70s. Today, many high schools offer even less than what's required, or allow students to replace PE with cheerleading or marching band. In some cases, a student can get out of PE if a parent sends a note that states the child works out at a gym.

Third graders are moderately or vigorously active for only 25 minutes a week in school, according to a 10-year study by the National Institute of Child Health and Human Development.[70] "Most schools have cut PE programs to save money, so academic teachers now have to lead PE and many don't know what to do. So they count recess as PE," explained Ron Wilkins, head of the YMCA of the East Bay, CA.

And PE still needs an overhaul in many schools. Research shows that in many classes, students spend more time standing in line or watching others than being active themselves. One study found that a 40-minute physical education class provided youngsters with an average of only three minutes of vigorous activity.[71]

Nonathletic and less fit youngsters are the ones who need PE the most. Yet they are often the ones most neglected. One in six children is so weak or uncoordinated as to be considered physically underdeveloped by the President's Council on Physical Fitness and Sports. "That cold statistic barely hints at the personal trauma and social problems behind it. Such a child is likely to become a sedentary, overweight adult with all of the added health risks those conditions entail," says the Council.[72]

Focusing on fun and creativity, not competition, is important to all students, but particularly to children who are physically underdeveloped. These are the students most likely to lead sedentary lives. Competition isolates and discourages them from being active. A

New York study in grades five through eight found that when children were criticized for their weight while being physically active, they were less likely to enjoy the activity or to participate in even mild-intensity activities. This criticism was more common for girls than for boys.[73]

The President's Council recommends fitness testing and remedial programs for students who don't meet standards.

The Children and Youth Fitness Study also found less than half the PE curriculum is based on *lifetime activities*, which are those defined as only one or two people and are readily carried into adulthood, such as biking, swimming, jogging, dancing and racquet sports. Children's group games and competitive team sports don't count as lifetime activities but are the major focus of most programs.[74]

Fitness Testing

In Austin, Texas, parents will soon receive fitness testing results along with report cards. A 1999-2000 study in three Austin schools found 32 percent of second graders were overweight and 24 percent were obese. Many schools around the country are taking steps to begin a report-card system to gauge their students' fitness levels. Fitness testing is useful in helping individuals and their coaches develop reasonable goals and evaluate improvement. Typically the tests include four measures: aerobic capacity, flexibility, strength and endurance.

But some tests add weight or body composition as a measure of fitness, raising unnecessary problems. Many experts point out that such scoring is unfair to the child who works hard and improves fitness scores, but still fails because losing weight is beyond his or her control.

Karen Petersmarck, PhD, RD, Public Health Consultant, Michigan Department of Community Health, says fitness needs to be separated from fatness and weight when evaluating children's progress in PE classes. "Let's give children goals they can realistically meet through plain hard work. Let's not add even more to the burden of shame and guilt heavy children are already carrying—in the name of 'fitness.' "[75]

Fitness tests that hinge on weight erroneously suggest that only slender individuals can be fit, and that good health is impossible at higher body weights. Teachers need to reassure students of the fallacy of this, and demonstrate that fitness has it's own rewards aside from changes in body shape. Furthermore, there is tremendous potential for misclassifying children based on weight and body fat measurements. Children may go through several growth spurts in a year, and each time fat may be depleted or deposited. Two fitness tests not dependant on weight in scoring are the Presidential Physical Fitness Award Program and Chrysler Fund AAU Physical Fitness Program.

Encouraging Girls in Sports

The days when boys played varsity sports and girls were delegated to be their cheerleaders are long gone in most schools. It's been thirty years since Title IX banned sex discrimination in schools receiving federal funds. Before the law, only 300,000 girls played on competitive U.S. high school teams. Now there are 2.78 million.

Half of all students do play on at least one school sports team during the year, with girls almost as likely as boys (50 vs. 61 percent). About half of high school students work on weights and toning activities at least three days a week in sports season. Boys are more likely than girls, Caucasian students than African-American, and freshmen more than seniors, to do this.[76]

Yet girls are still neglected in physical education and sports and receive far less encouragement from the institutions in charge of sports and health to stay involved than do boys. Often negative attitudes or disparaging remarks from family or friends dampen their enthusiasm. Gymnasium facilities and the encouragement to use them for pleasure may not be as available for girls. There is also the issue of putting too much emphasis on appearance for girls, and less on skill, ability, fitness and health.

The primary motivator that keeps teenage girls continuing in sports is that they are having fun. Research shows that other motivators are gaining approval and respect, making their parents proud, feeling good about doing well, making friends, and keeping in shape.[77]

Yet most girls still drop out of sports in their teens, and studies show their self-esteem drops at the same time. One study shows that while older girls agree that they enjoy sports, they also encounter major barriers by age twelve to seventeen. Among these are systems that favor male athletes and controlling behavior by boys.[78]

A demonstration that girls are not being taken seriously is the curious attitude some trainers take toward stress fractures. It is known that female athletes are at greater risk of stress fractures than males, due to smaller and thinner bones, undernourishment and calcium deficiencies, and excessive dieting and exercise. Instead of requiring that women athletes stop dieting and fully nourish themselves, some coaches and trainers are recommending they practice a three-step hip-hop to help protect fragile bones when they jump—this eases the impact by shifting weight quickly from one foot to the other.[79]

Sports Coverage Short-Changes Girls

Despite shining examples in the summer and winter Olympics, girls have relatively few athletic role models. Media coverage tends to ignore women's teams and women athletes.

It is important for girls to have many positive female role models, and to see healthy female athletes of all sizes in the media, not just thin ones. When the media does focus on women in sports, it is often in a confusing way that sends mixed messages to girls. Female athletes may be portrayed in ways that emphasize their femininity or appearance, rather than their athletic skill and excellence in their sport. This can cause much ambivalence for girls, uncertain whether their role should be primarily athletic—or looking attractive on the field.

Amy Terhaar Woodcock, a graduate student in sports management at the University of Minnesota, says reporters watch for female weaknesses and often exploit them in photos and stories. She charges that some sports writers try to find a way for female athletes to fit into feminine ideals by pointing out that women are too frail for contact sports. When a male athlete is injured, the injury is attributed to the sport, but for female athletes, the injuries are blamed on female weakness.

Sports magazines, such as *Sports Illustrated,* avidly read each week by sports-minded girls and women as well as men, typically devote far more space to swimsuit editions, pinup calendars, and cheerleaders and the clothes they wear, than to women athletes.

One study found photos of female Olympic athletes were often suggestive, emotional, or in poses where the women were away from their sport. Many focused on the female athlete's body in sexually suggestive ways. Emotional shots showed the athlete crying and being comforted by male coaches and family.

Women's sports are vastly under-represented in television, newspaper and sports magazines. A look at four daily newspapers found that women were the subjects of only 3.5 percent of all sports articles, and men, 81 percent. Men were pictured in 92 percent of all sports.

This unequal coverage is reflected in sports books—even picture books for very young children. A 1993 Melpomene study found girls portrayed only half as often as boys in children's picture books on sports. Often the girls were shown watching boys play. These were major improvements, however, the researchers noted; during the 1950s and 1960s, no girls at all were pictured in the same series of sports books.[80]

When Exercise Takes Over

At the other extreme from sedentary living are young people who exercise obsessively, and develop an activity disorder that takes over their lives.[82] Many girls try to "fix what's wrong" with their bodies through exercise. Boys join them, driven by today's emphasis on muscles and body sculpting.

Activity disorder

Activity disorder or exercise dependence can be defined as excessive, purposeless physical activity that goes beyond any usual training regimen and ends up being a detriment rather than an asset to health and well-being.[81]

Excessive exercise, also called obligatory exercise, is a form of obsessive-compulsive behavior that has pathological attributes. The individual with an activity disorder tends to follow rigid, stereotyped patterns and insist on continuing the activity even when it causes or aggravates a serious physical disorder. A missed exercise session causes emotional distress. Exercise takes priority over everything else and is often aimed at losing weight or sculpting the body. For some it is a form of purge behavior, a way to burn up calories, related to the drive for thinness, body dissatisfaction, perfectionism, and higher eating disorder scores. Others exercise obsessively as a way of releasing tension and getting a sense of "high" that makes them feel better. Typically the exercise is solitary. with severe calorie restriction. Girls caught up in excessive exercise are at increased risk for the female athlete triad: amenorrhea, osteoporosis, and eating disorders, and the associated loss of bone mass, bone fractures, and stunted growth. Signs are when the young person becomes preoccupied with exercise and spends so much time at it that he or she is no longer socializing, achieving in school, or pursuing other interests.

Activity disorders are closely linked to eating disorders. A warning sign that exercise is becoming a problem is when goals shift from enjoyment and becoming fit, to body shaping. It is critical that coaches emphasize health-promoting goals, and question weight loss and excessive muscle building. Eating disorder patients also need to be closely monitored for signs of overtraining.

Female Athlete Triad

Everywhere girls are taking part in athletics as never before. But there's a dark thread running through women's sports. It's the vulnerability for the female athlete triad and its separate components: eating disorders, amenorrhea and osteoporosis. Any of these can impair health and performance—together they compound the risk.

Amenorrhea, a ceasing of the menses, is associated with scoliosis and stress fractures in young ballet dancers. Delayed menarche, as late as age nineteen or twenty for very thin female athletes and ballet dancers, usually with a restrictive diet, is linked to osteoporosis and bone fractures. (At the same time, a somewhat later puberty, well over today's young average of 12.8 years, appears beneficial in reducing reproductive cancer risk.)[83]

Avoidance of meat, common among female athletes, is highly linked to menstrual abnormalities, warns a recent article in *The Physician and Sportsmedicine*.[84] One study cited by the authors finds over 26 percent of vegetarian women have menstrual irregularities, compared with less than 5 percent of nonvegetarian women.

Struggling to be best at a sport while coping with adolescent changes is difficult for young people, and is compounded by social pressures promoting thinness. Trying to control weight while focusing on training and performance can lead to a sense of frustration, guilt, despair and failure, and to undernourishment and eating disorders.

Bodysculpting

Weight training increases strength, endurance and bone density and is a valuable part of high school athletic programs. Yet working with the weights can become detrimental when boys or girls focus on reshaping their bodies for the sake of appearance. Coaches may also get caught up in muscle building, to the extent their influence can be harmful to youth. Athletic directors, coaches and parents need to be aware that the new emphasis on muscle building and body sculpting is strongly influencing teenage boys and adults through advertising, television shows and muscle magazines.

Joe McVoy, PhD, a Virginia eating disorders specialist, says he is seeing more boys with eating disorders caught up in bodybuilding. "This has become more epidemic in our society. There's a great increase in fitness and muscle magazines, fitness spas, and home exercise equipment all with a focus on shape and muscle building."[85] Bodybuilding often involves profound alterations to the natural body, extremely restrictive ways to eat so as to deplete fat under the skin, and dehydration so severe that skin is thin as paper. This defines rope-like muscles and makes blood vessels stand out like veined leaves just under the surface. Bodybuilders call this being "ripped" or "sliced."

Some teenagers, along with hours of high-intensity training, turn to illegal steroids and other drugs as a shortcut to building muscles. Anabolic steroid effects may be permanent. For boys, steroids can reduce sperm, shrink testicles, and cause impotence and irreversible breast enlargement. Girls can develop irreversible masculine traits. Dangers include stunted bone growth and potentially permanent damage to the heart, liver, and kidneys. There are reports that steroids may increase aggressive behavior and violence. Dependency is another risk, according to Jim Wright, PhD, an editor of *Muscle & Fitness*.[86] He cites a study indicating that at least one-fourth of high school users of steroids are dependent on the drugs.

Red Flags for Athletes

Obsession with a sport may indicate an athlete is overtraining in unhealthy ways. Athletes at risk tend to talk and think constantly about their sport, often spending hours upon hours in the gym perfecting their workout at the expense of school activities, friendships, and hobbies. Compulsive exercise beyond regular workouts may be a sign the athlete is trying to compensate for eating.[87]

Nancy Thies Marshall, chair of the USA Gymnastics' task force on eating disorders, who has herself struggled with disordered eating, says that other signals of include the following:

- ⋆ Drinking an overabundance of fluids
- ⋆ Laxative or diet pill use
- ⋆ Bathroom visits after meals
- ⋆ Menstrual dysfunction
- ⋆ Wearing baggy clothing to hide weight loss

Malnutrition may also cause chills, apathy, irritability, dry and pale skin, hair loss. Vomiting may cause callused finger, and sores on lips and tongue.

Testing Inactivity

The effects of prolonged inactivity have been studied by confining healthy young male athletes and sedentary volunteers to bed for up to three weeks, following a control period during which baseline measurements were taken. Results of bed rest studies show numerous physical changes including a profound decrease in cardiorespiratory function.

Within a few days metabolic disturbances became evident. These included insulin resistance, negative nitrogen balance that indicated muscle protein loss, and negative calcium balance that reflected bone loss. Though muscle deterioration occurs at a faster rate than loss of bone density, it also regenerates more quickly. Fairly rapid regeneration of muscle, as well as improvements in cardiorespiratory and metabolic functions were observed in individuals after they resumed normal activity, though restoration of bone minerals took longer.[88]

Genetic Pathways Break Down

It has been theorized that we humans inherited physical activity genes from our ancestors of the Paleolithic Age, when strenuous activity was essential for human survival. Booth, Chakravarthy, and their research team set out to identify the underlying reasons why inactivity produces chronic health disorders. They suggest that many people are now so inactive their normal signals fail to activate this genome, and the protein expression of cells changes. Altered proteins are linked to many of the chronic diseases that humans suffer from today.

They conclude that sedentary living negatively affects at least twenty of the most chronic and deadly medical disorders, including heart disease, stroke, hypertension, and breast cancer. These conditions share common genetic pathways that are supported by activity, Booth and Chakravarthy suggest. Their research indicates that a sedentary lifestyle leads to a breakdown in the body's biomedical system, which in turn leads to chronic disease.[89]

TABLE 4.2 **Conditions That Are Caused or Exacerbated by a Sedentary Lifestyle**[e]

Angina	Low physical endurance
Heart attack	Obesity
Chronic back pain	Osteoporosis
Coronary artery disease	Pancreatic cancer
Breast cancer	Peripheral vascular disease
Colon cancer	Physical frailty
Congestive heart failure	Premature mortality
Depression	Prostate cancer
Gallstone disease	Sleep apnea
High blood triglycerides	Spinal cord injury
High blood cholesterol	Stiff joints
Hypertension	Stroke
Less cognitive function	Type 2 diabetes
Low bone density	Vertebral/femoral fractures
Low blood HDL	Weak skeletal muscles
Lower quality of life	

Activity Links to Body Fat

Though obesity is often blamed for the associated metabolic syndrome and chronic diseases, a large and growing body of evidence suggests sedentary lifestyle may well be the mysterious third factor causing both metabolic problems and excessive body fat.

A recent Australian study suggests the amount of body fat that preschool children carry is determined by physical activity, rather than diet. The study looked at activity and food intake of 77 children, ages 1.5 to 4.5 years. Four-day weighted food records were kept. Habitual activity was determined through calculating ratio to predicted metabolic rate, and body composition was measured.[90] The results indicated that children who engaged in more physical activity had low fat levels; diet apparently had no effect. Neither total calorie intake nor percent of calories from fat, carbohydrate or protein made any difference in body fat levels for either boys or girls.

Regardless of the origins of obesity, the evidence is clear that physical activity helps protect against its related risks. So it makes a lot of sense for treatment to begin with an exercise program rather than with food restriction and dieting. Increasing the level of activity directly improves metabolic profiles and helps normalize these problems even without weight or fat loss.[91]

Health Benefits of Activity

Fortunately, just as there are severe consequences to leading a sedentary life, there are major health benefits in being active. For example, inactivity increases the risk of high blood pressure and type 2 diabetes, and regular physical activity lowers that risk. Both conditions improve with activity, which reduces high blood pressure and mitigates the effects of diabetes.[92] The body also responds to regular activity with dramatic improvements in the cardiovascular, metabolic, respiratory, endocrine, and immune systems.

Physical activity helps protect against the most severe health risks associated with obesity. It helps to control and stabilize weight; increases strength, endurance, flexibility, aerobic fitness and agility; and is associated with fewer hospitalizations and clinic visits. Bone density is improved—which is particularly important during adolescence, as these are important bone-building years. (See Chapter 14 for more information on the health benefits of activity.)

Underwhelmed by Physical Activity

"People don't wear out, they rust out," health advisors warn the elderly. At present, this admonishment can just as easily apply to sedentary children. Though our bodies are built for action, in this country we are *underwhelmed* by activity advice and *overwhelmed* by food advice. Whether the talk is of health or weight, most experts give lip service to the importance of physical activity—then they move on to discuss at length how to restrict calories, fat or certain foods. It's as if they don't believe their activity advice will be followed, but they know they can make an impact by probing the ever-growing list of "bad" versus "good" foods.

In 1992, the National Heart, Lung and Blood Institute convened a strategy development workshop to gear up for public education on weight and obesity. Several experts testified to the importance of physical activity, and the obesity specialists seemed to agree. But the teachers complained that, at the end of the day, the workshop recommendations focused far more on restricting food than on increasing physical activity.[93]

Unfortunately, this is the message most listeners seem to be hearing. Those with weight concerns often disregard recommendations on the importance of increased activity, apparently thinking it's easier—and of equal value—to simply make food restrictions. Blair says, "We believe that the public health would be better served with more comprehensive attempts to increase population levels of physical activity, rather than emphasizing ideal weight ranges and raising an alarm about increasing prevalence rates of obesity."[94]

Instead of encouraging large kids to lose weight, which often leads to failure, it seems more appropriate to encourage them to increase physical activity. Regular activity will lead to health benefits regardless of any changes in weight. Focusing on behavior also helps motivate youngsters of every size, and also makes them feel good about their efforts.

The good news is that youngsters don't have to reach competitive heights to achieve major benefits to health and well-being. They can improve the quality of their lives dramatically by including moderate activity throughout their day.

The stakes are high. So are the potential rewards: preventing premature death, unnecessary illness and disability; controlling health care costs; and maintaining a high quality of life from childhood into old age.

Chapter 5

♦ ♦ ❖ ♦ ♦ ❖ ♦ ♦ ❖ ♦ ♦ ❖ ♦ ♦ ❖ ♦ ♦ ❖ ♦ ♦

Dysfunctional Eating Behavior: An Overview

Children all too often make poor choices in *what* they eat today. But equally disturbing—and perhaps more so—is *how* children are eating. Eating patterns and eating behaviors have been ignored for far too long. Today's soaring rates of obesity and eating disorders make it imperative that we take a close look at the relationships children have with food—how eating habits become dysfunctional, the risks associated with such behaviors, and what can we do to help.

Over the last three decades we have seen great changes in the way kids eat—where they eat, when they eat, and how much they are being served. You may recognize some of these patterns in your children:

Jamal, age twelve, is always eating or roving the house scouting for food. He comes home to an empty house after school and feeds more or less steadily on snack foods, crackers, cookies, candy, and chips until mealtime. He keeps on eating through dinner and into the evening. It seems like he's never satiated. Whenever food is available, he eats it. Jamal is an overeater.

Monique, a fourth grader, regularly skips breakfast and lunch. She plays with her food and eats only a small amount of what is on her plate though she'd like to eat more. She never feels really satisfied and is deeply afraid of gaining weight because everywhere around her people talk about getting fat. Monique is an undereater.

Tara, age 16, is unpredictable. Some days she skips breakfast and lunch, grabs a candy bar and Diet Coke after school, finds a way to skip the evening meal with her family, then goes on a huge eating binge in the evening. Some days she fasts and other days she eats nonstop. In between, she's usually on a strict diet, bingeing, or gearing up to start a diet. She weighs herself every morning and evening. Tara is a chaotic eater.

Craig, age 17, is a wrestler who typically fasts and restricts water for two days before his matches to make weight at 119 pounds. After each match, he binges for a day or two and eats all the foods he was deprived of while fasting. Then he restricts again. Craig is a violently chaotic eater, but only during wrestling season.

Children like these have lost touch with their hunger and satiety signals; they no longer know when they're hungry or when they're full. They eat to relieve anxiety, or because they're tired. They eat to change the shape of their bodies, for comfort, from habit, or just because the food is there. These are the children of a generation of parents who are chaotic eaters, undereaters, overeaters, grazers, and dieters themselves.

Modern culture encourages dysfunctional eating with increasingly large servings of good-tasting food and advertising that promotes eating for recreation. What causes children to eat or not eat? What causes them to override what their stomachs are telling them?

Family Battlegrounds

Family attitudes and practices can set the stage for dysfunctional eating behaviors early in life. Frequent family dieting, food restrictions, compulsive eating, overeating to calm anxiety, and excessive exercising can all play a part—as can a father's disparaging comments, and a mother's obsession with appearance.

Some parents believe they need to control children's eating to keep them thin. A 1999 study shows how this can backfire. Forty percent of parents believe that restricting or forbidding certain foods will cause their child to like them less. But studies by Leann Birch, PhD, at Pennsylvania State University suggest that deprivation directs children's attention to restricted foods, making them want forbidden foods even more. The more control parents exerted over their children's eating, the less the children seemed to naturally regulate their intake, and the less self-control they had. They also snacked more when they had the chance.[95-98]

Parents disrupt normal eating patterns in children when they insist on rigid rules and give frequent instructions—"eat more," "eat less," "clean your plate"—or when they invest food with emotional value, offering food instead of affection. Parents need to remember the long-term goal: to help children become healthy eaters who listen to and trust their inner signals.

Making meals a family battleground can foster severe eating problems. In a healthy lifestyle program led by Christie Keating of Victoria, British Columbia, and quoted in the *HUGS Club News,* teenagers shared these unfortunate family eating experiences:[99]

- "My mom knows I hate mushrooms and I told her I would throw up and she made me eat it and I threw up."
- "If we eat too much, we get this story about being greedy."
- "My mom won't give me any more, even if I'm hungry."
- "We used to stuff our mouths with the foods we didn't like and then ask to go to the bathroom."
- "If I eat all my dinner, then I can have dessert."

Forced feeding of children is abusive on the part of parents. Disruption of normal eating may also occur when parents fear a child is gaining too much weight and begin to restrict food. Feelings of deprivation can promote disordered eating and weight gain, warns Laurel Mellin, RD, MA, University of California, San Francisco. She reports that obese youngsters are at greater risk for developing disordered or dysfunctional eating than are normal-weight youth.[100]

The "fear-of-obesity syndrome" is a term health professionals use to describe the stunted, underfed babies they've been seeing in the last decade or so—children whose parents are so afraid they will get fat, that they keep them half-starved.[101] " Even the fat child is entitled to regulate the amount of food he eats," insists Ellyn Satter, RD, MS, author of *Secrets of Feeding a Healthy Family,* and an internationally known specialist on feeding children. This might be difficult for parents to accept, but they should never put a child on a diet, she advises. "Diets are not an option. Restricting food intake, even in indirect ways, profoundly distorts developmental needs of children and adolescents."

Eating disturbances can begin soon after birth, especially when modeled by parents. A study that followed 216 newborns from birth to 5 years, suggests that eating inhibitions, secretive eating, overeating, and overeating-induced vomiting in the young child can be related to a mother's dieting, bulimic symptoms, body dissatisfaction, and internalization of the thin ideal.[102] Satter advises parents to normalize their own eating.

Dieting is a form of dysfunctional eating that sometimes begins in children as young as age seven or eight, and is so common by age eleven that some researchers are calling it the norm for girls in America today. Children are growing up with skewed attitudes toward food because of fear of fat. They are turning away from normal eating and mealtimes with family to a restricted and chaotic form of eating.

If dysfunctional, disordered eating patterns are so prevalent, why don't we know more about them? What are their effects? How can they be measured?

What is Normal Eating?

Eating serves to maintain good health, energy, strength and normal growth. When children eat normally, they eat at regular times—typically three meals and a couple of snacks to satisfy hunger. They are attuned to their inner signals of hunger, fullness, and appetite, and satisfy them normally. Because they eat meals, they are hungry at mealtimes. Eating until they are full, but not stuffed, holds them over comfortably to the next meal. If they happen to overeat or undereat, their bodies can be trusted to regulate calorie needs with calorie intake. After eating, they have renewed feelings of pleasure and well-being.

Instead of being triggered by normal hunger, dysfunctional eating often is set off by emotional or sensory cues. Any of children's five senses can start them eating: tantalizing smells of a bakery, tinkling sounds of an ice cream wagon, the smooth touch of a candy wrapper crinkling in the pocket, tasting the first cookie of a handful, sights of other children eating or a candy dish on the coffee table. Even a stray thought can do it—thinking about that pan of brownies waiting in the kitchen or a Krispy Kreme shop around the corner. It can be a habit to link eating with television or reading. Any of these promotes the desire to eat for the child who is a dysfunctional eater. And though the child may struggle to avoid eating, the desire becomes irresistible.

When does the dysfunctional eater stop eating? Again, it's not regulated in normal ways, by signals of fullness. Instead of trusting their own body signals, dysfunctional eaters rely on inappropriate internal and external controls to bring eating to an end. It may be will power, a diet sheet, or a certain number of calories or fat grams. In an out-of-control phase, binges may end only when the stomach is "full to bursting."

How Many Calories Make a Binge?

For some, a binge is really only a small amount. For others it may be 10,000 calories or more. But always there is the sense of being out of control and unable to stop. Often it follows a period of restraint and deprivation, when the diet is broken and the "floodgates" come down.

Instead of relieving stress, eating may make the situation worse. After eating, it is common to feel guilty, ashamed, and uncomfortably full, to regret or scold oneself or, if unsatisfied, to feel ravenously hungry and fear triggering a binge.

Dysfunctional eating can be located on a continuum of increasing severity (mild, moderate or severe), between normal eating on the left and clinical eating disorders (actually an extreme form of dysfunctional eating) on the right. The youngster may move back and forth across the continuum, returning to normal eating after short bouts of dieting. Or she may restrict food so severely that she moves into the dangerous realm of severe eating disorders from which she cannot recover alone.

Studies suggest that dysfunctional eating is extremely prevalent, especially among girls and women. It appears to be increasing and striking at younger ages as the cultural drive for thinness continues to intensify. As many as 50 to 81 percent of girls and women in the United States, age 10 and up, say they're trying to lose weight. They are increasingly being joined by boys and men responding to new pressures to have lean and muscular bodies.

A North Carolina college study found 23 percent of a large sample of women students, faculty and staff and 8 percent of men revealed disturbed eating patterns, testing high on the Eating Attitude Test. Of these young women, 80 percent reported they were terrified of being overweight, 85 percent were preoccupied with the desire to be thinner, 84 percent dieted, and 83 percent used diet foods. About 15 to 27 percent of the men were in these same categories.[103]

There are three general patterns:

Chaotic eating. Chaotic and irregular eating—fasting, dieting, skipping meals, snacking, restricting, bingeing.

Consistent undereating. Eating less food than a child wants or needs; ignoring and overriding hunger signals.

Consistent overeating. Eating more food on a daily basis than a child wants or needs. The child eats more than maintenance and growth needs, eats past satiety, and over-

TABLE 5.1 **Eating Behavior Patterns**[1]

	Normal Eating	**Dysfunctional Eating**	**Eating Disorders**
Eating Pattern	Eating at regular times, usually three meals a day and one or two snacks to satisfy hunger.	Irregular, chaotic eating—skip meals, fast, binge, diet; or consistent pattern of eating much more or much less that the body wants or needs.	Eating typical of anorexia, bulimia, binge eating disorder, other eating disorders.
How Eating is Regulated	Eating regulated by internal signals of hunger, appetite and satiety; eat when hungry, stop when full and satisfied.	Eating often regulated by inappropriate internal and external controls such as dieting, counting calories, emotional events, sight or smell of food.	Eating regulated mainly inappropriate internal and external controls.
Purpose of Eating	Eat to satisfy hunger, for healthy, growth, well-being and at times for pleasure, (social reasons). Feel good after eating.	Often eat (or restrain eating) for thinness; eat to relieve anxiety or stress; may feel too full after eating, or feel remorse, guilt or shame.	Eating almost entirely for purposes of body shaping and to relieve stress; eating may cause distress.
Prevalence	Small children and persons who don't interfere with natural regulations; likely more males than females.	Large percentage of girls and women, perhaps at times as 50 to 81 percent age 10 and over (who report trying to lose weight); increasingly boys and men.	Estimated prevalence: 10 percent of high school and college age youth, 90 to 95 percent female.
Physical	Promotes health and energy; growth and development of children.	Often feel tired, dizzy, chilled; may have weak bones, delayed puberty, if undernourished; increased risk of eating disorders.	Severe physical effects; mortality as high as 15 to 20 percent for anorexia, bulimia.
Weight	Normal, stable weight, expressing genetic and environmental factors.	Varies; eating pattern may cause weight to cycle up and down, decrease, remain stable, or increase.	Weight varies, depending on genetics, the disorder, and its expression.

Mental	Promotes clear thinking, and ability to concentrate.	Decreased mental alertness, concentration, narrowing of interests.	Diminished mental capacity, memory loss.
Thoughts of food, weight	Food thoughts low, usually at meal time, about 15 to 20 percent of day; less if no food preparation.	Preoccupied with food; thoughts often focus on eating, planning to eat, counting calories or fat grams, body image; may occupy 30 to 60 percent of time awake.	Thoughts focused on food, weight; as much as 90 to 100 percent of time awake in anorexia, 70 to 90 percent in bulimia.
Emotional	Promotes mood stability.	Greater mood instability; easily upset, irritable, anxious, lower self-esteem; increasing concern with body image.	Mood instability, risk of functional depression.
Social	Promotes healthy relationships with family and friends.	Less social integration; may be withdrawn, self-absorbed, lonely; diminished capacity for affection, generosity.	Social withdrawal, alienation, often eat alone; worsening family relations.

rides normal fullness signals. The outsize portions frequently being served today both at restaurants and home may contribute to this. It is important to note that body size does not identify overeating; it cannot be assumed that large youngsters overeat.

Chaotic Eating Affects Emotions

Dysfunctional eating affects children mentally and physically. They may be moody and irritable when they go too long without eating, or lethargic if they are eating continually and not allowing themselves to feel hunger. If your child diets, or cuts weight severely for a school sports program such as wrestling, the harmful effects of undernutrition can range from fatigue, moodiness and dulled mental alertness to delayed puberty, stunted growth and fragile bones. These effects of food deficiency are described more fully in the next chapter (see Chapter 6).

Food thoughts take up much of the time for children who are restricting food. There is increased preoccupation with forbidden foods, diet foods, delicious foods, good foods and bad foods. They are preoccupied with when to eat, and how to avoid or delay eating, and concerned with weight and their body image. Socially, children preoccupied in this way may feel isolated and lonely. Shame and guilt may surface because of their eating or thoughts about eating. They might feel stigmatized because of real or imagined body imperfections.

Dysfunctional eating affects weight, yet in its various forms, it is associated with a wide range of weights as genetics interact with lifestyle factors. Children may be thin—or large. Associated with-chaotic eating, dieting, and bingeing, fluctuations in weight often cycle up and down in "yo-yo" fashion. Consistent undereating can be expected to result in a weight lower than normal for that child, while consistent overeating may result in a higher weight, adding excess fat to normal growth, year after year.

"Going on a Diet" is Not Normal

Many children begin their chaotic, roller coaster eating with a diet. Dieting may seem harmless, and few parents consider how disruptive it is. But even without nutrient deficiencies, dieting and fasting can affect development. Dieting becomes a way of life.

Research by Janet Polivy, PhD, a University of Toronto professor who has studied the detrimental effects of dieting for over 20 years, shows that dieters respond differently than non-dieters in a range of situations. Chronic dieters are easily upset, emotional, moody, are more likely to eat when anxious, and have trouble concentrating on the task at hand if there is any kind of distraction. They are compliant, perfectionist, preoccupied with weight and body dissatisfaction, and have a diminished lifestyle.[105]

They salivate more when faced with attractive food, and have higher levels of digestive hormones and elevated levels of free fatty acids in their blood. They can go longer without food and eat less under "ideal" circumstances than nondieters, but once started, they binge or eat more, then experience guilt. The chronic dieter focuses on food, eating and weight, both for herself and in her awareness of others, and has lower self respect.[106] (See Chapter 9 for more on dieting and its effects.)

Dieting almost inevitably fails, causing weight to yo-yo up and down, or ratcheting it up even higher. And while people often feel they are improving health by their efforts to lose weight, research shows just the opposite. Weight cycling is linked to higher death rates (see Chapter 2).

Yet, ironically, as harmful as dieting is, it can make children feel they are doing the right thing. They feel good just for having made the decision to go on a diet. Pursuing thinness is widely perceived to be the same as pursuing good health. "That feeling of self-sacrifice can hook us into wonderful feelings of purity and goodness," notes Mary Evans Young, founder of No Diet Day in London, and author of *Diet Breaking.* "The diet becomes a kind of fanatical religion, requiring you to abide by a set of stringent rules or pay the penance of guilt. It's a guilt that starts by slowly nibbling and then steadily gnaws away at your body, spirit and confidence. Give yourself a break. You deserve much, much more."[107]

Eating Disorder Risks

As American parents continue to obsess about weight and diet, it is hardly surprising that eating disorders among their children have risen to crisis levels.

Eating disorder sufferers become lonely and driven to keep their disorder a secret. They irritate easily, and can be extremely rigid, determined to keep their own small rituals and rules. The father of one girl said, "She has withdrawn into her own world. She's lonely and is missing out on all the fun and exciting things during her teenage years . . . I have cried many times over this."[108]

An estimated eight million people in the United States suffer from eating disorders, including about 10 percent of high school and college-age youth, 90 to 95 percent of them female. Estimates are that anorexia nervosa affects about one percent and bulimia nervosa one to three percent of high school girls. In the third category called *other eating disorders,* eating disorder specialist Michael

FIGURE 5.2 **Teens: Find Out What Rules You**[9]

Score:
1 – always; 2 – very often; 3 – often; 4 – sometimes; 5 – rarely; 6 – never

__I am unhappy with myself the way I am.
__I am constantly thinking about changing the way I look (thinner, more muscular, smaller nose, etc).
__I weigh myself several times a week.
__The number on the scale influences whether I feel good about myself or not. (If the number is where I want it to be, I feel good about life and myself. If the number is higher or lower than I want it to be, I feel lousy about myself.)
__I think about burning up calories when I exercise.
__I eat for reasons other than being physically hungry (tired, bored, lonely, upset, because food is there).
__I can't tell when I am hungry or full.
__I eat too quickly, not taking time to pay attention to my meal and taste, savor and enjoy my food.
__I don't take time to do activities that I really enjoy that are just for me.
__I swing between times when I enjoy healthy eating and times when my eating is out-of-control.
__I spend a lot of time worrying about how I look.
__I go through periods of not eating anything to "pigging out" on food.
__I think all-or-nothing – like, if I can't do it all, or can't do it well, I don't even try.
__I try to do everything my friends ask of me.
__I try to do things perfectly and if I don't succeed I get really down on myself.
__I criticize myself when I don't achieve exactly what I set out to do (or don't reach my goals).

___TOTAL + 4 = ____ YOUR SCORE

Research shows that if you scored less than 75 you may benefit from an approach that points you in a new direction for eating. Discover the nondiet road to healthier living. It could change your life.

OMICHINSKI. 1995

Levine finds prevalence rates of 2 to 13 percent of middle school and high school girls.[109]

Recovery can be long and difficult. Less than half of patients with severe disorders recover well.[110] Death rates are relatively high, with an estimated mortality of 15 to 20 percent for anorexia and bulimia. Yet health agencies and the public have failed to come to grips with the severity and extent of eating disorders. They are even ignored in the Healthy People 2010 report, which sets the health agenda for the nation.[111]

Families of eating disordered youth are in a difficult situation. They see their child behaving in destructive ways and feel helpless and frustrated. They may try to gain control over what she eats, policing washrooms and searching drawers for diet pills or laxatives. The eating disorder tends to take over and dominate family life.

Anorexia Nervosa

"When I first started to eat strangely, all I would eat were sweets, and that wasn't any good. Then I got into just eating salads, just lettuce and diet pop and that wasn't any good. Then I got into pretty much not eating at all, and that wasn't any good," says a former anorexic patient.[112]

As the malnourished body shuts down in anorexia nervosa, changes occur in behavior, perception, thinking, mood and social interaction. One of the most striking features is how intently the individual is preoccupied with food, even though she eats very little and is in a semi-starved condition. She may develop odd eating rituals, positioning and cutting food into small pieces, chewing a certain number of times. Many of the bizarre behaviors common to anorexia nervosa, once thought to be caused by pre-existing psychopathy, are now recognized as the result of severe and prolonged food restriction, or semi-starvation.[113]

A sense of heightened control becomes important. Pleasure and enjoyment during eating are replaced by guilt, anxiety and ambivalence. The individual grows depressed, irritable, anxious and unstable, often leading to increased social isolation. Compulsive exercise may be part of the disorder.

Definition

In anorexia nervosa, by definition, the individual is more than 15 percent under expected weight; she fears gaining weight, is preoccupied with food, has abnormal eating habits, and has amenorrhea. Other common warning signs include chewing each bite a number of times, denial of hunger, and saying he/she is too fat, even when this is not true. If male, sexual drive decreases. There are two types of anorexia: one restricts food; the other restricts food and either purges regularly, or binges and purges both.[114] Note: the more warning signs a person has, the higher the probability that the person has or is developing an eating disorder.

Mental Complications of Anorexia Nervosa

Up to one-third of anorexic individuals also develop bulimia nervosa. When this happens they experience symptoms characteristic of both eating disorders.[115] Just a partial list follows:

Energy level. Fatigue, weakness, and apathy.

Mood, attitude and behavior. Mood swings (tyrannical); anxiety and ambivalence; critical and intolerant of others; depression; perfectionist behavior; fantasy that weight loss can cause or prevent some life event (prevent parental divorce, attract romance).

Mental ability. Inability to concentrate, loss of memory decline in ambition.

Weight. Increasing preoccupation with body; frequent monitors body changes (may check with scale and/or mirror many times per day.

Food, eating and hunger. Misperception of hunger, satiety and other bodily sensations; hunger and increasing hunger; fears food and gaining weight; eats alone; guilt when eating; may secretly binge; need to vicariously enjoy food (may collect recipes, dream of food, hoard food, enjoy watching others eat, pursue food-related careers—as dietitians, chefs, caterers).

Other. Hypersensitive to cold and heat, hypersensitive to noise and light; sleep disturbance.

Physical Complications of Anorexia Nervosa[116]

Electrolytes. May be low in potassium, sodium, chloride, calcium, magnesium, and high or low bicarbonate. Electrolyte imbal-

ance is more likely when there is dehydration and/or purging.
Gastrointestinal. Constipation is likely, and may promote laxative use. Commonly there is vomiting, feelings of fullness and bloating, and abdominal discomfort. There may be ulcers, and pancreatic dysfunction. Excessive laxatives over time may result in gastrointestinal bleeding and impairment of colon functioning.
Cardiovascular. Commonly symptoms are chest pain, arrhythmias, hypotension, edema and mitral valve prolapse. Electrocardiogram (EKG) changes. Heart rates lower than 40 beats per minute are common and as low as 25 reported in severe starvation. Prolonged QT intervals can lead to sudden death syndrome.
Metabolic. Abnormal temperature regulation and cold intolerance are common. Abnormal glucose tolerance, fasting hypoglycemia, high B-hydroxybutyric acid, high free fatty acids, hypercholesterolemia, hypercarotenemia are common. Diabetic patients with an eating disorder may have fluctuating blood glucose levels leading to serious long-term consequences.
Bones. Decreased bone mineral density may lead to fractures, growth retardation, short stature and osteoporosis.
Renal. Elevated blood urea nitrogen, changes in urinary concentration capacity, and decreased glomerular filtration rate are common.
Endocrine. Amenorrhea is 100 percent for females, by definition, although many anorexia nervosa patients menstruate over time. Amenorrhea related to weight loss but may precede weight loss (in one-third); may cause delayed puberty, contributes to osteoporosis, breast atrophy, infertility. Hypometabolic state resulting in cold intolerance, dry skin and hair, bradycardia, constipation, fatigue, slowed reflexes. High plasma cortisol, decreased cortixol response to insulin.
Hematologic. Anemia, leukopenia, bone marrow hypocellularity, common; these effects are usually mild, but can include bleeding tendency.
Neurological. EEG and sleep changes are common; epileptic seizures affect up to 10 percent.

Musculocutaneous. Muscle weakening, muscle cramps. Hair loss, brittle hair and nails, lanugo hair, dry skin and cold extremities are common.

Bulimia Nervosa

The individual with bulimia nervosa goes on an eating binge, eating a large amount of food in a short time. This is followed by recurrent inappropriate compensatory behavior to prevent weight gain, either purging with induced vomiting, misuse of laxatives, diuretics, enemas or other medications—or non-purging measures such as fasting or excessive exercise.[117] Both binge eating and the compensatory behavior occur on average at least twice a week for three months.

As bulimia progresses, it develops into a complex lifestyle that is increasingly isolating, with depressive mood swings and low self-esteem. "I can't stop throwing up. I try, I really do," insisted a bulimia patient from Lemon Grove, Calif. "Yesterday, I promised myself I wouldn't do it anymore. I tried to keep myself busy. I cleaned house, played with the cat, prayed. . .But I don't want to gain weight. I can't do that! I never want to be fat again. I'll never go back there. Nothing is worse than that pain. . .My joints even hurt. I feel so old. My hair looks horrible; and it keeps falling out. I find it all over the place. My mouth is so full of sores, it's gross! I can't even walk around the house standing straight any more. I'm in a daze. I can't focus. But I can't stop. I feel so trapped. Please help me."[118]

Warning Signs of Bulimia nervosa[119]

- ⋆ Makes excuses to go to the restroom after meals
- ⋆ Exhibits mood swings
- ⋆ Unusual swelling around the jaw
- ⋆ Laxative or diuretic wrappers found frequently in the trash
- ⋆ May purchase large quantities of food, which suddenly disappears.
- ⋆ Frequently eats large amounts of food (a binge), often high in calories, and does not seem to gain weight
- ⋆ Unexplained disappearance of food in the home or residence hall setting

* Weight may be within normal range

Mental Complications of Bulimia

The person with bulimia nervosa is often normal weight and may not experience the effects of starvation. However, if she has nutrition deficiencies due to purging, she may have symptoms typical of anorexia nervosa.

Following are mental and physical complications or traits commonly associated with bulimia nervosa, adapted from Kaplan and Garfinkel.[120]

Mood/attitude/behavior. Anxiety, depression; mood swings; low self-esteem, self-deprecating thoughts; embarrassment, shame related to behavior; persistent remorse; paranoid feelings; unreasonable resentments; makes excuses to go to bathroom after meals; may buy large amounts of food, which suddenly disappears; impulsive as compared to anorexics who are overcontrolled.
Mental ability. Loss of ordinary willpower, poor impulse control, self-indulgent behavior; recognizes abnormal eating behavior.
Social. Depends on others for approval; feelings of isolation; unable to discuss problem, others are unhappy about food obsession; social isolation; distances self from friends and family; fear of going out in public; family, work and money problems.
Weight. Feels that self worth is dependent on low weight; constant concern with weight and body image.
Food, eating and hunger. Eats alone; eats when not hungry; preoccupation with eating and food; fears binges and eating out of control; increased dependency on bingeing; binge eating of large amount of food in a short time, feeling out of control, cannot stop eating.
Purging. Feels need to rid body of calories consumed during binge (through vomiting, laxatives, diuretics, enemas, fasting or excessive exercise); experimentation with vomiting, laxatives and diuretics often leads to regular abuse.
Binge/purge cycle. Spends much time planning, carrying out, cleaning up after bulimic episode; eliminates normal activ-

ities; complex lifestyle may develop with episodes occurring several times a day; worsening of symptoms during times of emotional stress; feels soothed and comforted by binge/purge cycle — it may serve to relieve frustration, anxiety, anger, fear, remorse, boredom, loneliness.

Other. Dishonesty, lying; stealing food or money; drug and alcohol abuse; suicidal tendencies or attempts.

Physical Complications of Bulimia Nervosa

Electrolytes. Low potassium, low chloride, dehydration and metabolic alkalosis are common. May lead to cardiac arrest, renal failure. Dehydration is common along with hypotension, dizziness, weakness, muscle cramps. Cardiac arrhythmias affect 20 percent; unpredictable, may require emergency treatment. Hypochloremia is common; limits kidney's ability to excrete bicarbonate.

Gastrointestinal. Constipation and increased amylase common. Rarely gastric and duodenal ulcer, acute gastric dilation and rupture. Frequent abdominal pain. Severe abdominal pain may lead to rigid abdomen and shock which may result in death. Abuses of laxatives may lead to iron deficiency anemia, rectal bleeding and cathartic colon.

Pulmonary. Aspiration pneumonia possible from aspiration of vomitus.

Cardiovascular. Peripheral edema is common along with EKG changes and QT changes, which can lead to serious arrhythmias and congestive heart failure. Uncommon is sudden cardiac death. Ipecac syrup abuse may lead to death through cardiomyopathy, myocarditis.

Metabolic. High B-hydroxybutyric acid, free fatty acids. Less common edema, abnormal temperature regulation and cold intolerance.

Renal. Possible changes.

Endocrine. Menstrual irregularities with low body weight, dexamethasone nonsuppression common.

Hematologic. May be anemic with nutrition deficiency.

Neurological. EEG changes common. May have epileptic seizures with malnutrition and electrolyte imbalance.
Musculocutaneous. Calluses on dorsum of dominant hand are common from inducing gag reflex. Muscle weakening with ipecac abuse.
Dental. Enamel erosions from vomiting.

Other Eating Disorders[121]

Some eating disorders don't fit neatly into the diagnostic criteria of either anorexia or bulimia. Two of these, binge eating disorder and night eating syndrome, have been linked to overweight. Night eaters may eat over half their day's calories between 8 PM and 6 AM, suffer from insomnia, and eat several times during the night when they awaken.

Examples of individuals in the *Eating disorder not otherwise specified* category include those with the following:

* All criteria met for anorexia nervosa except amenorrhea.
* All criteria met for anorexia nervosa except, despite weight loss, current weight is in normal range.
* All criteria met for bulimia nervosa except frequency of binges is less than twice a week or for a duration of less than three months.
* An individual of normal body weight who regularly engages in inappropriate compensatory behavior (such as induced vomiting) after eating small amounts of food.
* Repeatedly chewing and spitting out large amounts of food without swallowing.

Binge Eating Disorder

As he hurried up the walk from the school bus, Jeremiah's thoughts centered on the cookies in the kitchen drawer. He'd have a just a snack. But at some level he knew he'd eat more, and the thought excited him. Pulling open the drawer, he took not one but a handful of double Oreos. He ate fast, filling his mouth with big bites, hardly taking time to chew or to swallow one cookie before he was eating another. He prowled the kitchen for candy and snacks, and before he knew it the whole package of Oreos was gone. He opened the refrigerator door, glanced around furtively, listening to make sure he was alone. He scooped a big helping of ice cream, pouring on caramel and chocolate syrup. Even while gulping down the ice cream, he could scarcely pause to taste it. He couldn't stop. He ate with almost a sense of panic, thinking only of what he'd eat next. More cookies? Peanut butter with chocolate chips? Marshmellows and graham crackers? He knew he should eat an apple, but it was too late. He didn't have time. He felt driven to eat all the foods he'd wanted the day before but hadn't eaten. It was as if now the barriers were down in this brief window of time he had permission to eat all he wanted, and he had to do it. He ate a few slices of bread, and tore open a sack of candy. He felt guilty. But he couldn't stop until his stomach hurt. Painfully full at last and disgusted with himself for what he had done, Jeremiah went to his room, turned on the television and opened a school book.

First described in 1959, binge eating disorder is included in the category of *Eating disorder not otherwise specified*. It meets most of the criteria for bulimia nervosa except that persons with binge eating disorder do not regularly purge or try to get rid of the calories they have eaten. They eat in chaotic ways and eat large amounts of food at least twice a week, in a relatively short time such as within a two-hour period with a sense of loss of control. They may be of average weight, but most often are overweight. They have high levels of body image dissatisfaction. Binge eating disorder is much more common in men than other eating disorders.

The individual has marked distress regarding binge eating, and engages in binge eating at least two days a week, on average for six months.[122]

Chapter 6

♦ ♦ ❖ ♦ ♦ ❖ ♦ ♦ ❖ ♦ ♦ ❖ ♦ ♦ ❖ ♦ ♦ ❖ ♦ ♦

The Death of Family Meal Time

The yellow school bus pulls up to a convenience store and out pours a hungry load of junior high students. They're on their way to a sporting event, traveling directly from their last class to a town eighty miles away. They're hungry. Time to stock up for an evening meal and snacks.

What foods do these youngsters bring up to the counter? One after another they lay them out: candy, chips, cookies, big bottles of soda pop.

Jill chooses only a diet coke and a candy bar—she's a cheerleader and says she needs to watch her figure. But Jill skipped breakfast and lunch, so she's famished. Another group of girls encourages each other to buy banana flips, Sara Lee pastries, cookie packs, and candies—they'll share on the bus.

As for the boys, their hands are filled with packaged treats and bottles. Chocolate donuts, chips, crackers, cookies, plastic-wrapped cakes, and heavily-oiled popcorn. They pour over the vast refrigerated walls of drink selections: Power Aid sounds like it would provide lots of energy; so do the dozens of "10-percent-juice" selections.

This is dinner? Where are the five food groups: bread and cereals, fruits, vegetables, meat and alternates, milk? Where are foods rich in calcium, iron, and the vitamins so desperately needed by growing teenagers? Many of these kids spend five dollars at this first stop. They'll buy more of these same foods during the game, and the bus will probably stop again on the way home.

Interestingly enough, they could purchase differently. The store offers tuna and ham sandwiches, milk and chocolate milk, 100 percent fruit juice, string cheese, beef jerky, even bananas and packets of washed baby carrots. Among main entree foods, it may be easier to find the high in fat deep-fat-fried chicken nuggets than the beef roast sandwich.

More Highly-Processed Foods

It's not that there is anything wrong with consuming candy, chips, and soft drinks as part of an otherwise nutritious diet. But most kids are falling far short of eating what they need from the five food groups. Some are not eating enough of any food—especially teenage girls. Others are overloaded with calorie-dense foods—excess amounts of fats, sugar and sweeteners (and alcohol) from the tip of the Pyramid—so nutritious foods get crowded out. The confused advice young people are getting from national health advisers as well as the media on the "need" to restrict food and avoid weight gain, rather than to eat for health, is simply overwhelming.

Kids are eating more added sugars of all kinds. They drink more sugar-sweetened soft drinks, as well as more low-calorie soft drinks (about three-fourths of soft drink consumption is sugar-sweetened). Teenage boys consume 34 teaspoons of sugar a day with 44 percent from soft drinks and teenage girls consume 24 teaspoons of sugar a day with 40 percent coming from soft drinks, according to Michael Jacobson, of the Center for Science in the Public Interest.[123]

The percent fat in the diet appears to have dropped since 1978. Kids have shifted from drinking whole milk to low-fat or skim, or have made the less desirable shift from milk to soft drinks. At the same time, they have shifted toward eating higher-fat mixtures like pizza, and eating out more, which means higher fat foods and larger portions.

They eat fewer eggs, and fewer cuts of beef and pork, slightly more poultry, and slightly less fish and shellfish. Fruit consumption is up, but many eat no fruit at all on any given day.

Food Advertising

These changes are driven by highly-targeted advertising. Not surprisingly, most advertising dollars promote the branded, highly-processed and packaged foods which are most profitable for big food companies, the dozen or so food giants who produce, distribute, and sell much of what the world eats.

Four out of five ads targeting kids are for soft drinks, fast food, snacks, or sugary cereals. Ordinary, wholesome foods in their natural states are not showcased. Advertising of fruits and vegetables is almost non-existent. Half of nutrition-related information in TV commercials aired in top-rated prime-time network shows and viewed heavily by two- to eleven- year-olds is misleading or inaccurate. Public service announcements are virtually absent from prime-time TV. [124]

Food manufacturers spend $13 billion a year bombarding children with ads for foods high in calories and fat, according to a recent CBS news story.[125] That money is considered well spent by advertisers. The food and alcohol market is huge, capturing about 12.5 percent of consumer income. Its advertising comprises nearly 16 percent of total advertising dollars, second only to the auto industry's 18 percent.[126]

Children see more than 40,000 advertisements a year on television alone, according to the national Stop Commercial Exploitation of Children coalition. One study shows that on Saturday mornings U.S. children see about 10 food commercials for every hour of TV they watch.

Television ads do prompt kids to eat. "Childhood obesity, eating disorders, violence, rampant materialism and other societal ills are all linked to excessive marketing to kids," warns Joe Kelly, head of the national nonprofit Dads and Daughters.[127]

And these are only children; they lack critical thinking skills. Often they cannot tell the difference between programs and advertising.

Alcohol advertising is targeted directly at underage youth, charges the Center on Alcohol Marketing and Youth, based at Georgetown University. A recent study shows American youth saw far more ads for beer, distilled spirits, and "malternative," or low-alcohol drinks, in magazines in 2001 than did people of legal drinking age.[128]

Outsize Portions

Modern culture encourages overeating. Youngsters are being coaxed to overeat and at the same time, are urged to restrict eating and stay thin. They are taught to distrust and override their natural signals of hunger and satiety. Ads for Pringles Right Crisps show young people eating 10 or 20 chips at a time. Ritz Air Crisp ads implore kids to "inhale them." And Baked Lays Potato Chips challenges, "Betcha can't eat just one—bag!"

Restaurants offer larger servings, larger meals, and more abundant buffets with many food choices. A study in *Restaurants USA* found customers expect larger quantities of food than they did in 1991, and that people think of large servings as getting better value for their money.[129]

Food portions commonly being served today are compared with standard portion sizes from the Food Guide Pyramid in a study published in the February 2002 American Journal of Public Health. The findings:[130]

* Cookies can be 7 times standard sizes
* Cooked pasta servings are often nearly 5 times standard sizes
* Muffins weigh over 3 times the standard size

Ethnic Influences

Ethnic foods commonly grow larger when Americanized. The bagel, when introduced from Poland, weighed 1 1/2 ounces and contained 116 calories, according to Melanie Polk, RD, director of nutrition education at the American Institute for Cancer Research.

Today's triple-size bagel weighs 4 or more ounces and may contain over 300 calories.[131]

In Mexico, a quesadilla is a 5-inch tortilla containing around 540 calories and 32 grams of fat. The American quesadilla is typically 10 inches, and one serving may contain over 1,200 calories and 70 grams of fat.[132]

In London, a news story titled "Portions out of all proportion" decried America's "elephantine cuisine." The writer compares foods: hot dogs (350 calories in the U.S. vs. 150 calories in Britain), cookies (493 vs. 65), ice cream cone (625 vs. 160), muffin (705 vs. 158), nachos (1,650 vs. 569), and a meal of steak and fries (2,060 vs. 730). The writer observed that Europeans are "a lot more quality conscious...Americans just want value for their money, and base value on size."

We Eat More When Served More

"There is something about our psychology that makes us eat more if it's put in front of us," says Marion Nestle, chair of the Department of Nutrition and Food Studies at New York University, and author of "Food Politics."[133]

This begins before age five, according to studies at Pennsylvania State University. Children up to three years old eat about the same amount no matter how much is in front of them. But when five-year-olds are served more food, they eat half again as much as usual. So do adults.[134] People also eat more when presented with a wide array of food choices. They eat more when a smorgasbord of foods is spread out in front of them. Many families eating out favor "all you can eat" buffets, where children learn from their parents to fill their plates with supersize portions, and maybe go back for more.

Eating Out

One of the disturbing trends in restaurant eating is the increasing popularity of appetizers and the large amount of fat and calories they contain. An appetizer of deep-fried onion rings contains 2,000 calories. A plate of cheese fries from Outback Steakhouse chain contains over 3,000 calories and 217 grams of fat, including 90 grams of saturated fat, according to the Center for Science in the Public Interest. Even split three ways, this appetizer still contains 1,000 calories—and the main course is yet to come.

Even a drink can become the calorie-equivalent of a meal. At Starbucks, a Venti White Chocolate Mocha with whipped cream contains 600 calories and 25 grams of fat, including 15 grams of saturated fat. Adding a scone brings the total to 1,130 calories, 51 grams fat and 31 grams saturated fat. It's easy to cut calories: a latte with skim milk is only 150 calories and a cappuccino with skim milk is 100 calories.

Between 1977 and 1996 consumption of food prepared away from home increased from 18 to 32 percent, according to the USDA.[135] This is one-third of daily calories. And when kids eat out, they consume more fat and calories.[136]

Boys at age eighteen are eating 40 percent of their meals away from home, compared with 23 percent two decades ago. Teenage boys are getting more of their food from fast-food places than any other place away from home.

Fast food restaurants, with their many deep fat fried options, are even more likely than other restaurants to serve food that is high-calorie, high-fat, high in saturated fat, and low in fiber and low in variety. However, nearly all restaurants today make heavy use of their deep fat fryers—for chicken and seafood as well as potatoes. Even take-out or delivered food is usually higher in fat than food prepared at home.

Cookies for Breakfast

Skipping breakfast can affect children's intellectual performance, lower their scores on standardized tests, and increase their rates of absence and tardiness.[137] Even moderate undernutrition can have lasting effects on children's cognitive development and school performance. One in five teenagers age 15 to 18 regularly skips breakfast.

When youngsters do eat breakfast, what are they eating? Typically it's a bowl of sugar-laden cereal, with most of the milk left in the bowl afterward—a sorry lack of nutrients to sustain a child through the morning hours. General Mills recently introduced chocolate chip cookie cereal, with 13 grams sugar and 10 percent of the day's sodium in every bowl. Somehow this sugar product is thought by its makers to merit a side panel "endorsement" from the American Heart Association for what it doesn't contain—no cholesterol or saturated fat.

Breakfast food companies are promoting cereal bars to eat on the run, such as Chocolate Granola Bars, Pop Tarts, Honey Nut Cheerios and Cinnamon Toast Crunch. Such meals-on-the-go tend to be high in fat, high in sugar, and high in calories. Like many of today's sugary cereals, they are more like eating cookies and candy for breakfast than ordinary cereal. Bars are more expensive, too, than a bowl of cereal and milk.

The energy and nutrition bars are another growing industry. PowerBar advertises, "A great way to kick start your day with the natural energy and nutrition that powers world class athletes." But remember that the term "energy" on the label is just another name for calories, many of them empty calories. Some energy bars also have unexpected ingredients, stimulants such as ephedra, which has been linked to numerous deaths, according to the Center for Science in the Public Interest.

If there's no time to eat breakfast, how about a sandwich as your child goes out the door?

Children Snack More Now

Children are snacking more today than twenty-five years ago. Researchers at the University of North Carolina compared information from three national surveys 1977 through 1996, and found that, while the average size of snacks and calories per snack remain relatively constant, the number of times kids eat between meals has increased. Snacks are higher in calories and fat and lower in calcium than meals. Thus the "calorie density" of what children eat over the course of a day has risen significantly, from 1.35 to 1.54 calories per gram.

Children today take in about twenty-five percent of their calories in snacks (600 calories), compared with about 18 percent (450 calories) in the late 1970's.[138]

Snacks are important in keeping children's energy levels high, but the kinds of snacks kids choose can be a problem. The authors note that the biggest changes in snacking patterns have occurred in the last 10 years and include more soft drinks, chips and salty snacks, and fewer snacks of fruit, vegetables and milk.[139]

Too Much Sugar

Added sugars include sweeteners of all kinds used as ingredients in prepared food or added at the table—fructose, sucrose, honey, maple syrup, molasses, glucose, brown sugar, corn syrup, and lactose. If one of these is the first or second ingredient on the label, or if several kinds of sugars are spread throughout the list, you know that food is high in added sugars. Added sugar turns up not only in candy, cake and desserts, but also in pizza, bread, soup, crackers, canned vegetables, flavored yogurt, ketchup and salad dressing.

American's consumption of added sugars went up to 32 teaspoons a day in 1996 from 27 teaspoons in 1970, according to the U. S. Food Supply data.[140] The Healthy Eating Index puts it somewhat lower: about 20 teaspoons for teenagers, and 19 for younger children ages six to eleven.[141] But Michael Jacobson, of the Center for Science in the Public Interest, puts it higher: 34 teaspoons of sugar for teen boys, with 44 percent coming from soft drinks, and 24 teaspoons for teen girls, with about the same percent from soft drinks.[142]

Regardless, sugar consumption by kids is too high, and since these are averages, many consume much more. A limit of 12 to 18 teaspoons a day is recommended for fully nourished teen girls and boys. And for the many girls who eat only 1,600 calories, the limit is 6 teaspoons. If they eat fewer calories, as many do, they should limit sugar even more.

Sugar is not a villain triggering hyperactivity in children, as many believe. (Hungry children do have behavior problems, and when they eat sweets it can quickly leave them hungry again, dissatisfied and frustrated.) But sugar does add empty calories, displaces other nutrients, and contributes to tooth decay.

Where's the Balance, Variety, Moderation?

The way many kids eat today violates the basic nutrition principles of balance, variety, and moderation. They are shifting away from the five food groups to rely heavily on highly-processed foods from the grain group—granola bars, Toastits, pops, crackers, chips, cookies, pasta, rice dishes, tacos, burritos and pizza. They are drinking three times as much soda pop and consuming more desserts and candy.[143]

Many children eat healthy diets until they reach their teens and have less parental supervision. The Bogalusa Heart Study documents this trend: the percent of youth who get less than two-thirds of recommended nutrients increases as they reach their teenage years. Food choices shift more toward higher-calorie, lower-nutrient food, toward more dessert and snack food, and more soft drinks.[144]

Teenage girls have the poorest diets in the nation, and are most at risk from nutrient deficiencies. Younger teen girls from ages twelve to fifteen are even worse off than older teens, because of their tremendous growth needs.

Missing Food Groups

Only two percent of school-age children meet the Food Guide Pyramid recommendations for all five major food groups. Overall, only 14 percent meet the recommendations for fruit, 17 percent for meat and alternates, 20 percent for vegetables, 23 percent for grains, and 30 percent for milk.[145]

Young children, age two to nine, score generally higher, and are lowest on meat. Only 18 percent eat enough from the meat group, even though it includes poultry, fish, eggs and meat alternates such as peanut butter, tofu and beans.[146]

Few American kids eat the recommended five-a-day servings of fruits and vegetables, except for these younger children, who do. Only about one in four high school students gets five—boys more than girls, white kids more than black or Hispanic, high school freshmen more than seniors.[147]

Only 16 percent of high school students report drinking three glasses of milk a day in the 2001 Youth Risk Behavior Survey (20 percent of boys and 11 percent of girls).

As Milk Drops, Soda Takes a Leap

Milk consumption has dropped off steeply in the last twenty years. Only half of teenagers drink milk today, compared with three-fourths in the 1970s. And those who do, drink only about 1 1/2 to 2 cups a day on average, not the 3 glasses recommended.[148]

Why this devastating drop in milk? Experts say teens are responding to aggressive mass marketing of soft drinks as "fun" foods, and switching over from milk. More sobering are school policies that promote higher-profit beverages rather than milk.[149]

Heavy soft drink intake is associated with low intake of calcium and other nutrients, and with a diet high in calories and fat. A national study shows children and teens who drink milk at their noon meal are more likely to have high quality diets.[150]

Healthy Eating Index Report Card

In the Healthy Eating Index, a score over 80 rates as a "good" diet, with less than 51 rating "poor"; a diet in between "needs improvement." A high score suggests the individual is eating well from all five food groups and getting variety in the diet. He or she is keeping fat, saturated fat, cholesterol and sodium at low levels. (Some experts believe these levels may be unnecessarily low.) A perfect score on each of these 10 components scores 10, for a possible total of 100 points.

As reported in 2002, teen scores average only in the low 60s out of 100. This does not improve after high school, when older teens score a national average of 61, college students scoring somewhat higher than noncollege youth.[151] Children from low-income households tend to have poorer diets.

TABLE 6.1 **Healthy Eating Index Scores**[h]

	Age	Average score
Children	2-3	74
	4-6	68
	7-10	67
Girls	11-14	64
	15-18	61
Boys	11-14	62
	15-18	61

Diets of young children at age two to three rate highest with an average Healthy Eating Index score of 74.[152] Yet many of these children have a poor diet or one that needs improvement. Quality declines as they grew older, especially between the age groups of 2 to 3 years and 4 to 6 years, when the percentage with a good diet drops from 36 percent to 17 percent.

Meat, fruit, grain, vegetable and sodium scores also declined between the ages of 2 and 9. Experts recommend that nutrition promotion activities be directed toward younger children to prevent a worsening of the diet as they grow older.[153]

Alcohol Adds Calories

Alcohol consumption is often ignored in counting calories, yet it makes up 6 percent of calories in the average American diet and as much as 10 percent for regular adult drinkers. Alcohol is not called a nutrient, as it doesn't promote growth, maintenance or repair. But it does add 7 calories per gram, nearly double the 4 calories of protein or carbohydrate.

Although illegal, many underage youth consume a significant amount of alcohol. The 2001 Youth Risk Behavior Survey shows heavy drinking episodes by nearly one-third of high school students, both boys and girls, in which they drank five or more drinks

TABLE 6.2 **Recommended Calorie Intake**[i]

	Age	Calories Recommended
Boys	7-10	2,000
	11-14	2,500
	15-18	3,000
	19-24	2,900
Girls	7-10	2,000
	11-14	2,200
	15-18	2,200
	19-24	2,200

For pregnancy, add 300 calories for 2nd and 3rd trimester; for lactation, add 500 calories.[39]

For adults, calorie intake apparently increased only slightly between 1977 and 1996, from an average of about 1,854 to 2,002 calories, an increase of only 148 calories, some of that judged likely due to improvements in the way dietary data are collected. Recommended daily intake for adults to age 51 is 2,900 calories for men, and 2,200 for women.[40]

NHANES III, PHASE I, 1988-91

of alcohol once or more in the previous month. Half of white and Hispanic boys and girls report current alcohol use, compared with less than one third of black teenagers.[155]

Calorie Intake Stable

While children have been getting heavier, they seem not to have increased their calorie intake. In 20 years of NHANES studies, 1971 through 1991, children's average calorie intake has declined slightly for most age groups.[156]

It's puzzling that even though the children in the Bogalusa study are heavier than those studied fourteen years ago, they eat fewer calories and less fat and cholesterol.[157] This trend is seen in other countries, too. A French study found that in 1995 ten-year-olds ate fewer calories, less total fat, and lower percent of fat than in 1978. Yet they had more than double the rates of obesity, at 14 percent, and a more dangerous abdominal fat distribution. What's going on here? Researchers say this puts the origins of obesity into question:

overeating and fat intake may not be the major culprits in weight gain they were once thought to be.[158]

For teen boys, their average intake of 2,716 calories is close to the 2,500 to 3,000 recommended, but for girls their calorie intake of 1,841 falls short of the 2,200 recommended.[159,160] Therefore, many experts are saying that to reduce obesity, children probably should increase activity, rather than cut calories.

Mineral Deficiencies

Among the most critical nutrients for health and growth that American girls lack are iron, zinc and calcium. These deficiencies can cause long-term health problems, and few teenage girls consume even two-thirds of what they need. Over 80 percent of girls today are not getting the calcium they need to build strong bones for a lifetime.

Why don't they drink milk? Often it is not expected or modeled at home. Parents don't drink milk and don't think it's important. In one focus group, a twelve-year-old girl said, "I have Mountain Dew with dinner because it tastes good, high in sugar…Mom drinks Pepsi."

Teenage girls also suggest negative social aspects. They said, you "look lame drinking milk," "most people drink soda," and it's "not cool to drink milk."

But the major reason: girls fear milk is fattening.[163] Pressures to be extremely thin from the media and federal health officials are taking their toll on girls' nutrition.

Iron is not well absorbed in the body, and as much as 80 to 98 percent of nonheme iron may be wasted. Adding just a small amount of heme iron from meat, poultry, fish or eggs enables the body to better absorb the nonheme iron from plant sources.

Certainly a diet without meat can be healthy when people practice good nutrition. But for many girls not eating meat is a way to avoid eating. The trend is so strong that eating disorder specialists watch for the avoidance of meat as one of the steps along the way to an eating disorder.

Girls especially need the highly-absorbable heme iron from meat to make up for monthly blood losses, yet they usually consume less food and get less of all nutrients than boys.

Iron carries energy-giving oxygen through the blood to cells. Girls with low iron stores are likely to feel fatigued, weak, listless, irritable and prone to headaches. They have more difficulties learning, and decreased verbal and memory scores.

In London, investigators recently found that one in four girls age 11 to 18 may be lowering their intelligence by dieting and depriving themselves of high-quality iron.

"We were surprised that a very small drop in iron levels caused a fall in IQ," said Michael Nelson, PhD, study author and senior lecturer in nutrition at King's College, London. "We conclude that poor iron status is common among British adolescent girls and that diet and iron status play an important role in determining IQ."[164]

The damage young children suffer from lack of iron may be irreversible. Mental performance fails to improve in treatment for many anemic children, some studies show. Iron-deficient children commonly have shortened attention spans, lower intelligence scores, and reduced overall intellectual performance.[165] Other problems of anemia or iron deficiency include fatigue, palpitation, impaired work performance, temperature abnormalities, and a compromised immune system.

Girls with low iron stores usually have low zinc levels, too, since zinc comes from similar animal sources. Zinc is need for optimal development and sexual maturation, and helps keep the immune system healthy. Research shows all major branches of the immune system are compromised by even mild zinc deficiency. Other risks are retarded growth, birth defects and decreased short-term memory, problem-solving and attention.[166]

Disease-based Nutrition Versus Full Nutrition

While nutritionists are concerned with how kids are eating, they are just as concerned by some of the solutions being put forward. One of the strongest is "disease-based nutrition," a movement in the health field that promotes a shift toward feeding kids for the prevention of chronic disease, rather than feeding them for full nourishment.

The influence of disease-based nutrition can be seen in the current emphasis on eating to restrict weight. It is evident in the Healthy Eating Index, in which 40 points out of a possible 100 are based on restriction—of fat, saturated fat, cholesterol and sodium—to levels that may be unnecessarily low for most people. It permeates the latest Dietary Guidelines for Americans in recommendations to aim for a "healthy weight," rather than to aim for an active, healthy lifestyle.

This has never happened before: that parents are told to feed their children to avoid the diseases of old age, rather than for good health now, for nourishment, energy, strength and healthy growth. The result is fear and confusion for parents, fear and confusion for children. Many resort to unhealthy, extreme solutions.

Some experts point out that disease-based nutrition is untested. There is no evidence that it will make children healthier, less likely to develop chronic disease, or even add weeks to their life span. Robert Olson, MD, PhD, professor of pediatrics at the University of South Florida, warns that restrictive eating may be risky at any age,

FIGURE 6.1. **Calcium Intake (White Girls age 12-15)**[i]

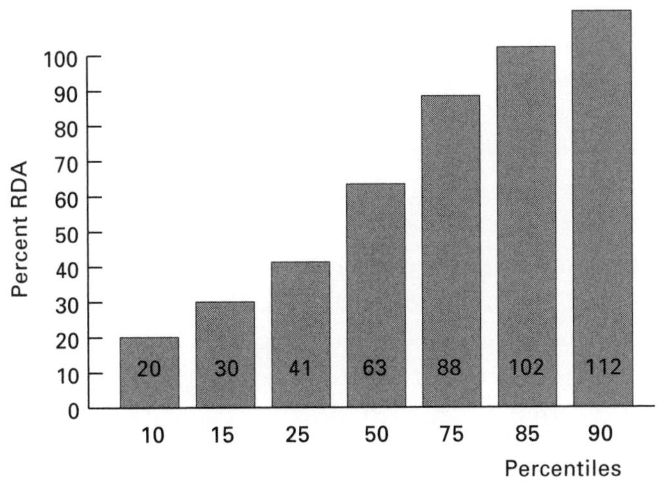

NHANES III, PHASE I, 1988-91

and especially for children. "The recommendation to modify the diets of children is without merit," he charges.

Even if the trade-off is longer life, it is not known whether this would be enough to matter. One study found an increased life expectancy of only three days to three months from a modified diet for a hypothetical person with elevated cholesterol. [167]

Undernourishment of Teenage Girls

Teenage girls have the poorest nutrition in America. Their diets are deficient in many important nutrients and in total calories. Yet this is a time in their lives when they have critical needs for growth and body development.

The appalling truth is that over half of teenage girls do not eat enough for health, energy and strength. They do not eat enough to feel or look their best. They do not eat enough for optimal bone growth, for energy, or even to warm themselves normally. They do not eat enough to be their best selves or to reach their greatest potential, and they don't eat enough to support a healthy pregnancy.

Instead, they are often weak and dizzy, light-headed, cold and anemic. Emotionally, they may feel anxious, irritable, moody, and depressed. And mentally these girls, nearly all students, may have difficulty understanding and concentrating on their studies. Moreover, they feel so badly about themselves that one-third of high school girls report having seriously considered suicide in the past 12 months—double the rates of boys who consider suicide.[168]

What is the problem? The answers are based in a culture that pressures girls to restrict their eating in unhealthy ways.

Girls age twelve to fifteen are at most risk from nutrient deficiencies. They have enormous growth needs. But a recent national study showed their median intake—what the girl in the middle is eating—provides only half to two-thirds of the recommended amounts of calcium, iron, vitamin A, magnesium, zinc, copper and other critical nutrients. She consumes about 79 percent of recommended 2,200 calories. Sixteen to nineteen year-old girls fare little better.[169]

This is a time when their bodies undergo major changes, when their childhood bodies mature. It's normal to put on some extra fat as a girl's body develops curves and readies itself for healthy pregnancies. It's all part of normal female development—and it's going to add a few pounds. Unfortunately, modern girls believe they must fight against the maturing of their own bodies with every weapon they can muster.

Lettuce and Diet Coke

Today these are frequent reports:

- ★ *Twelve-year-old girls who choose only lettuce and non-caloric dressing in the lunch line;*
- ★ *Teenage girls who eat only a bagel and apple all day — after they break a two-day fast of Diet Coke and cigarettes;*
- ★ *Female runners who exercise obsessively and refuse to eat a bite of any food they imagine might add a bit of fat, especially meat or eggs;*
- ★ *A college sorority in which members pay a penalty if they eat any fat at all;*
- ★ *Girls in a dancing troupe who eat fat, but don't swallow it.*

FIGURE 6.2. **Iron Intake (White girls age 12-15)**[k]

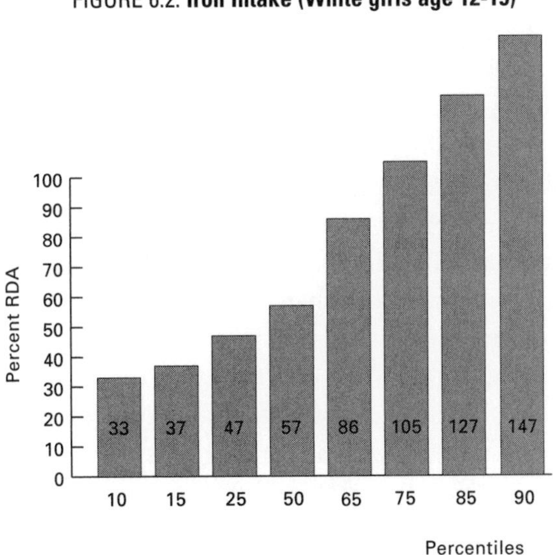

NHANES III, PHASE I, 1988-91

When these girls go on a binge, their nutrition would be much improved if they would binge on a boiled egg or beef sandwich, or even a stick of jerky. But it doesn't happen. Their favorite binge foods are nutrient-deficient sweets—cookies, cake, chips, snack crackers and candy.

Half of girls are not eating well. And even the half with better intake levels often eat erratically, fasting, then bingeing on foods that fail to add up to a high quality diet, cutting out entire food groups. They are dissatisfied and discouraged with their bodies, and yearn to make them less.

Perhaps in the past this could have been called a phase, or a concern affecting only a few girls. But today, undernutrition and malnutrition affect huge numbers of girls and they're not going away.

The Hungry 25 Percent

It is the lower 25 percent of girls—the hungry 25 percent—who are at most risk. Go to any high school basketball game or visit a classroom and you'll see them—the undernourished and malnourished girls. Bony, half-starved girls with hungry eyes and hollow cheeks. (They are not to be confused with girls who are naturally thin and well-nourished.) And larger girls are not exempt from self-starvation. At the 25th percentile (the best of the lower one-fourth) Mexican American girls are consuming only an average of 1,300 calories, white girls, 1,358 and African American girls, 1,400. None is even up to the lower range of needed calories (recommended daily intake is 2,200 calories, with a range of 1,500 to 3,000). At the 10th percentile, Mexican American girls get only 833 calories, white girls, 904 and African American girls, 1,064.

Looking at the calcium intake, girls at the 25th percentile, are getting only about one-third of what they need, and at the 10th percentile only 20 percent.

For iron, girls at the 25th percentile get less than half of what they need, and at the 10th only one-third. It's no surprise that iron deficiency and anemia are increasing among teen girls and now affect

FIGURE 6.3. **Calorie Intake** [1]

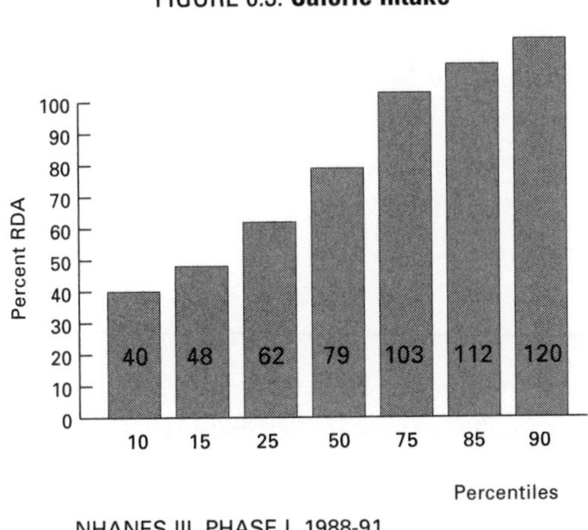

11 percent of girls and women, including 19 percent of Mexican American and 15 percent of African American females, according to Healthy People 2010.[170]

At the 10th percentile teen girls are getting barely half the protein needed, one third the vitamin B12, one-fourth of the zinc, and 15 percent of the vitamin A. Median values for girls and women are shown in Table 6.3. It should be noted that percentiles are not averages, but rather the top intake at that point. If we figured the average intake for the bottom one-fourth of girls, these figures would be much lower.

Pre-teen girls from age six to 11 have more adequate nutrition, overall. Their parents have more to say about what they are eating, and most are doing a good job of nourishing their children. Yet even in this younger group, many girls are dieting, skipping meals and restricting food. The hungry one-fourth of pre-teen white girls are getting only about one-half of the 2,400 calories recommended at this age. Their diets, too, are sadly deficient in many vitamins, minerals and protein essential for healthy growth. Our society's unfortunate overemphasis on reducing fat and increasing carbohydrates has meant that protein and animal product nutrients are being neglected by many girls and women.

Cutting Fat Has Risks

High fat intake combined with overeating apparently contributes to obesity, and is a risk factor for chronic disease; yet, low-fat eating has its own risks.

All things being equal, fat is stored as body fat much more easily than other nutrients. One-fourth is wasted in converting excess carbohydrate to fat and, even in excess, protein is seldom stored as fat. Before discovering this, Americans were eating about 42 percent of total calories in fat—plus 25 percent in sugars. This left only about one-third of calories for more nutritious foods.

FIGURE 6.4 **Median Daily Intake—Female**[m]

Percent of Recommended Dietary Allowances (RDA)

	12 - 15 years			16 - 19 years			20 - 59 years		
Nutrient	**NHW**	**NHB**	**MA**	**NHW**	**NHB**	**MA**	**NHW**	**NHB**	**MA**
Food energy	79	88	78	74	89	81	79	78	75
Protein	124	137	135	139	150	150	128	126	126
Vitamin A	63	64	59	73	60	54	75	52	66
Vitamin E	70	85	63	72	78	76	80	75	75
Vitamin C	106	180	144	102	140	127	110	97	110
Thiamin	108	120	107	105	118	107	112	111	112
Riboflavin	112	112	127	119	116	112	118	101	110
Niacin	97	115	100	100	112	96	118	111	103
Vitamin B_6	78	96	83	75	83	87	83	74	82
Folate	120	117	121	102	83	106	107	86	115
Vitamin B_{12}	169	145	170	170	154	148	156	146	150
Calcium	62	51	66	66	52	56	80	62	79
Phosphorus	87	81	94	88	87	90	130	113	134
Magnesium	64	70	74	62	58	66	85	66	85
Iron	67	65	68	63	69	68	74	66	72
Zinc	67	71	72	70	78	72	70	65	70
Copper	67	62	59	63	66	67	70	59	68
Sodium	108	124	106	103	129	106	110	111	106

NHW-non Hispanic White **NHB**-non Hispanic Black **MA**-Mexican American

Shaded values indicate median intakes that are below recommended amounts (for sodium, above) for girls and women. Considered to be current public health issues are the intakes of calories, calcium, iron, and zinc. Potential health issues for which further study is needed are the intakes of vitamin C, vitamin B_6, and folate. Values represent the percentage of Recommended Dietary Allowances (RDAs); for calories, values represent percentage ofthe Recommended Energy Intake (NRC, 1989a)

Source: NHANES III, 1988-1991

Many teenage boys eat particularly high levels of fat, saturated fat, cholesterol and sodium. More than 90 percent of teen boys exceed the Dietary Guidelines in these.[171] Yet, on average, kids are eating only about 32 percent fat in the Food Guide Index.

Much progress has been made in reducing fat intake. During the past decade, Americans have reduced fat intake to an average of 34 percent of total calories, bringing them closer to the goal of 30 percent fat and 10 percent saturated fat.

But unfortunately the new awareness has led to a deep fear of fat. At one extreme, fearful kids with "fat phobia" are deficient in needed fat and at the other, kids eat still eat high-fat diets.

FIGURE 6.5 **Median Daily Intake—Male**[n]

Percent of Recommended Dietary Allowances (RDAs)

	12 - 15 years			**16 - 19 years**			**20 - 59 years**		
Nutrient	NHW	NHB	MA	NHW	NHB	MA	NHW	NHB	MA
Food energy	102	92	84	106	89	82	90	84	82
Protein	184	160	187	173	163	156	149	140	152
Vitamin A	85	55	70	77	55	67	78	53	62
Vitamin E	68*	74	67	93	92	77	90	75	80
Vitamin C	194	204	180	112	188	137	140	153	148
Thiamin	146	122	134	148	120	109	119	108	109
Riboflavin	169	120	147	148	120	118	129	102	116
Niacin	140	115	120	135	122	96	140	131	120
Vitamin B6	110	92	95	104	93	83	100	89	98
Folate	203	133	169	140	106	132	146	114	144
Vitamin B12	242	188	212	258	248	244	248	210	225
Calcium	90	60	85	103	76	79	113	74	103
Phosphorus	118	97	114	141	126	122	188	155	196
Magnesium	103	85	97	78	68	70	95	74	96
Iron	128	110	119	146	119	114	161	139	152
Zinc	77	59	70	90	82	80*	87	75	84
Copper	81	76	79	93	87	84	100	82	97
Sodium	154	137	134	194	179	134	161	151	143

NHW-non Hispanic White **NHB**-non Hispanic Black **MA**-Mexican American

Shaded values indicate median intakes that are below recommended amounts (for sodium, above) for boys and men. Considered to be current public health issues are the intakes of calories, calcium, iron, and zinc. Potential health issues for which further study is needed are the intakes of vitamin C, vitamin B_6, and folate. Values represent the percentage of Recommended Dietary Allowances (RDAs); for calories, values represent percentage ofthe Recommended Energy Intake (NRC, 1989a). An asterisk (*) indicates a statistic that is potentially unreliable.
Source: NHANES III, 1988-1991

Fear of Fat

Many teenagers, especially girls, have taken their fear of fat to the extreme, cutting fat intake as close as possible to zero. This is painfully apparent in working with college students. Cynthia DeTota Sass, MA, RD, University Nutritionist at Syracuse University, New York, says their obsession with thinness is excruciating.

She says, "It's such a frustrating problem, because these young women don't seem to value their health enough to make any changes. I have analyzed some students' fat intakes to be only four percent of their needs. When I give them the results, they are proud instead of concerned. They have an intense fear of fat. They really think if they increase their fat intake, they'll immediately gain weight."

Supplementing with Pills

Many parents are taking a variety of herbal supplements today and giving them to their children, in hopes of filling nutrition gaps or solving health problems. One survey found nearly 20 percent of parents give their children herbal supplements. This surge in herbal use by children is causing rising alarm among pediatricians, children's health advocates and medical officials. In 1998, the American Association of Poison Control Centers reported 704 adverse reactions to herbal products involving kids age 6 to 18.[172]

Some supplement companies have begun aggressively targeting children and their parents with untested, unregulated products of unknown potency, some of them actually powerful drugs. They are alleged to cure illness, improve mood, or help kids gain strength and energy.

Herbal products are not standardized, although there is some movement toward requiring regulation and standardization. They have been shown to vary in potency, and there is risk of getting a dosage so high it is toxic. Tests show some products are contaminated by harmful substances. Even fiber, which is hardly toxic, can cause digestive and nutrient deficiency problems when a person overdoses. The nutrition committee that set the RDAs recommends that fiber come from fruits, vegetables, legumes, and whole-grain cereals and breads, rather than by adding fiber concentrates to the diet.[173]

Parents who try to fill their children's nutrition gaps with pills may be missing the point. Pills don't substitute for real food. For example, take phytochemicals, one of the hottest new areas in cancer research. It's estimated there may be over 100 different phytochemicals in just one serving of vegetables. Scientists haven't identified them all, much less which ones are most effective against cancer. This is why a balanced diet with variety is so important in food choices, to ensure getting the needed nutrients. If you substitute a pill for real food, you lose out.

Diet and disease

- ★ Diet and physical activity patterns together account for at least 300,000 deaths among adults in the United States each year; only tobacco use contributes to more deaths.
- ★ Diet is a known risk factor for the three leading causes of death—heart disease, cancer, and stroke—as well as for diabetes, high blood pressure, and osteoporosis.
- ★ Researchers have estimated that dietary changes could prevent as many as 35% of cancer deaths.
- ★ The annual economic costs to the nation from heart disease and cancer alone exceed $150 billion.
- ★ Early indicators of atherosclerosis, the most common cause of heart disease, often begin in childhood and adolescence and are related to young people's blood cholesterol levels, which are affected by diet.
- ★ Obese children and adolescents are more likely to become obese adults. Overweight adults are at increased risk for heart disease, high blood pressure, stroke, diabetes, some types of cancer, and gallbladder disease.

Diet and Academic Performance

- ★ Research suggests that not having breakfast can affect children's intellectual performance.
- ★ Even moderate undernutrition can have lasting effects on children's cognitive development and school performance.

- ★ Participation in the School Breakfast Program can improve students' standardized test scores and reduce their rates of absence and tardiness.

Eating Behaviors of Young People

- ★ More than 84% of children and adolescents eat too much total fat (i.e., more than 30% of calories from fat), and more than 91% eat too much saturated fat (i.e., more than 10% of calories from saturated fat). On average, young people get 33%-34% of their calories from total fat and 12%-13% of their calories from saturated fat.
- ★ Children and adolescents eat, on average, only 3.6 servings of fruits and vegetables a day, and fried potatoes account for a large proportion of the vegetables eaten. Only one in five children eats five servings of fruits and vegetables a day, as recommended by the National Cancer Institute.
- ★ Fifty-one percent of children and adolescents eat less than one serving of fruit a day, and 29% eat less than one serving a day of vegetables that are not fried.
- ★ The average calcium intake of adolescent girls is about 800 mg a day; the Recommended Dietary Allowance for adolescents is 1,200 mg of calcium a day.
- ★ Eight percent of high school girls take laxatives or vomit to lose weight or keep from gaining weight, and 9% take diet pills. Harmful weight-loss practices have been reported among girls as young as 9 years old.

Nutrition and the Health of Young People, School Health Program Guidelines, CDC Fact Sheet. U.S. Department of Health and Human Services, Centers for Disease Control and Prevention, National Center for Chronic Disease Prevention and Health Promotion, Division of Adolescent and School Health.

Chapter 7

♦ ♦ ❖ ♦ ♦ ❖ ♦ ♦ ❖ ♦ ♦ ❖ ♦ ♦ ❖ ♦ ♦ ❖ ♦ ♦

Feeding Our Kids at School: Who's in Charge?

Coke. Root beer. Diet Coke. These are beverage choices you expect at a fast food restaurant—not in an elementary school. But in a growing national trend, many school districts, strapped by funding cuts, have gone into the business of selling soft drinks to students to fund school programs. They sign detailed "pouring rights contracts" that give soft drink companies extensive rights to sell and advertise to children every hour of the day and in which the final stipulation is chillingly simple: *Don't tell.* Confidentiality clauses in many contracts prohibit public school administrators from revealing the details. Not only do they agree to give up control over the number and location of vending machines, but cannot move them without company permission. Signs that used to warn fans "No drinks in the gym," must come down.

Fast food franchises and snack food companies are following close on the heels of the soda companies. In the end, our most vulnerable citizens are subjected to sophisticated marketing tactics pressuring them to bypass healthful food and drink in favor of products that add money to the tab and scant nutrition to the meal.

Invasion of the Soda Machine

Once, soda machines stood out on the sidewalk for after-school treats. But now soda companies have opened the doors and moved inside with one vending machine for every 150 students, as stipulated by some of the new beverage contracts. And just as waiters and waitresses receive training to hawk these products in restaurants, market training is urged on the coordinator who handles the school's soda contract. Some companies guarantee a $30 commission per child—so students need to buy plenty to make it all work. An average of two drinks a day at $1 for 15 days or so should do it.

Pouring Rights

Pouring Rights contract is an agreement between a beverage distributor and an organization that allows the distributor to be the only one selling beverages at a given location. The beverage distributor generally also requires that the organization not endorse a competitor's product through the posting of logos or advertising. In return, the distributor pays a commission on each sale to the organization and may even guarantee a minimum commission per year. Frequently the distributor offers other inducements in order to be selected, such as providing athletic equipment or other donations.

Federal regulations require soda machines to be turned off during lunch time—when milk is offered—and most schools follow them. But others violate the law and allow soft drink purchases at any time. Why? Because it's locked into the pouring rights contract, sometimes for ten years. Soft drinks that should be consumed infrequently if at all, are replacing healthful beverages as staples in students' diets.

Bigger Isn't Better

Parents who investigate may be surprised to find that most of the bottles in their school soft drink machines are large: 20-ounces or more, well over a pint. When did one serving come to be two and a half cups, containing 16 teaspoons of sugar and 250 calories?

It's not a case of supply and demand, as one might expect—larger bottles because that's what children want and buy. It's the other way around: Children buy larger bottles because that's what is offered. Many contracts stipulate that 85 percent of the bottles offered for sale must be at least 20 ounces. Soda companies know that the tactic works. They employ extensive market research to ferret out what gimmicks will sell the most product to children in both short and long run.

Marketers in general are shifting from smaller to larger servings. Sizes have grown from Coke's 6.5-ounce bottle of the 1950s to the current 12-ounce can to 20-ounce bottles. Convenience Store 7-11's Big Gulp drink has ballooned from the 32-ounce size tested in 1976, to the 44-ounce Super Big Gulp, and now the 64-ounce Double Gulp. Many retail and vending machines outlets have dropped cans entirely.

It's not only available serving sizes that encourage children to buy large servings. Prices, too, induce them (and adults) to choose super-size. After paying the basic 75-cent price, a larger one priced at a dollar seems to cost less. At McDonald's a 12-ounce "child size" drink is 89 cents, but a 42-ounce "super size" costs $1.59. At Cineplex Odeon theaters a "small" 20-ounce drink costs $2.50, but the "large" 44-ounce drink is $3.25, less than a third more.[174] These prices make buying larger drink seem economically wise.

Iron-Clad Contracts

In 2001, the California Endowment, a health care foundation, commissioned the Public Health Institute (PHI) to examine school beverage contracts. Among its other findings, the report revealed that one company held exclusive rights to have its beverages available in any district location and "in the cafeteria lines of all schools," including elementary schools, and at all other special events conducted at any location on the campus. The contract stipulated that "campus" meant every school and facility owned or operated by the district, now or in the future, "including all elementary, middle, high, and alternative schools, athletic facilities, concession stands, and, for each building, the grounds, parking lots, dining facilities, athletic facilities and concession stands, food service outlets, and vending areas."[175]

Exclusive rights don't end with the school day. Far from it. They extend to school events, athletic concessions, booster club sales, and all other events held on school premises. No competitive products can be served or sampled on school campuses. Scoreboards, side line and court side rights, signs, advertising, and products from competing beverage companies are prohibited.

Contracts often stipulate that all athletic teams must use the company's sports drinks whenever such drinks are offered to athletes or at a sporting event. They require that the company's advertising panels be clearly visible to the public on athletic field scoreboards, marquees, and in gymnasiums. All fountain cups, paper cups, and concession cups—even when coffee is sold in them—must be 100 percent trademarked and purchased from the company. All sales of carbonated soft drinks, water, 100 percent fruit juice, fruit-flavored drinks, and sports drinks are controlled.

According to the United States Department of Agriculture (USDA), per capita soft-drink consumption has increased almost 500 percent over the past 50 years.

Soda Sales Increase, Milk Sales Plummet

Aggressive tactics and seamless marketing strategies have tripled soft drink use since 1967. Experts say that soft drinks—including soda, fruit-flavored and part-juice drinks, and sports drinks—now account for more than one-third of all refined sugars, and therefore empty calories, in the diet. (Part-juice offerings have exploded, but parents need to be skeptical of any so-called health benefits.)[176] As a result, milk consumption has dropped steadily in the last twenty years. Only one-half of teenagers drink milk today, compared with three-fourths in the 1970s. Teens who do drink milk consume only about 1.5 to 2 cups a day on average, not the 3 glasses recommended.[177] Young teens may have a new perception of milk as being "just for little kids," while soft drinks are "cool."

- ★ Teenage boys today drink twice as much soda as milk. The typical teen boy drinks 20 ounces per day. One-fourth drink 2.5 or more cans of soda per day; one out of twenty drinks 5 cans or more daily.
- ★ Teenage girls are not far behind. The typical teen girl drinks 14 ounces per day. One-fourth drink 2 or more cans per day; one in twenty drinks 3 cans or more.

This is twice as much as only twenty years ago when the typical teenager drank 9 ounces or 3/4 of a can per day.[178]

Calcium intake declines rapidly during teen years, at the very time it is urgently needed for building strong bones, especially for girls. During adolescence is when young bones grow and 15 percent of adult height is added, so it's important to get plenty of calcium-rich foods every day. Bones grow and develop only until about age 25, and after that bone mass begins to decline.

Follow the Money

Why do schools allow soda companies to take control like this? "Huge multi-national soda companies woo cash-strapped schools with the promise of money for concession, advertising, and pouring rights," says Dr. Carmen R. Nevarez, medical director and vice president of Public Health Institute, a non-profit agency that investigated California beverage contracts. "Soda companies are clearly in the best position to dictate terms to school officials that are favorable to soft drink companies but not the health of our children."

During the 1990s, tightened school budgets created the opportunity for increased commercial intrusion into public schools, the United States General Accounting Office (GAO) informed Congress in 2000.[179]

The money is no small potatoes. Pepsi offered $2 million to Sacramento, California, schools and $5 million to Oakland for exclusive rights to sell and advertise to students, according to the California study. Dr Pepper paid the Grapevine-Colleyville, Texas, school district $3.45 million for a 10-year contract. To reach after-school sales, Coca-Cola is paying $60 million over ten years for exclusive rights in more than 2,000 chapters of the Boys and Girls Clubs of America.[180] The amount of money generated for a school or district varied widely according to the GAO study. Some districts—which may have had better negotiators—were guaranteed $30 per student per year and other benefits. One high school principal reported the contract in his school netted about $67,000 in up-front money and commissions its first year, or about $12 per student.

Non-exclusive contracts are less lucrative. A school in Albuquerque, New Mexico, investigated by the GAO made an informal agreement that gives it about $3 per student, a scoreboard, cafeteria banners, and ten competitive grants of $1,000 for teachers. This school also had to maintain 40 percent of the vending machines. An elementary school principal said his school beverage contract, which covered only one machine, located in the teacher's lounge, generated about $12 a year.

Income is tied directly to the volume of beverages sold, so the more sales, the greater the revenue for the school. One large district received 55 percent and 56 percent commissions on 20-ounce and 12-ounce drinks respectively, with a guaranteed commission of $300,000, and additional commissions available with higher sales.

Then there are the bonus payments—special incentives for signing the contract, that the companies term sponsor fees, sponsorship cash, incentive monies, or support funding. These provide one-time signing payments from $55,000 to $1,000,000, plus yearly payments from $25,000 to $80,000. Longer term contracts—up to ten years—tended to have larger payments.

Where does all this money come from? It is an oversimplification to say that it comes from the soda companies. In the end, their profits come from one source—the wallets of parents and children who attend the school. Yet schools have a unique interest in promoting the health of children, which is directly related to a child's ability to learn and achieve his or her academic potential. Healthy children have increased attention, creativity, and test scores.[181] An overconsumption of soft drinks is blamed for health and nutrition problems in children that haunt parents and policy makers today.

Soft Drinks Take a Toll

Many experts say soft drinks have played a part in the increase in childhood obesity. A recent study reported in the British medical journal *The Lancet* found children who consume one extra soft drink a day have a 60 percent greater chance of becoming obese.[182] Adolescents on average get 11 percent of their calories from soft drinks.[183] Heavy consumers of soft drinks tend to have higher calorie intakes.[184] The National Institutes of Health (NIH) recommends that people trying to control their weight drink water instead of soft drinks.

According to the NIH, children and teens who consume soft drinks have lower intakes of important nutrients, compared with those who don't, suggesting that soda, including diet soda, displaces nutritious foods in the diet.[185] Both regular and diet sodas affect a child's intake of minerals, vitamins, and additives.

Failure to meet calcium requirements in childhood can hinder skeletal growth and bone mineralization and contributes to osteoporosis. Heavy soft drink intake is linked to low intake of calcium and other nutrients. And sugar sodas simply add too much sugar to the diet. The United States Department of Agriculture (USDA) advises that people who eat 2,200 calories a day (as recommended for teenage girls) not consume more than twelve teaspoons of refined sugar day, yet one can of soda contains ten teaspoons. Boys consuming about 2,800 calories, as recommended, should not eat more than eighteen teaspoons of refined sugar, but 1.5 cans of soda contain fifteen teaspoons. Many children easily exceed those sugar limits from soft drinks alone. When they add sugar cereal, candy, cookies, cake, ice cream, and other sugary foods to their daily intake, those recommended limits are exceeded by a wide margin.[186]

Sugar in soft drinks can also erode tooth enamel. A report by the American Dental Association (ADA) says even diet sodas are high in acid and can potentially cause dental erosion, to which fluoride offers little protection. The ADA opposes school beverage contracts that promote increased access to soft drinks.[187]

Selling beverages and foods in competition with school lunch foods conveys a mixed message to children. They are taught in the classroom about good nutrition and the value of healthy food choices but are surrounded by vending machines, snack bars, school stores, and à la carte sales offering low nutrient options. The message they get is that good nutrition is theoretically useful, but not really important to their health or education. Thus, they undermine the ability of school meals to contribute to student health, well-being and academic achievement.

Don't Tell!

By 2000, parents in California were becoming alarmed when they found their schools were promoting soft drinks to their children and, in effect, discouraging milk drinking. Those parents were even more upset when they learned the extent of advertising aimed directly at their children by soda companies. They uncovered confidentiality clauses in the soft drink contracts. School administrators had not only given up control of beverages for up to a decade, but they had also agreed not to reveal the details, even though these were public schools operating under open record laws. The more they investigated, the more outraged parents grew.

Parents discovered soda companies even were attempting to position their drinks as healthful. They encouraged teachers to put up posters from the National Soft Drink Association that claimed, "As refreshing sources of needed liquids and energy, soft drinks represent a positive addition to a well-balanced diet . . . These same three sugars also occur naturally, for example, in fruits . . . In your body it makes no difference whether the sugar is from a soft drink or a peach."[188]

Defending its marketing tactics in Africa, Coca-Cola's Chairman M. Douglas Ivester said, "Actually, our product is quite healthy. Fluid replenishment is a key to health . . . Coca-Cola does a great service because it encourages people to take in more and more liquids."[189]

Sports drinks, too, are often portrayed by their makers as being healthful. But experts advise that water is the preferred choice for most people during physical activity. (Sports drinks contain an electrolyte solution that may be useful for elite athletes engaged in an hour or more of vigorous exercise.)

Snack Attack, Fast Food Frenzy

Close by the soda machines stand candy and snack machines, packed with the latest versions of chips and cookies, but noticeably lacking in nutrition-dense foods like fruits, yogurt, string cheese, turkey, or beef jerky.

Food franchises, too, have taken hold in schools. McDonalds, Taco Bell, Kentucky Fried Chicken, and Pizza Hut claim space in many school cafeterias. It's not that there aren't plenty of nutritious foods available from these franchises, but there is a difference between buying it from the franchise as an à la carte item and as a part of the regular school lunch.

In schools today, many children select a noon "meal" of potato chips, cookies, and a candy bar, topped off with a 20-ounce bottle of soda. At 50 cents each for the snack foods and $1 for the drink, the total cost is $2.50 and 1,050 calories but provides almost no nutrition. By contrast, school lunch costs $1.25 to $1.50 in elementary school and $1.50 to $1.75 in high school, and provides one-third of the day's recommended nutrition.

Teachers lament that when children do bring lunch from home it is often more of the same: chips, processed bars, desserts, and a soft drink. Seldom seen is the time-honored sack lunch of twenty years ago: sandwich, apple, and cookie, plus a 5-cent carton of milk from the cafeteria. Even when children bring a healthful lunch, all too often they toss the sandwich and apple into the garbage and head for the conveniently enticing vending machines. It's not that children should never eat these "fun" foods or that they aren't fine as occasional treats. But where's the fun in a steady diet of foods like these, and what lasting habits are being formed?

Who's Paying?

In some cases, the availability of snack and fast food takes money from those who can least afford it. Free- and reduced-cost breakfasts and lunches are offered in schools that qualify for Title I funding, which have large numbers of low-income families. But sometimes lunch is neither free—nor nutritious—for these children. For instance, a La Puente, California, school that offers free meals under the Title I program keeps the vending machine room locked during breakfast, to encourage students to eat a good breakfast in the cafeteria. But the snack room door remains open during lunch time, and every day many of the free lunch children pass up the nutritious school lunch and spend their own money on potato chips, soft drinks, and candy from the machines. Often the uneaten lunches get reported as free meals served under federal regulations.[190]

Title I Schools

Title I of the Elementary and Secondary Education Act of 1965 provides financial assistance to schools on the basis of numbers of disadvantaged, at-risk, and low-income students attending the school. Federal funds provide educational assistance in reading and math, and free and reduced cost breakfast and lunch for students who qualify. Schools and districts receiving Title I funding are required to follow federal guidelines for nutrition and competitive foods.

Shrinking Nutritional Quality

Foods sold in competition with school meals are a concern to nutritionists and the health community. They should be a concern to parents, as well. In a 2001 report to Congress, the USDA, which is in charge of feeding school children, warned that these foods jeopardize the nutritional effectiveness of lunch programs and may contribute to the trend of unhealthy eating among children and subsequent health risks. It urged Congress to strengthen the law to ensure that all foods sold or served anywhere in the school during the school day meet nutrition standards, and that income from all such foods go into the school food service account.[191] Research shows clearly that eating school meals contributes to better nutrition, while competing foods tend to bring down diet quality.

Compared with other students, children who eat school meals:
* Are more likely to consume vegetables, milk, and milk products, meat, and other protein-rich foods, both at lunch and over the course of 24 hours.
* Have higher average intake of many nutrients, both at lunch and over 24 hours.
* Consume less added sugar and drink less soda.[192]

Eating a nutritious lunch is especially critical when one understands that only two percent of school-age children meet the Food Guide Pyramid recommendations for all five major food groups. Overall, only 14 percent of youth meet the recommendations for fruit, 17 percent for meat and alternates, 20 percent for vegetables, 23 percent for grains, and 30 percent for milk. Only two percent meet them all.[193] In 1997 the Institute of Medicine recommended that school meal programs should serve as a learning laboratory for developing healthful eating habits and not be placed in a profit-making or competitive situation with other food options in schools.[194] (See Food Pyramid in Chapter 16).

Targeting Younger Audiences

Long considered a high school phenomenon, competitive foods today are often sold in junior high, where students are especially vulnerable to peer pressure, and in elementary schools, where eating habits are most easily influenced. Rules set by the National School Lunch Program forbid the sale of foods of minimal nutritional value during meals. Some vending machines have automatic timers to shut off machines in accord with these regulations. But the rules aren't always followed. Increasingly, pouring rights contracts signed by school personnel stipulate that no time restrictions can be placed on when machines operate. That means students with money in their pockets are likely to head for the fast food counters and vending machines anytime during the day to pick up the popular foods advertised to them daily. Many schools now require meal programs to be completely self-supporting, but with school meals priced so low, revenue budgets often come up short. The easiest way for schools to compensate is by selling and profiting from fast food and à la carte food. Some even argue that having popular franchises in school food courts keeps teens on campus during the noon hour.

However, selling these attractive foods close by discourages students from eating the regular lunch (and thereby benefiting nutritionally). This has several additional ill effects. First, the stigma of poverty becomes attached to the low-priced school lunches—and to the children who consume them. Second, when students do not eat the offered school lunch, federal funding is cut, making it even harder to maintain high-quality nutrition. Financial decisions are not easy and may require trade-offs. For school administrators and communities in a financial pinch there may be no perfect solutions. But schools that are putting nutrition at the bottom of the list need to reassess their priorities.

Although beverage advertising was most pervasive, the 2000 GAO study found a variety of commercial activities in all schools it visited, more in high schools than in middle and elementary schools. Most advertising involved logo products, free equipment, or reducing the cost of products such as student planners or yearbooks. In some states school buses carry ads both inside and out. In one Texas district, selling ads on school buses and school buildings generates several hundred thousand dollars a year.

The study also noted that schools have had vending machines for decades, but that the terms and coverage are new in their demands. Also, traditional fund-raisers, candy bars, popcorn and pizza sales, run by student groups, parent organizations, and booster clubs, have increased over the past decade.

Stories of Success

Public outcry at the invasion of soft drink and snack food sales into schools has brought on newspaper articles, letters to the editor, parental investigative groups, and legislative action throughout the country.

In California, public protests failed to stop the signing of a November 2000 $1 million soda contract in Roseville. But in Sacramento, parents that same year exposed and stopped PepsiCo's proposal to pay the district $2 million for exclusive rights. Public resistance also halted a proffered $5 million contract in Oakland; instead the school board developed a nutrition policy committee that called for elimination of unhealthy snack foods and drink from district schools.[195]

In 2001, the California legislature passed a Senate bill limiting the sale of low-nutrition foods and beverages. The new law eliminates soda sales in elementary schools, limits them in middle schools, but does not affect high school sales. More measures may be on the way. Another bill, before the California senate at the time of this writing, proposes to extend its ruling to middle and high schools. Only water, milk, 50-percent fruit juice drinks, and certain sports drinks (no carbonated beverages) could be sold in schools. California State Senator Deborah Ortiz introduced a "soda tax" measure that would impose a 9-cent tax on every two-liter bottle of soda. She later dropped the tax idea in favor of ensuring that only healthy beverages are sold in schools.[196]

In Maryland, a Senate bill to eliminate "minimally nutritional foods" from schools, introduced in 2001, noted that:

- students spend 40 percent of their waking hours in school,
- they consume low-nutrient foods from vending machines throughout the school day;
- this trend has accelerated due to pervasive advertising by snack food and beverage companies; and
- using children as a captive audience for commercial purposes is a violation of the public trust.[197]

In a small revolt that began in the bush country of the Alaska interior, Athabascan parents tossed soda machines out of their schools and shredded contracts with vendors. "Let them drink water, milk, or fruit juice," became the rallying cry. Most of these schools are in villages with no road access, and whose people live a subsistence lifestyle—gathering wild berries and greens, fishing and hunting, depending on the largess of nature to "store-bought" foods.

More Work to Do

Nineteen states have statutes targeting commercial activities in schools. But the GAO report calls it a piecemeal approach. Most regulations are only general, with policy decisions largely delegated to school officials on a case-by-case basis. New York law prohibits commercial activities on school grounds, but permits commercial sponsorships of school activities. Virginia prohibits advertising on and in school buses. Tennessee restricts the size, location and appearance of school bus ads.[198]

Is it Really Harmful?

Whether over-consumption of soft drinks and non-nutritive snack foods contribute substantially to obesity is controversial. Eating too much of these kinds of foods may directly cause excess weight gain. It may be part of a group of unhealthy behaviors that put children at risk. Or the increase in child obesity may be caused primarily by other factors.

But aside from its effect on weight, this way of eating is clearly related to nutrition deficiencies. Nutrient-dense foods needed for healthy growth and development get left out when youngsters over-consume sweet and high-fat foods. There just isn't room for them all. Girls, especially, risk severe deficiencies of several nutrients, including calcium, iron, and zinc.

Some argue that poorly-financed schools need beverage contract money even more than schools in wealthier districts, that it is unfair to restrict access to lucrative soft drink contracts. But consider how the contracts are fulfilled: by encouraging students to spend more money while making poor nutrition choices. Are lower-income families—or any families—able to afford this?

The questions are: Who has pouring rights to your child, and what are the conditions of these "rights"? Do you want your child urged to drink soda instead of milk? To eat candy and chips instead of regular meals? Do you want your school activity programs financed by children buying soft drinks and candy bars? And, perhaps, the question of the moment: Will you send enough snack money to school today so your child can be just as "cool" as the other fifth graders?

PART III

♦ ♦ ❖ ♦ ♦ ❖ ♦ ♦ ❖ ♦ ♦ ❖ ♦ ♦ ❖ ♦ ♦ ❖ ♦ ♦

False Starts

Chapter 8

♦ ♦ ❖ ♦ ♦ ❖ ♦ ♦ ❖ ♦ ♦ ❖ ♦ ♦ ❖ ♦ ♦ ❖ ♦ ♦

Why Past Solutions Haven't Worked

The school bus swings up to their Michigan farm home to pick up John, age eleven, and his older sister Jillian, age thirteen. It stops right by the back door, and after school brings them back to the same spot. John rides nearly an hour on the bus each morning and evening. He's tired when he gets home, plays a few minutes with Thumper, a yellow lab who jumps joyfully all over him, then heads inside, grabs some snack foods and settles down in front of the TV with his arm around the dog, while Jillian hangs out in her room with a teenage fashion magazine and playing games on her computer. Mom is still at the nursing home where she works and Dad is out in the field. Both lead busy lives at work, at home, and in the community.

John will probably eat snack-type foods, high in fat and sugar, all evening, if his mom has a meeting and comes home late. Jillian eats half an apple, her first food of the day. She won't eat more, and can now tell Mom she's eaten, so can avoid eating with the family later. She's thin as a rail, while John carries the pudginess of "baby fat."

Their city cousins in a tree-lined Boston suburb and Seattle high-rise live almost precisely the same kind of lives—except for three cousins who play sports, hang out with jocks, and whose lives seem to focus around the gym and driving back and forth from competitions.

Since they no longer have cattle or other livestock, Jillian and John have no outside chores. Their land has become so costly, and farming so expensive, that Dad farms right up to the edges of the yard, and there are no big enticing areas to hike and explore as in the past. The big high-priced equipment he uses is not suitable for kids learning to drive or helping out in the field.

Big changes have come on that farm for Dad since he was a boy, busy with his 4-H calves before and after school, helping his dad and brothers and sisters around the corrals and machine shed, fencing, chasing cows, and riding horseback for fun. A few generations before that his great-great grandfather and grandmother cleared the land, plowed, planted, dug the well, and built house and barns. Children helped out from a young age. They worked in the garden and field and barns, cared for younger children, and walked two miles to and from country school. They lived frugally, but most of the time they had plenty to eat, simple, hardy fare, much of it raised right there on the farm—meat and potatoes, milk and homemade bread, abundant vegetables from the garden along with some wild plants and native fruits.

History of Lifestyle Change

Sedentary habits and abundant rich foods are luring too many of our kids down the pathway to poor health and excessive weight gain. Nearly all American children today, whatever their weight, whatever their income level, whoever their ancestors, are at risk because of lifestyles like these.

In caveman days, both work and recreation demanded strenuous effort. Anthropologists tell us that around 8,000 BC, men commonly hunted from one to four days in a row, followed by days of light activity and rest. Women gathered plant foods every two or three days, while all devoted much physical labor to butchering, tool making, home repair, food preparation, carrying firewood and water, traveling, and moving to new campsites. Visiting involved walking six to twenty miles round trip between villages to see relatives and friends and to trade. Dancing, often lasting hours, was a major recreational activity in many hunter-gatherer cultures.[1]

Our nation stands on its history of progress and technical achievement. We can't go back, and don't want to. Yet, genetically our bodies haven't changed much from those of our primitive ancestors in physically demanding times, subsisting on natural foods. They still need plenty of movement and activity to keep healthy.

History of Prevention

After World War II recovery, concern grew in Europe over the declining fitness of both children and adults. There the value of active living and fitness was well known. By 1966, the Council of Europe had adopted the long-term objective: *Sport for All*. The next year Norway promoted exercise nationwide with public campaigns. Within fifteen years *Sport for All* programs spread through the industrialized world and a number of third world countries, encouraged by UNESCO. In Canada, the nationwide physical activity program called *Participation* began in 1971. The Australian program, *Life Be In It*, was initiated in 1975 and went national in 1977.

Most of these programs emphasize health, fitness, and happiness through recreational sports and activity, and get the message out through schools, public campaigns, television and other media. They are initiated and supported by government, working with a broad network of private, corporate, community and volunteer sponsorship. It works. People take pride in walking and being active. Successful intervention began before the situation had deteriorated to the extent it has in the United States today.

Unfortunately, in the United States almost no unified effort was made to increase activity. "Physical fitness and physical education have no respected place in the American public health movement," lamented M. Terris in 1975, in the *American Journal of Public Health*.[2]

In the early 1980s, policy makers at the Department of Health and Human Services (HHS) added a goal for increased physical activity to the nation's Healthy People agenda. An unrealistic goal, as it turned out. That objective, aimed at getting 60 percent of adults exercising vigorously by 1990, had to be scaled back to 15 percent over the then-current baseline of 11. Still no public campaign ensued. Elsewhere, fitness campaigns proved effective. An Australian study found in 1977, that 38 percent of people said they exercised more often as a result of *Life Be In It*. For 47 percent, it had changed their thinking, and 97 percent were aware of the program.

By the 1980s the signs were clear. National statistics showed that obesity and its most closely related disease–type 2 diabetes–were rising swiftly for both U.S. children and adults. In one of the first HHS calls for obesity prevention, in late 1990, four researchers at the Centers for Disease Control in Atlanta urged that action be taken, "Obesity prevention [should] begin among adults in their early 20s, and special emphasis is needed for young women who are already overweight." They advised weight loss as the first step.

An editorial in the Nov/Dec 1990 issue of *Healthy Weight Journal* commended this fledgling step and urged more efforts in prevention, "The nationwide lack of interest in prevention by the medical community and health departments has been disappointing. Preventing overweight rarely is discussed in print or at conferences. The focus remains on treatment, however ineffective this has been in our field. Meanwhile obesity rates mount alarmingly. It should be a concern that the steepest rise in obesity is among children and young adults. What does this bode for the future? In fifteen to thirty years these young people will reach mid-life, presently the time of highest rates. Will obesity then be the norm?"[3] One expert warned, "If you think this is a problem now, just wait. You haven't seen anything yet. Wait till these kids grow up and have children of their own!"

That time is now, and at last, prevention is on everyone's mind. The Surgeon General launched his Call to Action to Prevent and Decrease Overweight and Obesity on Dec. 13, 2001. In July 2002 the CDC began a $190 million multimedia campaign called "VERB: It's What You Do" to get kids moving. The message is that verbs—run, skip, swim, dance, play, volunteer, join clubs—are active and kids should be too. Though this is timely, one can hardly avoid a sense of regret that an opportunity was missed to encourage activity a generation earlier, as elsewhere—for health, fitness and happiness. Now it is being launched with the rather grim purpose of reducing obesity rates.

The Diet Industry

Diet programs were successful in helping people lose weight—sometimes a great deal of weight. But nearly all patients and clients quickly regained their lost weight, often ratcheting it up even higher. Fortunately for the industry, most consumers willingly accepted the blame. Yet it was necessary to find ways to obscure the fact that weight loss was only short-term in most cases.

Diet companies intensified their marketing around the early 1980s and began forging stronger links to researchers and health policy makers through serious grant funding. Some obesity specialists aligned themselves financially with one or more of these companies. It was sometimes charged that their vested interests unduly influenced research outcomes, statistical analysis, and the way research was reported to the press, clinicians, and scientific audiences.

It's been said, and is probably true, that if this industry made cars, no one would buy them, and if they did, consumer groups would force a recall. If it offered any other health service, it would be required to prove safety and effectiveness before its products could be prescribed to millions of unsuspecting consumers—as were both the disastrous very low calorie diets and fen-phen/Redux diet pills in the last decade, and currently weight loss surgery. It would be held accountable for the many deaths and injuries it causes. But no agency keeps track.

Attempts At Control

In 1990, Congress attempted to gain some control over the weight loss industry. Chaired by Democratic Rep. Ron Wyden of Oregon, a series of hearings on *Deception and Fraud in the Diet Industry* exposed many deceptive promotions, unfair business practices, lack of accountability, high failure rates, and injuries.[4]

Wyden charged that the industry provides "A new mix of questionable products, untrained providers and deceptive advertising, exposing our citizens to unexpected health risks." Diet companies large and small promised fast, easy, permanent weight loss. Only the most fraudulent and dangerous found their way to court. The three regulatory agencies—the FDA, in charge of content and false labeling; the Federal Trade Commission (FTC), in charge of regulating advertising and marketing; and the Postal Service, with authority to prevent using the mail for fraudulent purposes—investigated, charged, and eliminated fraudulent promotions as best they could, on a tedious case-by-case basis. Promoters found guilty, paid fines and bounced back with a new company name, new twist on the product, or ownership transfer to a family member.

Mainline companies, too, made claims they couldn't back up. Very-low-calorie-diet companies, then at the height of their popularity, ran ads like these as a matter of course:

- ⋆ "The one that's clinically proven safe and effective." (Optifast/Sandoz)
- ⋆ "You will not experience a rebound phenomenon after you attain your goal." (Medifast/Jason Pharmaceutical)
- ⋆ "With the support of the *Ultrafast* Program, you get a new attitude. The weight stays off." (National Center)

At the hearings it was made clear that these diets were not effective, the weight didn't stay off, and for many patients they were unsafe. It was deceptive advertising. "With rare exceptions, none of the popular commercially available programs for treating obesity is based on current scientific knowledge," testified C. Wayne Callaway, George Washington University endocrinologist and obesity expert.[5]

Also testifying at the hearings, Peter Vash, MD, president of the American Society of Bariatric Physicians, charged incompetence and unethical supervision. "Make no mistake, abuse, incompetence, and irresponsibility is present in the area of weight loss throughout the treatment hierarchy, from top to bottom," he said. "The commercial diet industry has gorged itself on the vulnerability of people desperate to lose weight, and has grown fat with the easy profits that it has slickly extracted from them. There is no question that the weight-loss industry needs to have guidance and structure, and now is the time for health care professionals and the government to work together."[6]

Following the hearings, FTC took on the big guns. In 1992 and 1993 the FTC charged seventeen companies, including all the major commercial diet companies and weight loss centers, with making false and deceptive claims about safety and effectiveness. Charged were Abbott Laboratories, Beverly Hills Clinics, Diet Center, Diet Workshop, Doctors Medical Quick Weight Loss Centers, Formu-3 International, Health Management Resources, Jason Pharmaceutical, Jenny Craig, National Center, Nutri/System, Pacific Medical Clinics, Physicians Weight Loss Centers, Sandoz, United Weight Control, Weight Loss Centers, and Weight Watchers.[7] Each signed a consent agreement saying they would no longer make claims unless supported by reliable studies. Advertising improved, in that the major companies and many small supplement companies dropped false statements, although they used creative spins and weasel words that often seemed to suggest the same thing. Some elusive fringe companies advertised as they always did.

Prodded by Wyden in 1992, the FDA banned 111 diet pill ingredients of herbal supplements. Recommendations to remove these "natural drugs" from the market as potentially dangerous had been stalled at the agency for nearly twenty years. The FDA also agreed to review the safety and efficacy of PPA (phenylpropanolamine), which was approved for over-the-counter sales in 1979, but for which many adverse reactions were being reported. This proved challenging, as it took on powerful drug companies and popular products on the shelves of every grocery, drugstore and convenience store.

Wyden repeatedly asked FDA to speed up the investigation, but in May 1993 he received a letter from Donna Shalala, Secretary of Health and Human Services, saying he could expect more delays. They were still looking at the risk of stroke, she said. In the meantime, "The agency does not believe...there is a basis for removing PPA from the marketplace while this additional information is being collected. The PPA review was stalled for over 10 years, but was recently taken from the market.

Industry Gets Grip on Federal Policy

Prestigious researchers with vested interests in the weight loss industry helped determine federal health policy. Their research was funded by diet companies; they served as paid consultants, and collected company fees for lectures at multinational conferences. By this time, seemingly, the diet industry had a strong grip on federal health policy. Callaway said it bluntly, "The so-called clinical research in this field has been largely paid for by the formula and drug companies."

In her book, *Losing it: America's Obsession with Weight and the Industry that Feeds on It,* Laura Fraser writes, "Diet and pharmaceutical companies influence every step along the way of the scientific process. They pay for the ads that keep obesity journals publishing. They underwrite medical conferences...Some obesity researchers have a clear conflict of interest, promoting or investing in products or programs based on their research...while they also sit on the boards of the medical journals that determine which studies get printed. What it comes down to is that most obesity researchers would stand to lose a lot of money if they stopped telling Americans they had to lose a lot of weight."[8]

Now that the FDA has opened the door to diet drugs, large multinational pharmaceutical companies have their drugs in the pipeline, awaiting approval. Members of the federally funded National Task Force on the Prevention and Treatment of Obesity, which sets United States national policy, for instance, are well funded by the diet industry. In 1996, the nine members of the Task Force were required to disclose their financial affiliations for the first time. The list read like a Who's Who of the diet industry. Of the nine members, eight would seemingly have conflicts of interest. They were academic researchers who each had financial agreements with up to eight diet companies. They were consultants, served on advisory boards, conducted industry research, and received honorariums and grants from weight loss companies and drug manufacturers of diet pills. These companies were Amgen, Duke Diet and Fitness Center, Genentech, Hoffman-LaRoche, International Life Sciences, Knoll Pharmaceuticals, Lilly Pharmaceuticals, Neurogen, Parke-Davis, Procter & Gamble,

Roche Laboratories, Ross Laboratories, Sandoz Nutrition, Weight Watchers and Wyeth-Ayerst. Most funded several Task Force members.[9] By 1995 the Task Force was recommending the easing of federal and state regulations that restricted long-term use of obesity drugs.

Pat Lyons, RN, MA, regional health educator for Kaiser Permaente in Oakland, Calif., protested this action, "The course they are on at present—to advocate weight loss at any cost in a social climate that perpetuates discrimination against fat people—will indeed have high costs for millions of Americans." She was right; the fen-phen/Redux tragedy was just ahead.

Rise of a Drug Heyday

By this time doctors had begun prescribing fen-phen, a combination of fenfluramine and phentermine. The combination never was approved by FDA, but both drugs were approved for other purposes, so it was prescribed widely "off label" (meaning doctors can use their own discretion). Its popularity was based on widespread publicity given the four-year Weintraub study that combined the two drugs. Not an unimpressive study, but one that was strategically placed in many scientific and medical journals. In this study the majority of subjects dropped out, many because they could not tolerate the side effects. Only 26 out of 121 kept off as much as 10 percent of their weight.[10]

The pressure was on the Food and Drug Administration to approve dexfenfluramine, a related anti-obesity drug being used in Europe. Then in September of 1995 one of those well-staged media events hit American women like a bombshell.

A Harvard University team announced that their Nurses' Health Study showed women risk higher death rates if they weigh more than 119 pounds (at five-foot-five). "Even mild to moderate overweight is associated with a substantial increase in risk of premature death," JoAnn Manson, PhD, lead author, told the press. In fact, the study findings were quite different from their report, which referred only to a small subgroup. The larger study actually showed that being 20 to 40 pounds overweight made little difference, and a gain of up to 22 pounds did not increase the risk. However, the message most women took home that day was that they needed to lose weight fast or risk early death.[11]

The Fen-Phen/Dexfen Story

Dexfenfluramine should never have been approved in the United States. By the time it was, in April 1996, two of its terrible effects were well known, and a third was soon to surface.

The drug had been used over a decade in European medical clinics and was tested extensively before then. Known risks were primary pulmonary hypertension, a lung disease fatal within four years for nearly half its victims, and brain damage, found in more than eighty animal studies.

The FDA had held out for twenty years without approving any new diet drugs. Yet, approval was only a matter of time. Michael Weintraub, a University of Rochester pharmacologist who authored the study that launched fen-phen pills, was installed at FDA. Its own advisory board voted "no." But Redux was approved over this negative vote during a questionable meeting about the drug's safety from which doctors and scientists from health-advocacy groups were excluded. *U.S. News & World Report* says pressure and political donations to California Rep. Tom Lantos helped close that FDA meeting to possible dissenters.[12]

Once approved, Redux pills flew off the shelves. People lost considerable weight, but it was a familiar story. They lost weight mostly from dieting, and it quickly returned. The drug itself kept off an average of only about five and a half pounds over placebo.[13] The FDA listed the drugs as safe for only one year, but to be effective they had to be taken long-term. Once a person stopped taking them, the five or so pounds returned.

In a sizzling diet pill market, sales of fen-phen and Redux to U.S. pharmacies totaled over $214 million in wholesale dollars during the first half of 1996, filling 87 million prescriptions.[14] Diet pills were prescribed in medical clinics, in weight loss centers, and even at California flea markets.[15]

Meanwhile, the prestigious *New England Journal of Medicine* was caught in an ethics crunch. It published the European study showing that patients who took a form of the fen drug were twenty-three times as likely to suffer pulmonary hypertension as matched controls who did not, and the longer they took the drugs, the greater the risk.[16] But in the same issue an editorial by JoAnn Manson and Gerald Faich criticized the European study and assured physicians that the risks of being obese were far greater than any possible risks from taking the pills.[17]

Interneuron's stock rose 13 percent in the next few days.[18] Then the *New York Times* reported Manson was a paid consultant to Interneuron, and Faich was paid by two companies marketing the fen and dexfen drugs.[19] The editors of the journal, Angell and Kassirer, apologized and said this was the first violation in six years of their policy of requiring the authors of editorials to be free of associations with companies that stood to gain from a product mentioned.

What happened next was a shock. Abruptly, on Sept 15, 1997, FDA asked that makers of fen and dexfen take the pills off the market. Within hours both drugs were gone, and it is unlikely they will ever return.[20]

Without a doubt, the unsung hero of America's flirtation with fen-phen and Redux diet pills is sonographer Pam Ruff, of Fargo, N.D. She noticed it first in December 1994: an abnormal heart valve coated with a glistening white substance that prevented it from closing fully, unlike anything she had seen in more than ten years as an ultrasound technician. Curious, she asked the patient if she took fen-phen, and was told, yes. The same day she saw another nearly identical abnormality, and again was told the patient was on fen-phen. For nearly two years Ruff and her fellow sonographers at the MeritCare echo lab kept records on the strange heart valves, now numbering nearly two dozen, all patients using fen-phen.[21] Jack Crary, MD, a MeritCare heart surgeon, took an interest. He called a friend at Mayo Clinic in Rochester, Minn., who checked and found identical cases in Mayo files. The article they wrote for the *New England Journal of Medicine* so alarmed the editors that they contacted the FDA.[22]

The FDA notified the companies, even before the article was published. Later the FDA found that 25 to 30 percent of all patients who took the drugs may have abnormal echocardiograms, and the damage sometimes worsened after the pills were stopped. "Clearly, had the drugs stayed on the market longer, we would be seeing many more and more-serious cases of heart valve damage and pulmonary hypertension," said a senior official at the FDA. Even before Redux was approved, the companies and the FDA knew about heart valve damage, according to a 1999 expose' in the *U.S. News & World Report*.[23]

The story doesn't end there. More drugs are in the pipeline. One might think authorities would be extra careful. But just two months later, in November 1997, FDA approved sibutramine, under the brand name Meridia by Knoll, again over a "no" vote from the FDA scientific advisory council, and again with only one year safety and effectiveness data.[24]

Questioned why it was approved without longer studies, an FDA official explained that doctors *must* have an anti-obesity drug—they and their patients demand it. One can only wonder—is it too much to expect of those desperate doctors and patients that they consider moving ahead to health-centered treatment, instead of one more round of likely failure?

Why Clinicians Prescribe Radical Methods

One might wonder why health care professionals adopt programs like the fen-phen pills, very-low-calorie liquid diets, and various quick-fix weight-loss plans. In many cases, these weight loss regimens seemed to offer the best hope for truly desperate patients. Naturally, it's reassuring to see patients happy because they're losing weight fast. Often they were busy, and did not follow through to find what actually happened with their patients' weights.

A bias against large patients exists in health care. Among some providers, there may be a feeling that they deserve to be treated with experimental methods, since they have not responded to more conservative treatment. Others apparently believe the patients' health risks are so high that a high-risk method is justified, even if it takes off weight only temporarily. Further, many patients demand the new pills and programs they read of in the daily headlines.

Feds Promise Guidance

In an effort to help providers determine the best way to address obesity problems, *Weighing the Options: Criteria for Evaluating Weight-Management Programs,* was published in 1995 by the National Academy of Sciences, a health policy advisory group. This book reviews available weight loss programs and, despite much evidence to the contrary, finds nearly all of them safe and effective. It also seems to suggest that weight loss surgery is an underused option, that more people should be undergoing stomach reduction surgery.[25] About the same time, a new consumer brochure assured dieters, "Almost any of the commercial weight loss programs can work." Its title—*Choosing a Safe and Successful Weight-loss Program*—implies the reader can choose from any of a number of successful methods.[26]

Clinical Guidelines

Physicians still needed more help. It was time for a large, comprehensive report that would document the research, identify persons at risk, and make recommendations based on sound scientific research. Clinical Guidelines on the Identification, Evaluation, and Treatment of Overweight and Obesity, the official answer, was released on June 17,1998.[27]

This report is a curious hybrid that on the one hand sets out the scientific research clearly, on the other glosses over inconvenient facts, and then blends the two into a set of recommendations for health care providers. However, the major goal seems directed toward getting more people on weight loss programs. For example, they lower the bar on how many people will be considered overweight and obese. The long-standing definition of adult overweight was at a BMI cutpoint of nearly 28. Now they pushed it down to 25. The Guidelines are based on 236 randomized, controlled studies lasting four months or more, in which weights are measured. These studies show the BMI with the lowest death rate is about 25 for Caucasian men and women, 27 for African-American men and women, and 25 to 30 for adults at midlife. Perhaps this was higher than expected, so, incredibly, the authors brought in one more study.

The Nurses' Health Study is based on self-reported answers to mailed-in questionnaires from Caucasian female nurses in a few states. The final Guidelines recommendations embrace the conclusions of that single nonrandom, noncontrolled study.

The Guidelines classify weight this way:

BMI	
18.5-24.9	Normal weight
25-29.9	Overweight
30 and over	Obesity

"It's an absurd goal. Many people are at natural and healthy weights over a much wider range than this," Cliff Johnson, of the National Center for Health Statistics had said earlier, when these levels were first suggested. His agency held as long as possible to their long-standing definition of overweight as a BMI value of 27.3 for women and 27.8 for men. Even then they had assured Americans that health risks did not necessarily start at this point. The Guidelines themselves hardly defend the new definition, and do not discuss the contradictions. Instead, they almost exclusively discuss risks that begin in individuals with a BMI of about 30.[28] The Guidelines fail to advise that patients be screening for eating disorders, or warned of weight loss risks.

Doctors are urged to motivate their patients to lose weight in two ways:

* By warning them of the risks of overweight
* By explaining how the new plan will be different

No effective plans are put forward, however. Thus, one might suggest the report encourages physicians to manipulate their patients with scare tactics and false promises. In the end, they seem to serve the diet industry better than they do consumers or health professionals.[29-31]

Effectiveness Claims

The Guidelines define success as keeping off the lost weight for a period of just one year. This apparently can begin on sign-up day, and include the months of weight loss. More realistic definitions of long-term success in weight loss are available from FTC and the American Heart Association. FTC says it means keeping off lost weight for two years *after the end* of any maintenance program. American Heart Association guidelines call for five years, and state bluntly, "If there are no data to demonstrate that program participants maintain their weight losses for five years or more, there is no scientific evidence of long-term results of the program."[32]

The Guidelines recommend losing about one to two pounds a week for six months, and then beginning a weight maintenance program. "No plan has demonstrated significant success in weight maintenance beyond six to 12 months," writes Ann Coulston, MS, RD, senior research dietitian with the General Clinical Research Center at Stanford University Medical Center.[33]

Manipulations of Truth

As in the Guidelines, government obesity reports often say one thing in the body and another in the conclusion. It's as if they are written by two opposing factions—one documenting weight loss risks, for example, and the other advising weight loss.

Wayne Miller, PhD, professor at George Washington University School of Medicine, points out these contradictions in the report from the 1992 NIH Conference on Methods for Voluntary Weight Loss and Control, which investigated the weight loss industry. One statement truthfully sums up the conference: *Long term weight loss following any type of intervention was limited to only a small minority.* Then comes the non sequitur, the inference that does not follow: *Regardless of products used, successful weight loss and control is limited to and requires individualized programs consisting of restricted caloric intake, behavior modification and exercise.*[34]

Dr. Miller says, "It is puzzling how the NHLBI could come to any effectiveness conclusion based on the paucity of data they received which they themselves judged to be inadequate, questionable, and inconclusive. Dr. Miller adds that, from the evidence given, only two conclusions are possible: First, there can be no conclusion, because there is no data on which to base it; or no commercial program is effective at producing long-term weight loss, because no company can provide data to show otherwise.[35]

Reports investigating the risks of a certain diet or pill often end with a warning that it can be dangerous, so should be used only on severely obese patients. But wait a minute. If it's risky for healthy people, why is it not even more so for high-risk individuals? And if it doesn't work for moderately overweight people, why would it work for people who are obese?

Size activists have labeled this last paragraph, the non sequitur that doesn't follow, the *PS phenomenon*. It means, they say, "P.S. Keep dieting. We hate you." Perhaps the message hits another theme: These are our best paying customers. We can't afford to lose them. Put your research out there if you must, but we get the final paragraph.

Guidelines Suggest Harm

The new federal Guidelines can do a great deal of harm, especially to children, and there is no evidence they will benefit them in any lasting way. It seems unlikely that many experienced doctors will follow the guidelines' advice. But if they do, and tell millions of already weight-obsessed Americans to lose weight, these are likely outcomes:

1. More children will be harmed by their weight loss attempts.
2. More will begin smoking, and be less likely quit.
3. More teenage girls will be malnourished, and suffer stunted growth, arrested sexual development, and fragile bones.
4. More kids will develop eating disorders and dysfunctional eating.
5. Weight cycling will increase, along with its risks, ratcheting weight ever higher.
6. The health community, the public and the media will intensify their focus on weight, rather than health; on treatment rather than prevention.

7. Media and advertising will increase the pressure on girls to be thin, and continue to promote weak, passive, self-absorbed, sexually vulnerable role models.
8. Large children will suffer even more from size prejudice, stigma and harassment.
9. Health care costs will increase as more drugs are prescribed long term.
10. Preventive efforts will remain stalled.

How Does Quackery Fit?

The quackery segment of the diet industry is as much an integral part of this field as are the big companies. Business is booming for these players—the diet gurus, con artists, miracle pill entrepreneurs. Kids are especially susceptible to their advertising messages—the persuasive infomercial, the seductive voice of the quack. Kids are often their victims.

So it is curious that the legitimate diet industry never speaks out against this questionable and fraudulent segment. Is it because the industry knows that public faith is fragile, and fears to shake it? Is there fallout to be gained from the outrageous advertising, continually whipping up excitement, fantasy and hope?

Replicating the Minnesota Starvation Study

While promoters continue to claim success for weight loss programs, credible information on potentially harmful effects is simply not available. Even though much federal money has been spent on treatment research in the past twenty years, this research has seldom looked at potentially adverse effects. A good place to start would be by replicating the Minnesota Starvation Study. That study found numerous harmful effects from dieting—physical, mental, emotional, and social.

But the testing techniques used in that study are now over a half century old. That same meticulous testing needs to be repeated with modern techniques and the results made available. Clinicians and researchers need this information. Consumers need it. But this idea meets with disfavor in the industry. When it was suggested, obesity researchers replied it would not be ethical to replicate a study that caused such distress. Not ethical? In the Minnesota Study 36 healthy young men were put on a diet of 1,500 calories for six months. These same obesity researchers were prescribing 300 to 800 calorie liquid diets to thousands of high-risk patients for six months or longer. Why were they *not* testing all possible physical and mental effects, and furnishing clinicians with accurate information on what really happens during a diet?

False Starts

Currently, there is great impetus in federal health policy to launch childhood obesity prevention programs in schools. Research on child obesity is also needed. Some obesity specialists who author the kinds of policies discussed here are pressing hard for programs in schools to include screening kids and getting those who are overweight and at risk for overweight (85th percentile and up) on weight loss programs. They would insist that insurance companies pay. No evidence suggests this would be successful, or even safe, and it is quite certain that large children would be further stigmatized and shamed.

Research into childhood obesity has not gone well. The Office of Human Research Protections (OHRP) recently stepped in to stop a federal study testing 200 children. The children were average weight and overweight kids with obese parents. The National Institute of Child Health and Human Development study aimed to find how obesity develops in high-risk children, and why some do not gain excess weight. It would extend over a period of fifteen years. Sounds like a good idea, so far. However, the children repeatedly had to undergo a battery of procedures that included psychological testing, x-rays, blood sugar tests, and an MRI of the abdomen. Some tests involved overnight hospital stays, the insertion of intravenous bloodlines and hours-long duration of extremely high and low blood sugar levels. "This testing posed a larger risk to the children than is allowed by law," said OHRP investigators.[36]

Two Paradigms

The experts involved in weight and eating issues split into two schools of thought, with differing philosophies and differing approaches to weight problems. First, is the *traditional approach*, which views obesity as a disease that needs to be cured with weight loss. Advocates emphasize the health risks of overweight, and the need for food restriction. Rules and numbers are important: which foods to eat and not eat, calories, fat grams, calories burned in exercise, pounds lost, calculating body mass index. This has also been called the *medical model* or *weight-centered approach*.

On the other hand stands the nondiet *health at any size approach*, which is more flexible. It emphasizes active living, tuning in to one's own body signals, supporting children's abilities to self-regulate food, and the need for nurturing and self-esteem. Advocates focus on wellness, and improving health and well-being regardless of weight. They cite research that shows weight loss programs are ineffective and often unsafe, that weight-cycling can shorten lives and may cause increased weight gain, and that some health risks of overweight may be exaggerated. This is also called the *health at every size*, or *health-centered approach*.

Traditional vs *Health at Any Size*

★ *Traditionalists* are concerned primarily with weight loss. *Health at any size* advocates are concerned with the health and well-being of the whole child.

★ *Traditionalists* define adult healthy weight as a BMI of 18.5 to 24.9. *Health at any size* advocates define healthy weight for both children and adults as: *The natural weight the body adopts, given a healthy diet and meaningful levels of physical activity.*[37]

★ *Traditionalists* favor weighing and measuring kids in school, categorizing them as "at risk" (BMI at 85th percentile) or "overweight" (95th percentile), and notifying parents of steps to be taken. *Health at any size* advocates discourage weighing and labeling kids in schools because of the high potential for error and stigmatizing effects.

★ *Traditionalists* count calories, restrict food, and teach kids about "good foods" and "bad foods." *Health at any size advocates* support children's abilities to self-regulate their eating, and teach that "all foods can fit."

★ *Traditionalists* say even if there are risks to their programs, it's worth it if some children lose weight. *Health at any size* advocates say: Do no harm.

★ *Traditionalists* say even though older weight loss programs didn't work, their new plans are better and new drugs will be better. *Health at any size* advocates say: Show me the data.

★ *Traditionalists* urge that insurance pay for all weight loss programs. *Health at any size* advocates say insurance should pay only when and if programs are proven long-term safe and effective.

★ *Traditionalists* assure parents that weight loss will bring self-esteem, self-acceptance, and good health. *Health at any size* advocates initiate measures to improve self-esteem, self-acceptance, and health right now.

★ *Traditionalists* promote large and rather sudden lifestyle changes, as being motivating for weight loss. *Health at any size* advocates promote gradual lifestyle change, as being lasting.

★*Traditionalists* promote physical activity for weight loss and to burn calories. *Health at Any Size* advocates promote activity for fun, energy, improved health, self-care, strength and endurance.

★ Both approaches are aimed at better health. Both have the goal of improving children's health now and for a lifetime, and of alleviating and preventing weight problems. Yet these philosophies are very different. Their histories are different, so are their goals.

This nation stands at the brink of putting preventive programs in place in schools all across the country. It does make a difference what kinds of programs these are, and the philosophy that drives them. These two philosophies call for very different approaches. The questions are: Which philosophy will guide preventive efforts in your school? What prevention measures will be used? Will the children in your school be better off for prevention efforts, or might some be harmed?

Chapter 9

♦ ♦ ❖ ♦ ♦ ❖ ♦ ♦ ❖ ♦ ♦ ❖ ♦ ♦ ❖ ♦ ♦ ❖ ♦ ♦

Dieting is Not the Answer

Janelle was excited when she read about mystical ways to lose weight. Her imagination raced—she read of blue water techniques and aromatics. It sounded like fun, very convincing; if you could just get your mind to work with you...She sent in her hard-earned $39 for the kit, a booklet and aromatics—to burn as a candle, or put in bath. It didn't do anything. Disappointed and ashamed, she threw it all away. But at least it didn't injure her.

More dangerously, an array of pills and teas, sold as food supplements to avoid drug regulation, offer "safe, all natural" quick fixes for weight loss. Often they contain plant-derived drugs that threaten severe injury. Far from being reassured by the word "natural," parents need to remind their children that poison mushrooms and many other naturally toxic plants are deadly. *Natural* and *safe* don't necessarily go together, especially in the quickly shifting world of weight loss quackery.

Ten teenagers in Texas were rushed to emergency rooms in one month with severe reactions to an herbal diet pill containing ephedrine. Soon after, in a related case, an Austin woman died of a heart attack. Other fatalities were reported around the country about the same time from the same ephedrine-laced pill. When

Baltimore Orioles pitcher Steve Bechler died during spring training in Florida, Feb. 17, 2003, after his temperature shot to 108 degrees, his death was blamed on the ephedrine-based weight loss pill he was taking. Sixteen-year-old Illinois football player Sean Riggins died in 2001 of what the coroner called an ephedra-induced heart attack.[38]

Formula One, Mini Thin, Xenadrine RFA-1, and Thermojetics are just some of the popular sellers boasting the ingredient ephedra, or ephedrine or Ma Huang. Side effects are heart damage, stroke, high blood pressure, seizures. In 1996, the FDA reported 330 adverse reactions and about a dozen deaths related to ephedrine-containing pills.

Questionable and fraudulent weight loss schemes multiply in another direction with the Internet. The information highway chokes everyone's morning email with the traffic of con artists and easy promises of weight loss.

No Help for Children or Teens

It is indeed unfortunate that, in their sometimes-desperate struggle to lose weight, kids have not received much helpful guidance from teachers, parents, or health providers. Policy makers at federal levels have failed to provide the needed leadership. Perhaps they hoped some of this confusion would shake out in slimming down some kids over time.

There are hundreds of ways to lose weight fast. This alone should tell us something. *None work.* If even one method worked in a safe way, the others would simply disappear. That happened with polio. Fifty years ago all kinds of methods were promoted to prevent this dread disease. Quacks profited handsomely from parental fears. Then along came Salk vaccine, and just like that, profits dried up. The quackery stopped. Now there's no quackery left in polio.

> *Alisha, 14, 5-foot-1, 160 pounds, discovered diet pills on the shelves of the corner convenience store. She confessed taking them to a friend, who said she was taking them too. "The pills are labeled 'natural,' so they must be harmless," she said. They didn't seem to help much, so she took 10, and the next day, 23 pills. The active ingredient: Ephedrine. Her heart began to beat rapidly, and she felt*

faint. She was a little scared—but it must working. Faster metabolism was just what she wanted. Sure enough, Alisha lost four pounds in four days. She began spending her allowance on the pills buying several boxes at once. Her weight rocketed up and down. One day her mother found her lying unconscious on the kitchen floor.

Children fall victim to the many high-risk ways to lose weight, from fad diets to gadgets, diet pills, smoking, and purging—methods that can damage the body, mind and pocketbook. Unfortunately, the medically monitored, scientifically tested, weight loss treatments available today are not effective long-term either. And they may be far from safe. None of these methods works in a safe and lasting way for very many people, but each time, kids are led to hope for a new miracle. Promoters are persuasive and kids easily tempted.

Many of today's quick fixes are dangerous, causing severe injury and sometimes death. The irony is that weight loss programs seem to work for a time, so kids, and often their moms and dads, keep trying something new, hoping to get past their own "failure."

Nothing Works Long Term

Americans, including children and teenagers, spend $30 to $50 billion annually experimenting with weight loss. And this doesn't even include smoking for weight control, that unacknowledged and highly lucrative windfall for tobacco companies, or weight loss surgery. The thinness culture has created a desperation in people at every age, from children to senior citizens, and opportunists are quick to take advantage.

Through nearly two decades *Healthy Weight Journal,* a publication for clinicians, has reported the facts on medical obesity treatment, and at the opposite end of the spectrum, on a steady stream of over 200 fraudulent and questionable products. Nothing has been able to show long-term safety and effectiveness. In sixteen years of incisive investigation, *Healthy Weight Journal* reported that the best statistics any obesity treatment program can show is weight loss up to six months, then a steady regain back to baseline weight or higher.

Most popular plans make about a four-year swing. Two years on the upswing, hyped by vigorous advertising and the endorsement of medical authorities and media personalities, followed by two years at peak excitement as more and more patients come on board. Then comes a swift decline as reality sets in, and the program is quietly dropped by medical centers and clinics.

An early "miracle" of the '80s was the Garren-Edwards gastric bubble—a balloon inserted into the stomach, then inflated. Within a short time, severe health problems forced a withdrawal of the hastily-granted FDA approval.

Enthusiasm moved on to the very-low-calorie liquid diets, known as VLCDs—with their "amazing, miracle" results. Patients taking in only 300 to 800 calories lost one-third of their size within a few months. Just as rapidly they gained it all back, with sometimes terrible side effects—including sudden death. Hundreds, probably thousands, of short-term studies, most of no more than six weeks to four months duration, appeared in the medical journals attesting to the great success of VLCDs.

Then came Slim Fast and its stacks of liquid meal replacement imitators filling grocery aisles for a couple of years. Three or four cans, all tasting the same, proved too much for most people. There were surgeries, intestinal bypass, stomach stapling, liposuction, jaw wiring, and thigh cream. Fen-phen and Redux then took center stage. At least five million American adults, and uncounted teens, took these prescription diet pills before they were abruptly withdrawn. New drugs were soon approved by the FDA, and others are in the pipeline, awaiting approval.

Even a the wedding can be a dangerous event, as each woman in the bridal party tries to fit into the smallest dress possible for the wedding pictures. Newspapers headlined the deaths of two brides who died on the eve of their weddings. One lost weight at a commercial diet center; the other was prescribed fen-phen.

Weight Loss Can Boost Death Rates

Most large, long-term studies suggest that losing weight is a risk factor for earlier death. The best way to defend against this may be to lose weight slowly with any weight loss attempt, while gradually increasing physical activity to minimize muscle and organ loss and improve overall health. The NIH conference on Methods for Voluntary Weight Loss and Control first compiled this evidence in 1992. It showed that weight loss is associated with increased risk of death, rather than lower risk, as had been assumed.[39]

During 18 years of follow-up in the ongoing federally-funded Framingham Heart Study, which in 1948 began surveying the population of Framingham, Mass., both men and women who lost weight through 10 years had the highest death rates.[40]

Similar findings were reported from other long-term comprehensive studies including the Harvard Alumni Study, MRFIT, CARDIA, the NHANES I followup, and a 10-study review by Reubin Andres, MD, clinical director of the National Institute on Aging. All exhibited higher mortality with weight loss. Most controlled for age, smoking, race, early deaths, and other possible confounding factors. Andres concluded, "For the general population, the results of the 10 studies do not support the idea that losing weight will increase longevity ... (but) the opposite."[41]

The question is *why?* Why, when short-term studies show benefits from weight loss, do long-term studies show the opposite? Some have thought it was bone loss and the increased risk of fragile bones and osteoporosis that comes with weight loss, intensified by repeated weight loss.[42] The answer may involve muscle loss.

When a 300-pound person loses 100 pounds rapidly or without exercise, as many did on the very-low-calorie liquid diet, the hope is that the loss all comes from visible rolls of fat just under the skin. Unfortunately, this is not the case. Instead, the person who loses one-third of her size loses a large amount of muscle from internal organs and throughout the body. A shrunken heart can easily be thrown off stroke and into irregular rhythm. Sudden death is a real risk.

A recent analysis of two large longitudinal community studies led by David Allison, PhD, of the Obesity Research Center in New York, found higher death rates with weight loss in both. But fat loss did provide benefits. In the first, the Framingham Heart Study, weight loss of a standard deviation meant a 39 percent *increase* in mortality risk, while fat loss provided a 17 percent *decrease* in mortality risk. The net result: a 22 percent *increase* in risk. In the Tecumseh Community Health Study, comparable figures meant a 29 percent average increase in risk with weight loss, and 15 percent decrease with fat loss. The harmful effects outweighed the benefits by 14 percent. Thus, while loss of fat appears to be healthy, the loss of muscle, organ and bone is not.[43]

To confirm their results, the researchers tried again using different analysis techniques. They controlled for smoking, age, gender, initial weight and fat. Each time they arrived at the same outcome.

"The body powerfully defends its fat," explains David Garner, PhD, director of the Toledo Center for Eating Disorders. He cites studies that show fat is defended at the expense of lean muscle and vital organs. Autopsies of emaciated patients show a shrinkage of vital organs, including heart, liver, kidneys and spleen, equal to the percent of weight loss.[44] Weight cycling or yo-yoing weight up and down may compound the problem. After weight loss, regain of fat appears to outstrip the regain of muscle mass.[45]

For the first time, in January 1998, a major scientific journal questioned weight loss treatment in a realistic way. "Until we have better data about the risks of being overweight and the benefits and risks of trying to lose weight, we should remember that the cure for obesity may be worse than the condition," wrote Marcia Angell, MD, and Jerome Kassirer, MD, editors of the *New England Journal of Medicine*, in their New Years Day editorial. Their report said bluntly that weight loss is not effective, it involves serious health risks, and it is untrue that the risks of obesity are so high this kind of treatment is justified. They concluded that the $30 to $50 billion dollars being spent on weight loss is wasted.[46]

Who's Trying to Lose Weight?

About two-thirds of all teenage girls are trying to lose weight, even though many are average or underweight. So are one quarter of teenage boys. Half of adults diet, and small children as young as six or seven are keying in to all this anxiety and following suit.[47] A nationwide study of 8th and 10th graders found 61 percent of girls and 28 percent of boys had dieted to lose weight in the last year.[48]

What is happening to these kids as they restrict nutrients, pop pills with unknown ingredients, and yo-yo their weight up and down? What happens to their growth, their bones, their brain development, *their lives?* Is this supposed to be normal? Why are parents and health care providers accepting this without protest? At the very least, the strenuous efforts kids make to reshape their bodies are diverting many from their important tasks of physical and mental development.

In Cleveland a survey of high school students found that 70 percent of Caucasian girls and 60 percent of African-American girls had lost at least five pounds in a weight loss attempt; so had 40 percent of all boys. More than one third of these girls were currently dieting. Many used dangerous methods — semi-starvation, vomiting, diet pills, laxatives, diuretics and smoking. One-third of dieting girls and one-fourth of dieting boys said they fast for 24 hours at least once a week.[49]

A national survey of 13,454 Native American junior high and high school students finds 27 percent of girls (and 12 percent of boys) vomit to lose weight, 11 percent use diet pills, and 7 percent diet more than 10 times a year.[50]

FIGURE 9.1 **Dieting and Purging (Percent of high school students)**[◦]

	Girls		Boys	
	White	Black	White	Black
Dieting	77	61	42	41
Liquid diet	14	24	6	9
Diet Pills	23	16	6	0
Laxatives	7	18	5	2
Diuretics	5	11	1	2
Vomiting	16	3	7	0
Monthly or more often	8	1	-	-
Fasting monthly or more often	35	40	29	25

Potentially harmful dieting behaviors are widely practiced by U.S. high school students. Total 1,269 students, Cleveland State University study.[1]

Lillian Emmons, PhD, RD, the nutritional anthropologist who directed the Cleveland study, said the high dieting rates among boys are much above earlier reports, and yet may be under reported. Of particular concern, she suggests, are the 10 percent of male dieters who lost 62 pounds or more through dieting, and lost 10 pounds twice as often as any other group. Emmons recommends that meaningful education on the dangers of dieting and reasonable expectations for body size and shape should be taught in schools, before the pre-adolescent growth spurt. But it's certainly not happening, or if it is, she warns, "is not as powerful as other cultural pressures. The amount of purging shown in this study is cause for concern because of the potentially damaging effects purging can have on health."

As noted earlier, not only are more kids dieting today, but they are starting younger.[51]

> *Sandra is only eleven years old, but already a medal-winning figure skater. Her slim, boyish figure is starting to change, to fill out, to be more rounded. She's panicky. She must be slim and graceful, and fit her spangled costume tightly. She's judged on appearance, after all. Sandra collects diet fads with a frenzy, but finds it works better to eat almost nothing when an event is coming up. Her skating friends are restricting food severely, too. Some vomit after eating so they can eat more, but she hasn't been able to do that yet.*

Young athletes in sports and performance arts that emphasize leanness are at special risk for harmful attempts to control the size and shape of their bodies. These activities include gymnastics, wrestling, judo, boxing, weight lifting, bodybuilding, figure skating, diving, ballet, dance, horse racing, and distance running. Vomiting and laxatives are commonly used by female college athletes in several sports.[52]

Summer Camp

In the hope that they will lose weight, many parents send their children to summer weight loss camps.

"Most camps are costly, stress excessive weight loss and fail to include an intensive family component," warns Laurel Mellin, RD, Director of the Center for Adolescent Obesity, San Francisco.[53] Mellin says that the typically severe dietary restrictions actually stimulate binge eating after camp is over. Such camps, Mellin points out, "are most likely to attract families that are desperate about their adolescent's weight and want to have their child 'fixed.' The overweight adolescent becomes the victim as parents first delight in initial weight loss, then despair and blame him or her as weight regain predictably occurs."

While some camping programs recognize the vulnerability of young people and hire qualified health professionals, many others do not. They may focus on restrictive diets and strenuous exercise that cannot be maintained.

An Associated Press story tells of a 10-day weight loss camp for sixty children, ages eight to fourteen, directed by Dr. Yan Chun, chief endocrinologist at Beijing Children's Hospital. Yan restricted his young campers to an 800 to 1,000 calorie, high protein, low starch, no-sweets diet. He exercised them four to five hours per day, and medicated them with a "new appetite suppressant." Appallingly, the visiting AP reporter wrote that the program "seems to be working," because "the children's main topic of conversation was how much fat they'd shed."[54]

Making Weight in Sports

Athletes often bring together several dangerous techniques for quick weight loss. Wrestling is at the top of this list. "If there's a way to lose weight, a wrestler will find it," warns Don Herrmann, associate director of the Wisconsin Interscholastic Athletic Association. "I've seen vomiting, laxative abuse . . . even a self-induced bloody nose."[55]

A Pennsylvania study found 42 percent of high school wrestlers had lost 11 to 20 pounds at least once in their lives. One-fourth were losing six to 10 pounds every week. They used a variety of aggressive methods including dehydration, food restriction, fasting, vomiting, spitting, laxatives, and diuretics.

A study of college wrestlers found food intake was extremely chaotic. One 118-pound wrestler ate 334 calories the day before the match, 4,214 calories in the evening after his match, and 5,235 the next day. His weekly loss was 12 pounds, followed by rebound after each match. Many were deficient in needed nutrients, which was more severe because of their strenuous training.[56]

Competing or training while dehydrated is an extremely hazardous practice. It inhibits sweating and increases risk of body temperature problems and heat stroke. Dehydrated wrestlers also lose stamina. Muscle endurance in these studies dropped 31 percent after a 4 percent loss of body weight from dehydration. Even four hours after rehydration, endurance was depressed as much as 21 percent.

The deaths of three college wrestlers within six weeks in 1997 shook the sport of wrestling. All three were restricting food and fluid and were trying to dehydrate in supervised training sessions when they died. In the wake of these tragedies, the National Collegiate Athletic Association revised the guidelines to prohibit hot boxes, hot rooms over 79 degrees, saunas, steam rooms, vapor-impermeable suits, use of laxatives, emetics, diuretics, excessive food and fluid restriction, and self-induced vomiting.[57]

The rapid weight loss wrestlers undergo can cause kidney and heart strain, low blood volume, electrolyte imbalances, increased irritability, depression, inability to concentrate, and increased vulnerability to eating disorders. Severely restricting food and fluid can also affect metabolism, body temperature and overall health. Fluid losses and resulting electrolyte disturbances can increase risk of cardiac arrhythmias, renal damage, impaired performance and injury. For young wrestlers, concerns are also raised about stunting of growth at a time in their lives when growth should be active and natural. Working with a sports nutritionist throughout the season is strongly recommended for athletes in sports in which weight is a concern, especially wrestling and gymnastics. Unfortunately, young kids are continually lured into ill-advised weight loss efforts by the promise of a quick fix.

Methods Kids use

While many overweight children are taken by parents from specialist to specialist for medical treatment, most are using do-it-yourself methods to lose weight. There is a whole world of treatments and gimmicks out there that claim to help people lose weight. Some are simply a waste of money. Others are deadly. Here are some of the favorites—and most dangerous.

Diet Pills

Kids don't need a prescription to buy diet pills off the shelf. They are cheap and handy. Diet pills are readily available at grocery, drug, chain and convenience stores, under such names as Dexatrim, Accutrim, PhenSafe and Cellulite Burner. Many teenage girls confess they shoplift diet pills and swallow them by the box.

Often sold as "natural" or "herbal," diet pills are usually labeled as food supplements, and claim no drug effects, to avoid FDA regulation. However, in advertising they may illegally make drug claims, such as that they suppress appetite, speed up metabolism, block digestion of fat or calories, flush fat out of the cells, or otherwise alter body functions to bring about "safe, easy, fast" weight loss.

One in three teen girls has taken diet pills.[58] In a Michigan State University survey, nearly half of college women and 6 percent of men had taken a diet drug. One in five said they'd started using these pills between age twelve and sixteen. None had ever consulted a physician, even though labels advise it under age eighteen, and many took far more than the recommended daily limit.

Diet pills may cause fatigue, hyperphagia (overeating), insomnia, mood changes, irritability and, in large doses, psychosis (a severe mental disorder), say Allan Kaplan and Paul Garfinkel in *Medical issues and the Eating Disorders.* Other documented side effects include fatal strokes, dangerously high blood pressure, heart rhythm abnormalities, heart and kidney damage, hallucinations, seizures, headaches, nervousness, cerebral hemorrhage, nausea, vomiting, anxiety, palpitations, renal failure, disorientation and death.

A popular drug that was long allowed in non-prescription diet pills, PPA (phenylpropanolamine) is now off the shelves, after a long process and much pleading from bereaved parents and alarmed health professionals. In November 2000 the FDA asked companies to stop marketing PPA. Most reformulated their best-selling pills by removing PPA and adding ephedrine or other active ingredients—with new names such as Dexatrim Natural, and Acutrim Natural.[59]

Tests proved PPA increased the risk of hemorrhagic stroke, or bleeding into the brain. First warnings had come back in the 1980s when medical journals cited several dozen young women who suddenly had strokes soon after taking their first diet pill. Some strokes hit within three days of taking the diet pills.[60] With PPA off the market, ephedrine has increased in diet pills.

Yet diet pills containing ephedrine, also sold as ephedra or Ma huang, have proven dangerous, even deadly. Life-threatening conditions include irregular heartbeat, heart attack, angina, stroke, seizures, hepatitis and psychosis. The FDA warns consumers that ephedrine overdosing, common with diet pills, can start the heart racing, cause heart palpations and death. An especially dangerous combination, says the FDA, are diet pills that contain both Ma huang (ephedrine) and kola nut. Pills containing ephedrine are now outlawed in Texas for sales to minors.[61]

Bee pollen, too, has caused fatal reactions, even though promoters claim it is "naturally safe" and "safe for any dieter." The FDA warns that bee pollen holds hazards for anyone with allergies, asthma or hay fever.[62] Pills like these are often spotlighted in the Slim Chance Awards given each January by Healthy Weight Network and the National Council Against Health Fraud. Awards go to the four so-called "worst" weight loss products of the year. Always in hot contention are the latest versions of herbal pills.[63]

Weight loss fraud works because kids and adults want to believe there are easy ways to lose weight. Con artists exploit this with a mixture of pseudoscience, mysticis, and sensationalism, says Burton Love, Midwest Regional FDA Director. Authorities say there is more fraudulent and misleading information about nutrition and weight today than ever before, and it is being marketed more effectively in high-tech, highly targeted ways, with enormous profits.

Laxatives and Diuretics

Taking laxatives or diuretics is dangerous and does not help kids lose weight. Laxatives cause weight loss through dehydration due to a large volume of watery diarrhea. Calories are not really affected, although nutrients may be poorly absorbed. Abuse of laxatives can cause both acute and chronic lower gastrointestinal complications, including abdominal cramping, bloating, pain, nausea, constipation and diarrhea.[64] They can cause loss of electrolytes, including potassium, essential for heart function.[65] Nerve damage may result in a sluggish bowel that can get so severe it requires removal of the colon. Diuretics or "water pills" are used less by youngsters, but their abuse is extremely dangerous.

In the Cleveland study, African-American girls were the ones most likely to use laxatives and diuretics for weight loss—18 percent had used laxatives and 11 percent diuretics, compared with 7 and 5 percent, respectively for Caucasian girls. About half of these girls took them at least every month.[66] In the Youth Risk Behavior Survey, laxatives and diuretics were taken most often by Mexican-American girls.[67]

Tolerance to laxatives develops over time, so young people who abuse them may increase their dosage to 60 or more tablets daily. Laxatives are probably the most common type of drug abused by bulimic patients.[68] Using several purging techniques together intensifies the effects. The big concern is potassium loss leading to heart arrhythmias and kidney damage. A physician should be consulted immediately on signs of potassium loss, such as muscle weakness, fatigue and chest pain.

Vomiting

At the very least, repeated vomiting can cause sore throat, difficulty in swallowing and dehydration. It can progress to heartburn-like pain, rupture of the esophagus, tooth decay, loss of potassium, cardiac arrhythmias and sudden death.[69] Forceful vomiting may tear the mucosa of the gastrointestinal tract, showing blood in the vomitus. Occasionally, the force of vomiting breaks small blood vessels in the eyes, and injures the esophageal sphincter, allowing stomach contents into the lower esophagus. The esophagus may rupture after ingestion of a large meal and subsequent forceful vomiting. This creates a medical emergency with severe upper abdominal pain, worsened by swallowing and breathing. It has high death rate if left untreated. Surgery is usually required. Low levels of potassium, essential for muscle and heart functioning, can trigger cardiac arrhythmias, from prolonged vomiting.

One in six Caucasian girls in the Cleveland study vomited in their desperate efforts to avoid digesting the food they ate.[70] Some kids use Ipecac syrup to induce vomiting, a practice that is especially dangerous and can cause cardiovascular, gastrointestinal and neuromuscular toxicity.[71]

Those who vomit three times a week or more will eventually cause erosion of their tooth enamel from acid vomitus in the mouth. Experts say this erosion can take as little as six months, or several years. Teeth become sensitive to heat and cold, then open up spaces, lose fillings, and eventually deteriorate down to painful cores. Patterns of vomiting become visible as "chipmunk" cheeks, likely from repeated gland stimulation by the acid contents of the stomach.

Jamie, age seventeen, a beautiful, bright girl, weighing 145 pounds, hated her body, her hips, and her stomach. Always wanting to lose a few pounds, she had begun purging her food six months ago.

"Every night that I throw-up I can't help but be afraid that my heart might stop or something terrible might happen. I just hope I can stop this throwing up before it kills me.... I feel crazy when I have a panic attack. Each time I have an incredible binge, I immediately take laxatives to rid myself of all that forbidden food."

She fasted all day, and when she got home from school weighed herself. When the scale showed no weight lost, Jamie went into the kitchen and began to binge. She could eat two bowls of cereal, a large bag of animal cookies, a quart of ice cream, and two-thirds of a frozen cheesecake. She really needed to lose five pounds. Eating rapidly, stuffing more and more food in her mouth, she felt ashamed; she had to purge. It became a pattern in which she'd fast most of the day, drinking only diet coke, then go on binges in afternoon and evening, eating up to 5,000 calories, then vomiting and taking laxatives to purge herself of the horrible food and guilt.

On weekends, sometimes Jamie would binge 10 times a day. Her voice became raspy, her glands swollen, her cheeks pouched out, chipmunk-like. Her stomach, throat and nasal passages all burned from the constant vomiting. She worried about damage done to intestines by laxative abuse. She was tired of always being dehydrated, exhausted—tired of being chained to bathroom, sneaking in and out—tired of craving foods she knew she'd just throw up again if she ate. She spent all her money on food, laxatives, and diet pills. Her bingeing and purging interfered with all areas of her life. Yet she felt relaxed and comforted when she binged for a while. Then she'd feel ashamed and would wish she hadn't eaten so much. No way she could stop, she feared that only with laxatives and vomiting could a ballooning of her weight be prevented.[72]

Smoking

Smoking delivers that most popular of all weight loss drugs—nicotine. And it's more popular than ever, especially with girls, as the pressure to lose weight intensifies.

The jump in girls' smoking began during the late 1970s, "to the point where for almost two decades teenage girls have been puffing away at rates exceeding or equal to those of teenage boys," mourns Joseph Califano, Jr., former secretary of Health, Education and Welfare. Targeting girls and women with cigarette advertising began in the late 1960s, and in the next 20 years, death rates from lung cancer increased 500 percent for female smokers.

Smoking rates declined for young Americans in the 1970s and 1980s, then went up again. In 1991, only 27 percent of all high school students were smoking. By 1997, 36 percent were lighting up. African-American kids were smoking much less than others, but now they're on their way to catching up. Smoking levels are also higher for college students (at 29 percent), than for adults (25 percent). With teenage girls leading the way, 3,000 American adolescents become regular smokers every day.

For the first time ever in 1995, Caucasian high school girl smokers caught up and surpassed the boys. That year, forty percent of Caucasian girls were occasional smokers, compared with 37 percent of Caucasian boys in the Youth Risk Behavior survey.[73]

Three studies make it clear why so many girls are smoking today. In a recent study of over 15,000 children, reported in *Pediatrics*, preteens who worry about their weight are most likely to experiment with smoking at early ages. Ten percent had smoked by age nine to fourteen, and they were the ones who were more concerned about weight and more likely dieting, purging, or exercising to lose weight.[74]

Increasingly, African-American girls are embracing the drive for thinness. Their weight concerns are the primary reason many become daily smokers by age eighteen or nineteen, reports a new federal study. The researchers followed the smoking practices of 2,379 girls for nine years in three cities, Cincinnati, Washington, DC., and Richmond, Calif.[75] Caucasian girls are more likely than African-American girls to become daily smokers.

Smoking has its own powerful industry promoting nicotine as a method of weight control. In magazines targeted to girls and women, smoking ads feature thin models and often the word *slim* used in a subliminal way. "That's what makes Virginia Slims and Capri Superslims—with their names, slim cigarette outlines, and extremely thin models—so attractive to teenage girls," says Califano.[76]

Girls and women are not as likely to quit smoking as boys and men. And when they try, studies show they are less likely to succeed. A major reason is their fear of weight gain. Yet there is evidence that women who smoke have nearly double the risk of lung cancer as men.[77]

Tobacco companies face a dilemma. How can they line up a generation of young new smokers without seeming to recruit them? In the $206 billion tobacco settlement of 1998, tobacco companies were banned from taking "any action, directly or indirectly," to target youth. But they often manage to advertise aggressively in magazines that reach teens as often or more often than adults. They sponsor sporting and concert events that attract young people, and get wide exposure as background for televised sports events.

Health policy makers face a dilemma, too. How can they discourage smoking for weight control, while keeping up the pressure on kids to lose weight? But it's not such a dilemma after all. When the larger goal is to improve the overall health and well-being of all children, including children of all sizes, then the choice is easy. Smoking needs to be discouraged. But what benefits and what harm accrue from keeping up that pressure on kids to lose weight?

Califano says he regrets not dealing with the fear of weight gain in the fight against smoking back when he was HEW Secretary during the late 1970s.[78] The irony is that thirty years later, health leaders still hesitate to acknowledge that people smoke to control weight. Why? Perhaps they fear lending credence to nicotine as a weight loss drug. Or perhaps they are conflicted over how to deal with the fact that smoking does indeed tend to keep off a few pounds.

It's true that upon quitting smoking, most people gain some weight, an average of about 6 to 10 pounds in national studies. They'll weigh about the same as persons who never smoked. This is consistent with studies that show people who quit smoking catch up with their peers who never smoked.[79] Thus, nicotine acts much like prescription diet drugs. People keep off a few pounds, and regain them when they stop the drug. The weight control effect is not much compared with the economic and health costs.

Some researchers note that children's weight concerns underlie both smoking and dieting, and advise that unhealthy weight concerns be addressed in prevention programs.[80] Why not admit a major reason why girls smoke is their drive for thinness, and develop educational programs to convince them this is a poor reason for choosing a lifelong addiction that will do them harm? Instead of pretending no effect, which gives kids a secret they can't talk openly about, we need to help them realize how foolish it is to smoke for weight control. Not only do they incur health risks, but eventually will also find that smoking ages the face, causes deep vertical wrinkles, and muddies the complexion with deep gray and purplish tones.

Healthy People 2010 goals for the nation are to decrease smoking to 16 percent of high school youth from 36 percent, and to increase the average age of first use to sixteen from fourteen years.

To meet these goals we need to be talking to kids about their unhealthy weight concerns.

Tobacco is responsible for more than one of every six deaths in the U.S., and smoking during pregnancy accounts for up to 30 percent of low birth weight babies and 10 percent of infant deaths, according to the Healthy People report.

Miracle Diets And Quick Fixes

Kids are tempted by an array of fad diets found in magazines or books, and given them by friends. They fall for all sorts of unbalanced and gimmicky ways to restrict food. Teens eat the magic combinations—grapefruit and steak, bananas and milk, fruits and fructose, rice and grapefruit, and the cabbage diet. They drink many cans of liquid meal replacer. Most of these are unbalanced, deficient in nutrients and lacking variety. But luckily, they are so boring kids don't stick with them long. Two or three days on the cabbage diet or subsisting on rice and grapefruit is enough. The drama and excitement of launching a new diet can't be sustained for long.

There are also ways to "detoxify" the body, an unsound notion that involves a fast of several days, then taking various combinations of herbal pills, up to 30 a day. This gets expensive, and supposedly rids the body of the pollution of modern life.

Other quack weight loss methods are herbal teas and mushroom tea, which have been linked to deaths. The FDA warns of at least four deaths and adverse effects ranging from diarrhea, cramps and fainting to permanent loss of bowel function related to herbal weight loss teas. Many contain large doses of stimulant laxatives, but since they are sold as food supplements, they're not regulated and contain unknown amounts. Potency varies widely with growing season, amount used, and steeping time.[81]

Sixteen-year-old Maria, the child of a single teenage mother who moved a series of live-in boyfriends into the house, died after drinking herbal tea. Maria longed to have better luck with boys than her Mexican-American mother had, and thought if she was thinner, it might happen. She ordered herbal tea from an ad in the Sunday paper supplement.

Advertised as "safe, all natural," it made no mention that the active ingredients (senna, cascara and buckhorn) are strong laxatives. Maria steeped three bags of tea (triple strength) in a cup of boiling water, and let it sit half an hour before drinking. She went to bed with terrible cramps. Her mother found her dead in bed the next morning.

Also in the quack arena are numerous gadgets such as slimming insoles, vacuum pants, appetite-suppressing earrings, appetite patches, passive exercise tables, electrical stimulators, acupressure devices, battery-driven spot-reducing belts, body wraps, hypnotism, meditation, mystical panaceas, aroma therapy, seaweed soap, spot reducing creams and lotions. Most of the gadgets are probably harmless, yet they involve scams, deception and false promises. The voice of the quack is seductive in enticing youngsters to waste money on worthless schemes.[82]

Medically Monitored Programs

Many overweight children are treated within the health care system, rather than with do-it-yourself methods. Their weight loss programs are medically monitored, but this does not mean they are without risk. In the best plans, physicians, dietitians and other health care providers trained in the area focus on encouraging healthy lifestyles. In many others the focus seems to be on rapid weight loss, at any cost to health and well-being.

Very Low Calorie Diets (VCLDS)

The semi-starvation diets of 300 to 800 calories, very low calorie liquid diets, were prescribed widely in the 1980s and early 1990s to both children and adults, and are still being used to some extent. They have the highest risk for sudden death syndrome, warn researchers at the National Institutes of Health Obesity Research Center in New York. Sudden death can come without warning. The heart, which loses volume during the large and rapid weight loss, may be thrown into an irregular stroke. Cardiac arrhythmias may lead to heart attacks and death. In 1995 a federal health book,

Weighing the Options, recommended this very low calorie diet for the "more serious cases of childhood and adolescent obesity, for which rapid weight reduction is essential." It was not explained why rapid weight loss was essential for higher risk children.

The book suggests that for children a part of the advised 600 to 800 calories be made up by two to four cups of low-starch vegetables. This is termed a "protein-sparing modified fast," to suggest that it will take off fat and spare the child's muscle, although no evidence is given as to how or why this is supposed to happen (it doesn't).[83] Sadly, many young children were put on these semi-starvation diets, some of them scarcely overweight. No child was too young, according to *Options*. "In children, the protein-sparing modified fast has been used on children as young as six and by children whose weight ranges from 120 percent to greater than 200 percent of ideal." In England, it was not recommended for children under thirteen.

Finally, in 1998, federal policy makers at the National Institutes of Health declared they could no longer recommend diets of 800 calories or less. They said these diets are unsuccessful, usually more weight is regained than was lost, and they increase risk of gallstones and nutrient inadequacies.[84]

Gallbladder disease is high risk with any low-calorie diet, and much more so with a VLCD. Children rarely develop gallstones, but one thirteen-year-old girl had to have her gallbladder removed after losing weight through a weight loss center diet, as described in the 1990 Congressional hearings on the weight loss industry. Her mother, Loretta Pameijer testified, "We're angry because it never occurred to us to be suspicious of a doctors' clinic."

A New York City investigation also turned up numerous problems with severe diets, including the case of a fifteen-year-old Long Island girl who had to have her gallbladder removed after losing 72 pounds in six months.[85]

Kelly, age sixteen, 260 pounds, persuaded her well-to-do Long Island parents to pay the $3500 bill for a very-low-calorie diet, assuring them the doctor would be checking her health closely as she lost weight. She picked up her cans of liquid protein, totaling 600 calories per day, at the doctor's office. The first day or two she felt *hungry, then was astonished and delighted to find that she had lost her appetite for food. She had no interest in eating. On a high, she lost weight rapidly. Every day the scale dipped lower. Although she often felt faint and dizzy, and was having out-of-body experiences as if viewing herself from afar, it was exciting. She lost 90 pounds, down to 170, in four months. It had all been so easy. She bought a wardrobe of new, smaller clothes, and was amazed and proud modeling them in front of the mirror.*

She still had 30 pounds to the goal weight she and the doctor had set when she reached a plateau. No matter what, she couldn't lose even a half pound more. What had seemed so easy was now impossible. By this time she was having trouble in school. She couldn't concentrate on her lessons or tests. Still, her teachers and classmates praised her weight loss.

Two weeks later she began to regain. One pound, then two, then three. Frantic, she drank even less of the diet liquid, and went back to the doctor for help. He thought she was cheating. She knew that right away, from the blaming way he kept questioning her about what she ate.

Ashamed, she went home, and that night she did eat some solid food. Just one slice of bread tasted so good. It was her first bite of real food in five months. Then the floodgates opened and she ate ravenously. The thought of even one more sip of the hated diet liquid almost made her sick. Kelly blamed herself, of course: It was her fault—no willpower. Everything was just fine, until she began bingeing. Only, of course it wasn't. She had wasted five months of her life and $3500. Yet she was lucky. Her immune system was still intact, and she had no other long-term adverse effects from the experience, unlike many others on the same diet. She had lost 90 pounds in four months; five months later she weighed 270 pounds, more than she had ever weighed in her life.

Primary pulmonary hypertension

A rare lung disease potentially fatal within four years to nearly half of patients. It was known to be linked with dexfenfluramine prior to FDA approval of the drug.

Phentermine

Phentermine, an amphetamine-related appetite suppressant, gained FDA approval in 1959. Popular in combination with the fen and dexfen drugs, its use declined after they were withdrawn in 1997. It is still the most common drug being prescribed for weight loss, even though it is approved for short-term therapy only. Phentermine was withdrawn from the market in the European Union in 2000.

Sibutramine / Meridia

Approved by FDA in 1997, Meridia works on brain chemicals to suppress appetite. But it tends to raise blood pressure, speed the heart rate, and is advised only for severely obese patients—but not if they suffer from poorly controlled hypertension, heart disease, or irregular heartbeat, or if they have survived a stroke, according to the FDA.

In one study of 82 overweight adolescents age 13 to 17 treated with sibutramine, the drug had to be reduced or discontinued for 44 percent of the young patients during the first six months because of increases in systolic blood pressure (versus a decline in blood pressure for control patients on placebo).[86]

Sibutramine has been taken off the market in Italy after two deaths and 50 adverse events linked to its use. The FDA received reports of 29 related deaths and 397 adverse events between 1998 and 2001, including the deaths of three women under age thirty.[87]

Today's approved prescription diet pills don't keep off much weight either. Average weight loss over placebo is 7 to 11 pounds for sibutramine sold under the brand name Meridia, by Knoll. People demand more weight loss than this, so a diet is prescribed to go along with the pills. The patient loses weight for a few weeks or months from the diet, then gains it back.[88]

Only one-year studies of safety and effectiveness are available, which means one should not take Meridia for more than one year and especially not a child. However, in catch 22 fashion, weight is regained when the pills are discontinued. But weight loss is also not assured even if pills are taken continuously; in the past, having only one-year data usually means an eventual regain anyway.[89]

Although many children are now being treated with sibutramine and other drugs for weight loss, experts recommend that weight loss medications should be used only on an experimental basis with children and adolescents. The FDA has not approved such drugs for children under age 16.[90]

Orlistat / Xenical.

Studies show orlistat, sold under the brand name Xenical by Hoffman-LaRoche, keeps off an average of about 8 pounds.[91] Approved by the FDA in 1999, it acts on the intestine, blocking up to 30 percent of the fat absorbed into the intestines. Xenical has been criticized for having the unpleasant side effects of soft stools and oily leakages as it sends undigested fat out of the body. Marketers say this purging effect teaches the patient to eat less fat. Others have pointed out similarities with purging in eating disorders.[92]

Amphetamines

Amphetamines are no longer recommended because of potential addiction risk, but are still available and being prescribed by some doctors.

In the book *Real Women Don't Diet,* a woman named Gloria says she was prescribed her first diet pills at age twelve. "They weren't called 'yellow jackets' or 'uppers' back then. They were just some little yellow pills given to a physically healthy twelve-year-old to lose weight. . . Withdrawing from years of diet pills, which meant having vivid hallucinations and periods of extreme paranoia and finally becoming bulimic, were the most dangerous, physically damaging aspects of my war with my body, but the psychological damage and pain have been far more lasting."[93]

It's hard to believe that it is helpful to take prescription pills indefinitely, just to keep off eight or 10 pounds. Will it really benefit the child who weighs 250 pounds? We don't know of any health benefits in taking these diet pills. Nor do we know what the long-term risks may be, especially for a child. As of April 2002, there were 27 weight loss drugs in the pipeline in or about to begin clinical trials or awaiting FDA approval.[94] Perhaps in the future we may have weight loss drugs that are safe and effective for some or most people. But not yet. Our vulnerable children have time to wait. They need not be victims of these drug experiments.

Weight Loss Surgery

Gastric bypass, known as stomach stapling, and other weight loss surgeries carry real risks and are not recommended for children under age seventeen, according to the 1991 Gastrointestinal Surgery Consensus Development Conference. Yet children are having the surgery, which reduces their stomachs by as much as 99 percent, and do die from it.

Surgical Techniques

The most acceptable weight loss surgeries are vertical banded gastroplasty and gastric bypass, based on available outcome data, according to the National Institutes of Health. Most common today are the Roux-en-Y gastric bypass, vertical banded gastroplasty, the biliopancreatic diversion and its variations, and the various gastric banding procedures. (American Society for Bariatric Surgery, Gainesville, Fla., www.asbs.org)

Weight loss surgery may be restrictive or malabsorptive, or a combination of both. In restrictive procedures the stomach is stapled or banded off into a pouch so small the patient can eat only a limited amount of food at one time—about one ounce or two tablespoons initially and later double or triple that much. With malabsorption the body absorbs fewer calories and fewer nutrients. Both surgeries may alter food choices.

The gastric bypass operation combines both food restriction and malabsorption. A small stomach pouch is created by stapling off a section at the top of the stomach. Attached to the pouch in Roux-en-Y gastric bypass is a Y-shaped bypass that allows food to bypass part of the small intestines. This is more effective in weight loss, but with higher risks.

A 1994 review of weight reduction surgeries at the University of Florida Department of Surgery, Gainesville, showed three deaths within the first year among eleven children. Three others had severe complications requiring reanastomosis or a reopening. Thirty-nine surgeries for weight loss were performed on adolescents from age eleven to nineteen at that institution during the previous 11 years.[95]

Weight loss surgery is increasing rapidly. About 47,200 procedures were performed in 2001, 62,000 in 2002,[96] and estimates are for an expected 98,000 in 2003. Death rate for this elective surgery is up to 2.5 percent in published studies, or as many as five patients for every 200 who undergo the surgery.[97] An estimated 10 percent or more have serious complications. A common complaint of patients who suffer debilitating side effects is that they were not informed beforehand of the risks and what can happen.[98]

Weight loss surgery has not been researched with controlled studies, or even adequate animal testing, charge many experts. Long term consequences remain uncertain. Paul Ernsberger says a number of trials have been started, but the final results were never reported. "I think it's because it's bad news."[99]

The federal Weight-control Information Network (WIN) is calling for a comprehensive study to be coordinated through selected centers that are involved in large numbers of weight loss surgeries. Even establishing a database to track bariatric surgery patients is much needed, says WIN.[100] It is suggested that surgeons solve the ethical dilemma by telling patients upfront that this is investigational surgery and they do not know if it will help the patient or not.[101]

Over 60 complications of weight-loss surgery have been documented, including infections, leaks in the digestive tract, intestinal obstruction, blood clots in the lungs, hernia, persistent nausea and vomiting, diarrhea, ulcers, anemia, and other nutritional deficiency diseases. Long-term risks include osteoporosis, pernicious anemia and stomach cancer. Malabsorption is considered especially dangerous for children. When they are lacking certain key nutrients before their bodies are fully developed, well documented to occur after weight loss surgery, very serious problems can result. Further, medical science has not provided convincing evidence that patients who undergo weight loss surgery live longer or have fewer diseases. Weight loss peaks after two years and then tends to gradually return.[102]

Experts urge patients to investigate the background and medical qualifications of the surgeon before opting for this surgery.[103] Surgery performed at major surgery centers usually involves fewer complications. Long-term pre- and postoperative care needs to be part of every program. Before making a decision, patients should have a clear understanding of expected benefits, risks, and long term consequences. A multi-disciplinary approach is essential, with appropriate lifelong follow-up to monitor potentially serious problems, operative failure, and nutrient deficiencies.

Liposuction

The suctioning out of fat from under the skin—may seem fairly simple and benign to a large teenager reading the local newspaper advertisements for liposuction. But it can cause death and lasting injury, particularly when the provider has failed to get specialized training. A study released by the American Society of Plastic Surgeons reveals 95 deaths between 1994 and 1998 in liposuction procedures performed by board-certified plastic surgeons. This is a rate of one death for every 5,000 surgeries. Not all who advertise are certified.

"Choose your surgeon carefully," warns Rod Rohrich, MD, plastic surgeon and co-editor of *Plastic and Reconstructive Surgery*, the journal that published the study.[104]

Why Diets Don't Work

Diane, age fifteen, 203 pounds, started her diet on Monday, and it is going well. She found it in a magazine—a good diet, 1200 calories, written by a dietitian. The week before Diane and her boyfriend had a fight. Angry and frustrated, she went home and binged on cookies and ice cream. The next morning she dug out the diet she had clipped. It was easy to follow, using mostly food her family already had in the kitchen. She's enjoying learning to cook some new recipes. Things are going better with her boyfriend, too.

Julianne, age thirteen, 160 pounds, joined a weight loss group that meets in a shopping mall. Her mother found a group with three other young teens like herself, so she feels good about that. She buys package foods at the center, which gets expensive, but it's working. At first she lost weight rapidly, 10 pounds in three weeks; since then it has tapered off.

Ten-year-old Jose, 195 pounds, goes with his mom to a health care team at their medical center. He had a doctor's checkup, and met with the dietitian and physical therapist. He's learning to eat more slowly, take small bites, sit at one place while eating, and follows a special low calorie diet his mom fixes for him. She says it's a good one for her, too.

Most would agree these are sound, sensible weight loss diets. They are well balanced with foods from all five groups. They include plenty of fruits and vegetables, lots of variety and fiber, and the food tastes good. Diane, Julianne, and Jose are learning good eating habits, too. And all three are walking half an hour or more every evening.

On these diets all three youngsters lose weight at the recommended rate of about one or two pounds per week—15 to 20 pounds in three months. They're pleased (although they had hoped to lose a bit more). They're getting much positive encouragement from program directors and favorable comments from friends and adults. Diets like these offer potential to improve a child's lifestyle. Even if weight loss is not maintained, long-term benefits can be gained, says Ellen Parham, PhD, RD, dietetics professor at Northern Illinois University, DeKalb. Establishing healthy lifestyle goals as well as weight loss, she suggests, helps kids:

- ⋆ Increase fitness and flexibility through exercise;
- ⋆ Improve nutrition;
- ⋆ Achieve a sense of control over eating;
- ⋆ Relieve a health problem;
- ⋆ Increase self-esteem;
- ⋆ Develop a family lifestyle that will reduce the risk of obesity for children and others.[105]

Children on these diets begin to improve their lifestyle habits. They gain long-term benefits if these habits are maintained—they will eat better, live more actively, and feel better about themselves—the same benefits a child gets from a healthy lifestyle program that does not focus on weight loss.

Sad to report, Diane, Julianne and Jose don't keep off their lost pounds. After three or four months of eating less than their bodies seem to want, the scale stops dropping. It begins a slow reversal. They binge, secretly, once or twice. They let slip the good habits they've learned. Instead of eating slowly, deliberately, they rapidly devour their food, scarcely chewing, and can't seem to stop.

No longer do they walk after school or in the evening. What's the use? It didn't help. Their best hopes are dashed. They soon regain the weight they lost and a few pounds more. They blame themselves for lacking will power, for "blowing" a diet that was doing so well for them. Worse, they've disappointed everyone who tried to help. It's a shameful, guilt-filled time, and they feel like failures, until the drama of the next diet begins.

Dieting Failure

It's a sad fact that diets almost inevitably fail. Even on the best programs, most dieters are unable to keep off the weight they lose. Within a few weeks or months of that exciting moment they start a new diet, weight regain begins. It continues until all lost weight is regained, and often adds extra for good measure. Thus, dieting is a major cause of weight cycling or yo-yoing, with all of the related health risks. (See Chapter 2 for the health risks of weight cycling.) The depressing statistic that 95 to 97 percent of diets fail, has held for over forty years.

Albert Stunkard, MD, pioneer obesity researcher, warned in the 1950s that most people who begin a weight loss program do not complete it, most who complete it do not lose weight, and most people who lose weight do not keep it off. This still holds.

One popular diet doctor of the 1980s, who had a busy metropolitan practice for many years, was so pleased with his success as coach, cheerleader and magician that he decided to run a check of former patients. He was appalled, and utterly disillusioned, by what he found.

Not one of his former patients—not one—had kept off for five years any of the weight they lost so successfully under his direction.[106]

Some programs try to count one year as proof of long-term success. But that's much too soon. *Rule One* in weight loss is: *The first year of weight loss doesn't count; wait at least till the end of the second year to celebrate.*

The Federal Trade Commission gives us a reasonable standard:

★ *Long-term weight loss means keeping off lost weight for two years after the end of any maintenance program.* (In other words, first comes the weight loss phase, then maintenance phase, if any, then start counting.)

The American Heart Association raises the bar even higher:

★ *If there are no data to demonstrate that program participants maintain their weight losses for five years or more, there is no scientific evidence of long-term results of the program.*[107]

Setpoint as a Settling Point

For adults, our natural weight seems to be what we weigh right now, at this time in our lives, when fully nourished, moderately active and not dieting. If we lose weight, there are many regulatory processes in our bodies working to restore that natural weight.

This natural weight is called our *setpoint.* Mohey Mowafy, PhD, a nutritionist at Northern Michigan University, has dubbed it the *settling point,* suggesting a somewhat flexible range, at least for some people.

"The body has an opinion about what it should weigh," says Richard E. Keesey, PhD, a setpoint researcher and professor at the University of Wisconsin, Madison.[108] He explains that most people maintain a stable weight, despite wide variations in calorie intake. This is because the body makes its own adjustments to match food intake. With overeating or undereating, adjustments are made, and metabolism speeds up or slows down, temperature rises or drops, heart rate adjusts to try to balance calorie intake. Keesey says a five percent drop in weight ordinarily results in a 15 percent drop in metabolism.

One of the most convincing arguments for a setpoint concerns the remarkable stability of weight. Many people vary only two or three pounds in weight throughout most of a lifetime. Stunkard has calculated that a person eating 3,000 calories a day consumes a million calories a year. An error of only 300 calories either way from an exact daily balance of food to physical activity, would add or subtract 30 pounds in a year. Obviously, this does not happen. Weight rarely varies more than a couple of pounds a year, if that. Stunkard reported that when a person's weight does go up or down through diet or various life events, it soon returns almost precisely to its previous level.[109]

It may be just as hard to gain weight as to lose it. Researcher Ethan Sims tested this with inmates at Vermont State Prison. The men volunteered to gain 20 to 30 pounds. Eventually twenty did reach that goal, but almost all found it extremely difficult. One 132-pound man ate great amounts of food and reduced his activity to less than half its former level, but could not get his weight above 144 pounds, a gain of only 12 pounds. One who gained more easily increased his weight from 110 to 138 pounds, but had to eat 7,000 calories a day to do it. As the men gained weight, they became lethargic, apathetic, and neglectful of their duties.[110] Weight at the natural setpoint is optimal for activity and mood, Sims suggests, and people become apathetic if weight goes much above or below that point.

When the overfeeding period ended, most of the volunteers dropped quickly and naturally back to their original weight. Only two men, who had gained more easily, stabilized slightly above their starting weight. Perhaps they were experiencing *setpoint creep*, a drift upward. Investigation showed they had a family history of obesity or diabetes.

In the same way, the person who eats a huge holiday dinner does not usually gain weight. Rather, it seems that excess calories are somehow wasted, partly through higher body temperature, partly through speeding up of the "inner clock." Also the person may eat less and be more active the next day. People who add 10 pounds of holiday weight gain over Thanksgiving and Christmas may be frantic to lose it in a January diet. Their New Year diets often do take off that excess, but perhaps it would come off naturally anyway as they resume normal life.

The almost inevitable regain after weight loss also furnishes strong evidence for a setpoint. A careful sixteen-year study of academic and commercial weight loss programs by *Healthy Weight Journal* finds that, no matter how hard they try, none can show long-term success past one year. Even on the strongest programs maximum weight loss comes at about six months, followed by inevitable regain until nearly all participants have gained back what they lost. This takes a few months to as long as two or three years, or in some cases, up to five.

The setpoint, or settling point, seems to be the weight at which an individual is able to maintain a high quality of life, keep well nourished, feel a sense of well-being, and be at his or her personal best. Attempting to suddenly displace this can have serious repercussions. Sustaining a lower weight than this does not lower the setpoint and requires a lifelong commitment, warns Keesey.[111]

It is not known how setpoint affects growing kids. But since weight loss for children is equally unsuccessful, it seems likely the body defends weight for children as rigorously as for adults. Again, it makes evolutionary sense—in primitive times children would have been especially vulnerable to weight loss. Thus, the advice for large children is usually to try to keep weight stable with improved lifestyle while the child grows into that weight. Prevention appears to be the most effective way to decrease what may otherwise be a higher adult setpoint.

Our setpoint or settling point is not fated at birth, but is the result of both genetic and environmental factors up to this time in life. It's the weight our bodies want to weigh now. Environment makes a difference, so does lifestyle later in life. It appears that setpoint can be gradually lowered somewhat, through increasing activity, and perhaps changed eating patterns and other changes. *Setpoint creep* is the gradual weight gain that often happens through the years.

Certainly some people do lose weight and keep it off successfully, apparently lowering their setpoint in a healthy way. But there are also haunting "pseudo successes"—gaunt, hollow-eyed shadows of girls and women, who are keeping their weight unnaturally low by eating less food than their bodies need. They experience a body shutdown to some degree that affects them physically, intellectually, emotionally, socially and spiritually. Anyone who works with eating disorders knows these symptoms all too well. With weight kept below setpoint, a person lives within the limits of a starvation mode, or what might be called the *starvation syndrome.*

The body's defense mechanism seems to kick in to restore the person's normal weight. Isn't it logical that the human machine, which can regulate precisely the amount of salt in the bloodstream, and maintain exact body temperature under blistering sun or Arctic blizzard, can also make adjustments to bring disrupted weight back to normal? The evidence suggests the body has some kind of weight-thermostat that regulates this. After weight has been threatened with a severe diet, the body may become more efficient next time. It appears that we cannot easily change this weight, whether we want to or not, although most people can possibly keep it quite stable and avoid setpoint creep.

Food Preoccupation

Food preoccupation is one of the most striking traits of dieting and hungry teenagers. Food craving drives their days, and they spend a major share of each day thinking about food, hunger and weight.

The food preoccupation of teenage girls has been studied by Dan and Kim Lampson Reiff, a husband-wife eating disorder team in Mercer Island, Wash. In their book, *Eating Disorders: Nutrition Therapy in the Recovery Process,* the Reiffs use a food preoccupation scale in which eating disorder patients are asked to write down the amount of time spent thinking about food, weight and hunger at three periods in their lives. This includes time spent shopping, preparing food, eating, thinking about eating, food cravings, purging, weighing, reading diet books, suppressing feelings of hunger, using strategies such as smoking or chewing gum to distract from hunger, and thinking about or discussing weight.[112]

The Reiffs tested more than 600 eating disordered girls on this scale. Untreated anorexia nervosa patients report spending 90 to 110 percent of waking time thinking about food, weight and hunger (the extra 10 percent includes dreaming of food, or sleep disturbed by hunger). Bulimic patients report about 70 to 90 percent. Dieting kids probably devote 20 to 65 percent of their waking hours to this, depending on how severe their food restriction, the Reiffs suggest. By contrast, kids who eat normally think of food and eating only about 10 or 15 percent of their waking hours. It's usually around mealtime. In girls with eating disorders, they find that the intensity of food preoccupation is directly related to how much weight they have lost, and how severe and long-lasting has been their food deprivation.

Eating Disorder Risk

Dieting is increasingly being regarded as an important risk factor for eating disorders, although this is still controversial. The current high rates of eating disorders in the United States are the inevitable result of 60 to 80 million adults dieting, losing weight, rebounding, and learning to be chronic dieters, say many experts. Most chronic dieters are girls and women, as are most who suffer from eating disorders.[113]

Clearly, many girls and young women who begin dieting and restricting food go on to develop full clinical eating disorders. A recent review showed that up to 35 percent of normal dieters advance to pathological dieting. Of pathological dieters, 20 to 25 percent progress to partial or full syndrome eating disorders.[114] Even the effects of one bout of dieting can perpetuate more disturbed eating, say Linda Smolak and Michael Levine, eating disorder specialists. "Children who are already dieting during elementary school may be at risk for developing eating disorders because of the physiological and psychological effects of caloric restriction and weight loss failures."[115]

The American Dietetic Association warns against promoting weight loss to persons with binge eating disorder or other eating disorders. When youngsters request help with weight loss, the ADA position paper on eating disorders recommends counseling on body image issues and how to stop the pursuit of thinness, rather than helping them try to lose weight. It may be healthier, ADA says, to help young people accept themselves at or near their present weight, stop binge eating and learn how to prevent future weight gain.[116]

Minnesota Starvation Study

What happens when dieting is so severe it becomes semi-starvation, as in the very-low-calorie diets (VLCDs) of under 800 calories? It's not uncommon for a plus-size child to stop eating. It's not uncommon for a growing teenage girl to subsist on a daily apple and bagel, or for her calorie intake to hover in that 600 to 1,000 range, instead of her recommended 2,200 calories. It's not uncommon for a physician to convince parent and child to opt for the rapid weight loss of severe calorie restriction. Everything that sabotages a moderate diet to prevent its effectiveness is multiplied in the very-low-calorie diet. The damage that a moderate diet does to health and well being is intensified in the VLCD. The body's defense against starvation, and the subsequent physical, mental and emotional changes that take place, has been called the *starvation syndrome.*[117]

The classic study of what it is like to live in a state of semi-starvation took place at the University of Minnesota in 1944 and 1945, during World War II. In the *Minnesota Starvation* study, aimed at recovery efforts for war-torn Europe, thirty-two male volunteers cut their daily food intake in half, to 1,570 calories, for six months, and lost one-fourth of their weight.[118] Their metabolism dropped by almost 40 percent, heart output per minute dropped in half, their pulses slowed, strength dropped by half, and body temperatures fell. Mental and social effects were even more profound, and heart wrenching. The formerly idealistic, good-humored young men became argumentative, sarcastic, self-centered, and intolerant of each other. They grew highly nervous, restless, and anxious, with an increase in apathy, fatigue, moodiness, and depression. Many experienced profound mood swings, from elation to "low periods." They no longer enjoyed group activities, but became loners, complaining that dealing with others was too much trouble.

These were well-educated, idealistic young men. Over half were college graduates, at a time when this was rare, and all had completed at least one year of college. Many were members of the pacificist Brethren Church. They opposed war, and expressed a deep desire to help heal the war's devastation. But during six months of semistarvation, their idealism dried up. General apathy extended to appearance and the men often neglected to shave, brush their teeth, or comb their hair. They continued bathing as one source of pleasure, because in their chilled condition they enjoyed the warm water and soothing of aches, pain and fatigue.

Personality tests revealed significant increases on the depression, hysteria, and hypochondriasis scales, confirming what the researchers observed. Before the study was over, personality profiles measured an average rise toward the neurotic end. Six men reacted with severe character neurosis. Two developed psychotic disturbances that included violence and hysteria. One man developed major personality disturbances after just ten weeks. He was so depressed he cut off three fingers so he could be released from the program. Yet this man had lost only 10 pounds, 7 percent of his weight, and his diet of 1,570 calories was much higher than that of many weight loss regimens.

Eating disorder specialists often see the same neurotic personality traits in women and girls who are undernourished through self-starvation. Therapists used to believe they were pre-existing problems, but now they understand semi-starvation can bring on these disturbances. These girls act out the same obsessive concerns, the same irritability, distrust and intolerance. Many deliberately injure themselves, and they show high tolerance for pain and discomfort.[119]

Starving in Africa

Even deeper social devastation was reported by anthropologist Colin Turnbull in his vivid account of the Ik, a starving tribe of east Africans he lived with in the 1960s. Turnbull relates in *The Mountain People* how even children and the elderly were abandoned as starvation advanced. The Ik came to fear and distrust each other. They seldom spoke. Cruelty took the place of love as their culture broke down. They lost their religion and all sense of moral obligation. Men and women went out alone to forage for food, hiding any extra bits of food they found and returning empty-handed to avoid sharing with crying children, weakened parents or spouses.[120] As starvation wore on, there was less and less that could be called social life among the Ik. Turnbull says there was simply no community of interest, family or economic, social or spiritual. They no longer practiced any religious rituals after the three old priests died of starvation.

Today, United Nations relief teams working with starving populations see this same sad desertion of family. Asked whether women or men survive longer under starvation conditions, a U.N. official who works with starving people in central Africa, sighed, "It's the men who survive longer. They are stronger and can better find food and get to relief centers to save themselves." They save themselves, and don't always return to bring food to their desperate families. It's the way starving people behave.[121]

Insatiable Rebound Appetites

Bingeing began as soon as the men were allowed to eat more in the Minnesota study. Their appetites grew insatiable. They ate voraciously. All wanted more food than they were allowed and most found it hard to stop eating even when physically full and "stuffed to bursting." Table manners and eating habits had deteriorated and now during refeeding became worse. These highly educated young men continued to lick their plates at the meal's end. During the 13th week after the starvation period ended, when all food restrictions were lifted, the men consumed a daily average of 5,218 calories. On weekends they sometimes ate 8,000 to 10,000 calories a day. They ate nearly continuously, as many as three consecutive lunches, and spent most of their time eating and sleeping. By the 15th week, table manners improved to normal for most, yet over one-fourth still gobbled their food, and had the desire to lick knives and plates. Four of the fourteen men retained for longer testing at the laboratory were still overeating eight months after the diet ended. One ate 25 percent more than initially and gained so much weight he tried to reduce, but grew so ravenous he couldn't stand it, and returned to excessive eating.

Seeing this same kind of bingeing in their overweight patients, some obesity specialists have laid it to psychological disturbances, but this evidence suggests it normally follows restriction. Again, it makes evolutionary sense. Our starving ancestors needed to recover quickly by consuming as much of a downed mammoth or whale as possible before the next time of hunger.

The refeeding period did not immediately revive their spirits. For about six weeks morale slumped even lower, and many of the men grew more depressed and irritable than before. Slowly humor, enthusiasm and sociability returned, and they began looking forward to their plans for the future again. But not until the 20th week, nearly five months after the restrictive diet ended, did the men all say they felt nearly normal and less preoccupied with food.

FIGURE 9.2 Starvation Syndrome: How the Human Body Defends Itself[p]

Calorie restriction and weight loss cause the body to close down into a defensive state.

Metabolism, heart rate, body temperature and other processes slow down, and the drive to eat increases (after initial loss of appetite.)

Physical Effects
amenorrhea, anemia, chills, cold hands and feet, constipation, depression, diarrhea, dizziness, fatigue, hair loss, headache, loss of bone mass, muscle and abdominal pain, nausea, reduced sexual function, weakness, risk of sudden death

Mental, Emotional, Social Effects
anxiety, decrease in mental alertness and memory; decreased sexual interest; diminished sense of generosity, spirituality, love and compassion; distrust; inability to concentrate or comprehend; intense food and weight preoccupation; intolerance; irritability; loneliness; low self-esteem; moodiness; narrowed interests; reduced ambition; self-absorption; self-centeredness; withdrawal from outside interests

In times of food scarcity or restriction, the human body strives to protect itself against starvation by closing down into a defense state that burns fewer calories. The more severe the calorie restriction, the more severe and lasting these effects. If food continues to be restricted, individuals may remain in this defensive state, or they may return to it repeatedly during diet and weight loss cycles.

Downward Spiral

Typically, people believe dieting will make them happier. They feel exhilarated and uplifted as the drama of a new diet unfolds.

Pursuing thinness is widely thought to be pursuing good health. "That feeling of self-sacrifice can hook us into wonderful feelings of purity and goodness," notes Mary Evans Young, author of *Diet Breaking*. "The diet becomes a kind of fanatical religion, requiring you to abide by a set of stringent rules or pay the penance of guilt. It's a guilt that starts by slowly nibbling and then steadily gnaws away at your body, spirit and confidence."[122]

It's easy to get caught in a downward spiral. Repeated dieting leads to more body dissatisfaction, leading in turn to more dieting, warns Polivy. Dieters begin their diets feeling bad about their bodies, but for a time are buoyed up by a false sense of hope. Then hopes are dashed once again by the inevitable transgressions and weight gain. Self-image drops lower. Then, as one diet fails, another beckons, again feeding false hope. It's a downward spiral of negative self-esteem marked by repeated failure, depressed mood, loss of hope, worsened self-image, and commonly, an even stronger resolve to begin another diet.[123]

What Does Work

The Minnesota Starvation Study challenges the popular belief that if people will just show a little initiative and will power, they can easily lose weight and keep it off. The alarming information from this study needs to be investigated further. Unless we can fully understand the effects of weight reduction programs, how can they succeed in a way that ensures health and well-being?

It seems that each person has a baseline of adequate nutrition, and when this is breached there is severe disruption of normal life and a diminishing of mind, body and spirit. These effects are well known to eating disorder specialists and directors of very-low-calorie diets. Now they need to be known as well by all health care providers and the general public.

As a responsible and caring society, we need a wider understanding of dieting issues so we can begin to find solutions that make a real difference, instead of continuing with failed solutions.

Chapter 10

♦ ♦ ❖ ♦ ♦ ❖ ♦ ♦ ❖ ♦ ♦ ❖ ♦ ♦ ❖ ♦ ♦ ❖ ♦ ♦

Challenges for Overweight Children

"For me, living is literally hell," says Jonelle, a teenager. "The insults I must endure, the pity, the loneliness, the self-hatred and the loathing are all punishments I would not wish on anybody. I didn't do anything wrong. I am fat...My life is a Catch-22. I'm lonely and don't have friends because I'm fat, and I eat because I'm lonely. Nobody wants to be seen with me including some of my family...There is nothing I would not give to be thin."[124]

Echoes from his youth, writes Dan Davis of Salinas, California, are the shouts: "I don't want you on my team. You're too fat to run. Look at the fat tub. Your belly looks like a watermelon." Today he says, "My stomach still knots when I remember. . .I'll carry the scars to my grave, (but) today's kids have it worse."[125]

Research confirms what we all know, that there is strong prejudice, harassment, and even oppression against large youngsters regardless of age, sex, race, and socioeconomic status, which can interfere with their ability to grow into self-assured, successful adults. Many struggle with discrimination in education, employment, health care and social relationships. Even young children feel the stigma of obesity and fear being a target. In a 1961 study, children as young as six described silhouettes of an overweight child as "lazy, dirty, stupid, ugly, cheats and lies." When shown drawings of a normal weight child, an overweight child, and children with various handicaps, including missing hands and facial disfigurement, children rated the overweight child as the least likable.[126] When this study was replicated recently it showed the incidence of children stigmatizing obesity has increased significantly over the last 40 years.[127] Sadly, even the larger children felt the same prejudice against overweight kids.

Leaner kids think it's fair to treat large children with scorn and abuse, that they deserve this treatment. Abuse is even seen as a humanitarian gesture, since supposedly the inflicted humiliation might drive them to lose weight. The shame of fatness is so intense and pervasive that sometimes the victims themselves come to believe they deserve this treatment.

Large children and teens can be healthy, eat normally and live active lives, but the stigma may be overwhelming. "Clearly obese children are blamed for their condition. It is an unusual person who does not fashion this into serious self-doubt and a persistent concern with dieting," says Kelly D. Brownell, an obesity researcher and professor of psychology at Yale University.[128]

Large young children may be oppressed—teased on the playground, called names, and chosen last to play on teams. Still, studies show that their sense of self-worth is similar to that of average-weight young children. But in adolescence, the powerful social messages become internalized and a lifelong negative self-image can develop.[129]

This is especially difficult for large teenagers in advanced countries, where both feminine and masculine ideals have become very thin. Male stars of movies, television, sports and pop music are not only lean, but usually appear muscular and fit.

Obesity is the last socially acceptable form of prejudice, charge Albert Stunkard and Jeffery Sobal, in *Eating Disorders and Obesity:* "Obese persons remain perhaps the only group toward whom social derogation can be directed with impunity."[130]

Teachers Reinforce Prejudice

Harassment is illegal, no longer allowed in many schools, but is often ignored by teachers and staff. In fact, discrimination has been shown in the way teachers interact with large students and the grades they give for comparable work. Acceptance into prestigious colleges is lower in one study for large females, even when they do not differ in academic qualifications, school performance, or application rates to colleges.[131]

In 1993, the National Education Association launched an investigation into size discrimination against students and teachers in the schools as a human rights and civil rights issue. The next year, NEA published its 27-page "Report on Size Discrimination," which describes size discrimination in schools at every level.[132] The report says the school experience is one of "ongoing prejudice, unnoticed discrimination and almost constant harassment" for large students, and "socially acceptable yet outrageous insensitivity and rudeness" for large teachers.

"At the elementary school level, children learn that it is acceptable to dislike and deride fatness. From nursery school through college, fat students experience ostracism, discouragement, and sometimes violence. They are deprived of places on honor rolls, sports teams, and cheerleading squads and are denied letters of recommendation."

A member of the investigating team sympathized with large teens who are uncomfortable in showers and don't want other students to stare at or ridicule them. Another told of a high school drill team that for ten years excluded overweight girls from the team. Those who were progressing toward their goal weight were allowed to practice at school, but not perform in public.

Carol Johnson, a Wisconsin therapist who founded Largely Positive support groups for large people, writes in her book, *Self-Esteem Comes in All Sizes*, how her cheerleading ambitions came to an abrupt end.[133]

> *"One of my dreams was to be a cheerleader. When tryouts were announced in the seventh grade, I signed up immediately and practiced night and day. After tryouts, I knew I had given a flawless per-*

formance. However, the physical education teacher who was judging the competition took me aside and gently told me that although I was one of the best candidates, she simply could not choose me. The reason? I was too chubby . . .

"Shortly thereafter, I became intrigued by the baton and decided to take twirling lessons. You would have thought the cheerleader episode would have deterred me forever, but somehow it didn't. I dreamed of leading the marching band down the football field, and adept as I was, I thought there was good chance this dream would become reality. Reality did set in, but not the one I had dreamed about. Once again I was trying to do something chubby girls weren't supposed to do—put themselves on display. This time I was told not to bother because the uniforms wouldn't fit me. I didn't even try out. And the message pierced deeper: You're not acceptable.

"The truth is that my weight in high school exceeded the weight charts by no more than 30 pounds. Now, when I look at my high school pictures, I don't think I look at all heavy. Yet at the time those extra 30 pounds felt like the weight of the world on my shoulders. Losing weight had become the most important thing in my life."

The NEA report quotes a *New York Times* article about a girl named Aleta Walker as an example of the "outrageous behavior" to which large children are subjected in schools.

Aleta never had any friends during her childhood and adolescence in Hannibal, Mo. She was ridiculed and bullied every day. When she walked down the halls at school, boys flattened themselves against the lockers and cried, "Wide load."

But the worst was lunchtime. "Every day there was this production of watching me eat lunch." She tried to avoid going to the school cafeteria. "I would hide out in the bathroom. I would hide out behind the gym by the baseball diamond. I would hide in the library."

One day, schoolmates started throwing food at her as she sat at lunch. Plates of spaghetti splashed onto her face, and the long greasy strands dripped onto her clothes. "Everyone was laughing and pointing. They were making pig noises. I just sat there," she said.

One leader in the size acceptance movement, Cheri Erdman, now a therapist and college teacher, was actually sent away from home at age five, on the advice of a kindergarten teacher, to live for more than a year in a residential weight treatment facility for children with "special nutritional needs." In her book, *Nothing to Lose: A Guide to Sane Living in a Larger Body,* Erdman, describes the sadness of being separated from her family for so long.[134]

Ironically, it is in health care that large kids seem to suffer most. Unfortunately, humiliation often has been the chief result of encounters with health providers. Doctors and other health professionals are often seen as part of the problem. Sally Smith, editor of *BBW (Big Beautiful Woman),* recalls:

> *"When I was seven, I was sent to a dietitian for my first diet. There were weekly weigh-ins...rare praise and more often, scoldings. When I was nine and alone with my pediatrician in the examining room, he told me to take off my gown, get off the table, stand up and bend down and touch my toes, so I can see how fat you are. There I was, a naked nine-year-old, being degraded and humiliated by my doctor...*
>
> *"When I was sixteen, my doctor told me that I was so fat I'd never live to see my 18th birthday. When I was twenty-six, a different doctor told me I'd drop dead if I didn't buy the liquid diet program she was selling and lose weight immediately. This was the same doctor who had me on a high blood pressure medication unnecessarily for three years. It was a new doctor who used the proper blood pressure cuff and said, 'What are you doing on medication? Your blood pressure is low.'"*

Worse than poor health care, says Lynn McAfee, Director of the Council on Size and Weight Discrimination, is the amount of sheer, inexcusable cruelty that large children and adults endure at the hands of health professionals. They are often forced to suffer severe verbal abuse from angry and contemptuous physicians who seem to blame every condition on obesity. While she agrees that many diseases are associated with obesity, naming obesity as a cause without offering a successful, affordable cure puts the blame squarely on the victim. McAfee points out that health providers need to help large kids be as healthy as possible, right now. With each visit they should feel empowered, more determined to take care of their bodies. "Studies show clearly that isn't happening. Physicians have been counseling people to lose weight for decades now, and the result has been that we are fatter, not thinner."[135]

What large kids need from health providers is a change in attitude, as well as better lifestyle guidance. Health professionals need to examine their own prejudices and understand how social discrimination affects the care they are giving to large children. Their attitude also affects an obese child's response: fear, anxiety and stress can damage the heart and immune system through continual increased cortisol exposure.[136]

No Safe Haven at Home

For some children, fat oppression, teasing, and ridicule comes from inside the family circle, so there is no escape from tormentors. Pat, age thirty-four, describes her father's disdain of her size in *Real Women Don't Diet.*

> *"My experience of prejudice for being fat started at a very young age. The sadness and teasing . . . [came] from within my family, by the people who are supposed to most love you. At the age of nine, I did not consider myself overweight, but in my father's opinion I was not only overweight but also a 'fat cow' and a 'fat pig.' His ridicule and teasing continued as I grew older and larger. High school was the worst. I not only had to tolerate the hatefulness of my classmates calling me 'fat Pat,' but then I would go home and hear my father threaten to send me to Missouri. He wanted to have his mom lock me up and feed me bread and water so that I could lose weight.*
>
> *"My father's threats were always at the tip of his tongue. One time he had a new idea: 'If I tie you to the back of my truck and make you run around the block a few times, you'll really lose weight.' Although he never did, just the horror of knowing it might happen was never far away. During all the years of growing up, I never was able to defend myself. I felt like I was a leper or some-*

thing very bad, just for being overweight. I spent years taking drugs. I overdosed many times. Why should I care? My life wasn't worth that much. After all, I was different. I was fat."[137]

Effects of this stigma carry over into adulthood, especially for girls. Women who were overweight as adolescents or young adults earn less, are less likely to marry, complete fewer years of school, and have higher rates of poverty than their normal weight peers. Fewer of these effects occur for overweight males.[138]

One study shows adults who were large children, but normal weight as adolescents, had a body image comparable to that of individuals who had never been overweight. But adults who had been large adolescents had an extremely negative body image and feelings of low self-worth. Some of them experience a great deal of unresolved anger and rage. Jean Rubel, age thirty-six, describes turning this anger against herself:

"Under my loneliness simmered a lake of molten rage. Sometimes I turned it loose when I felt ignored, criticized, misunderstood, or unloved. Most of the time, though, I held it in the pit of my stomach, where it became the only defense I could find against my belief that I was flawed in some critical way that kept me from joining the human race. Unfortunately, I too often turned this hateful energy against myself in storms of self-criticism and loathing. I began to blame my body for all my problems. If I weren't so ugly, so big, so soft and flabby, I would be happy and popular. I was six feet tall and 145 pounds. According to yearbook pictures I was slender and reasonably attractive, but I couldn't see it. I wanted to be thin, admired, and loved. Instead I felt awkward, shy, fat, defective and extremely lonely."[139]

Too Much Pain

Large kids often experience the pain and humiliation of size prejudice from an early age. At times it may seem unbearable, such as in the following example:

The Fort Lauderdale Sun-Sentinel reported a tragedy on August 27, 1996, that took place the day before school opened in the fall.[140]

To twelve-year-old Samuel John Graham, starting at the new middle school meant being called fat and getting teased by kids again. Broward County Sheriff's detectives said Samuel so dreaded the idea of walking into the first day of classes on Monday that he got up in the middle of the night and hanged himself from a tree in the back of his home.

Samuel, 5-feet-4, 174 pounds, had talked of suicide before and his humiliation at the teasing from kids at school. His parents had tried. They had met with his teachers, showered him with affection and love, took him to physicians and sent him to Jamaica that summer to spend time with an uncle who was a fitness buff, hoping he would build muscle and self-esteem. Now they are setting up a center where shy, overweight children can swim without shame. Sammy loved to swim, they said, but only after dark. He was too ashamed to let anyone see him in his bathing suit.

While many boys do suffer extreme size prejudice, size activists say a double standard exists. Society criticizes overweight girls and women severely, while often overlooking it in boys and men. In school, boys are often allowed more body fat than is permitted to girls. They tend to be less subject to abuse, teasing and humiliations, compared with girls. At larger sizes boys may be considered strong and powerful, and to feel this way themselves, especially if they are athletes.

The larger the child or teen, the more severe is discrimination in all areas. Those with higher fat levels may have work- and recreation-related disabilities, more health problems, and they must deal daily with a constraining physical environment that limits mobility and subjects them to humiliation. Many cannot fit through subway turnstiles, or sit in theater seats or waiting room chairs. In almost every aspect of living they are made to feel different and as if they don't fit in.

Invisibility for Large Kids

Charisse Goodman contends that large people in America are in many respects, invisible in today's thinness-obsessed culture, in her book *The Invisible Woman.*[141] Regardless of her unique personal qualities, a large girl or woman is often not seen as an individual, but as a stereotype, portrayed as having physical and emotional problems, as being unattractive, compulsive, self-indulgent, even anti-social. Thus, often she is not treated as an ordinary human being with normal needs, desires, virtues and vices, but rather as a failure, an example of what not to be, not to become. She may be discreetly or unconsciously excluded from office or extracurricular social interaction. She may be automatically passed over for promotions, even paid less than thinner people for equal work.

On the other hand, says Goodman, large people become all too visible when someone is looking for a scapegoat. Then they are easy targets for the neighborhood bully, the insecure classmate in need of a cheap ego boost, and for the weight loss industry. "It takes a powerful character not to vanish beneath this avalanche of stereotypes, which is all that American society sees when it looks at a fat woman," she concludes.[142]

Stigmatizing Myths

Some of these myths include the following:

★ *Romance is not important to large people.* Large teens like any others long for romance, love, admiration, appreciation and fun. Yet they may be routinely left out of social activities. It sometimes takes courage for others to date the larger girl or boy for fear of ridicule or disapproval from peers.

★ *Large kids are unhealthy.* Often the health issue serves as a smoke screen for discrimination. But if large kids are physically active there may be little or no added risk. Research shows that for moderately active people there is little difference in longevity between the different weight categories; active people are much more likely to live long lives than inactive people of any size.[143] With severe overweight, health risks are more likely to be serious. However, no research has investigated the damage done by a lifetime of hazardous weight loss attempts—yo-yoing one's weight, or ratcheting it upward through repeated weight loss and gain cycles. None has counted the costs of lower access to preventive health care, or the price of added stress from discrimination.

★ *Large kids have unhealthy lifestyles.* Many large children and adults are fit and maintain healthy lifestyle habits. Others may be sedentary, as are other people of all sizes. Leanness does not mean good health or a healthy lifestyle. Some people say that if large kids would just adopt healthier habits and live more actively, they would automatically lose weight. This is not necessarily true.

★ *Large kids overeat.* This is still controversial, but the latest official word is that there's little or no correlation between weight and calorie intake. Calorie intake fails to predict weight, and vice versa. This comes from the Healthy Eating Index, the nation's newest "report card" on how Americans are eating. It pulls together extensive recall data based on national intake studies, compiled by the Center for Nutrition Policy and Promotion, CDC.

★ *Rapid weight loss is healthy for large kids.* One of the most dangerous myths among health professionals, which has caused much injury and death, is the myth that obese kids and adults are at such severe health risk that radical weight loss methods are justified. Any doctor who has practiced a few years should spot the fallacy in this thinking at once. The severely obese patient who has high-risk factors is not well served by the severe shock to the body that comes with large, rapid losses. Rather, it is even more critical that this person get conservative treatment and that weight loss be gradual and lasting.

★ *Large kids have psychological disturbances that keep their weight high.* There are still traditional psychotherapists who take a Freudian view, following theories such as that fear of sexuality, suppressed rage, aggression, oral fixation, or Oedipal impulses are involved in obesity. Many still believe that the conscious wish to be thin is sabotaged by the unconscious desire to be fat. However, research finds no common patterns to explain obesity is a result of personality factors, emotional conflicts, faulty training in self-care, or dysfunctional family systems.[144]

After reading all this you might wonder that any large kids are able to live their lives with smiles on their faces and hope in their hearts, but of course they do it every day. It's not always easy, but strong and supportive families help them cope with difficulties. Teachers who care and enlightened health providers do much to empower them in fulfilling their potential.

This information might make you sad, it might make you angry, it might leave you feeling overwhelmed. But knowledge is power. Knowing what the research says can help us all to move ahead.

Research tells us that large kids are no different than any others. Each is a unique individual and deserves to be regarded this way and treated with respect.

PART IV

♦ ♦ ❖ ♦ ♦ ❖ ♦ ♦ ❖ ♦ ♦ ❖ ♦ ♦ ❖ ♦ ♦ ❖ ♦ ♦

A New Perspective

Chapter 11

♦ ♦ ❖ ♦ ♦ ❖ ♦ ♦ ❖ ♦ ♦ ❖ ♦ ♦ ❖ ♦ ♦ ❖ ♦ ♦

Wellness and Wholeness

Wellness—the combination of physical fitness and sound mental health—is your birthright...A lifestyle that encompasses sound health and outstanding physical and mental fitness costs little to maintain, it can't be stolen from you or taxed, it's enjoyable almost from the first moment, and it's well within your grasp. A healthy lifestyle not only will add to the length of your life, but also will improve the quality of life, the richness and simple joy of being alive...Living longer—and living fit—allows you thousands more hours of vibrant and active living, a wider range of activity, and the opportunity for greater accomplishment.

—Blue Cross/ Blue Shield of North Dakota

It's time to move ahead with vision and direction. In the bigger picture it is wellness—the child's overall health and well being that counts. This is what concerns parents. Weight may seem important but it's only part of the total picture. It needs to be kept in perspective.

It's time to take a new approach to wellness and wholeness. Time to focus on promoting healthy, happy lifestyles for our children, on preventing weight and eating problems, instead of causing them. This is an urgent challenge for America and countries around the world. The traditional ways of dealing with weight through food restriction and the dieting mentality have not worked, and are causing grave harm.

The new approach asks: How can we help the child shift to healthier habits that can last a lifetime? How can we prevent weight and eating problems? How can we help each child be healthier at the size he or she is now?

A healthy body is only part of good health. The World Health Organization (WHO) defines health as a state of complete physical, mental, and social well-being and not merely the absence of disease or infirmity.[1] Wellness involves guiding the child toward making healthy choices in all these areas.

By choosing a wellness lifestyle, we can prevent much disease and disability, and can cope better with inescapable experiences of illness, disability or trauma. The wellness approach to life combines sound physical, mental and emotional health in a positive relationship with family and community.

Wellness is free, or costs very little, and is enjoyable from the first moment. It improves the quality of life, the richness of life, the simple joy of living well. The journey of wellness begins in infancy. It's a journey that parents can enjoy in the moment and look forward to with pleasure. The wellness approach takes a positive view, avoiding a focus on the negative:

- ★ Wellness is not about perfection.
- ★ Wellness is not about numbers.
- ★ Wellness is not about fearing disease.
- ★ Wellness is not about criticism, blame, or shame.

The Wellness Wheel

It's helpful to think of wellness as a wheel, to visualize how the six dimensions of wellness complement and interact with each other. When one aspect is strong, it strengthens and positively affects the others. Yet all are needed, and a balance of growth in each dimension helps the wheel roll along smoothly.

FIGURE 11.1. **Wellness Wheel**[q]

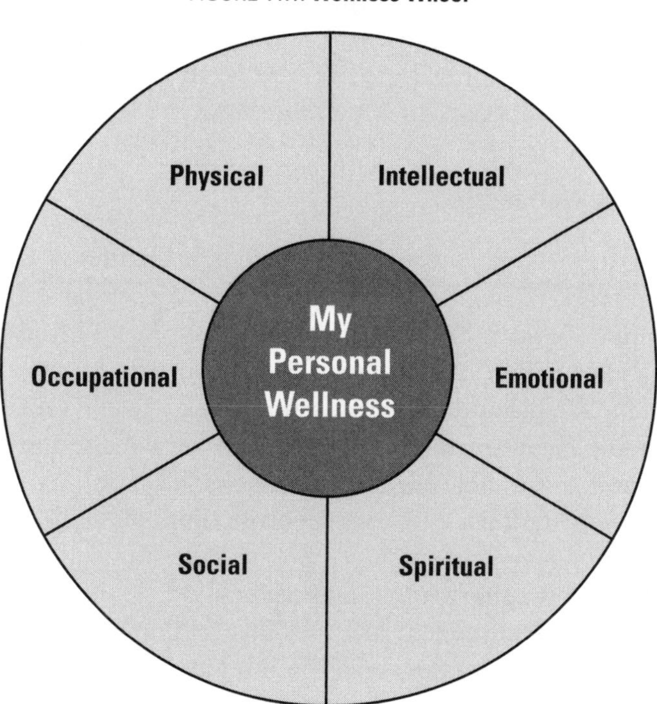

Physical Wellness

The wellness challenge is to build the child's health from infancy on a strong foundation of physical health, incorporating the basic elements of a wellness lifestyle. Wise parents take early responsibility for good physical health, then gradually shift responsibility appropriately, as the child grows older. Taking care of one's own body involves regular physical actively, healthy eating, getting adequate sleep, stress management, sexual health, freedom from substance abuse (smoking, alcohol, use of illegal drugs), regular medical care, and attention to safety—wearing seatbelts, not riding with a drinking driver, avoiding risks and violence. Wellness involves living responsibly. Children who live with illness, disability or trauma may need special help to cope in positive ways. They can benefit, as can all children, by learning to reduce negatives in their lives, and to take responsibility for their health as appropriate to their age.

Negatives arise and disrupt their sense of wellness when children get into habits of being sedentary, consuming a deficient diet high in fat and sugar, missing sleep, being overstressed, smoking, using alcohol or illegal drugs, or taking unnecessary risks.

Intellectual Wellness

Engaging in creative and stimulating mental activities at the child's level is important. Helpful parents will encourage verbal skills, showing interest in scientific discoveries, keeping up with the news. Reading to the child and helping older children find time every day for reading for pleasure, not just schoolwork, creates valuable lifetime reading habits. Help the child expand knowledge and improve skills in and out of school, through classes, informal learning, and travel. In most families this may involve computer skills, high tech learning and television, which can be mentally stimulating and educational when programs are chosen carefully.

However, recommendations are that children and teens not watch more than two hours of television a day. Parental supervision is critical. For young children, some experts are now questioning whether the busy movements of television may interfere with brain development, and advise no television for the first two years.

Emotional Wellness

Emotional wellness means the child has a solid sense of self-identity and self-esteem, and feels secure in the love and affection of family and friends. The child has an awareness and acceptance of his or her own feelings, is able to express them, and is considerate of the feelings of others. Laughter and a sense of humor help to enrich life and relieve tension. As the toddler grows older he or she learns to cope with anger and frustration in positive ways. Emotional self-care includes attention to relaxation and stress reduction.

Negatives intrude when the child does not get needed love and reassurance, feels unloved, is unable to express emotions, or meets too much criticism or stress in life.

Social Wellness

Social wellness means the child feels she or he is getting comfortable support from family, friends, teachers and classmates. She or he has the perception of belonging and being valued and supported by others. The safer and more supported the child feels, the more likely that child will develop higher levels of wellness. The socially comfortable child cooperates well with others, takes instruction, feels comfortable in groups, and communicates feelings easily.

Social wellness includes contributing to community improvement and being able to touch others through service, as appropriate to a child's age. Children can early discover the joy and sense of accomplishment in helping others.

Social negatives occur when a child becomes lonely and withdrawn, and does not feel supported by family, classmates, or teachers. The child may be bullied, picked on, criticized, isolated by classmates, or discriminated against. This can happen to the child who for one reason or another does not conform to appearance standards, such as a larger child; if it does, parents need to protest and take immediate steps to work with school to stop this illegal behavior.

Occupational Wellness

A child's occupation is how he or she spends the day. For small children, play is their work. Later, they take on school and home responsibilities and hobbies. As children grow, a special joy of parenting is to help them develop special interests they can enjoy and in which they can lose themselves. This may begin with coloring pictures or helping bake cookies, and extend to training seeing-eye dogs, planning travel adventures, or playing the violin.

Choosing their life's work, whether temporary or long-term, is the task of older teens, although the foundations are laid much earlier. Helping children to be comfortable, successful and confident in play, school and home will help them be successful later in the workplace.

Negatives occur when children fail to begin this process, and adults fail to help them—or actually place roadblocks in the way, perhaps by expecting children to keep quiet and not make a mess.

When time is too rushed, activities become stressful, rather than fun. When children fail to fulfill their responsibilities, and are not required with patience and love to follow through (or have tasks that are too heavy or time-consuming), it's difficult to develop the confidence of knowing they can succeed.

Spiritual Wellness

Spiritual wellness gives children a profound sense of who they are. It addresses the strength of values and ethics being taught in the family, whether in a religious or other context, and the degree that actions are consistent with these values. Teaching in family faith helps give meaning and purpose in life. Children as well as adults have a need for spiritual connection and a sense of being part of a larger whole or purpose. They can learn to access it in nature, music, a religious environment, prayer, meditation, quiet contemplation, or through community service and helping to make the world a better place.

While being part of a religious community does not guarantee problem-free teen years, it increases the opportunities for positive outcomes. Studies show teens involved in religious organizations are less likely to abuse drugs and alcohol, have fewer delinquency problems, and are more likely to delay sexual activity.[2]

Sometimes teens buy strongly into the values of appearance perfection and material gain, which our culture seems to teach, then are left with feelings of emptiness when they find that neither bring happiness. Thinking about spiritual abundance can put such disruptions as body dissatisfaction into perspective. In the bigger picture, when a young person has strong spiritual grounding, and is involved in service-oriented activities, why would she or he waste time on body hatred?

Readiness To Change

In helping children make lifestyle changes, it is important to consider their readiness to change. For small children, parents can initiate change gradually in direct ways. Older children and teenagers will be involved at appropriate levels. Approaching the idea of change in the spirit of adventure is most likely to have positive results for both child and parent. Consider how to make a change in small increments, breaking it down into small steps. Criticism should be avoided.

Not everyone is motivated to seek personal changes in level of health and well-being. Some will be motivated to make changes in one area, but not in others. Let the child decide, and work with him or her on consistent follow-through. Achieving success is a good motivator for moving ahead with other changes, so make sure goals are easily reachable, and rewarded with praise and appreciation of the effort made.

For example, after a period of encouragement from her mom, twelve-year-old Janie said she'd like to be more active. As a first step, they decided to walk for 10 minutes before the evening meal every night for two weeks, and then see if they want to extend the time longer. It was an enjoyable time for both as they walked out the door and down the sidewalk, with their yellow Labrador Alex dancing on a leash beside Janie. Mom kept time for five minutes, then they turned around and walked back. Soon Janie knew just how far five minutes would take them in any direction, and became responsible for the distance. They usually greeted two or three neighbors on the walk. By the third and fourth week they were walking 15 minutes, and talking about extending this to 20 minutes.

To the mother's surprise, she was the one who balked. "I can't take that much time just before dinner," she said. "But I would like to walk longer. How can we do this?"

"Well, I could go on farther, and you could come back. Or we could walk again after dinner," Janie offered. "Or we could take another 5 or 10 minutes after dinner marching in place while we watch TV."

For the next month they tried different options that eventually added up to 30 minutes a day for each of them. Sometimes they walked together, sometimes not. After two months, Janie joined the 7th grade volleyball team. Her mom took over the daily job of walking Alex, who was by now so eager to go walking that she hadn't the heart to disappoint him. Both Janie and her mother felt good about their success in becoming regularly active.

They were making their way through the stages of change. These stages of readiness are:

Precontemplation. There's no thought of making change in a particular area. In the above example, Janie was initially quite sedentary; she did not miss being active, or even think about it.

Contemplation. The person has thought of making a change and intends to do it sometime within the next six months. Under her mother's gentle and persistent encouragement, Janie began to think about the benefits and possible pleasures of activity, and what she might be missing.

Preparation. The child wants to change and intends to begin within the month. Janie and her mother made the decision to begin the before-dinner walk.

Action. Changes are started, but not complete. Three months of regular activity gave both Janie and her mother an excellent start with the new habit.

Maintenance. Desired changes have been maintained for more than six months. Support is important. Janie is supported now in her changed behavior, not only by her mother and their dog's eagerness, but also by her coach and other players on her volleyball team.

Relapse. Backsliding will happen. Expect and plan for it. But when dealt with successfully, relapse incidents occur less and less often. Again support is important, for Janie as volleyball season ends, for her mother as time constraints intrude. Success cannot be taken for granted, even after six months.[3]

Instead of trying to make several changes at once, it's better to make one small change and then progress to another once you have succeeded with the first one. The teenager who tries to quit smoking, change eating habits, and begin a physical activity program all at one time, may be setting himself or herself up for failure. Trying to change in several areas can be so overwhelming that the child (or parent) gives up on them all and is worse off than before, because of a new sense of failure.

Support is needed at all stages, especially at the maintenance and relapse stages. Determine at the beginning how support will be sustained. Some lifestyle programs for youth include group and individual support, or can be followed online, as in the HUGS *Teens No Weigh* program for teens and preteens *(see resources).*

Choosing Parental Wellness

Parents are the most important role models for their children, even through the teenage years. As a parent, consider your own wellness wheel. How are you doing? Are the six wellness dimensions of your life within your comfort level? Are there areas you'd like to improve? When you are comfortable with your own wellness it positively affects all those around you, especially children. If there are areas you'd like to improve, ask yourself how can you move ahead in gradual and lasting ways. (The book *Women Afraid to Eat* can help both women and men; see resources.)

Are you modeling positive ways of solving problems? For instance, if you feel angry with someone and cannot forgive because of some past injury or incident that looms large in your life, it may prevent you from growing and moving on in your dimension of social wellness. This affects your wellness in other areas, as well. Don't allow this relationship to continue to fester and build negative feelings.

Positive ways of dealing with such problems include forgiveness and reconciliation, often the most beneficial course, although it may be difficult. Or it can include a silent forgiveness that lets you diffuse and forget anger and pain. Or it may be a simple acceptance that this is the way things are going be: "I'm not going to think or talk about it any more. I can leave it alone and move on."

The negative approach is to continue to replay the injury over and over in your mind, to talk about it endlessly, and to show anger at the individual involved. (And don't forget there's a certain warped pleasure here that can trap its victims into a cycle of resentment combined with perverse satisfaction.)

The Serenity prayer can help children and parents deal with difficult situations: *Grant me the serenity to accept the things I cannot change, courage to change the things I can, and wisdom to know the difference.*

Your example of dealing with problems in positive ways, accepting the outcome, and moving on will not be lost on your children.

Choosing for yourself a lifestyle of wellness in all six areas will help you cope more easily with life's challenges, and result in immeasurable benefits to your family.

Dealing With Change

As one goes through life, important areas in the wellness wheel will shift and change. Sometimes the changes in a child's life are so abrupt that it seems as if the bottom has dropped out of everything, and nothing will ever be right again. A sudden shift in life's realities can be extremely upsetting for a child at any age. Divorce, financial distress, moving, or the illness or death of a parent can swiftly change the child's priorities in every dimension.

For the pregnant teen or preteen a major life change comes when the baby is born. Few events are more life changing. Even young marriage can't compare with taking on the responsibilities of being a parent. When such events occur, parents can help to pull things into balance again. Good communication is important. Talking about feelings is important, too. Don't hesitate to get professional help if it seems needed. Help is available from school counselors, a pastor, or mental health professional.

Many things of importance are going on in your child's life. Weight is only one part and must not be allowed to distort the many other dimensions of your child's health and well being. Think about the big picture. Think about wellness. Help your child grow and blossom in all six dimensions of wellness—physical, social, emotional, occupational, spiritual, and intellectual.

Chapter 12

♦ ♦ ❖ ♦ ♦ ❖ ♦ ♦ ❖ ♦ ♦ ❖ ♦ ♦ ❖ ♦ ♦ ❖ ♦ ♦

Health at Any Size

A dramatic change is taking place in the way many health professionals deal with weight problems. They have moved on to success stories, after struggling too long with dieting failures. Healthier lifestyles have replaced dieting, counting calories, "good foods/bad foods" thinking, and yo-yoing their patients' weight up and down.

They are part of the Health at Any Size movement, now beginning to sweep the country. We are in the midst of a movement that will not be stopped. A movement that promotes health and well-being, wellness and wholeness, for everyone of every size. It's a movement that meets people where they are in their health journey, and encourages them to eat well, live actively, and feel good about themselves and others.

Mona steeled herself, and dialed the first dietitian on the list she'd picked up at the doctor's office.

"I'm calling because of my son, Jason, age 12. The doctor said he needs to go on a diet and lose weight."

"Has Jason been on a diet before?"

"Yes, twice."

"So, what happened?"

"He lost weight. They were good diets. The last one, he was doing so well. If he could have just stayed on it."

"In your opinion it was a good diet because he lost weight?"

"Oh yes. We had a diet sheet...lists of food he could and couldn't eat."

"Can he stay on any diet for the rest of his life?"

"No. I don't think so. He doesn't have the will power."

"It's not about will power. No one can stay on a diet the rest of their life. Have you ever been on a diet?"

"Yes. Lots of them." Mona laughed.

"And could you stay on any of them?"

"No, I guess not."

"It's because dieting causes deprivation, which leads to bingeing. Bingeing is the normal response to deprivation."

"Oh, I get it. I lost weight on those diets. Then all of a sudden I'd go on a binge, blow the diet, and gain back the weight. Usually I gained back more than I lost!" She sighed, remembering the despair and feelings of failure.

"That's right. Diets don't work. You haven't failed. Dieting has failed you. You don't want Jason to start this same dieting cycle, do you?"

"No! But what am I going to do?"

"What you can do for him is show him how to become a confidant, energetic boy who isn't ruled by a number on the scale."

"How do I do that?"

"I can help you. I'll show you how. Jason can learn to live a healthy, happy lifestyle without diets."[4]

In the Health at Any Size approach, also known as Health at Every Size, people are free to take pleasure in food again. They rediscover normalized eating—tuning in to hunger and satiety cues, eating to meet energy and nutrient needs, and trusting their bodies to make up for times of eating too much or too little. They rediscover the joys of living actively, happily discarding the miserly goals of exercise for calorie burn.

For people schooled in weight-centered, control thinking, Health at Any Size is a 180-degree shift that profoundly changes not just their thinking, but their knowledge and behavior as well. They become advocates for a lifestyle free of dieting.

What is Health at Any Size?

Health at Any Size affirms the truth that beauty, health and strength come in all sizes. That health is not defined by body weight, but by physical, mental and social well-being. The Health at Any Size approach asks: How can this child be healthier at the weight he or she is now? How can we help this child gradually shift to healthier habits that improve health and weight, and last a lifetime? How can we prevent weight and eating problems for this child and every child?

Health at Any Size rejects the false notion that thin children are healthy and large children unhealthy. Rather, it accepts the truth that large children and thin children are a normal part of the human spectrum, and all deserve respect and consideration. It celebrates diversity as a positive characteristic of the human race. It reassures parents that, of course, children can be healthy at their natural size and weight. That children are healthiest at the weight that develops from a healthy lifestyle. Restrictive thinking is left behind.

Health at Any Size helps people recognize that we don't know how to make large kids thin, but we do know what *doesn't* work. It helps health professionals recognize that much harm has been done in attempts to help large kids lose weight, and that failed experimental methods perpetrated on children need to stop.

As the wheel on page 231 demonstrates, the goal of healthy children of all sizes is supported when they receive consistent messages of encouragement to live actively, eat well, and feel good about themselves and others. When these positive messages come from those important to them—health providers, teachers, family, peers and the entertainment media (around the outside of the circle)—then weight and eating problems diminish or are prevented. Negative aspects of the culture are dealt with more effectively.

A focus on Health at Any Size frees children from struggling to fit unrealistic size expectations. It frees parents from the confusion of conflicting advice. It frees young girls who have kept themselves thin, but limited, by living in starvation mode. It frees large children to get on with what's important in their lives, no longer paralyzed by scorn or waiting to be thin. Through this new approach, children of all sizes move on to a more enriching life of wellness in its many dimensions. Health at Any Size principles embrace the following:

- ★ Wellness of body, mind and spirit are important to health.
- ★ Healthy lifestyle is achievable by everyone, unlike "ideal weight."

- ⋆ Accept, respect and celebrate each child's unique qualities.
- ⋆ Rediscover normal, healthy eating and regulate energy needs by tuning in to hunger and fullness. Live without diets, and avoid food restriction.
- ⋆ Rediscover normal physical activity. Normalize activity, as natural, beneficial and enjoyable.
- ⋆ Celebrate diversity. Everyone deserves acceptance and respect from others.
- ⋆ Everyone of every size deserves respectful, objective health care.
- ⋆ Parents and providers: do what you can to help children be healthy, and leave size alone. Do no harm while attempting to help.

These convictions have evolved into the Health at Any Size paradigm, truly a philosophy for the 21st century.

Trust the Child

Ellyn Satter, registered dietitian, family therapist, and international authority on feeding children, explains that the difference between this and the control approach is *trust.* In her health professional workshops, she teaches that parents need to trust that each child has the innate ability to regulate eating according to that child's needs. Wise parents help children strengthen this ability, so they eat when hungry and stop when full, just as they did when they were babies and toddlers. If all children would eat this way, there'd be fewer weight and eating problems. But by age five, studies show, many children already have been taught to distrust these natural signals and override them.[5]

"The task for the growing child is not to remain slim, but to maintain energy balance in response to variations in caloric density of the diet, activity level and growth," says Satter.

"It means listening to your body," agrees dietitian Linda Omichinski, founder of the HUGS healthy lifestyle programs, and an educator of nondiet Health at Any Size leaders. "It means discovering individual patterns for food and activity levels that keep you energized. It means finding the strength to accept yourself just as you are and get on with life."[6]

Parents also need to trust their intuition and knowledge of what's best for their own children. Often they wonder how to deal with a child who is struggling with overweight, size prejudice, chaotic eating behavior or an eating disorder, and they receive much conflicting advice from experts. Wise parents will use only what makes sense in light of their own experience with their child, which allows them to maintain homes that are safe and comfortable places where children know they are loved and accepted unconditionally. The nurturing family is a critical force in defusing the public health crisis created by today's obsession with thinness. Secure in this foundation, children and teens find the confidence to grow and bloom in the varied dimensions of wellness.

The new approach recognizes that a child's body cannot be shaped at will. It rejects the current demand that large children and their parents focus vigilant and constant effort in trying to reshape those youthful bodies. It rejects misguided advice that children keep trying methods that have repeatedly failed and repeatedly caused harm. It rejects the current control paradigm that says all bodies should be in an "ideal weight range" and large children must lose weight to be healthy, even though have tried many times and cannot do this in a healthy and lasting way.

This is no new radical approach to living. The concept of Health at Any Size is natural, nurturing and wholesome. It recalls a time before this debilitating cult of thinness began—perhaps the 1950s, when war-weary parents were happy to nourish their children.

Nondiet programs based on this concept offer a fresh approach to weight problems that is flexible, open, accepting, individualized and family-centered. The message is trust yourself and trust and empower your child. Support your child in solving his or her own problems. Parents gain confidence that they and their children can make good decisions.

Defining Healthy Weight

Healthy weight is defined as *the natural weight the body adopts, given a healthy diet and meaningful levels of physical activity.*[7] For some children this weight will be higher, and for others, lower. This moves on from the narrow definition that classifies weight in terms of numbers (body mass index), and inaccurately discounts the superb health of athletes, children's growth spurts, the role of body fat, genetic heritage, and current evidence that some kinds of obesity are not associated with health risk.[8]

Satter proposes that obesity may be defined as *fatness that is abnormal or unnecessary for the individual.* Fatness may be just as normal for children at the highest 5 percent as thinness is for the lowest 5 percent, provided they grow in a consistent and predictable way, and any growth adjustments are gradual and occur over time. If fatness is the result of unstable weight with abrupt or acute gains, then it is more likely to be abnormal, Satter explains. Children who are grounded in their internal regulatory processes are more likely to avoid eating errors and to sustain their natural and appropriate body weight regulation throughout life, she points out in her book, *How to Get Your Kid to Eat—But Not Too Much.*[9]

The Nondiet Revolution

The Health at Any Size movement is the natural outcome of the anti-diet or nondiet revolution, which has been periodically erupting across America during the past twenty years; it exploded on the scene in the mid-1980s, when the public first realized that diets don't work—that they only weight-cycle their victims. The mantra grew: "Diets don't work."

Many nutritionists joined the revolution early on, advocating for wellness solutions to take the place of food restriction and rigid control of overeating.

Health Canada launched a model through its *Vitality* public awareness campaign in the early 1990s. *Vitality* emphasized healthy eating, active living and positive self and body image, through an integrated approach to healthy living that shifted the focus away from rigid dieting and prescriptive exercise and toward normalized eating and activity and acceptance of a range of body sizes. *Vitality* encouraged people to be healthy at the weight they are, to get on with enjoying life and stop obsessing about weight. It is the basis for many of today's nondiet and Health at Any Size treatment programs. The *Vitality* chart illustrates this shift to the Health at Any Size approach.[10]

Figure 12.1. **The Shift to Vitality From a Weight-Centered Approach**[r]

Weight Centered Approach	**Vitality**
DIETING	**HEALTHY EATING**
• Restrictive eating • Counting calories, prescriptive diets • Weight cycling (yo-yo diets) • Eating Disorders	• Take pleasure in eating a variety of foods • Enjoy lower-fat, complex-carbohydrate foods more often • Meet the body's energy and nutrient needs through a lifetime of healthy enjoyable eating • Take control of how you eat by listening to your hunger cues
EXERCISE	**ACTIVE LIVING**
• No pain, no gain • Stringent workout regimens • Burn calories • High attrition rates for exercise programs	• Value and practice activities that are moderate and fun • Be active your way, every day • Participate for the joy of feeling your body move • Enjoy physical activities as part of your daily lifestyle
DISSATISFACTION WITH SELF	**POSITIVE SELF/BODY IMAGE**
• Unrealistic goals for body size and shape • Obsession and preoccupation with weight • Fat phobia and discrimination against overweight people • Striving to attain impossible "ideal" body size • Accepting the fashion, diet, and tabacco industries' emphasis on slimness	• Accept and recognize that healthy bodies come in a range of weight, shapes/sizes • Appreciate your strengths and abilities • Be tolerant of a wide range of body sizes and shapes • Enjoy the unique characteristics you have to offer • Be critical of messages that focus on unrealistic thinness (in women) and muscularity (in men) as symbols of success and happiness

For the general public, the momentum of revolution was swept aside temporarily by the hype that was spun over new "miracle" treatments—especially very-low-calorie diets and fen-phen/Redux pills. When all that came crashing down, they picked up their wounded with renewed anger.

Encouraging Trends

The response is positive to the Health at Any Size approach, largely due to diets that don't work, pressures to be thin, and the eating disorders crisis. Baby Boomers are rebelling against the thinness obsession. They want more comfortable, normal lives and healthy solutions.

Federal health policy has changed, too. Policy makers at the National Institutes of Health and NIDDK, the institute in charge of diabetes, have come a long way from the time they claimed that basically all weight loss methods were safe and effective.

The 1990 Congressional hearings exposed a great deal of deception and fraud in the weight loss industry. The Federal Trade Commission charged all of the major diet companies, a total of seventeen, with false advertising about the safety and effectiveness of their programs. In 1992 the National Institutes of Health investigated the industry, and reported that not one company could produce research showing the safety and success of any program.

In 1997, a conference report from the National Health, Lung, and Blood Institute, attacked dieting from a new direction. "Little information is available showing that intentional weight loss improves long-term health outcomes...In fact, a growing number of critics in both the scientific community and the lay press are questioning whether obesity should be treated at all."[11]

This led many health professionals to call on the federal government for a new philosophy of wellness. (Virtually alone among federal agencies, the U.S. Department of Agriculture, through all the controversy, has maintained its even-handed policy of providing positive health messages to the public.) Today there is overwhelming agreement among both health professionals and the public about the failure of weight loss programs to bring about lasting change. There is widespread concern for the harm they cause. This is clear in the new federal obesity prevention programs.

It's true, many who have not been able to make the shift, or are tied to industry, are still trying to make diets work. But clearly they are in the minority. Many leaders in national policy and the health and medical community today have shifted all the way to the Health at Any Size philosophy.

Every Child Qualifies

Health at Any Size advocates insist that every child deserves nondiet, health-centered treatment. Everyone qualifies. No exceptions. What's good for the thin child is good for the large child, as well. *Do no harm,* is an important precept. In contrast, federal recommendations promoting healthy nondiet lifestyles often add the qualifying word: *except.* A restrictive or dangerous method is not recommended—*except* for overweight children, *except* for children with health risks, *except* for those who "need rapid weight loss" (whatever that means). In its *Pediatric Nutrition Handbook,* the American Academy of Pediatrics has moved forward when it reports: "No evidence supports the role of radical surgery or pharmacologic therapies..." But then it adds, "*except in extremely obese children in whom all other interventions have failed.*"[12]

This kind of phrase causes knowledgeable people to do a double take. The truth is that no evidence supports the safety and effectiveness of either surgery or drugs in children, period. So why would they be perpetrated on extremely obese children? Further, all other weight loss interventions have failed everyone. So why would any sensible physician use this to justify the radical treatment of a severely obese child, especially if that child has serious health risks?

Just in case—against all odds—it might work? Or because that child is already at such high risk it doesn't matter? If a weight loss method doesn't work for moderately overweight kids and can harm them, then it won't work on severely obese kids and can harm them even more. A failed diet is a failed diet.

Need for Policy Change

It is clear that restrictive national policies promoting weight loss as the means to improve health are not working. So, in the face of these problems, and almost complete weight loss failure, why isn't the Health at Any Size approach more widely accepted at federal levels? "Mysteriously, nutrition professionals proposing 'Health at Any Size' received a lukewarm reception on a government policy setting level," reported Mary Anne Clairmont, RD, in June 2000 in *Today's Dietitian*. "The missing piece in the puzzle [is that] Health at Any Size is not financially advantageous to the weight loss industry." She called for "an entire revamp" of government policy.

Some argue that were Americans to lose their fear of fat and accept size diversity, there would be tremendous increases in obesity. Yet, the fear of fat has not prevented obesity. On the contrary, evidence suggests it may have escalated excess weight gain during the last three decades through increases in dysfunctional eating, dieting and weight cycling.

Another argument holds that the public needs to keep believing in currently ineffective obesity treatments, because someday there will be drugs that work and people must be kept in a mood to take them. Again, this is a faulty argument. The public will recognize and respond to honesty in an area where it has so often been deceived. When some future treatment is proven safe, long-term effective, and health promoting (for a minimum of three to five years), it will fit into the Health at Any Size approach, and size-accepting people will certainly use it when appropriate.

It's true the industry may be damaged by a more open approach. But they have held back progress for too long. (See Chapter 9 for more information.)

National Policy Moves Ahead

Fortunately, obesity prevention programs are now moving swiftly ahead throughout the country. National efforts, long delayed by the inability of policy makers to separate treatment from prevention, are focusing powerfully on ways to increase physical activity in schools, community and home. Improved nutrition is another goal. But obesity prevention alone is not enough. One more step is needed.

Eating disorders and the widespread undernourishment of teenage girls need to be recognized as serious health concerns. Long kept off the table, both need to be added to the Healthy People 2010 agenda for the next decade, which claims to identify "the most significant preventable threats to health and establish national goals to reduce these threats."[13] It is time for health policy makers to recognize that eating disorders cause far more deaths among children and teens than does obesity. Eating disorders affect an estimated 10 percent of young people, with death rates as high as 18 to 20 percent for anorexia and bulimia. Health risks are much higher than for illnesses that get far more attention and funding. If preventive efforts continue to exclude the prevention of eating disorders and related problems, they will not succeed, but only exacerbate the problems of young people. Once eating disorders are officially recognized as the health risks they are, we can expect dramatic improvement in national obesity policy, as well as in obesity treatment. Even the media will alter the way it reports these issues. This happened in Canada, where a shift in health policy brought a remarkable shift in schools, community and health care.

What we need to do is understand that overweight, size prejudice, the undernutrition of teenage girls, hazardous weight loss, eating disorders and dysfunctional eating are not separate issues. They are all part of the same problem, and our diet mentality and unnatural obsession with weight impact them all.

Viewing them in an integrated way means fewer failed treatment methods for children. It means fewer hysterical news reports warning parents and children about increases and risks in obesity. Only when all of these issues are examined openly can comprehensive policies be developed that make sense and are supported by health professionals.

Research Supports the Health-Centered Approach

Research confirms the wisdom of the Health at Any Size approach. A growing body of evidence also confirms the link between health and positive attitudes, optimism, and good relationships. People who expect to be well, generally are, and they live longer.

Feeling good about ourselves relieves stress, which appears to boost the immune system. Studies show people with hopeful, positive attitudes recover more quickly from surgery, have less damage after heart attacks, and live longer. On the other hand, negative thinking can be harmful, as research also shows.[14]

There is no justification for inducing weight fears among large children who are perfectly healthy, whether the warnings come from parents, classmates, teachers, health providers, our national leaders, or the media—particularly since we have no current solutions for their plight. It's false, barbaric, and needs to end.

If fitness, not weight, is the key to health and longevity, as many studies and over thirty years of research at the Cooper Institute for Aerobics Research in Dallas suggests, then setting activity goals rather than weight goals is far better for children.[15]

Weight loss may be a deceptive and unnecessary goal. The Health at Any Size approach helps large children grow into their weight. For the most part, we need to focus efforts on prevention.

Shifting to Health at Any Size

If you are a parent, teacher, or health provider who has tried everything, and know diets don't work, you probably don't want diet failures being endlessly perpetrated on your child, or any child. You're ready to move on.

For others, the shift comes more gradually. They may fear loss of control: *If I didn't diet, count calories, and keep track of fat grams, I'd go out of control and gain a lot of weight.* Others might believe in the nondiet method intellectually and implement it with patients and clients, but hesitate to adopt it for themselves. The shift from a weight-centered mentality to the new health-centered philosophy can take months, or in some cases, even years.

In considering shifting to the new philosophy, the six stages of change come into play: precontemplation, contemplation, preparation, action, maintenance and relapse. (See Chapter 11 for more information about these stages.)

FIGURE 12.2. **Health at Any Size wheel (merged with wellness wheel)**[5]

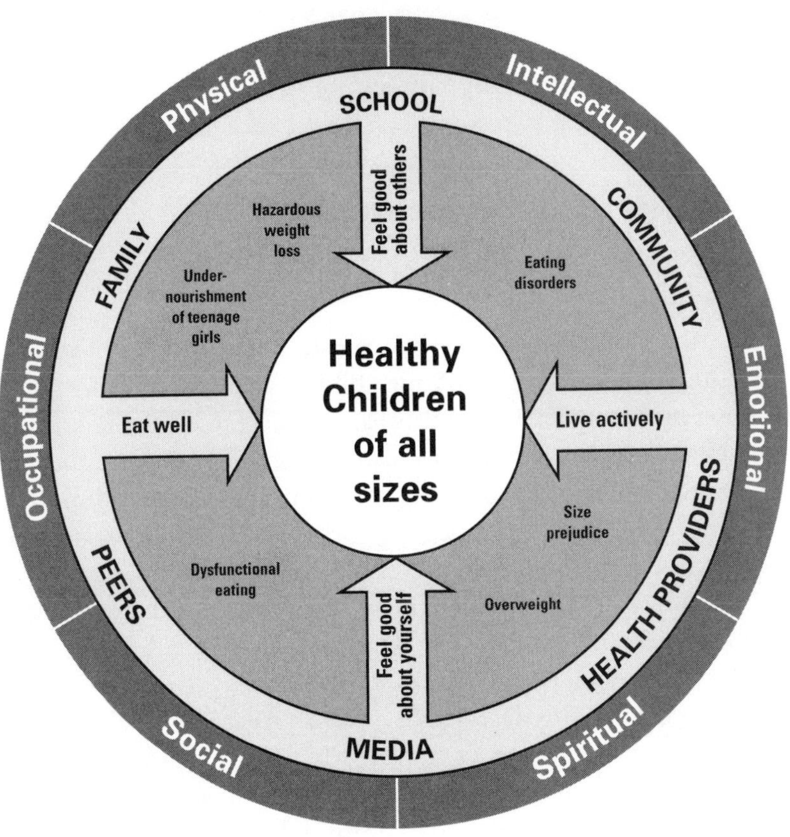

Every Body is a Good Body

Parents hold the key to helping their children move ahead in refreshing ways. The most basic step is accepting for themselves—and teaching—that every body is a good body; that whatever its size or shape, this body does wonderful things for the child, and can do even more with a healthy lifestyle.

This begins with the small child and is especially critical for girls. As puberty approaches, prepare your child for changes, which may come earlier or later than those of classmates. Assure them that individual differences in rate of change, and in body shapes and sizes are natural and desirable. You can help your teenage daughter or son shift out of the diet mentality, and move on to develop self-esteem, healthy coping skills, trust, and respect for size diversity. And yes, parents need to be willing to accept what has long been unacceptable: that overweight youngsters may not lose weight permanently or grow up to be thin. Helping kids feel good about their bodies motivates them to maintain healthy behaviors.

Key Principles of a Healthy Lifestyle

Following these principles will help parents guide their children in a healthy lifestyle:

Shape a nurturing environment. Help children feel good about themselves and others. Your child is okay just as he or she is, and deserves acceptance, love, trust, and respect. Celebrate and enjoy each child's special traits and talents. Support each as a unique individual and encourage open communication with unconditional love.

Parents set a good example, too, by being accepting and respectful of diversity, including size diversity. They can insist on zero tolerance for size bias in school and the workplace, and make it clear that every person of every size deserves acceptance, respect, and a sense of well-being, peace and tranquility.

Live actively. Physical activity comes naturally to all children. Encourage them with plenty of time for active play, especially playing outside. Help children take pleasure in being active in their own way, as a normal part of every day. Limit television to no more than one or two hours a day, and help them break up long periods of inactivity.

Share the benefits by having active fun together as a family. Reject the goal of weight control as a major reason to be active. Instead, live actively for better health, and because it makes you feel good.

Eat well. Think of food as a friend—celebrate, enjoy, taste, savor. Eating well has two aspects: *how* and *what* we eat.

How to eat: Normal eating means eating at regular times, usually three meals and one or two snacks, and responding to internal signals. It means tuning in and trusting our bodies, so we eat when hungry and stop when full and satisfied. Children naturally self-regulate, and can rediscover it if they have forgotten how. If Americans would do this, many of the weight and eating problems that plague our culture today could be prevented. Normal eating enhances our feelings of well being and promotes clear thinking and mood stability; it furthers normal growth in children and stable weights for adults.

What to eat: Choosing foods from all five groups—fruits, vegetables, grains, meats and alternatives, and milk—ensures that children are getting a balance of the many nutrients needed for health, energy, and a strong immune system. Take pleasure in eating a variety of fruits, vegetables, and other foods. Encouraging moderate eating, an amount that feels "just right," helps kids avoid the disruption of extremes, neither overeating nor undereating; neither overindulging in high-fat, high-sugar foods nor fearing to eat these foods, which may be favorites and can certainly fit into a healthy eating plan.

PART V

Effecting Change

Chapter 13

♦ ♦ ❖ ♦ ♦ ❖ ♦ ♦ ❖ ♦ ♦ ❖ ♦ ♦ ❖ ♦ ♦ ❖ ♦ ♦

What Works; What Doesn't

How is your state handling obesity prevention? What is about to happen in your schools, your neighborhood, your medical community? If you don't know, it may be smart to find out before problems surface. Overzealous interventions aimed at larger kids in school can be detrimental.

In the United States, each state has been given the task of developing and implementing a plan for childhood obesity prevention. It is important that selected programs focus on the health and well being of every child, physically, mentally, and socially. It is important that they avoid doing harm to vulnerable children.

Two excellent plans are already in place in Iowa and Michigan. They both adopted the Health at Any Size approach. Both advocate size acceptance and lifestyles without diets. The Iowa plan looks at childhood obesity prevention in five settings—home, child care, school, community, and health care. The Michigan plan confines its scope to prevention in schools.

The Iowa Program

In *Prevention of Child and Adolescent Obesity in Iowa*, the components of a healthy lifestyle are set forth. They include regular physical activity, healthy eating (based on the Food Guide Pyramid, regular meals with reasonable portion sizes, and using the division of responsibility that respects each child's right to decide what, how much, and whether to eat), and a positive and healthy emotional lifestyle (in which differences are accepted, and children are taught self-reliance and resistance to society's pressures to diet or be obsessed with weight).[1] In the five settings addressed, the task force emphasizes the importance of adults as role models in establishing healthy lifestyles. It spells out specific choices in the three areas of promoting physical activity, promoting healthy eating, and creating a positive environment that considers psychological impact and body image.

In Iowa, where children now spend an average of three hours a day watching television, parents are advised to limit television and computer time to one to two hours a day; child care providers are urged to limit TV and video time to one hour or less.

A sampling of Iowa recommendations include:

At Home

- ★ Include physical activity in family outings on a regular basis, even if only for short periods of time.
- ★ Limit sedentary activities, such as television or computer time, to 1 to 2 hours a day.
- ★ Start early to establish healthy eating practices in the home. Young children are quick learners.
- ★ Plan healthy snacks. Snacks are needed to meet a child's nutritional needs, add variety and satisfy hunger between meals without spoiling a child's appetite. Be wary of continuous snacking, which may lead to overeating.
- ★ Provide praise and positive comments to children that focus on their strengths and do not refer to body size either as a strength or weakness.
- ★ Recognize that a child's body shape will change as he or she grows. A short stocky child at age nine may grow to be tall and lanky.
- ★ With older children discuss how the media uses unrealistically thin models to sell their products.

In Child Care

- ★ Provide daily opportunities for large muscle motor activity daily through outdoor playtime or alternative activities during severe weather.
- ★ Limit time spent watching TV or videos to one hour or less a day.
- ★ Children and adults eat together and eat the same foods.
- ★ Limit high sugar and high fat foods without being overly restrictive.
- ★ Children are allowed to refuse to eat a new food, but the caretaker serves the food again. Repeated exposures to a food usually result in a child accepting new foods.
- ★ Caretakers refuse to prepare additional foods for a child who chooses not to eat.
- ★ Food is not used to punish or reward children. Instead, favorite activities or time with adults are rewards. Withholding food causes a child to fear hunger and overeat at a later time. Sweet foods appear more attractive to children when they are used as a reward.
- ★ Do not refer to body size either as a strength or weakness.
- ★ Avoid teasing a child about his or her body size.
- ★ Recognize that children may be healthy at a variety of weights.

In School

- ★ Offer a variety of experiences including both team sports and individual activities.
- ★ Provide both indoor and outdoor facilities.
- ★ Include physical education grades in the overall grade point average.
- ★ Form a committee of students and adults to ensure that healthy eating messages are supported by food sold in vending machines, a la carte meal offerings, and snack bars.
- ★ Prepare students for anticipated body changes through human growth and development and health education classes.

- ★ Increase awareness of how the media and advertising influences cultural norms.
- ★ Be alert to signs of eating disorders and refer appropriately.

In the Community

- ★ Market physical activity through positive portrayal in the media.
- ★ Plan new development to promote walking.
- ★ Flood a park for winter skating.
- ★ Promote after midnight recreational programs or other alternative recreational programs for teens.
- ★ Use parenting classes provided through hospitals, schools, alternative schools and community action agencies to stress the importance of healthy eating and foster parenting styles that promote healthy feeding relationships.
- ★ Encourage grocers and restaurants to offer healthy fast food options.
- ★ Encourage local media to positively portray children with a variety of body sizes.
- ★ Ensure that mental health professionals in the community are familiar with issues of body image disturbance, weight problems and their relationship to self-esteem.

In The Health Care Setting

- ★ *Intervention at primary level—children 85th—95th percentile:* Nutrition assessment conducted by a licensed dietitian to assess etiology of excessive calorie intake including basic pattern of meals and snacks, frequency of fast food intake, frequency of juice or sweetened beverage consumption, leisure time activities, and caregiver nurturing style/feeding interactions; Establish goals: primary goal—develop healthy eating and activity patterns (general lifestyle changes); weight goal—maintenance.
- ★ *Intervention at secondary level—children over 95th percentile:* Increased frequency of structured monitoring by health

professionals (every one to three months).

★ *Intervention at tertiary level—children over 95th percentile with complications, strong family history of obesity:* Establish goals: primary goal—change in one to two identified problematic eating/active behaviors; weight goal—slow weight loss of one to two BMI units, stabilize for six months with weight maintenance and repeat with slow weight loss.

Recommendations in state structure include adding a nutritional consultant position at the state department of education and area agencies to provide technical assistance to schools in selecting and implementing nutrition education curricula so nutrition is taught throughout school health programs.

The Michigan School Plan

The Role of Michigan Schools in Promoting Healthy Weight, is based on the "healthy weight concept" developed by the Michigan Advisory Council.[2] Three separate, but related problems are addressed jointly:

★ Excessive weight gain;

★ Social pressure for excessive slenderness and weight discrimination;

★ Unhealthy weight loss practices.

Improvement in health and well being for all children, both immediate and long-term, is the desired outcome of addressing childhood overweight and obesity. These Guidelines for obesity prevention programs encourage a health-centered, rather than weight-centered, approach that focuses on the whole child, physically, mentally and socially. The emphasis is on living actively, eating in normal and healthy ways, and creating a nurturing environment that helps children recognize their own worth, and respects cultural foodways and family traditions. It is recognized that obesity, eating disorders, hazardous weight loss, nutrient deficiencies, size discrimination, and body hatred are all interrelated and need to be addressed in comprehensive ways that do no harm.

—Guidelines for Childhood Obesity Prevention Programs: Promoting Healthy Weight in Children. Society for Nutrition Education (2002)

If schools address only weight, the advisors warn, they could inadvertently cause damage in the second and third areas. Schools are urged to adopt the concept model to more easily visualize the meaning.

The Michigan plan defines six overall recommendations:

★ Create an environment where students can be physically active;
★ Increase student participation in physical education;
★ Create a healthy nutrition environment;
★ Strengthen nutrition education;
★ Create a safe and supportive learning environment;
★ Work with families to promote physical activity and healthy eating.

In order to foster a safe and supportive environment, important procedures include:

★ School staff should model respectful behavior by refraining from making disparaging comments about their own weight or the weights of other adults;
★ Create a policy that all students and staff are to be treated with respect;
★ Educate athletic coaches, cheerleading coaches, drama directors, and other program advisors in body weight and size sensitivity to eliminate weight discrimination from all school activities. Refrain from using labels for students such as "overweight," "fat," "obese," "underweight," "too thin," or "anorexic;"
★ Create a zero tolerance policy for criticizing, bullying, name-calling, and shaming others about weight or size;
★ Define and enforce clear consequences for disrespectful behavior;
★ Create a process for students to report bullying or disrespectful behavior. The process should protect the victims and those who report the behaviors from reprisal.

In the physical activity and nutrition areas the important points include:

- ★ Provide recess at least twice each day for elementary school students and once each day for middle school students;
- ★ Offer intramural and physical activity programs that feature a range of competitive, cooperative, and individual physical activities;
- ★ Encourage students to walk or ride bikes to school where it is safe for them to do so. Encourage parents to assess routes for safety. If unsafe conditions are found, the school health team may be able to take steps to improve them;
- ★ Create a nutrition integrity policy. This would spell out the principle that all foods available in the school should be consistent with what students are taught in nutrition lessons;
- ★ Teach developmentally appropriate nutrition concepts at every grade level;
- ★ Use active learning strategies and activities that students find enjoyable and personally relevant.

Throughout, the reader is referred to Michigan resources that will provide more detailed information on how to accomplish these objectives. Michigan schools are urged to establish local policies that support some or all of the prevention measures given in the paper.

The Michigan Weight Advisory Group acknowledges that schools cannot completely solve weight-related problems faced by students, and that family influence is far more powerful. Yet schools have the potential to be part of the solution. Their main role is in prevention.

Pursuing Activity in Kentucky

The state of Kentucky was recently ranked lowest of 16 states by the Centers for Disease Control and Prevention on a quality of life index. The index showed Kentuckians as having fewer years of healthy life at ages twenty-five and sixty-five than the residents of the other 15 states. As the current population of overweight and obese youth move toward adulthood, it is feared the quality of life related to health may become even more dismal. Current data on overweight and obesity among Kentucky children are limited, but available data indicates they have higher prevalence than the national average. Nearly 70 percent of Kentucky high school students are not enrolled in a physical education class, compared to 51 percent of high school students nationally.

Thus, the Kentucky draft position paper *Kentucky Children at Risk: The War on Weight,* proposes directing the state board of education to require 30 minutes of structured, moderate to vigorous physical activity per day, beginning in 2003-2004 for preschool through intermediate students, beginning in 2004-2005 for middle and junior high schools, and beginning in 2005-2006 for high schools. Alternate plans and activities would be developed to address how this can be integrated into the school day in at least 15-minute segments.

The paper also proposes improving nutrition in schools, where nearly three-fourths of students eat school lunch daily, well above the national average of 54 percent. Twice as many Kentucky children also eat in the school breakfast program, 27 percent versus 13 percent nationally. Enforcing United States Department of Agriculture standards, and improving these meals in other ways are seen as ways the state can ensure that students are provided with healthful foods and beverages.[3]

Ethics and Boundaries

Wary of the pitfalls in the sensitive area of obesity prevention, and concerned that well-intended efforts may be carried out in ways that are counter-productive to the overall health and wellness of children, Connecticut officials are considering a statement of values, beliefs and boundaries.[4] It emphasizes respect for each individual and reminds those who work with children and adults in obesity prevention programs to look at the whole person and not just their size, stating the following values:

- The decision to change or not change your eating or physical activity is your decision. It is not our decision.
- Our job is to provide leadership and support to help peo-

ple achieve success in their efforts to increase their healthy eating and physical activity.

* Our job is to provide accurate and useful information for individuals and communities to make their own decisions about their eating and physical activity.
* Our job is not to pressure or force anyone to change their eating or physical activity patterns. Our job is not to criticize anyone's decisions about their eating or physical activity patterns.
* Our job is to trust that others are doing the best they can in the context of their own lives.
* Our job is to move towards enjoyment of eating and being active and to be comfortable with our own eating and physical activity decisions.

Special Interest Pitfalls

Currently health insurance providers resist paying for weight loss treatment. But they do cover any harm that ensues from treatment. They pay for stomach surgery, and for the repair and often lengthy hospital stays for surgery gone wrong. Some planning groups wrestle with the question of whether to recommend insurance coverage. On first thought, this may seem reasonable. But planners need to ask: Do we really want insurance to pay for more of the same failed treatments? How much will this drive up health insurance cost? Will it improve the health of children?

Any task force dealing with obesity risks being overloaded with professionals who may have vested interests. The Society for Nutrition guidelines for obesity planning groups suggest they include a broad spectrum of individuals—health professionals, eating disorder specialists, classroom teachers, health-at-any-size advocates and the general public—to ensure a diverse make up of people who will be dealing with the program and affected by it. This caution is added, "As with any planning group, membership disclosure policies are advisable, especially addressing members with special interests, such as financial affiliations with the weight loss industry."

Help for Prevention Planners

Planning groups faced with the task of developing child obesity prevention programs can find help with the paper *Guidelines for Childhood Obesity Prevention Programs: Promoting Healthy Weight in Children,* from the Society for Nutrition Education. Parents can also use the guidelines to review prevention programs in their state or community. Developed by nutrition professionals, the paper encourages a health-centered, rather than weight-centered, approach that focuses on the whole child. It explains how to deal with the interrelatedness of weight and eating problems (obesity, eating disorders, hazardous weight loss, nutrient deficiencies, size discrimination, and body hatred) in comprehensive ways that do no harm. The guidelines emphasize: living actively; eating in normal and healthy ways; and creating a nurturing environment for all children (these guidelines may be accessed online at www.sne.org and www.healthyweight.net).

Buying into the Plan

Health teams in charge of developing state programs can easily adapt for their own use fully developed programs such as those from Iowa and Michigan. Yet each program needs the local touch. Although obviously it could save huge amounts of time, in most cases it probably will not be sufficient to simply adopt such programs as they are. A great deal is to be gained when a working team takes the time to focus close attention on each section, hammering out what it will mean to local people, developing a consensus, and making sure it says what they want it to say. Such a process makes it uniquely their own. Involving everyone down the line in development, decisions, and progress, helps everyone buy into and stay enthusiastic about implementing the program. For example in initiating the physical activity program *Physical Dimensions* in Kansas high schools, Bobbie Harris, Program Director, explains that it was begun as a pilot program nearly 10 years ago. It is now in nearly half of Kansas high schools, and a similar program is expanding into middle schools.

Why did it take so long? Harris says you must first get people to recognize that they need a change. Once that happens, bring representatives of relevant groups together to create a plan, she advises. In Kansas, a number of teachers and administrators initially gathered for a two-day retreat. Before introducing the curriculum to schools statewide, it was tested in a variety of settings—large and small communities, rural and suburban areas, and in areas with diverse populations.

The key to success is to involve people at every level and get them to buy into the program, from grassroots to state government. It is unrealistic to rush in with new programs and expect them to work without laying the groundwork. Getting teachers to come to training sessions was critical to success, Harris explained. "A key decision we made was to provide the curriculum only to teachers who attend the training. Most importantly, you have to involve the teachers in the development of the program. This greatly improves the quality of the program, as well as its chances for being widely implemented."

A good plan is only as good as its implementation at the grassroots. Leaders throughout the community need to buy into the program or it won't fly. From state planners to classroom teachers to parents, everyone needs to be committed to sustaining a long-term program. Schools have an important role in preventing overweight, eating disorders and related problems, but cannot do it alone. Successful intervention programs will involve families, schools, health care, workplace, communities and the media.

Chapter 14

♦ ♦ ❖ ♦ ♦ ❖ ♦ ♦ ❖ ♦ ♦ ❖ ♦ ♦ ❖ ♦ ♦ ❖ ♦ ♦

The Benefits of Active Living

Second-grader Max Fenton is excited to be walking to school today with his dad, Mark, rather than taking the bus. Along the way, they will pick up his best friend, Jackie, her mom, and six other neighborhood children. The parents, two at a time, take turns walking the eight children. They remind them to stay on the sidewalk, watch for traffic from driveways, and line up in pairs and stay in a group when crossing a busy street. After a comfortable eighteen-minute walk, Max and his friends arrive at school alert, full of energy, and looking forward to their day. During their brisk walk back home, their parents accumulate thirty minutes of physical activity, which is the Surgeon General's recommended dose for adults. After school, two other parents walk the children home.[5]

Max is learning about his neighborhood and how to get around it safely on foot. His parents feel comfortable with his skill and awareness, and he has a growing circle of friends' homes and neighborhood places where he is allowed to walk on his own.

Max is active, healthy, and physically fit. Because of these walks, he and his friends are more likely to stay well and healthy, and are less likely to be overweight. There's also less traffic around the neighborhood and school, which means less pollution and less chance of being hit by a car. By the time he's a 5th grader, getting around on foot or by bicycle will be a way of life for Max.

Walking to School

One of the easiest and most appropriate ways to build physical activity into a child's day is for that child to walk or bike to school. Getting to school under their own power gives children a chance to get out in the fresh air, stretch their legs, and arrive at school refreshed and ready to learn. It makes for closer, friendlier communities. Children get to know their neighbors, especially older people, and exchange greetings with them as they go by.

If kids live a mile or less from school they should be walking where it is safe for them to do so. If they live two miles or less, they should be biking or walking. If unsafe conditions are found, steps should be taken to correct them. This is the recommendation of health officials in the United States and in countries around the globe.

But today most children, and over two-thirds of children who live only a mile or less from school, ride in vehicles. Less than one-third walk who live under a mile away, and many are inactive the rest of the day. (See Chapter 4 for more information on children's activity statistics.)

Curbing Traffic Nightmares

A national health effort is underway to get more kids walking or biking to school. But a parent's first question is: Will my child be safe? *Kids Walk-to-School*, a new federal guide from the Centers for Disease Control and Prevention, explains how parents can mobilize their communities and work with media, police, and local officials to improve the walking environment. Creative programs include the "Walking School Bus," in which children walk to school in groups accompanied by adults. Three states—California, Texas, and Washington—recently enacted legislation to make it easier to create safe routes to school.

Walk-to-school programs encourage neighbors to get to know each other and become friends. Senior citizens are encouraged to sit on their porches or work in their yards during the time children are going and coming from school, bringing back the days when children traveled safely through their neighborhoods. Crime drops because of the increased presence of adults on the streets.

Taking up this cause in nine schools, the Marin County [California] Bicycle Coalition in one year increased the number of children walking and bicycling by 57 percent and decreased by 29 percent the number of private car trips to schools.[6]

International Walk to School Day, the first week in October, is a great time to kick off a walking or biking program. On that day, kids in Oakland, Calif., walked to school with their Mayor, Elihu Harris. Children in Las Vegas walked and shared refreshments with then-Governor Bob Miller. In Silver Spring, M.D., McGruff the Crime Dog walked to school with children of East Silver Spring Elementary School.

The sight of children arriving at school in a large parade is enough to inspire parents to re-think their travel behavior, say community leaders. The amazing lack of traffic that day makes a big impression. Many schools follow-up with a weekly or monthly Walk and Bike to School Day. They put on bike rodeos and contests.

At the Queen Mary school in Vancouver, British Columbia, school officials enacted a successful program, now in its fifth year, encouraging children to walk at least part way to and from school each day. Streets near school have been designated as Safe Walking Zones, where walking is encouraged and facilitated by parent patrols.[7]

Implementing a Plan

Walking to school programs involve four key issues:

- ⋆ Physical activity
- ⋆ Safe and walkable routes
- ⋆ Crime prevention
- ⋆ Healthy environments

One of the first jobs is to map out the routes kids currently take to school. A planning group can recommend improvements and suggest safer routes when necessary. Next, this task force works with local officials to address safety issues such as speeding traffic and lack of visible crosswalks, sidewalks, or bike lanes. In the classroom children learn basic pedestrian and bicycle skills and safety.

Major barriers to children walking or biking are identified by parents as: long distances, traffic danger, inclement weather, crime danger and school policy.

The "Walking School Bus" or "Bike Train" requires parents and adult volunteers. Often retirees enjoy a daily walk while accompanying children to school. At designated points and times, other children join the group. Parents of children who live farther from school are encouraged to drop kids off at these designated points, and to carpool. Volunteer or paid crossing guards help children cross key intersections.[8]

Babies Need Action, Too

Young children are the most active Americans of any age. Babies, toddlers, and preschoolers need simple activities that move large muscles every day. Too many children are stuck in the stroller, baby seat, or playpen for long periods, says the National Association for Sport and Physical Education. In 2002 NASPE issued *Active Start*, the first physical education guidelines for young children. They include this advice:

- ⋆ Part of an infant's day should be spent in structured activity with a parent or caregiver playing peekaboo or pattycake, being carried to and exploring new environments.
- ⋆ Do not keep infants or toddlers in baby seats or other restrictive settings for long periods. Even when very young, they move differently when placed on a blanket on the floor than when restricted in a baby seat.
- ⋆ Toddlers should accumulate at least thirty minutes of structured physical activity, and preschoolers at least an hour, during each day. Play follow-along songs, or chase a ball; for older children, balancing games or tumbling increase strength and body control.
- ⋆ Toddlers and preschoolers should spend at least one hour daily, preferably more, in free play, exploring, experiment-

ing, imitating. Caregivers should provide safe objects to ride, push, pull, balance on and climb.

* Toddlers and preschoolers should not be sedentary for more than an hour at a time except when sleeping.

The goal is not to have baby workouts, but to play actively, have fun and use common sense. Physical activity will then be a routine part of daily life, not forced; never used as punishment. Parents are urged to join in, not just sit on a park bench and watch children romp.[9]

Because young children naturally move around a lot, many people assume they are getting all the physical activity they need. But today TV and videos often keep them still for longer periods than parents realize.

Many parents assume that skills such as rolling, sitting, and walking will just come naturally as babies grow, but encouragement helps, says Jane Clark of the University of Maryland, who led the panel of experts who wrote the Active Start guidelines. For instance, a baby who spends much of the day in a bouncy seat may like watching suspended or musical toys, but probably will roll over or sit later than babies who spent more time stretching out on a blanket.

In child care, choose providers who encourage physical activity and other good health habits. If care is provided by a grandparent or relative, express your interest in the child being active during the day. Entertaining with television or videos should be used sparingly, limited to one hour or less a day, according to the Iowa recommendations for day care.

Get Involved

As a parent, you can break the trend toward sedentary living by being active yourself and involving your children in the activities you enjoy. Set a good example by walking to the grocery store or a friend's house. If you have two or three miles to go, consider biking. A regular evening walk can be a great time for the whole family. Working out at a fitness center may be a useful choice for some. Exercise equipment in their own home works well for others. (But invest cautiously in equipment. Much sits unused, taking up space and adding to guilt, in homes around the country.)

Parents and teenagers lead busy lives, so it's most helpful to weave regular activity into the fabric of each day, within the normal scope of school, work, and recreation. Park farther from your destination and walk part way. Choose a distant spot in the parking lot. Bike, ride a scooter or rollerblade to the park. March in place or pace when on the phone or watching commercials. An accurate step-counter can help you see how you're doing, and inspire improvement.

Enjoy active vacations. If you're driving across the country, break for play in a park, a walk or hike once or twice each day.

Work counts, too. Many teens have jobs that keep them active, such as waiting tables, aiding in hospitals and nursing homes, construction, landscaping, or farm work. The Behavior Risk survey divides occupational activity into three categories: mostly sitting, mostly walking, and mostly heavy labor.[10]

Reduce Sedentary Time

It's not enough to have one period of physical activity during the day. Even if that activity takes an hour, there are twenty-three more hours left in the day. What happens during this time does make a difference. Experts tell us we need to go one step further and reduce sedentary time throughout the day. Parents especially need to reduce the time kids sit very still in front of a screen. One to two hours of recreational screen time is enough for young people, especially on school days, according to *Healthy People 2010.* This includes games and recreational time on the computer.

"We used to hear about couch potatoes, but increasingly, we have mouse potatoes," says Mellisa Olson, coordinator of the cardiovascular health program for the North Dakota state health department. "Mouse potatoes are youth who spend too much time in front of the computer or playing video games."

"What we need is people watching television while on exercise equipment. We also need to incorporate some low level aerobic exercise while we work on a computer," urges Mitchell Goldflies, MD, of the American Running and Fitness Association. To make it easier to limit children's screen time, you may want to cut down on your own television watching. If your child has a television set in the bedroom, this may be the time to phase it out. When a child has been reading or doing homework for an hour or so, encourage him or her to get up and move around before going back to it.

Girls and Activity

Girls typically grow less active as they enter adolescence, and become less and less engaged into their later high school years. Young pregnant teens and young mothers need even more help and motivation to stay active. It is critically important for their health, and so they might avoid the burden of excess weight gain so common with pregnancy and childbirth.

The benefits of physical activity for girls include energy and endurance, strong bones, maintaining a high quality of life, and preventing obesity, disease and premature death.

Molly Barker, founder of a running program for girls called Girls on the Run, says girls get pushed into what she calls "the girl box" at age eleven or twelve. They feel pressured to leave behind their spirited playfulness of girlhood, tomboyishness, and the natural and uninhibited exploration of the world they have known. They step into the female stereotype of MTV images, trying to live up to commercial advertising images and social expectations.[11] This is a time when girls especially need active moms as role models. They need involved dads keeping them inspired and motivated in sports. Alert parents can help them make the shift into female adolescence while remaining true to their authentic selves.

How To Get Kids More Active

Life is more fun when we're active—with friends, with a pet, or alone. It's the natural way to live. After all, it's just for fun that twelve-year-olds play softball all afternoon in a vacant lot. It's for the social and rhythmic pleasure that young people dance for hours on a Saturday night.

The Canadian *Vitality* program puts it this way, "Being active means enjoying physical activity and finding fun ways to be active every day of the year—at home, at work, within your community. Whether it's bowling, mowing the lawn or playing hopscotch with the kids, an active lifestyle pays off. Kids are motivated by three factors, experts say:

1. Children want to develop and demonstrate physical competence, such as athletic skills, physical fitness and physical appearance. They want to be good at sports.

2. Gaining social acceptance and support is important to them including friendships, peer group acceptance, and approval, reinforcement and encouragement by adults such as parents, teachers and coaches. They enjoy the camaraderie and mutual support of being part of a team effort.

3. Children want to have fun when playing. Being active is just plain fun, especially when there are few negative experiences related to activity.[12]

Think "Active Living," Not "Exercise"

There's a new way of thinking about physical activity that has swept the professional field in the last ten years. Active living is concerned with long-term quality of life and total well-being. What began as a revolt by a few leaders against the rigidity of the "no pain-no gain" thinking that had taken over the health field, has long since reached the tipping point in professional opinion, and is now being taught in colleges and to the public. This kinder, more practical, more flexible philosophy, or paradigm, emphasizes lifelong active living for everyone, including the most sedentary among us. The word "exercise" is seldom used, except in training regimens. (A similar revolt against food restriction in the nutrition field has had more difficulty reaching the tipping point, although there are encouraging signs that it may be close.) New attitudes embrace these concepts:

- ★ Celebrate activity as a natural part of your life;
- ★ Be active your way, every day;
- ★ Move for the sheer joy and power of it; fitness feels good;
- ★ Choose pleasurable activities; pace yourself;
- ★ Spend quality active time with family, friends, nature;
- ★ Be creative—increase activity throughout your day;
- ★ Enjoy the benefits—to health and well-being; take time to care for yourself;
- ★ Share the benefits with family and friends;
- ★ Have more fun!

In the new approach, everyone can succeed, explains Gail Johnston, a health and fitness consultant in Walnut Creek, California. It's not necessary to count target heart rates, calories burned, or work up to training levels. Nor is it necessary to lose weight to achieve the benefits of fitness, she points out.[13] In fact, focusing on weight loss tends to backfire and take the fun out of activity. So can focusing too much on excelling and winning.

The New Physical Education

Big changes are taking place in physical education. Many schools embrace the new approach, and others are well on their way. They focus more on getting all students involved and active, and less on winning games or showcasing spectator sports; more on cooperation and less on competition. They don't excuse youngsters with special needs from PE, but rather, broaden programs to include all children with disabilities and special needs.

Important features of the new approach:

- ★ Provides different physical activity choices;
- ★ Keeps students active for most of class time (Healthy People 2010 calls for students to keep active for at least 50 percent of the time in class);
- ★ Meets needs of all students, especially those who are not athletically gifted;
- ★ Features cooperative, as well as competitive, games;
- ★ Develops student self-confidence and eliminates practices

that humiliate students (such as having team captains choose sides, dodge ball, and other games of elimination);

- ★ Is based on national standards that define what students should know and be able to do;
- ★ Assesses students on their progress in reaching goals, not on whether they achieve an absolute standard;
- ★ Promotes physical activity outside of school;
- ★ Emphasizes knowledge and skills for a lifetime of physical activity;
- ★ Teaches self-management skills, such as goal-setting and self-monitoring;
- ★ Focuses at the high school level, on helping adolescents make the transition to a physically active adult lifestyle;
- ★ Actively teaches cooperation, fair play, and responsible participation in physical activity; and is an enjoyable experience for students.

At Cabell-Midland High School in Ona, WV, students are challenged to don wet suits, skis, and bicycle helmets and take to the great outdoors. One of the school's PE classes introduces students to outdoor activities like mountain biking, whitewater rafting, and cross country and downhill skiing. Children develop the skills and endurance needed for safe participation.

In Kansas, the Physical Dimensions program reinforces skills aimed at keeping students active throughout their lives. Begun in 1992, it was first piloted in five Kansas high schools and now is used in 40 percent of public high schools in the state. "The program de-emphasizes team sports and focuses on keeping everybody moving," said Bobbie Harris, Program Director. The curriculum consists of four three-week segments for each of three areas: health-related fitness, lifetime physical activity, and health/wellness concepts and skills. A similar program for middle school children is now being piloted in seven schools in Kansas.

The new PE has a way to go before becoming the norm in schools across the country. "There is still a sports-page mentality among some PE teachers," says Don Hellison, a professor of kinesiology at the University of Illinois at Chicago. "There are more fitness-oriented teachers these days, but too many educators still equate PE with sports."

Michigan experts recommend that all children have quality PE every day. At the elementary level emphasis should be on student learning of fundamental motor skills, activity-related knowledge, personal and social skills, and physical fitness. At secondary grade levels the focus shifts to personal responsibility for achieving adequate fitness and mastering lifetime activities such as swimming and racquet sports.[14]

We need more children signed up for daily PE classes and more schools requiring it, according to our national health agenda. Healthy People 2010 calls for an increase in the number of students taking daily physical education to 50 percent of all students, with a current baseline of 29 percent of high school students. Going a step farther, it calls for an increase in the number of public and private schools that require daily PE for all students. For middle and junior high schools the target is 25 percent, from a baseline of 17 percent. For senior high schools the target is 5 percent; only 2 percent currently have this requirement.

Budget cuts and full schedules still reduce or eliminate PE programs. Increasing the requirements may not seem in the picture for schools suffering budget crunch, yet it can save money in the long run. Convincing research shows that regular activity helps kids learn better, behave better, and may even improve brain development.

A Mile Run Before Class

Sometimes one person with commitment and enthusiasm can make a big difference—and it costs nothing. In a special education class at Los Robles middle school in the Hacienda—La Puente school district in Los Angeles County, teacher Jeanie Thiessen noticed her children seemed lethargic in the mornings. It affected their learning. She talked to the students about the benefits of active living, and asked, "Would you like to spend more time outside after the starting bell rings?" They were delighted. They went back outside and walked with their teacher and aide Julie a couple of times around the one-fourth mile playground fence." Some ran a mile—four times around the playground that first day. When asked how they felt the students replied, *"tired...happy...great...smarter...like I want to run some more."*

"We didn't want to wear them out, so we began slowly. After about 20 minutes we brought them in," says Thiessen. "Pretty soon, everyone could go the whole mile. They loved it. The air was clear, and the San Gabriel Mountains north of us were beautiful in the mornings.

"It would have taken too long to walk a mile, so we told them to build up their stamina by running 'till you're tired and walking 'till you're rested." "Before long even our very overweight Samoan girl was running partway and by the end of the year she could run most of it. She said her family noticed her loss of weight, and she was also much more alert and responded better in class."

Before long other teachers at Los Robles noticed the benefits and began turning their students on to activity. One classroom at a time, they began taking their students out for a morning walk and run.

Take 10!

A program called "Take 10!" encourages elementary teachers to get their students up once or twice during the day for ten minutes of activity combined with learning. Activities might be jogging in place, dancing, marching, clapping hands, jumping jacks, stretching, desk push-ups, or playing active games. Learning going on at the same time may involve memorization, calling out multiplication tables, spelling, history in action, solving math problems, financial fitness, and listening to the teacher read aloud.[15]

Proven Programs: SPARK

In twelve schools on the Navajo reservation near Window Rock, Ariz., the Sports Play and Active Recreation for Kids (SPARK) program has helped 1,250 children integrate activity with their tribal culture. Of the thirty minutes they spend three times a week on moderate and vigorous activity, half is devoted to sports skills and half to aerobic activity, including native dancing.[16]

"A sedentary lifestyle, lack of facilities in which to exercise, and a diet high in fat foods coupled with a large number of fast food restaurants on the reservation conspire to make it very difficult for both Navajo children and adults to maintain a healthy weight," said Paul Rosengard, a fitness specialist with the project. Studies show about 27 percent of Navajo children are overweight, and another 12 percent, severely overweight.

The SPARK program is an ongoing curricula for kindergarten through 6th grade, federally-funded, and offered on a non-profit basis through the San Diego State University Foundation. It emphasizes increasing the amount of time children are active in PE, as well as promoting regular activity after school, on weekends, during holidays, summers and after the program ends. Rosengard says the aim of the program is to turn the children on to movement, so they find activity fun and exciting. "And I think that modest goal has already been achieved." New programs include Early Childhood for children ages three to five and Active Recreation, after school activities for children ages five to fourteen.

Intramurals

Fitness experts are calling for more after-school intramural sports to supplement, or even replace, the traditional A, B, and C squads that schools usually field. Those teams involve intense training and require most of a student's spare time.

Megan's large school has an intramural system in which all students are encouraged to join after-school teams, playing each other two or three times a week. There's no travel. Megan can commit time to a sport of her choosing, train, and play hard. Best of all, she is active and still has time for other activities. She finds her life better balanced than when she played on the volleyball team and was committed to training four nights a week, competing the other nights and weekends, and riding the bus for hours, sometimes late into the evening. Megan's school sets sport for all as a primary goal, and is still able to field elite teams. For smaller schools it may not be possible to do both.

Communities that choose intramural sports over the traditional system find that more kids get to play and they often have more fun.

There's less pressure on coaches to produce outstanding athletes and win games. It lessens the sometimes-bitter rivalry between nearby schools, and benefits them with a stronger spirit of cooperation. Dedicated athletes can enjoy a more open system that frees up some training time for other interests and activities. Although easier to implement in large schools, this system works in the smallest schools when the first priority is regular activity and fitness for all students.

Assigning a sports nutritionist to work with school athletic teams is another urgent need that helps prevent problems of undernutrition and the dangerous weight loss practices common in sports like wrestling, running, and gymnastics. The sports nutritionist consults with athletes, coaches and parents at the beginning of each season and as needed to teach and encourage sound sports nutrition. She helps identify and find ways to solve or refer problems, such as obsessive exercise behaviors or disturbed eating patterns, which are all too common on high school sports teams.

Active Communities

Take a close look at your community. In what ways might it be improved to provide an environment in which most children and adults walk and are active in a variety of ways?

Surgeon General David Satcher urges communities to create walking trails to benefit health. "If we can get sedentary people of all ages up and moving for at least thirty minutes a day, five days a week, we can reduce cardiovascular disease and deaths from cardiovascular disease by one-half in this country." It's just as important for communities to provide physical activity for adults as for youth. This helps young people see how they can move seamlessly into adult activities. The United States is often criticized for focusing fitness efforts primarily on youth, and elite athletic youth at that, compared with European countries, which embrace a "sport for all" approach.

Communities have the opportunity to enhance leisure time activity for all youth, parents and other adults through league sports, gymnastics, dance, swimming, biking, canoeing, fishing, cross country skiing, skating, sledding, walking, marital arts classes, local events and games, and providing safe biking and hiking trails. Some communities promote after-midnight recreational programs or other alternative recreational programs for teens.

Concerned parents are getting involved in community plans, working with city officials and police, and involving their children in these efforts. For teenagers, serving on planning groups or helping to improve a hiking trail can be immensely rewarding. Local policies can set standards for green space and sidewalks in new housing developments. Walkable communities is one idea being tested. Planning that co-mingles housing, shopping areas and business offices, schools, and park areas encourages the people who live there to become more active in their daily routine. These communities provide wide streets, sidewalks, and a safe environment for children to walk to school, and play. They offer evidence that people are viewing the environment in different ways and the potential for enhancing physical activity.

Overcoming Barriers

People are more active in neighborhoods perceived as safe, says CDC. In unsafe neighborhoods, about half of women and elderly are inactive. They stay inside their homes when possible, and keep children inside.[17] Turning this around can be challenging. Yet community leaders are doing it every day.

People are also more likely to be active if they have recreational facilities close to their homes, CDC research shows. In neighborhoods with square city blocks, people walk up to three times more than in neighborhoods with cul-de-sac streets or other features that keep streets from connecting.[18] And transportation needs make a difference. Up to twice as many people walk or cycle in neighborhoods that are transit-oriented as in auto-oriented neighborhoods. They ride the subway or bus as close to their destinations as they can, then walk.[19] However, if people can drive, they usually drive all the way.

The need to get somewhere and lack of auto transportation to get there is what spurred physical activity in the past. It still does in many neighborhoods. Today the question is sometimes, not whether people can walk, but whether they can drive. If they can conveniently drive, unfortunately, most seem to do it.

American society has a troubled marriage with the automobile, says Katie Alvord, author of *Divorce Your Car!* She urges people to "re-meet their feet," by biking, taking trains, using the car less, or not owning a car at all. Alvord says divorcing your car can be fun, healthy, money saving, and helpful to the planet in the process.[20]

A national youth media campaign called "VERB: It's What You Do" is a campaign by "tweens" for tweens (age nine to thirteen), aimed at popularizing activity. The message is simple: Verbs are active and children should be too, so pick your favorite verb—run, skip, swim, dance, play, volunteer, join clubs—and do it. Action verbs morph into a child's form on television ads. The aim is to make it fun for children with ads on billboards, radio and in magazines children read. TV commercials air after school, during primetime, and on weekends. School-based promotions give messages on book jackets, school lunch menus and Channel One. Special commercials are created for children from various ethnic backgrounds. Print ads also target parents. VERB celebrates the June 21 summer solstice as the "Longest Day of Play" when tweens can cram every possible minute of daylight with fun and play.[21] (For more information visit www.verbnow.com or www.cdc.gov/youthcampaign)

A physical activity movement is well underway, despite the barriers. Parents can do much to move it along to the benefit of their children.

Available Resources

Interested parents and community leaders can find helpful resources through city, county, state and federal agencies (see resources). For example, the CDC has initiated the program Active Community Environments to promote accessible recreation facilities, including more opportunities for walking and cycling. Projects include promoting close-to-home parks and recreational facilities and promoting neighborhood recreation facilities.[22]

Activity or Training Programs

In planning an individualized activity or training program at home, school or community, Chester Zelasko, PhD, director of the Human Performance Laboratory at Buffalo State College in Buffalo, NY, offers these recommendations for parents and health professionals:[23]

Emphasize consistency first. Since the goal is to maintain a lifetime of increased physical activity, develop an easy, minimal workout and a consistent pattern of activity before moving to any in-depth, progressive fitness program.

Encourage duration, intensity and frequency. These factors are also important in building fitness and improving health as the program progresses.

Intermittent exercise is okay. If the individual cannot sustain ten or twenty minutes at one level, it is okay to break the sessions into segments. Alternating low or moderate intensity work is interval training, often used by athletes to increase strength and endurance.

Respect the large youngster. Everyone deserves respect no matter what his or her body weight. Nurturing is important. Maybe the child will lose weight or grow into the weight. Maybe not. But they can be healthier by exercising regularly and should be reassured of these benefits.

Understand physical and emotional needs. For kids who have been inactive, it takes time to gain confidence in moving the body. They may need to overcome shyness about using their body. As they become more successful, they enjoy activity more, and are more likely to continue. When choosing a fitness facility, it is important to find one where trainers respect the emotional and physical needs of the child.

Benefits of Living Actively

Rosarita, age 16, began taking long walks after school with her friend in September when school began. As with over half of high school students nationwide, she takes no physical education class. She rides the bus to school from the Latino community where she lives in Albuquerque. At 180 pounds, Rosarita has a soft maternal shape. She lost no weight in the first few months of walking, but after the first month her jeans fit more loosely, and after two she could wear a size smaller. She had gained lean muscle, which is heavier but smaller than fat, and burns more energy.

Best of all, she felt stronger mentally as well as physically, no longer as helpless as she had before. She felt more confident in making other changes in her life. Since she was strong enough to do this one thing, she decided maybe she could do something about that older man, a neighbor and friend of her father's, who leered at her every day as she walked by and called out obscenities. Frightened, she turned her head and hurried by. But now she began feeling angry. She confided her anger and fears to a teacher, who urged her to talk to her parents. She did, and abruptly the harassment stopped.

Just as Rosarita was empowered by being more active, so many other people have found that once they've succeeded in bringing regular physical activity into their lives, they begin to think of other ways they might succeed. They feel renewed energy.

Physical activity is becoming known as a *"gateway behavior,"* a behavior that when changed, empowers children to make other changes more easily. Understanding gateway behavior helps professionals and parents work more effectively in improving children's health.[24]

When kids improve their athletic skills and see their bodies grow stronger, they feel more confidence in making other lifestyle changes. (Note that this is *not true* of restricting food and dieting, which increases stress and negatively impacts other behaviors.)

Prevent Weight Gain

Regular physical activity is critically important in preventing and managing weight problems. It affects weight change in three ways—by preventing weight gain, promoting weight loss, and maintaining weight loss. Of these, its most important role is in preventing weight gain throughout life. Until now this critical role has been devalued in the United States. It is most unfortunate that national health agencies have delayed so long in advocating—or even measuring—physical activity. No more. The role of regular physical activity in preventing excess weight gain and fat gain is widely recognized today, with the results of the delay now obvious in soaring obesity and diabetes rates. "One critical answer to this problem is that we all must work together to help our children make physical activity a life-long habit," urges Dr. Julie Gerberding, director of the Centers for Disease Control and Prevention in Atlanta.[25]

During the last thirty or forty years, few voices were raised in concern, as baby boomers embraced laborsaving devices as trophies of their progress in every aspect of their lives—at work, at home, in transportation, and in their recreation. Their children took it all for granted, and some of them now have children with no conception at all of what an active life might mean.

Physical activity reduces body fat and increases lean body mass, which is more metabolically active. Thus, the child who becomes more active will have a higher ratio of muscle to fat than before, and burn more calories. This is why working out on weights can be especially effective in weight loss and management: it increases muscle mass more than aerobic activity alone. Again, the amount of change will differ depending on the individual child's genetics, variability in metabolism, and other lifestyle behaviors.[26] Both children and adults differ widely in their responses. No doubt some have strong genetic vulnerabilities that favor fat storage, while others have genetic resistance to weight gain. Steven Blair, who served as senior scientific editor of the U.S. Surgeon General's Report on Physical Activity and Health, has observed the variation in weight gain for both staff and clients over more than twenty-five years of research at the Cooper Institute. "Some individuals never exercise, yet also do not gain any weight over their adult years, while others gain a substantial amount of weight despite daily jogging," explains Blair.

It is important to help children maintain enough regular activity so that food intake will be regulated naturally in balance. The average healthy child can regulate food intake to match his or her energy and growth needs. It works out just right without excess fat gain. For example, most five-year-olds consume close to half-million calories a year. But despite this huge energy intake, and large fluctuations day by day in what they eat and how active they are, they balance it all naturally and without effort. They grow in a normal pattern according to their natural heritage.[27]

Will My Child Lose Weight?

Just as the causes of obesity are complex, so are its solutions. Excess fat does not come off quickly through exercise. But the long-term cumulative effects, day after day, add up to big differences. If you consider that walking a mile burns about 100 calories, then a person would need to walk 35 miles to burn a pound of fat, or 3,500 calories. Theoretically, then, at two miles a day, one would burn off a pound of fat in 18 days, or 21 pounds a year. But it doesn't necessarily work this way in the real world. The body is continually readjusting, and genetic differences can change the outcome.

Increasing activity levels appears to be the best way to lose weight and keep it off. It may be the only way to lower the setpoint. Yet, we cannot promise that children will lose weight with increased activity. The answers are not simple. For most children with high body fat there will be losses of weight and fat with increased activity. Weight lost this way is gradual, but lasting, as long as the activity is sustained. Other children will maintain their weight, while growing into it. Still others, who have kept their weight unnaturally low through food restriction, may gain some weight. Health and weight improvements that come with lifestyle changes provide far healthier, less stressful and more lasting results than restricting food or dieting. But changes will come more slowly.

A 1997 review of the 3-to-4-month weight loss programs using diet or exercise reported in the scientific press over the past 25 years, found that aerobic exercise produced an average weight loss of about 6.5 pounds, compared with a 24-pound loss from dieting.[28] Adding 30 to 60 minutes of physical activity to the diet increased weight loss by about 4 pounds.[29] These are short-term studies that give a picture of typical initial results. Longer-term research suggests we can expect that the 24 pounds lost through dieting will be regained during the next months. Likely the 6.5 pounds lost through aerobic activity will stay off, and more may be lost over time, if the activity is sustained. (In addition, increased activity can also prevent further gains of excess weight.) Yet this loss may well be less than expected.

Parents determined to make weight loss happen may need to revise their priorities and consider what is really beneficial in improving the overall health and well-being of their child. The role of exercise in weight loss has often been exaggerated, bringing much disappointment and discouragement, warns Chester Zelasko, PhD, director of the Human Performance Laboratory at Buffalo State College in Buffalo, N.Y.

It is important for parents, coaches and health providers to avoid suggesting that increasing activity will bring about major weight changes. Children may become disillusioned and give up sports activities for good. Also avoid suggesting that the purpose of physical activity is to burn calories. Adding up calories burned, or keeping track of dials and numbers on fitness equipment to predict pounds lost is an exercise in futility. It doesn't work, is discouraging and self-defeating. No wonder dieting has been far more popular as a weight loss method. The fast results are obvious, even though short-lived.

Maintaining Weight Loss After Dieting

Regular physical activity appears to be critical in maintaining any successful weight loss. The National Weight Control Registry, a group of 1,047 people nationwide who were able to lose weight and keep it off at least one year, confirms the importance of being active. These people, who have maintained an average weight loss of 64 pounds for over 6 years, spend at least an hour daily in moderate to vigorous physical activity. Unfortunately, it cannot be assumed that these results are typical, since the number of these weight loss maintainers is very small compared to the number of people who diet. To prevent relapse for the average dieter may require more intense activity than this. Parents who choose the dieting route for their children, need to recognize this. Will it be helpful to set them on a course such as this?

People make a common mistake when they think, "First I'll lose weight, then I'll change the habits." It doesn't work that way. They blow the diet long before they have time to develop healthy habits. Instead, tell your child, "We'll change habits first, and let the weight come off as a result." This works because the right amount comes off for that child, and when the new habits are maintained, so is the new weight.

What We Can Promise

Must the larger child lose weight to improve his health? If health is truly our concern, probably not. Regular physical activity is necessary. Research shows clearly that activity improves health for the larger person independent of weight loss. It should be reassuring to parents that what counts for health is living actively, not numbers on the bathroom scale. When obese persons are physically active they tend not to have the typical related risks.

Researchers suggest there is compelling evidence that the health risks of obesity can be managed through physical activity. An overweight child or adult can have a healthy heart and lung system as long as he or she is active. Heart and lung health may be independent of changes in body composition. Further, researchers note it has been erroneously assumed that overweight or obese individuals are generally unfit; this is not the case.[30]

Blair and Leermakers make the case that sedentary living and obesity may have been confused from the beginning by scientists researching obesity and health, because obese persons are more likely than normal-weight persons to lead sedentary lives. About

10 percent of lean individuals they studied were in the low-fitness category, compared with 80 percent of obese women and 90 percent of obese men with a BMI of 40 or more. "In many of the studies on obesity and health, physical activity was not mentioned at all, and when it was included, it was measured by crude and imprecise methods."[31]

Instead of focusing on losing weight, Zelasko encourages young people to exercise for the right reasons: "For the health of it! To improve the cardiovascular system; to improve the strength, endurance and flexibility of the muscular system; to effect positive changes on other body systems such as skeletal, digestive and immune systems; for other manifestations of improved health such as lower serum lipids and lower blood pressure." Since the health risks of overweight are so closely related to sedentary living, it makes sense for any treatment for weight or related health problems to begin with a physical activity program. Losing weight—which is so difficult—may not be necessary for dramatic improvements.

Unfortunately, research is yet not sufficient to evaluate changes in activity levels and what this means for weight problems. Blair severely criticizes federal obesity researchers for not developing tools to measure energy expenditure, and for not attempting, except in the crudest ways, to measure physical activity of national population samples.

Benefits: Physical, Mental, and Social

The benefits of activity extend far beyond any role in prevention and management of weight problems, and it is these that need to be emphasized. Otherwise activity is sometimes abandoned because it does not give the quick results expected. The body responds to regular physical activity with dramatic improvements in the cardiovascular, metabolic, respiratory, endocrine, and immune systems.

Research offers abundant proof that active people live longer and have higher quality of life, regardless of weight. Despite the common thinking that obesity is dangerous, being a couch potato is more life-threatening.

TABLE 14.1 **Iron Sources**[1]

Sources of heme iron	
Iron in one (3 oz) serving	(milligrams)
Beef liver	5.8
Sirloin, lean, broiled	2.9
Hamburger, lean, broiled	1.8
Chicken, skinless, dark meat	1.1
white meat	1.0
Pork, lean, roasted	1.0
Salmon, canned with bone	0.7
Sources of non-heme iron Iron in one serving (milligrams)	
Fortified breakfast cereal	4.5 - 18
Bran	3.5
Molasses, blackstrap	3.5
Spinach	3.2
Egg yolk	0.7
Raisins	1.1
Rice, enriched	1.2
Bread, whole wheat	0.9
white, enriched	0.7

Iron from animal sources (heme iron) increases total iron absorption and is better absorbed than the non-heme iron. Recommended dietary allowance is: 10 mg, infant to age 10; 12 mg, girls 11-14 and boys 11-18; 15 mg, girls 15-18.

Blair and his colleagues at the Cooper Institute find that active people have low risk of premature death, and it doesn't make much difference what they weigh. Their studies followed 25,389 men for more than eight years, and found disease and death rates were related directly to physical activity, not to weight or fatness. Obese men who were moderately or vigorously active had no higher death rates than lean men at these same activity levels. Their risk of early death was far lower than that of sedentary lean men. At every weight, fit men outlived those with lower levels of fitness.[32]

Blair finds the same for women. Of 3,120 healthy women at any weight, those with moderate and high fitness levels had much lower death rates than women with low fitness.[33] In another long-term study of obese women, exercise normalized their abnormal plasma glucose, insulin and lipid levels even though they did not lose weight.[34]

Trying to isolate other possible independent factors, the Cooper studies adjusted for smoking and alcohol, and excluded previous heart problems, stroke or cancer. They looked independently at the effects of weight (body mass index), fatness, fat free mass, waist circumference, and at the disease factors of hypertension, cardiovascular disease, type 2 diabetes. With every condition, it was the level of activity that most predicted longevity.

In a review of the 24 available research articles which evaluated the effects of physical activity and body fatness on health outcomes, Blair and colleagues reported the studies consistently showed that active men and women were protected against health risks associated with obesity. The studies included coronary heart disease, hypertension, type 2 diabetes, cancer, and deaths from all-causes. In every case, activity, not fatness, was the critical factor in health and longevity.[35]

Diabetes Improvements

Physical activity is key to treating and preventing type 2 diabetes and pre-diabetes, both increasingly common in young people. Both are closely associated with obesity and inactivity.

Muscle insulin sensitivity improves with any form of physical activity. This is due to improved aerobic fitness, muscle tone and strength. In one 15-day program, moderate exercise improved insulin sensitivity for diabetic patients by almost 90 percent and aerobic capacity by over 10 percent. The exercise consisted of treadmill walking for 35 minutes a day, 5 days a week, at 60 percent capacity. As is typical, many individual differences were found.[36]

Benefits of regular physical activity:

- ★ Lowers blood pressure and hypertension risk
- ★ Helps prevent heart disease and diabetes

- ★ Improves cholesterol levels, increases good cholesterol (HDL)
- ★ Lowers heart rate
- ★ Keeps heart and lungs working efficiently
- ★ Improves blood glucose levels
- ★ Improves diabetic symptoms
- ★ Reduces risk or symptoms related to some types of cancers
- ★ Strengthens immune system
- ★ Increases longevity
- ★ Increases strength and endurance
- ★ Increases productivity
- ★ Improves muscle function and joint problems
- ★ Builds bone, slows bone loss, helps prevent osteoporosis
- ★ Increases lean body mass and reduces body fat
- ★ Prevents or delays weight gain, overweight and obesity
- ★ Promotes weight loss
- ★ Reduces regain after weight loss
- ★ Increases resistance to fatigue
- ★ Improves sleep
- ★ Reduces stress and tension
- ★ Lessens anxiety and depression
- ★ Improves self-image
- ★ Boosts self-confidence
- ★ More energy and zest for life
- ★ Improved appearance
- ★ Refreshes, relaxes, energizes
- ★ Brings family and friends together
- ★ Brings new friends

The effect of exercise on bone density is particularly important during adolescence, because this is the time in life when bone mass builds most rapidly. We can think of bones as muscles. If they are actively used or stressed, they grow stronger. If not, they weaken. Tennis players, for instance, have much thicker and stronger bones in the tennis arm, the arm used more often, than in the non-tennis arm. In addition to aerobic activity, weight-bearing exercise has a powerful effect on strengthening bones. Working out with weights is especially beneficial for girls, who often lack strength, and are more subject to fragile bones.

Academic Benefits

Being active may even make kids smarter. Brain research suggests that exercising the large muscles during adolescence helps increase nerve connections for higher brain development.

Physically fit children performed better academically in a recent California study. Reading and math scores were compared with fitness levels for nearly one million children in grades five to nine. Higher academic scores were associated with higher fitness levels at each grade level. Girls showed even higher scores than boys, especially at higher fitness levels.[37] This supports studies that show girls involved in sports do better in academics. They are also less likely to drop out of school, take drugs or get pregnant while in school. But for many young people, the mental, emotional, and social benefits they gain, are even more important than the physical. Being active energizes kids. It builds self-confidence and gives them more zest for life. It lowers stress and anxiety, lifts the mood, and is especially beneficial in promoting psychological well-being for youngsters who are anxious or depressed. It relieves tension and helps young people put problems in perspective.

When kids list the benefits, a boost to self-esteem and mental outlook and a gain in friendships usually top the lists.

Self-Respect Grows For Girls in Sports

Girls who are physically active are more likely to have high body image, a positive sense of self-satisfaction, higher perceived competence, and to like most things about themselves, according to a recent study of girls age eleven to seventeen by Melpomene Institute and *Shape* magazine. Being in an athletic program enhanced their self respect.[38] All these positives were increased when the girls combined sports with other after-school activities. Girls in six or more after-school activities that included athletics were the most likely of all to feel good about themselves.

The authors suggest that after-school activities allow girls to develop their interests, express commitment, and work with a group of friends toward a common goal—all pursuits unrelated to appearance. The encouragement of parents in their activities also had a big impact on the girls' enjoyment and self-esteem.

Save Health Care Costs

Being active saves health care costs, too. A recent study found that Americans fifteen years and older who engage in regular physical activity—at least 30 minutes of moderate or strenuous physical activity three or more times a week—have lower medical costs. Their average annual direct medical costs were $1,019 each compared with one-third higher costs at $1,349 for those who are inactive.[39]

How Much is Enough?

A teenager doesn't have to run the Boston marathon or be a basketball star to get real health benefits from physical activity. In the new thinking, emphasizing the amount of time spent rather than stressing intensity offers more options for fitting activity into children's daily lives. For our overall health as a nation, there are far more benefits to getting sedentary children moderately active, than in improving the skills of athletes.

For teenagers, especially girls, a major goal is to avoid the drop in activity that typically comes between grades 9 and 12, and the subsequent drop after high school graduation. Sustaining the higher level of activity they learn in childhood will help them avoid problems of excessive weight gain and chronic disease as adults.

Healthy People 2010 Objectives

Increasing physical activity and fitness among young people
Increase the percent of adolescents who:

* Engage in moderate physical activity for at least 30 minutes, 5 or more days a week;

- ★ Engage in vigorous physical activity for at least 20 minutes, 3 or more days a week;
- ★ Participate in daily school physical education;
- ★ Spend at least 50 percent of school physical education class time being physically active (more than 20 minutes);
- ★ View television 2 or fewer hours on a school day.

Increase the percent of schools that:

- ★ require daily physical education for all students.
- ★ provide access to their physical activity spaces and facilities for all persons outside of normal school hours (before and after the school day, on weekends, and during summer and other vacations).

Some children love movement and will keep naturally active throughout the day. For others, who tend toward less active pursuits, parents may need to help them enjoy activity by taking extra time for active family fun, and joining them in walking, biking or skating.

The good news is that youngsters don't have to reach competitive heights to achieve major benefits in health, weight and well-being. They can improve the quality of their lives dramatically by including moderate activity into their day. It is critical that parents respond to the national call to increase activity at every age, and especially for their children, now setting patterns for a lifetime.

Chapter 15

♦ ♦ ❖ ♦ ♦ ❖ ♦ ♦ ❖ ♦ ♦ ❖ ♦ ♦ ❖ ♦ ♦ ❖ ♦ ♦

Normalizing Your Child's Eating

In the public mind, *what* kids are eating is the overriding cause of the obesity crisis. *How* they eat gets ignored. Yet, eating behaviors are at the root of many of today's childhood problems—an important factor in both the rising rates of obesity and eating disorders.

In normal eating, children are attuned to internal signals of hunger, appetite, and satiety. They eat what they want and as much as they want. Usually they eat at regular times, typically three meals and one or two snacks. If all Americans ate in this simple way, many of the eating and weight problems that plague our society today would disappear.

Give Up Control

Yet many parents fail to understand that the child knows best when he/she is hungry and how much he/she needs to eat. When parents give up control, trust the child, and provide with patience, then the child is free to choose. Mealtimes become pleasant and less stressful for the family.

The teenager who overeats or restricts eating is overriding his/her natural controls in another way and internalizes the power struggle.

Jody, 13, and a pudgy 150 pounds, had been on several diets when her mom took her to the dietitian recommended by her pediatrician. She usually skipped breakfast and lunch, and tried hard to restrict what she ate in the evening. She weighed herself twice every day—once in the morning, and again when she returned home after school. Then she'd eat what started out to be a small snack, but almost inevitably it triggered a binge in which she'd lose control.

After taking Jody's history, the dietitian asked for ideas on how she could get more active.

Jody thought about it, "Volleyball season is starting—and I've always wanted to be on the junior high volleyball team. I think I'm pretty good at it."

Jody expected to be given a diet and a lecture on what foods to eat, but instead, her dietitian told her not to worry about what she was eating. "First we'll work on normalizing your eating. Just eat what's on the table, whatever you want."

They talked about past diets, and Jody agreed to stop skipping meals.

"You'll need some kind of snack before volleyball practice. How do you think you can manage that?"

At the next week's session she learned how to pay attention to how her stomach was feeling. She practiced with a cracker. First, she felt its texture, smelled it, and thought about how her stomach felt. She took a drink of cold water, and was surprised to discover she could trace its course down her throat and into her stomach. Next she took a small bite of the cracker, chewed it thoroughly, swallowed, and checked with her stomach again. She was amazed that she felt quite full after eating just one cracker.

This was the beginning of big changes for Jody. Now she ate a granola bar after school as she went to volleyball practice, which included some weight training and running. She ate breakfast at home and lunch at school. Hungry at meals, she enjoyed eating whatever was served, along with a glass of cold milk. She ended her mindless snacking.

She didn't diet and she no longer felt like bingeing. In fact, she felt good. She forgot about eating for most of the time, and got involved in other, more interesting activities with her friends.

Benefits of Normal Eating

Normal eating enhances children's feelings of well-being and nurtures their good health. It furthers clear thinking, mood stability, and healthy relationships with other people. Normal eating promotes natural weight and stable weights as young people mature.

What is normal eating?

- ★ Normal eating is usually eating at regular times, typically three meals and one or two snacks to satisfy hunger.
- ★ It is regulated mostly by internal signals of hunger, appetite, satiety—we eat when hungry and stop when satisfied.

How does it promote health and well-being[40]?

- ★ Normal eating enhances feelings of well-being. We eat for health and energy, also for pleasure and social reasons, and afterward, we feel good.
- ★ Normal eating promotes clear thinking and mood stability. It fosters healthy relationships in family, work, school, and community. Thoughts of food, hunger, and weight take up only a small part of the day.
- ★ Normal eating nurtures good health, vibrant energy, and the healthy growth and development of children. It promotes stable weights, within a wide range, expressing both genetic and environmental factors.
- ★ Normal eating—eating meals—means that food choices will likely provide variety, moderation and balance.

Tuning In to Hunger and Fullness

Learning how to eat well—for children and teens who habitually overeat or restrict eating—begins by stopping all diets, meal skipping, chaotic eating, and restoring normal eating as a priority.

To help kids get back in touch with their hunger and satiety cues, parents need to accept their setpoint weight range, say nutritionists Karin Kratina, MA, RD, and Nancy King, MS, RD. "If a client is keeping her weight unnaturally low through restriction of calories or excessive exercise, her body is in a state of depletion, resulting in distorted hunger and satiety signals."[41]

Help Your Children Understand What They Eat

Linda Omichinski, author of *You Count, Calories Don't*, says any bite of food that goes into your mouth deserves attention. When you eat, do nothing but eat, even ift it's a handful of raisins. "Sit down, take a deep breath, relax, and focus on the raisins...Experience the different taste sensations, textures, and aromas."[42]

Nutritionists call this attuned eating (or attentive, intuitive, or purposeful eating). Getting in the habit of eating attentively helps the child feel satisfied, knowing he enjoyed what he ate, and that this meal will stick with him a few hours.

"Having enough food available helps you feel comforted, well taken care of and secure. Not having enough of what you want to eat may make you feel deprived. Eating foods you don't enjoy leaves you feeling unsatisfied after the meal," says dietitian Karen Siegel.[43]

It is essential for parents to maintain a positive feeding relationship through the growing up years that will allow kids to feel relaxed and comfortable about eating and in touch with their internal cues of hunger, appetite and satiety, says Ellyn Satter, registered dietitian and therapist, and internationally-known expert on the dynamics of feeding children, in *How to Get Your Kid to Eat . . . But Not Too Much.*[44] Underfeeding interferes with this, just as surely as does urging a child to eat more than he or she wants.

Satter explains that parents are responsible for food shopping, preparation and serving meals, and getting everyone to the table.

Then they need to stop, and trust that the child will eat what he or she needs.

Stress-Free Feeding teaches parents that no matter how young, every child gives cues. Parents need to learn the cues and respond appropriately.

For babies, response is simple. The parent provides breastmilk or infant formula when baby signals it's time to eat—by crying, fussing, or making sucking motions. Baby decides when she's done by

Tips for Stress-Free Feeding

Stress is a part of everyone's life. Planning, preparing and providing meals can become an unpleasant task, and mealtimes can increase our level of stress. Use the following tips so that you and your family will have a more enjoyable feeding experience.

- ★ Plan what you will serve in advance.
- ★ Make a list before you leave and only shop for those items.
- ★ Set a schedule for meals and snacks and follow it as closely as possible.
- ★ Changes take time. Don't try to change everything at once.
- ★ Sit at the table for meals and snacks—turn off the TV.
- ★ Start the meal in a positive way: say a blessing, talk about something good that happened during the day, say something nice about family members.
- ★ Set rules for the table: no arguing, no complaining about the food, don't bring up problems.
- ★ Decide how long your child will need to sit at the table—15 to 20 minutes is reasonable.
- ★ Don't allow your child to return to the table once he leaves. If he chooses not to eat, ask him to sit and keep you company.
- ★ Remember that your child knows when he is hungry and when he is full—let him choose to eat and choose how much.
- ★ Your child will be cautious about trying new foods. Remember that your job is to offer a variety of healthy foods. Let your child choose which foods he wants to eat.
- ★ Be a good role model for your child.

Reprinted by permission. Children's Healthcare of Atlanta; www.choa.org

closing her mouth, stopping sucking, or turning away. Urging babies to eat more when they are full makes them angry and frustrated. It may cause them to eat more than they want or need.

Mind your Ps and Cs

The Atlanta providers divide the jobs into "3Ps" for parents—plan, prepare, provide—and "3Cs" for the child—choose to eat, choose what to eat, choose how much to eat. They explain what they mean by the parents' 3Ps.

1. Planning for positives includes deciding what foods to prepare, what to buy, when to have meals and snacks, where you will eat, what foods and drinks you will offer, rules for meal behavior, and what habits and traditions you want to pass on to your children. Planning helps your child be a good eater.
   ⋆ Plan menus for meals and snacks and shop ahead of time; don't rely on fast food.
   ⋆ Schedule meals and snacks; don't allow your child to grab what she wants whenever she wants it.
   ⋆ Offer new foods and previously refused foods; don't serve only what you know he likes.
   ⋆ Make a family rule to eat meals and snacks at the table; don't allow your child to take food to other rooms.
   ⋆ Keep water available for your child to drink between meals and snacks; don't allow her to drink juice or other sweetened beverages between meals and snacks.

2. Preparing and putting food on the table and getting the family to sit down together may be hard for busy moms and dads. Sometimes it's tempting to let everyone decide what they want to eat and fix it themselves, or pick up fast food. But the Atlanta providers remind parents that when you take the easy way out you may end up turning all control over to your child, spending more money than you need to, or not serving what your child needs to be healthy.
   ⋆ Prepare the same meal for the whole family, making sure there is something in the meal that your child will usually

eat; don't get up and prepare something else if your child is not eating what you have served.
★ Allow your child to help with food preparation and setting the table.

3. Providing with patience pays off for parents. Supporting your child with patience will help him have a stress-free eating experience.
★ Let your child serve himself and feed himself; don't worry too much about neatness or your young child making a mess.
★ Present new foods positively and eat them yourself; don't pressure or force your child to eat.
★ Allow your child to touch and smell foods; don't expect your child to accept new foods right away.
★ Teach your child proper table manners (to say "Please," "Thank you" and "No, thank you."); don't allow whining, crying, begging or complaining at the table.
★ Sit and eat with your child; don't have your child eat without a parent or caregiver.

Following these Stress-Free Feeding principles establishes healthy mealtime behaviors so that all family members can enjoy their meals in a positive setting.

The Atlanta's 3Ps and 3Cs help children develop healthy eating habits

Ps are parents' jobs:
Plan for positives
Prepare and put food on the table
Provide with patience

Cs are children's jobs:
Choose to eat
Choose what to eat
Choose how much to eat

Both Children's Healthcare of Atlanta and Ellyn Satter make their training available to health professionals nationwide.[45,46] Buechner and her team have developed a variety of educational tools and materials to assist families with concerns about overweight. Parents can read and print off materials online at www.choa.org.

Positive Eating

Satter explains that parents should not interfere with the natural eating and regulation process by urging, bribing, scolding or praising for eating. Allow children to respond to their internal cues of hunger and satiety.

Parents who urge children to eat more or stop eating before they are satisfied, insist they clean their plates or refuse second helpings, set the stage for disruptive and disturbed eating patterns. Satter says it is sometimes hard to convince parents that "Even the fat child is entitled to regulate the amount of food he eats."

Moms and dads may want to talk about how their stomach feels when it's "just right," and when they've eaten too much. Being "stuffed" does not feel good. Yet, everyone overeats at times, and we can trust our bodies to balance it out over a few days. When kids come home from school, ask if they are hungry, and when they ate last. This is a good time to schedule a regular snack. If the child goes to day care, make sure the caretaker understands your child is being taught the division of responsibility. If she stays with a relative or neighbor, help her understand that you prefer Nancy not be praised or scolded for the way she eats, or urged to eat more. But she must always come to the table for meals. Explain that stress-free feeding makes the meal more pleasant for everyone, and it helps Nancy learn to regulate her own eating.

Eating Meals Together

Getting the family together for meals may not be easy for parents who have long workdays or long commutes and teenagers involved in sports and other activities, but it is critically important. All kids, teenagers as much as toddlers, need the structure of planned eating times to help them develop wholesome eating patterns, learn to like a variety of foods, consume a nutritionally adequate diet, and eat the right amount to grow well. Families who eat together value these times. Nearly all say they appreciate meals as a time to talk over their day's events. One study found the number of family meals eaten together predicted whether a teenager was doing well or poorly in academic motivation, peer relationships, substance abuse and depression.[47]

"Children who eat meals with their parents and siblings tend to eat a more varied and nutritious diet," says Kathy Walsh, Family Consumer Science teacher in Harvey, ND, and busy mother of three. "Let the kids help prepare the meal and they are more likely to eat it."[48]

For families on the run, Walsh suggests being creative and flexible. "Bring the family together for a late dessert or eat breakfast together. Make weekend meals the family focus."

Long-Term Goals

Take time to develop a long-term strategy and keep your eye on those goals for the bigger picture. This means dad's goal moves ahead from making sure Carol eats those green beans on her plate *tonight,* before she's allowed to leave the table. Instead, his new goal is to help Carol learn to enjoy eating green beans and a variety of other foods through all her growing up years. This takes patience and caring, and is much more pleasant for everyone.

Often a child won't like a new food the first few times it's offered. Be patient and attentive to opportunities. Satter says a child may need to taste a new food 10 or 15 or more times before liking it. But children do want to eat, and they want to eat grown-up food. Keep presenting it, sometimes preparing it in different ways or mixing with other foods that are enjoyed. Don't urge her to eat. Just offer the new food and don't make an issue of it. If others at the table are eating and enjoying the food the child will begin to eat it, too. But don't offer too many new foods at once (not more than one a week), and serve other foods that the child eats.

Parents can de-emphasize food in the home between meals by keeping snacks and food reminders out of sight and not talking excessively about eating. Avoid food symbolism by avoiding use of food to reward, punish, express love or comfort: A kiss is better than a cookie for a hurt finger.

The secret of feeding a healthy family is to love good food, trust yourself, and share that love and trust with your children, Satter tells parents. Do your job, let your children do theirs, and be relaxed about it. "You have to take the guilt out and put the joy back in."

Tips For Dads—Preventing Eating And Body Image Problems

- ★ Listen to girls. Focus on what is really important—what your daughter thinks, believes, feels, dreams and does—rather than how she looks.
- ★ Encourage her strength and celebrate her savvy. Help your daughter learn to recognize, resist and overcome barriers. Help her be strong, smart and bold!
- ★ Respect her uniqueness. Urge her to love her body and discourage dieting. Make sure your daughter knows that you love her for who she is and see her as a whole person, capable of anything. Your daughter is likely to choose a life partner who acts like you and has your values. Remember, growing girls need to eat often and healthy and dieting increases the risk of eating disorders.
- ★ Get physically active with her. Play catch, tag, jump rope, basketball, frisbee, hockey, soccer, or just take walks . . . you name it! Physically active girls are less likely to get pregnant, drop out of school, or put up with an abusive partner. Studies show that the most physically active girls have fathers who are active with them.
- ★ Get involved in your daughter's school. Volunteer, chaperone, read to her class. Ask tough questions, like: Does the school have and use an eating disorder prevention or body image awareness program? Does it tolerate sexual harassment of boys or girls?
- ★ Get involved in your daughter's activities. Volunteer to drive, coach, direct a play, teach a class—anything! Demand equality.

- ★ Help make the world better for girls. This world holds dangers for our daughters. But over-protection doesn't work, and it tells your daughter that you don't trust her! Instead, work with other parents to demand an end to violence against females, media sexualization of girls, pornography, advertisers feeding on our daughters' insecurities, and all boys are more important than girls attitudes.
- ★ Support positive alternative media for girls. Join with your family to watch programs that portray smart savvy girls. Subscribe to healthy magazines like *New Moon* and visit online girl-run 'zines and websites.

Scale Down Portion Sizes

Reducing portion sizes is on the minds of many nutrition and health leaders. Larger portions are being served today both in restaurants and at home. Barbara Rolls and Leann Birch, nutrition professors at Pennsylvania State, have shown that most people, even those who regulate well, will eat more when they are served larger portions.

"There is a strong tendency for people to try to finish all the food on their plates," says Rolls, author of *Volumetrics: Feel Full on Fewer Calories*. When eating out, she suggests asking for small or half-size portions, taking some of the food home, or leaving food on the plate. Or you might order salad along with an appetizer and entrée to share with your dining partner.[49]

When eating is normalized and the young person is attuned to body signals, occasional larger portions should not be a threat. Everyone overeats at times, such as during holidays or at special meals, and in general the body will adjust in the next day or so. But when servings continue to be too large day after day, children as well as adults can get in the habit of eating more than they want or need.

Nutritionists recommend that children serve themselves, or be served smaller portions and allowed to take more if they wish. In the Atlanta stress-free feeding program parents are encouraged to set food on the table family style, and let children take what they want.

One mother, who considered her 5-year-old son an overeater, was reluctant even to try. "I have to serve Jacob. If he filled his own plate, I don't think he would ever stop—he'd just keep right on eating. As it is, he eats every bite I put on his plate—everything."

Finally she had the courage to try, and the next week she came back to class amazed. "You'll never believe it! Jacob is serving himself now, and he puts less on the plate than I did. He seems more satisfied, too."

Coping With Eating Disorders

Parents who are concerned their child has a serious eating problem or eating disorder should consult their family doctor, dietitian or an eating disorder specialist for professional help. The National Eating Disorders Organization (NEDO) advises choosing a therapist with care: "You have the right to choose the gender of your therapist. You have the right to ask to talk with the therapist ahead of time to clarify his or her experience in this area and treatment approach. Listen to your feelings... If you feel you can work well with this person, then make a commitment to treatment."

A teenager may feel uncomfortable talking about her eating with anyone, and refuse to see a professional. Try negotiating, suggests Stephanie Fortin, MA, a Canadian eating disorder specialist, in the *National Eating Disorder Information Centre Bulletin*.[50] Rather than demanding your daughter enter treatment, she says, negotiate slowly, one step at a time, while reassuring her of your concern for her health and well-being.

Once the child is in treatment, the helpful parent will be there to listen, keep communication open, and share in supportive ways, says Fortin. Parents may wonder whether they are too involved or not involved enough. They need to allow their eating-disordered teen to grow up, to do the things others her age are doing. Giving advice and opinions in a respectful manner, as with another adult, will help.

NEDO cautions parents that recovery can take time. "Working through an eating disorder is very difficult, an 'up and down' process." Parents may want to examine their own feelings about weight and food, and work toward self-acceptance and size-acceptance. Modeling healthy behavior means having regular meals and ordinary nondiet foods in the home, and being active for fun and fitness, not appearance. Relapse back to baseline or worse is a recognized pattern, even after seemingly successful treatment. But Fortin cautions that parents are not responsible for making the eating disordered patient well. "The therapist will be responsible for that portion of the recovery process. This does not mean that you ignore the eating disorder altogether: Your support is important."

The therapist can help parents with coping strategies. Don't let the eating disorder take over all of family life. Focus on other interests you share. If family communication has broken down, family therapy may be advised. Recovery may be slow, and parents should not be discouraged by good progress followed by a plateau or setback. This is part of normal recovery. This is hard work, so families can celebrate small improvements.

Fortin offers these tips for parents of eating disordered youth:

- Learn as much as you can about eating disorders. You can be supportive by just learning about the issues your teen will be facing in therapy.
- Focus on health and well being. Avoid commenting on weight or appearance. She/he is already overly focused on it.
- Understand the eating behavior as a coping strategy for dealing with painful emotions and conflicts. Do not blame or shame.
- Encourage discussion of conflicts and concerns. Be ready to help problem-solve and find supportive professional help.
- Be prepared to seek help and support for the entire family. This is a good way to develop mutually respectful coping strategies.
- Youth with eating disorders may benefit from structure in meals. Regard meals as a relaxed time when family mem-

bers can catch up with each other's interests. Do not focus on food, or force or withhold food.

- ★ Avoid power struggles over food. Do not prepare or buy food for the adolescent and other food for the rest of the family.
- ★ When the eating disordered person's behavior affects others, she/he is responsible. Bathrooms and kitchens should be left clean by everyone. Household or shared foods depleted by bingeing should be replaced by the person who binged.
- ★ Take your child to your doctor if you are at all worried about her health. Signs of medical instability can be subtle, and might include dizziness, tingling sensations and blacking out.

One new approach to eating disorder treatment enlists parents in therapy. It doesn't work for all families, particularly if there is enmeshment or other disruptive forces, but when properly trained, parents can monitor and guide the eating process, says Amy Baker Dennis, PhD, an assistant professor at Wayne State University Medical School in Detroit. Parents are with their daughter for hours each day; they intimately know their daughter and her social life. When a truce is called in the battle for control, they can help her solve problems and surmount the hurdles she faces.[51]

The most effective and long-lasting treatment includes some form of psychotherapy or psychological counseling integrated with nutritional and medical care. Many patients respond well to outpatient therapy. For others, inpatient care at a hospital or residential center is needed.

Preventing eating disorders

8 Things Parents Can Do

1. Avoid conveying an attitude about yourself or your children that "I will like you more if you lose weight, eat less, wear a smaller size, eat only 'good' foods." Avoid negative statements about your own body and your own eating.

2. Educate yourself and your children about (a) the genetic basis of differences in body shapes and body weight; and (b) the nature and ugliness of prejudice. Be certain your child understands that weight gain is a normal and necessary part of development, especially during puberty.

3. Scrutinize your child's school for posters, books, contests, which endorse the cultural ideal of thinness. Make sure the school includes images of successful females in the curriculum.

4. Encourage children to ignore body shape as an indicator of anything about personality or value. Phrases like "fat slob," "pig out," and "thunder thighs" should be discouraged. Being teased about body shape is associated with disturbed attitudes about eating.

5. Help your child develop interests and skills that lead to success, personal expression, and fulfillment without emphasis on appearance.

6. Teach children (a) the dangers of trying to alter body shape through dieting; (b) the value of moderate exercise for health, strength, and stamina; and (c) the importance of eating a variety of nutritious foods.

7. Encourage your children to be active and to enjoy what their bodies can do and feel like.

8. Make family meals relaxed and friendly. Refrain from commenting on children's eating, resolving family conflicts at the table, or using food as either punishment or reward.[52]

The revised Practice Guidelines for Treatment of Eating Disorders are available in the January 2000 edition of the *American Journal of Psychiatry.* A wealth of information for parents, coaches and friends in how to help and how to prevent eating disorders is available from the National Eating Disorders Association in Seattle (www.neda.org).

Dads and Daughters is a campaign to help fathers understand and become more involved in their daughters' lives in an effort to prevent body image problems and eating disorders. Headquartered in Duluth, MN, this organization urges fathers to listen to their daughters, focus on what's important (not appearance), give them confidence in valuing their true selves, know and respect their friends, and get involved with their activities and schools. It urges men to: "help make the world a better place for girls by demanding an end to violence against females, media sexualization of girls, advertisers making billions feeding on our daughters' insecurities, pornography, and all 'boys are more important than girls' attitudes."[53]

The Will to Change

As a nation we need to develop the will to change. This can bring us to impacting problems at an earlier stage than is being done today. All kids who eat in dysfunctional ways will benefit greatly from a shift to normalized eating. Specialists consider this critically important if we are to prevent eating disorders. Normalizing eating while your child is at a mild stage of dysfunctional eating is far more successful than waiting for her to develop a level of severe concern. Treating a full-blown eating disorder is difficult, expensive and often unsuccessful.[54]

Numerous forces have contributed to the increases in dysfunctional eating, its engulfing of ever-younger children, and increases in adverse related effects over the past two decades. Reversing this trend will not be easy. It needs to start with parents who understand how severely their own dieting disrupts their children's lives.

Table 15.1 **Moving from Weight-loss Focus to Normalized Eating**[u]

Focus on weight	Focus on health
Restrictive eating	Enjoy a nondiet lifestyle; take pleasure in eating a variety of foods and foods from all 5 food groups
Dieting, counting calories, fat grams	Think of food as a friend—celebrate, enjoy, taste, savor
Rules, rigidity, control, stress, eating guilt	Tailor taste toward moderate fat, sugar intake; make gradual changes
"Good" foods, "bad" foods thinking	All foods can fit; there are no "good" or "bad" foods
Disturbed and dysfunctional eating	Listen to your body: eat when hungry, stop when full
Eating disorders	Meet your body's energy and nutrient needs
Yo-yo-ing weight (weight cycling)	Maintaining a natural, stable weight is worthwhile
Food is the enemy; willpower needed	Eat at regular times, typically three meals and one or two snacks
False hopes, failure, disillusion	Trust your body to make up for mistakes over time
Hazardous diet products, diet books, diet foods, scales	Enjoy home cooking, eating with friends and family

Chapter 16

♦ ♦ ❖ ♦ ♦ ❖ ♦ ♦ ❖ ♦ ♦ ❖ ♦ ♦ ❖ ♦ ♦ ❖ ♦ ♦

The Basics of Good Nutrition

Healthy food choices help children and teens grow, develop, do well in school, and feel at their best. They prevent child and adolescent problems such as obesity, eating disorders, dental cavities, and iron deficiency anemia, and may prevent health problems later in life. Health choices nourish both body and the spirit. Establishing positive eating habits and the enjoyment of nutritious eating in childhood is critical to long-term health.

When your child sits down to three meals a day, and you put food on the table from the five food groups with trust that your family will enjoy it, good nutrition just naturally follows. You can relax about it.

Add Foods, Don't Take Away

To improve your child's nutrition, focus on the positive aspects—adding fuel foods that will make eating more nutritious and give the child more energy. "This way people are less likely to feel deprived and are more likely to make changes." Cindy Byfield Darrow, a dietitian who worked many years in a clinical setting with overweight heart patients.[55]

Hints For Parents

In their brochure *A Parent's Guide to Children's Weight,* Carol Hans and Diane Nelson of the Iowa State University Extension Service offer these suggestions for parents in helping children make healthy food choices:

- ★ Be enthusiastic about eating a variety of foods. Help children learn what foods are in the different food groups and why it's important to eat some of each group daily.
- ★ Introduce new foods gradually. Offer the child a small portion but do not force the child to eat it. Tasting will come more readily as the food becomes more familiar.
- ★ Serve realistic portions. The appropriate serving size depends on the child's age and size. One possible guideline is to offer one tablespoon of meat, fruit and vegetable per year of age up to age five. Physical activity and growth spurts also influence appetite. Plan meals to include some lower calorie food items that can be offered for second helpings.
- ★ Buy fewer high-calorie, low-nutrient foods. Encourage children to think of such foods as occasional treats, not regular fare. Involve children in planning, shopping, and label-reading.[56]

Hans and Nelson caution parents that children grow at different rates and may have very different body structures from their own brothers and sisters. Parents confused about how to feed their families nutritionally and within their means can get sound assistance from their county extension service.

Nancy and Jim signed up for the Idaho Food and Nutrition Program (IFNP), concerned about their eight-year-old daughter Jennifer's weight problems. The IFNP advisor learned that Nancy and Jim both worked at grocery stores in their town. They often were so tired after work that they picked up dinner at the local deli. This habit was taking a big chunk of their paychecks, and their deli choices were high in calories and fat. They also brought home outdated "free" potato chips.

After taking the IFNP lessons Nancy and Jim learned to plan ahead with easy menus. They shopped once a week to have on hand what they needed, which made the evening meal easier to prepare at home. With home cooking they could control the calorie and fat content and the cost of the meal. They learned the chips were for them "false economy" because they were high in fat, sodium and calories they didn't need. The nutrition advisor shared ideas on how they could enjoy relaxed non-critical family meals with Jennifer.

Together they came up with these ideas: 1) prepare only as much food as they need; 2) involve the entire family in fun sports; and 3) involve the entire family in growing a garden. When the family finished the program they were working hard on their goals. So far they have had good success with their garden and family activities. Jennifer has grown taller without gaining weight.[57]

Balance, Variety, and Moderation

Balance, variety, and moderation are the guiding principles of good nutrition. Balance ensures that a young person gets enough fuel food for growth, energy and health from all five groups of the food pyramid—bread and grains, fruits, vegetables, meat, and milk. Variety means choosing many different foods from these basic groups to get the more than 50 essential nutrients. Eating moderately avoids the extremes. It means children eat until their stomachs feel just right—not too much or not too little.

Pyramid Power

The Food Guide Pyramid from the latest Dietary Guidelines for Americans shown here and on many food packages helps us visualize the five groups: bread and cereals, vegetables, fruits, meat, and milk.

Unfortunately, today's teens come up short in many areas. Kids in general are consuming more added sugar, more soft drinks, less milk, and fewer eggs and cuts of beef and pork. Their diets continue low in vegetables and fruit. Some eat no fruit at all.

Teenage girls especially lack healthy nutrition. Only about one-fourth of girls are getting the required minimum in four of the food groups. In the fifth, bread and cereals, half of teen girls achieve the minimum. (See Chapter 6 for more on the unhealthy ways children are eating today.)

Helping your child eat nutritiously is easy when you offer all the five food groups, or as many as you can, at each meal. This doesn't mean your child will eat some of everything you set on the table. She probably won't. Be patient. Be flexible. Trust that over time your child will eat a nutritious diet. She wants to eat, and she wants variety. She can balance out needed foods over several days.

The pyramid gives a range of servings for each food group. The range does not suggest an upper limit, as some people think, but recommended amounts for people of different ages, sizes and activity levels, according to the national Healthy Eating Index.[58]

For example, teen girls are advised to eat:

- ★ 9 servings of bread and cereals
- ★ 7 servings of fruit and vegetables
- ★ 6 ounces of meat, poultry or fish (or its equivalent in dry beans, eggs and nuts).

Teen boys are advised to eat:

- ★ 11 servings of bread and cereals
- ★ 9 servings of fruit and vegetables
- ★ 9 ounces of meat, poultry or fish (or its equivalent in dry beans, eggs and nuts).

In general, the lowest number given is about right for sedentary women and older people, depending on their calorie intake. The top number is advised for teenage boys, many active men and some very active women. In between is the amount suggested for most children, teenage girls, active women, and sedentary men. (Preschool children need the same variety of foods as older children, but a serving is about two-thirds in size.)

The number of servings depends on calorie needs. The Healthy Eating Index recommends an intake of about:

- ★ 1,800 calories for children age 4
- ★ 2,000 calories for children age 7-10
- ★ 2,200 calories for girls age 11-18
- ★ 2,500 calories for boys ages 11-14
- ★ 3,000 calories for boys ages 15-18

FIGURE 16.1. **Food pyramid and serving size information**[v]

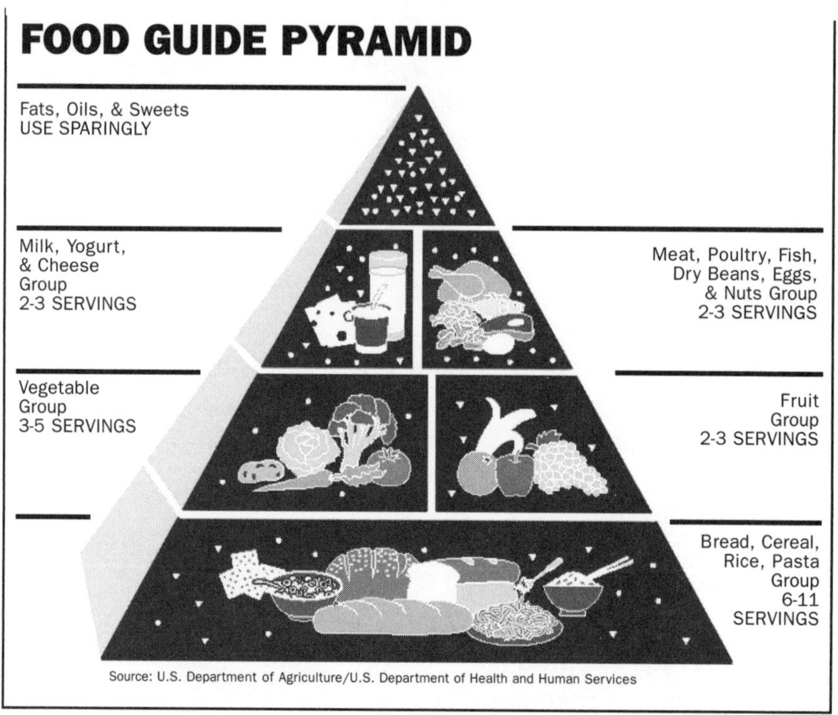

The dairy group is an exception. In this group the needed servings are based on age, not calories, and are increased during pregnancy and breastfeeding. Children need 2, and teenagers 3 servings a day.

Since pyramid serving sizes are generally smaller than the portions most people eat, a teenage boy often eats two or three servings of a food during a meal. Servings given in each group are sufficient for most children's needs, but some may eat more to fulfill their calorie needs. Others get their calorie quota all too quickly by pulling down more calorie-dense foods from the tip of the pyramid. These foods can fill them up quickly before they get the nutrients they need from the 5 food groups.

Nutrient-dense "fuel" foods should be selected most often from the five groups. These are foods high in nutrients and low in calories, fat, and added sugars. Many are bulky, high in fiber, and filling, such as apples, corn, beans and cereals. Others pack a lot of nutrition into small size and are very satisfying, such as eggs, fish and lean meat.

Help your children fit the foods they eat on the food pyramid. Pinning a food pyramid up on the kitchen bulletin board or refrigerator and using it often will help them understand how to balance their eating.

Bread and Cereals

Bread has long been known as the staff of life, and that's why grains—breads, cereals, rice, pasta—make up the foundation for healthy eating at the broad base of the food pyramid. They are good foods to fill up on.

Foods in the bread and cereals group provide complex carbohydrates and are an important source of the calories, vitamins, minerals and fiber we need every day. Eating a variety of grains is advised, including some whole grains. Whole grain foods include whole-wheat bread, bran cereals, oatmeal and brown rice. They contain the entire grain kernel, unlike refined grains in which the bran and germ are removed. Some refined grains, including all-purpose flour used in white bread and cereals, are enriched with B vitamins and iron.

Eating some whole grain foods every day is helpful because they are high in fiber—and most young people need much more fiber than they are getting. But don't take this to extremes. Too much fiber can cause digestive problems and interfere with iron and zinc absorption. Most grain products are low in fat unless fat is added in processing, cooking, or at the table. For instance, bread and bagels are low in fat, while cookies, cakes and pastries tend to be high in both fat and sugars.

The guidelines recommend eating at least 6 to 11 servings from the bread and cereals group, depending on calorie needs. For teen girls, 9 servings are recommended as a minimum, for teen boys, 11 servings. About half of girls and three-fourths of boys meet the basic minimum of 6 servings, but fewer meet the higher minimum based on their calorie needs.

Vegetables and Fruit

In looking at improving child nutrition, a good place to start is with those five-a-day fruits and vegetables—and no need to stop with five. Most Americans eat less. Teenagers actually need 7 to 9.

Include all kinds, the cancer-protective vegetables from the cabbage and broccoli family, deep-yellow and dark-green leafy, starchy potatoes, corn and beans. Add two or more servings of fruit, including citrus fruits. (Recommended minimums are 3 to 5 servings of vegetables and 2 to 4 of fruits.)

Only about one-third of teenage girls and half of boys meet the bare minimum of 3 servings of vegetables. And only about one-fourth are eating as much as 2 fruit servings. Over half eat less than one serving of fruit a day.

Five a day isn't much. It's only a small glass of orange juice with breakfast, an apple at lunch, and a salad, green beans and mashed potatoes for dinner. Even without snacks it should be easy. For teens, 7 to 9 servings is better. Try to include them at every meal.

Fruits and vegetables are excellent sources of many nutrients—vitamins, minerals, carotenoids, antioxidants, phytochemicals, protein, starch and fiber. People whose diets are high in fruits and vegetables appear to have lower risk for heart disease, diabetes, and certain types of cancers.

Choose a rainbow of colors in both fruits and vegetables, and offer them fresh, canned or frozen. Choose nutrient-packed dark greens and deep-yellows—green beans, corn, green peas, lima beans—and cancer-fighting vegetables from the cabbage family—cabbage, broccoli, cauliflower. Help your children enjoy less familiar vegetables and fruits occasionally. Not only do many children not eat enough, but they may eat only two or three kinds of vegetables and fruits. Yet it is from eating a variety that they get the many different nutrients they need.

Milk, Yogurt, and Cheese

Milk and milk products like cheese, yogurt, puddings and ice cream provide us with our best source of calcium for strong bones and teeth, as well as eight other essential nutrients. Other compounds found in milk fat such as conjugated linoleic acid (CLA), sphingomyelin and vitamin D may have anti-cancer effects as well.[59] Fat free or low-fat milk products are low in calories and satisfying. (Minimum 2 to 3 servings.)

Today's preteens and teenagers don't drink enough milk, falling far short of the recommended three daily servings of dairy products. (Cheese accounts for more than one-third of their intake.) Only half of teen boys and one-fourth of girls consume as much as 2 servings; 40 percent of girls get less than one.

Thus calcium intake declines at the very time it is urgently needed to build strong bones, especially for girls. During adolescence is when young bones are growing fast. Fifteen percent of adult height is added during this time, so it's important to get plenty of calcium-rich foods every day. Bones grow and develop only until about age 25, and after that bone mass begins to decline. Girls who fail to drink milk, and are thin, or often dieting, may never develop the strong bones they need to protect them from stress fractures and osteoporosis.

Recently there is evidence that milk, cheese and yogurt may play a critical role in preventing overweight. Children with a diet rich in calcium from dairy foods have lower body fat than children with lower dairy calcium intakes.[60] In another study it was found that diets high in low-fat dairy foods cause fat cells to make less fat and turn on the machinery to break down fat. These diets were associated with lower risk of obesity.[61]

For lactose-intolerant problems, try serving small amounts milk during meals, lactose-reduced milk, buttermilk and yogurt.

Meat and Alternates Group

Foods in the high-protein meat and meat alternates group pack a great deal of nutrition into a small package. Eating at least small amounts of meat, especially beef, provides many nutritional benefits in high-quality protein, easily-absorbable iron and zinc, and vitamin B_{12}, which is only available in animal foods. The Bogalusa Heart studies in Louisiana found that children who eat more meat are less likely to have nutrient deficiencies than children who eat little or no meat. Heme iron from animal sources in this group helps a child's growing body better absorb the non-heme iron from plant sources.

The Food Guide Pyramid suggests that children and teens eat at least two or three servings a day from this group, equivalent to 5 to

7 ounces of cooked lean meat, poultry or fish. Count 2 to 3 ounces of cooked lean meat, poultry or fish as one serving. That's about half a chicken breast, an average hamburger, or two eggs. Remember that it takes one-third cup of peanut butter, or one and a half cups baked beans or tofu to equal one 3-ounce serving of meat. So the youngster who chooses not to eat meat needs to double these amounts to get in their two servings each day.

Lean meat is not fattening, as many teenage girls fear. Rather it improves weight loss. In a recent study at the University of Illinois, including 9 to 10 ounces of meat each day helped dieters lose more body fat than a control group on a diet with less meat, and they maintained twice as much lean muscle. "Muscle helps burn calories, but is often compromised during weight loss," said Donald K. Layman, professor in the College of Medicine, UI, who conducted the study.[62]

This entire group, both animal- and plant-based, is being neglected, especially by girls. Only about one-fourth of teenage girls and half of boys meet the minimum (equal to 5 ounces of meat) from this group. Three-fourths of teenage girls fail to get what they need. They especially lack the high quality protein needed for healthy growth from animal sources, and the high-quality, absorbable heme iron and zinc from the same foods.

Iron deficiency anemia is one of the most common deficiencies for girls and women in the United States and worldwide. Signs are fatigue, pale skin, headache, weakness, lack of concentration, irritability and susceptibility to illness.

Annette, a distance runner, stopped eating meat as a college freshman when she discovered half of her teammates did not eat meat and were dieting. A senior told her that lean runners have an advantage. Keeping calories under 1200 a day and avoiding meat kept her thin, she said. When Annette began losing her edge, the coach took her aside and asked what her problem was.

"I just feel weak and dizzy. It seems like I can't run five miles anymore," she confessed. "Maybe I'm not good enough for college running."

"What are you eating?" her coach demanded. When he found out, he seemed angry. "You're an athlete—and athletes need to fuel

their bodies! Stop dieting. Go back to eating hamburgers, and all those foods you ate when you were winning races in high school."

She did, and was surprised how much better she felt. She began running better and enjoying it again. When two teammates asked for help, she told them that eating well worked for her.

Top of the Pyramid Adds Fat and Sugars

At the tip of the pyramid are the empty-calorie foods that add little if anything in the way of nutrition: sugars, fats, oils, soft drinks, and alcohol (illegal for underage youth). It's easy to consume so much of these that they crowd out nutrient-dense foods. It's better to eat them less often and in smaller quantities.

Many kinds of sugars and syrups, fats and oils, are added to foods in processing or preparation, especially snack and dessert foods. Candy, cake, ice cream and cookies are major sources of added sugars. But soft drinks now top them all as the number one source of added sugars. Drinking more milk and water, and less soda and fruitade drinks will quickly improve the diets of many youth.

Unfortunately, trends today are for kids to eat more and more processed high-fat, high-sugar snack foods, crackers, desserts, candy and soft drinks, and less fruits and vegetables, less milk, less meat and eggs than even 15 or 20 years ago.

Most children need to cut down on sugar. (See Chapter 6 for their current sugar intake.) Sugars add empty calories, displace other foods, and when eaten to excess, seem to dull the taste and discourage eating a variety of fruits and vegetables. Research shows that youngsters eating high-sugar diets are less likely to get the vitamins, minerals and variety they need.

The Food Guide urges Americans to limit added sugars to:

⋆ 6 teaspoons a day if they eat about 1,600 calories

⋆ 12 teaspoons a day for 2,200 calories

⋆ 18 teaspoons a day for 2,800 calories.

The lower percent in the minimal 1,600-calorie diet reflects the difficulty of getting in all needed nutrients in a diet this low. There's little room for added frills like sugar and fat. Yet many teen girls eat many fewer calories than this.

The problem for many kids is not so much what they eat as what they *don't* eat. They fill up on empty-calorie foods, and there's no room left for enough food from the five food groups. Further, evidence suggests that a sedentary lifestyle along with a diet high in sugars and fat may be a triple threat leading to obesity. Yet, humans have an innate taste for sugar and fat, likely as a survival trait. Of course, it's okay to eat moderately of both in the context of active living and a healthy diet. Children benefit from eating some fat and sugar, and under age 2 require a high-fat diet.

Good Foods, Bad Foods

When learning to make food choices, children can be taught that there are no good foods or bad foods. We can eat what we want, and it's okay. All foods can fit in a wholesome and varied eating plan. The idea that some foods are healthy and others unhealthy suggests that some foods can be used for medicine, while others are toxic and disease producing. This is false and unscientific, although this notion is often promoted in the press, and even by health professionals who have an axe to grind or fail to understand nutrition.

While a balanced diet will usually be moderately low in fat and sugars, there's nothing wrong with including some high-fat, high-sugar foods in an overall nutritious diet.

People often refer to snack foods as junk foods, but it's better to take the approach that there are no *junk foods*—but there are *junk diets*. It's not specific tip-of-the-pyramid foods but a diet filled with them, and omitting essential foods, that causes problems.

Foods eaten as close as possible to their natural state are usually the healthiest choices. They tend to have less added fats, sugars, salt and preservatives, and more fiber than highly processed foods. For example, nutrition is usually improved by choosing a baked potato over potato chips, a slice of roast beef over sandwich salami, and an apple over apple crisp. And they cost less, too. On the other hand, processed foods can be just what is needed for a busy day or occasional treats.

Food Pyramid Makes Sense

Disease-based nutrition has from time to time challenged the USDA Food Guide Pyramid and its nutrition recommendations. Various experts have drawn other pyramids and generated excitement for a time over the Mediterranean, Asian, vegetarian, high carbohydrate and high protein diets. Some have fashioned new pyramids featuring such items as whole grain foods or banning white flour and sugar.

Nevertheless, the health benefits of the USDA Pyramid recommendations are well known. They have stood the test of time. For over 60 years the Dietary Guidelines for Americans have provided a science-based foundation of good nutrition, with very few changes. During this time, they have helped three generations of Americans become among the strongest, tallest, healthiest and longest-lived people in the world.

The pyramid works for Americans. While other nutrition recommendations may be appropriate with other populations, where traditions and available foods differ, it makes sense to feed children everywhere for good health, growth, strength and energy. The benefits are numerous and proven many times over.

Fat in Moderation

It is quite clear that excess fat in the diet should be avoided. The Dietary Guidelines emphasize the continued importance of choosing a diet with less total fat, saturated fat, and cholesterol. Fat converts easily into body fat, and at 9 calories per gram, it's more than twice as high in calories as protein and carbohydrate (both 4 calories per gram). When fewer calories come from fat, there's more room for healthy food choices.

However, America has sadly overreacted to the low-fat message. Some dietary fat is needed for good health. Fat is not a four-letter word. It's an important nutrient that helps cells use vitamins and minerals more effectively. It also enhances the flavor, texture and appearance of foods. Certain fats may also protect against disease.

Babies need a high-fat diet until at least age two because of their tremendous growth needs. These needs continue throughout childhood, so the transition to low-fat should be gradual. Canada advises a gradual transition that extends through the entire growth period until adult height is reached, before a lower-fat adult diet is recommended.

The Dietary Guidelines advise cutting dietary fat to 30 percent of total calories. However, many nutritionists have long considered up to 35 percent more reasonable, especially for children. This is supported by the new guidelines released in the fall of 2002, by the National Academy's Institute of Medicine Food and Nutrition Board, a private, nonprofit organization that has been responsible for the development of the Recommended Daily Allowances in the United States for the past 60 years. The new Dietary Reference Intakes (RDIs) support a wider range for fat intake, from 20 to 35 percent of total calories.[63]

One fat that apparently has no redeeming qualities is *trans*-fatty acid, produced in partially hydrogenated vegetable oils, such as solid shortening and margarine. Found in many processed and deep-fat-fried foods, it appears to increase low-density lipoprotein cholesterol and increase the risk of heart disease.

Studies show monosaturated and polyunsaturated fatty acids are beneficial fats that reduce blood cholesterol and lower heart disease risk. Limiting saturated fats from animal foods is advised. Yet it is animal fats that almost exclusively provide conjugated linolic acid (CLA), one of the most potent natural anticarcinogens ever identified.[64] More recently, CLA also has been found beneficial in lowering blood sugar levels, possibly benefiting diabetes, reducing leptin, and increasing weight loss in studies at Ohio State University.[65] Higher levels of this fatty acid, which comes primarily from beef, lamb and milk fat, means lower levels of leptin, a hormone thought to regulate fat levels. Cutting out animal foods and using only fat-free products from the milk group can deprive children of the protective benefits they get from CLA.

The Importance of a Healthy Breakfast

Begin the day with a breakfast that includes sufficient protein to keep the child energized until lunch. Students who eat breakfast perform better in school. They have increased problem-solving ability, recall, memory, verbal fluency, and creativity and are less likely to be absent, reports the American Dietetic Association in a review of the scientific literature.[66] They are more attentive in the classroom. Hungry children are more likely to have behavioral, emotional, and academic problems at school, according to the Centers for Disease Control and Prevention.

Many teenage girls believe skipping breakfast will help them lose weight. It doesn't work that way. Studies show kids who eat breakfast have better overall nutrition, eat fewer calories and less fat through the day, and indulge in less impulsive snacking.[67]

A typical child's breakfast consists of a bowl of cereal and toast with jelly and juice. To improve it, add some protein for staying power. Adding cheese or peanut butter, a boiled egg or slice of left-over roast beef or hamburger adds the protein that will satisfy him the four hours till lunch. It's a good idea, too, to include some fiber via bran cereal, whole wheat toast, a bran muffin, or an orange.

Mary Friesz, PhD, RD, in *Food, Fun n' Fitness: Designing Healthy Lifestyles for Our Children* recommends skipping the sugary, brightly-dyed breakfast foods.[68] It's better to buy plain corn, oats, rice or wheat cereals and dress them up with slices of fresh fruit. Cheerios, the plain, slightly sweet oat cereal, is still the number one choice for children, according to Don Voorhees, author of *Why Does Popcorn Pop?* Or better yet, go with cooked oatmeal—and other foods in their least processed state.

Foods that Satisfy Hunger

Some foods have a larger effect on satiety than others, so we feel full and stop eating sooner. Foods that are naturally high in water are highly satisfying. Fruits, vegetables, low-fat milk and cooked grains, and prepared foods like soup, stews, casseroles, pasta with vegetables, and fruit-based desserts fill the stomach quicker than dry, dense foods like crackers, chips, or cookies.

"The surprising thing is that a lower-calorie portion of food will satisfy you as much as a higher-calorie portion," says Barbara Rolls, PhD, a Pennsylvania State University nutrition professor who has researched weight issues and why people eat as they do for over twenty years. Her research shows that people tend to eat about the same weight and volume of food every day, regardless of how calorie-dense it is.[69]

Water is helpful because it dilutes the calories in a given amount of food, says Rolls. But just drinking water doesn't work—it needs to be incorporated within the food, so it digests more slowly. Water is only one of many food elements that affect satiety. Adding fiber provides filling bulk without adding many calories. Even air adds volume, as in popcorn and whipped desserts.

In her book *Volumetrics*, written with Robert A. Barnett, Rolls advocates strategically increasing water and fiber by adding fruit to cereal and extra vegetables to casseroles. "When you add water-rich blueberries to your breakfast cereal, or water-rich eggplant to your lasagna, you add food volume but few calories. You can eat more for the same calories."

High protein foods are also highly satisfying. Lean meat, poultry, fish, eggs and beans decrease hunger and prolong satiety. The new Dietary Reference Intakes (RDIs) support higher protein intake—from 10 to 35 percent of total calories, compared with the 12 to 15 percent of calories previously recommended—based on new information about chronic disease risk.[70] Some individuals need more protein and feel better with higher intake. Higher protein intake helps to preserve muscle mass, and research shows that protein, even in excess, is not stored as fat, unlike fat and carbohydrate. If we take in more protein than needed, the extra calories are essentially burned off as heat.[71]

Good Taste Matters

If your family seems to eat excess fat or sugar, consider how you can make gradual changes to tailor everyone's tastes toward healthier eating. Reducing fat can be done more easily if we bring less fat into the house, add less fat in cooking, and use less table fat. In eating out, avoid frequent eating of deep fat fried foods. Don't attempt sudden change, because it takes time to adjust taste preferences.

For example, begin spreading half as much butter on the toast. You may find you can better appreciate the subtle differences in taste, texture and flavor of the toast not buttered so heavily. After a few months, when your family is used to this, again cut the butter or margarine in half. If you reach a point where taste diminishes, it's time to stop and return to good taste.

Eating too much fat and too much sugar leaves the mouth with a heavy, creamy feel and lingering strong sweetness that overpowers other flavors, tastes and textures. When children become accustomed to this kind of eating, they may prefer it and come to dislike other foods, especially vegetables and fruits with their distinctive flavors.

Changing taste preferences takes time and patience. It's better to avoid such problems by helping your children enjoy a wide variety of foods from the time they are young. Yet preferences can change.

Fast Food

There's no need to ban fast food. Food eaten at a fast food chain or family restaurant can be part of your child's balanced diet.

Fast food restaurants offer nutritious food that's low or moderate in calories and fat. You can order a chefs salad with julienne ham, garden salads, yogurt with fruit parfaits, a medium hamburger (patted with a napkin if greasy) stacked on the bun with lettuce, onion and tomato, a baked potato piled with broccoli and topped with cheese—and hold the sauces or add them yourself and use sparingly.

However, studies show the average fast food meal contains about 1,200 calories, and is usually high in fat, cholesterol and sodium, according to Lincoln University of Missouri Cooperative Extension. Lower-fat, lower-calorie alternatives recommended by Missouri Extension include:

TABLE 16.2 **Healthy Fast Food Options**[w]

Calories	Fat	(grams)
Wendy's grilled chicken salad, with fat free or reduced fat dressing	190	8
Wendy's grilled chicken sandwich	300	8
Wendy's small chili	227	7
Wendy's sour cream and chive potato	370	5
McDonalds grilled chicken Caesar salad, with fat free or reduced fat dressing	100	2.5
Burger King BK broiler, without mayo	390	8
Burger King BK broiler, with mayo	550	25
Burger King Whopper Jr., without mayo or cheese	350	16

The Vegetarian Alternative

When teenagers choose a vegetarian eating style, it is natural that parents may have concerns. At the same time, they need to keep in mind the basic principle that children are responsible for deciding what and how much they will eat. Parents need to respect these decisions, while guiding children toward healthy choices by having a variety of good-tasting foods available, from both plant and animal sources.

Not all vegetarians eat in the same way. Semi-vegetarians base their usual eating on plant source foods, occasionally eating meat, poultry or fish. Some vegetarians eat no meat, poultry or fish, but eat dairy foods and eggs. Vegans are most restrictive and eat no animal products at all, even foods containing milk or eggs.

When parents choose vegetarian diets for their children, it's important to remember that the more restrictive vegan diets are not recommended for children and teens who are still growing. It is possible to plan a diet entirely of plant foods that supplies most nutrient needs, but such a diet is so bulky that experts say it is unlikely a young child would eat enough calories, so growth may be stunted.[73]

For vegetarians who consume dairy foods and eggs, planning a healthy diet can be much like that for non-vegetarians. As with any kind of eating, choose a balance of foods from all 5 food groups in variety, and eat them in moderation—remembering that moderation means eating sufficient fat and calories, as well as not overeating. To improve iron absorption, encourage plenty of plants containing iron, such as legumes and dark-green leafy vegetables, and include a food rich in vitamin C, such citrus fruit, at each meal. You'll want to consider a reliable source of vitamin B_{12}, an essential vitamin missing in plant foods. Other nutrients that need special attention for these diets are protein, vitamin D, calcium and zinc. A science-based vegetarian cookbook written by a registered dietitian can be helpful.

A common error for new vegetarians is to incorrectly replace meat with foods from other groups. Beans, tofu, soymilk, eggs, and nuts are in the meat and alternates group, and should be consumed every day in equivalent amounts.

Vegetarian eating can supply a teenager with the nutrients needed to build, maintain, and repair body tissues, and keep the immune system functioning well, but it's difficult when other foods are restricted as well. As noted elsewhere, vegetarianism can be a marker for an eating disorder, so parents need to be aware of what is going on. The important thing is for youngsters to keep well-nourished and to fit normal eating into their lifestyle for own good health and well-being. Common sense is always the best guide.

If you have concerns, consult a dietitian. Supplements may be an option for vegetarians, remembering that they do not substitute for real food.

Supplements

Parents who want to give children supplements should choose a simple multivitamin that provides levels no higher than 100 percent of the recommended daily allowance (RDA), and from a company for which ingredients are regulated and reported fully on the label. Larger amounts of vitamins and minerals over 100 percent can be harmful.

Herbal supplements have appeal because they are "natural," which many people assume means safe and healthy. However, they may not be safe for children. There are almost no federal standards for herbal supplements. So even if they "work," they vary tremendously in potency, ingredients, quality, and whether there may be contamination.

Most children who regularly eat a healthy, balanced diet will not need supplements. They'll have the many nutrients they need in balance and variety. If they are not fully nourished, then improving food choices is the place to start. Parents need to be clear that a poor diet with supplements is still a poor diet.

Real food is better than supplements for at least three reasons. First, it works better: nutrients from food are nearly always absorbed better by the body. Second, it has wider benefits: each food contains many nutrients, some we may not even be aware of yet, such as the 100 or more phytochemicals in some vegetables that appear to be effective against cancer and possibly heart disease. Third, it's safer: the nutrients from food are in natural balance, so we are not in danger of overdosing or risking toxic effects. Besides, real food tastes better.

Weight Loss Options

Going on a weight loss program is an option that a child may choose, or a parent may choose for the child. Many weight loss methods are available, and many are promoted by various experts. But not many allow the child to continue eating normally, attuned to hunger and satiety, along with continuing regular pleasurable physical activity.

True nondiet, healthy lifestyle programs do this. If you and your child have come this far in establishing these two critically important habits—normal eating and active living—and then have taken the third step of ensuring that she is fully nourished, you've achieved a great deal. Over time, this healthy lifestyle in itself can result in the desired weight loss, or stabilizing weight till she grows into it.

Consider following the Healthy Weight Kids seven-step program explained in Chapter 20. This is a plan for helping children and teens normalize their lives and develop a healthy, happy, diet-free lifestyle that fits into the big picture of total wellness in their lives. Based on gradual habit change, it promotes self-esteem, self-acceptance, stress reduction, the ability to communicate, and enjoying positive relationships.

The way to succeed in weight loss is:

- Establish or maintain normal eating. Help your child become attuned to hunger and satiety, to eat when hungry and stop when full, rather than trying to eat less.

- ⋆ Increase or maintain physical activity and reduce sedentary activity. Children and teens should be active at least an hour a day. If your child is not in an organized sports program this may be a good time to join an after-school sport that includes regular training and competitions.
- ⋆ Establish or maintain full nutrition. All children need to be eating at least the recommended amounts from all five food groups of the pyramid. Consider increasing lean meat over minimums.
- ⋆ Learn about calorie density and what foods satisfy most. Follow the principles of lowering density and increasing volume by adding water, fiber, fruits and vegetables. High-quality protein such as meat adds satiety.
- ⋆ Tailor tastes gradually. Help your child shift toward an enjoyment of foods lower in fat and sugar, and rich in fiber, fruits and vegetables.
- ⋆ Make small changes, step by step, that the child accepts well and can live with on a long-term basis. This is the way to ensure that lost pounds stay off, and to avoid bingeing.
- ⋆ Decide to wait and see what happens. Don't set weight goals. Each individual responds differently to shifts in activity and calorie intake.
- ⋆ Slow weight loss is preferable, not more than a pound or so a month. Fast weight loss just sends the body into a defensive state.

For further guidance consult a dietitian or health professional who uses a nondiet health at any size approach for youth.

Chapter 17

♦ ♦ ❖ ♦ ♦ ❖ ♦ ♦ ❖ ♦ ♦ ❖ ♦ ♦ ❖ ♦ ♦ ❖ ♦ ♦

What Schools Can Do

Fresh strawberries are a big favorite in Princeton, Ohio, where students "are begging us for more," says Linda Bass-Wiley, a dietitian for the school district. "They also love clementines and blood oranges."[74]

On a February day when snow delayed school opening two hours at Muscatine High School in Iowa, the question students asked as they arrived was not about delayed class or sports schedules, but whether they'd get their morning snack. "All they wanted to know was, 'When are we going to get our fruit today?'" said Muscatine principal Dennis Heiman.

Both schools are part of a U.S. Department of Agriculture (USDA) pilot program that provides fruit and vegetable snacks for 65,000 students in five states. At a time when nutrition surveys show that three out of four American youths fail to eat the minimum five servings a day, the agency is looking for ways to improve eating habits as well as to prevent childhood overweight. The $6 million program is testing whether offering healthful snacks—baby carrots, star fruit, dried plums, fruit smoothies and even broccoli and cauliflower—means students will eat them.

They will, it seems. Since fruit and vegetable snacks were introduced at Muscatine High, sales of candy, snacks and soda have dropped 25 percent. The drop prompted school officials to get rid of a candy machine and to replace a soda machine with one dispensing milk.

No More Candy Sales

Some schools have banned the popular candy sales—traditionally easy moneymakers for student organizations. At first there may be complaints—in Oakland, administrators said junior prom ticket prices went up because students could no longer sell candy to fund the prom. But such complaints usually disappear when students discover the benefits of healthier options.

Healthy food sales during recess are a moneymaking project of the student government at Horace Mann Elementary School in Southeast Glendale, Califorina. Students wash apples and organize food items into plastic bins.

"We're trying to establish healthy patterns and encourage them to look for things like sugar and fat content," said Principal Kim Bishop.

The bins contain granola bars, applesauce, crackers, fat-free string cheese, yogurt-covered raisins and bananas. Each snack sells for 50 cents. Profits will go toward annual class trips to places like Six Flags, California missions or whale-watching trips.

Students line up for the snacks and don't seem to mind at all the lack of sugary candies, soda or cookies. It's a typical snack break, but with much lower fat and sugar content.[75]

Federal Program Brings Fresh Fruit Snacks

In the USDA pilot program, federal grant funds provide $89 to $152 per student to buy fruit and vegetables snacks for the academic year. Each school makes its own purchases. One hundred schools are in the pilot program—in Indiana, Iowa, Ohio, Michigan, and on the Zuni Indian reservation in New Mexico, where the problems of overweight and obesity have hit particularly hard.

It aims at giving schools a new way to improve nutrition, while reducing student demand for the high-calorie snack foods and sweetened beverages that have become standard vending machine fare in many schools. The program "has made kids aware of different eating options," Heiman said. "It's been a real eye-opener. Some kids have never had a tangerine before. And it's actually become somewhat of a biology lesson. If the bananas are too green, then we say, 'Let's put them in a paper bag and tomorrow they will be okay.'"

Among fruit and vegetables served are raisins, grapes, dried cherries, caramelized apples, star fruit, dried banana chips, baby carrots and fat-free ranch dressing. Snack boxes are distributed to classrooms, where students eat the snacks while watching Channel One, which broadcasts news-oriented programs to schools.

Students are enthusiastic. April Beason, a 16-year-old junior, praised the program. "It's pretty neat…Instead of having junk food and stuff, I eat the snack."

At Summit Country School, a kindergarten through grade 12 private school in Cincinnati, students are greeted every morning with huge trays of fresh strawberries, pineapple, cantaloupe, kiwis or honeydew melon. At 2 p.m., carts of vegetables and dips are in the halls as students change classes. Fewer kids are eating desserts and French fries at lunch. When and how schools serve the fruits and vegetables is up to them.

"Everyone seems to be eating healthier," says Melissa Geers, head of the school's food service.

In another positive outcome, teachers see evidence the program may help parents successfully introduce more fruit and vegetables at home.

As federal grants end, the USDA is asking Congress to fund the program nationally. Meanwhile pilot schools are looking for ways to continue the healthy snacks. With enthusiastic students, parents, teachers and administrators behind the program, it seems likely they will find a way.

Civilizing the Lunchroom

Some schools are trying to teach students better ways to eat lunch. In Pennsylvania, school teams are formulating a comprehensive nutrition and activity program. A focal point is lunch environment, finding ways to change the commotion that is a typical school lunch—kids waiting in long lines and hasty meals left half-eaten. A quieter, calmer environment does make a difference, they find.[76]

Haverford township schools are replacing long tables with round ones that encourage conversation. Sixth graders can opt for Literary Lunch Club, where about a dozen eat in the quiet of the library two or three times a week while librarian Sue Kratzinger reads a novel aloud over several weeks. "It gives them a little break from being in a noisy, crowded lunchroom," she says.

"We shove kids in lunchrooms, feed them as quickly as we can, and we don't care what they learn," charges Karen Evans Stout, an associate professor of education policy at Lehigh University and one of those leading the call for change. "It's this wasted half-hour. We don't use that time to teach a thing about sitting and eating and talking."

Stout has studied more than 2,000 lunch periods, including in Europe, where the midday student lunch can run as long as 90 minutes. "Teachers sat down with kids. There was an emphasis on how to behave, how to have a conversation… Lunches were more humane." She advocates 25 minutes of actual table time close to noon.

First grade teacher Harriet Horton at Marshall Street Elementary School in Norristown, Pa, is choosing to eat a tossed salad among her charges rather than retreat to the calm of the faculty lounge. "Goodness flows from you to them when you eat with them," she says.

An Appleton, Wisconsin, school tossed out the fast foods and hired a private company that switched to fresh salads, meats "prepared with old-fashioned recipes," and whole grain bread. Fresh fruits were added to the menu. Vending machines were removed.

Teachers there say student behavior has improved with the meals. Grades are up, truancy is down, and they are able to spend more time teaching. Principal LuAnn Coenen sums it up: "I can't buy the argument that it's too costly for schools to provide good nutrition for their students. I found that one cost will reduce another. I don't have the vandalism. I don't have the litter."[77]

Teachers in two South Dakota schools that began holding recess before lunch, instead of after, are pleased with the change. Students immediately began eating in a more relaxed way and wasting less food, than when they were hurrying to eat so they could get out in the playground. Now most students eat the entire lunch, including all their vegetables, and they drink much more milk.

The American Academy of Pediatrics and other medical and nutrition groups have joined with USDA in endorsing 10 keys to achieving healthy eating in schools. Among these are a call for longer lunch periods, shorter lunch lines, fewer very early or very late lunch periods, more pleasant surroundings, and more adults eating with students.[78]

Schools Can Soda Sales

Dr. Pepper is getting expelled from public schools. So are Coke, Pepsi and Mountain Dew. Parents' rebellion over unhealthy school nutrition has focused on the commercial take-over of their campuses by beverage contracts. Soft drinks (known as "soda," "pop," "coke," or "cola," depending where you live in the U.S.) are being tossed out, although so far only a handful of districts have been able to make it stick.

It's happening in the Los Angeles Unified School district, which with 748,000 students is the second largest in the United States.[79]

"It's going to set a national trend," said Francesca de la Rosa of the Center for Food and Justice at Occidental College's Urban and Environmental. "People will say, if you can do it at LA USD, you can do it anywhere."

The transition can be painful for schools. More than 200 middle and high schools in the district have contracts with Coca-Cola or PepsiCo. Los Angeles High School stands to lose funding from Coca-Cola—$50,000 up front for a three-year exclusive contract and nearly $5,000 a month from soft drink sales. The money funds school sports, dances, clubs and field trips. The district will phase in the new rules slowly, in part to find alternative sources of money.

Financial benefits can come from selling healthier options at lower prices, a pilot program in a large inner-city San Diego school suggests. Soft drinks were limited to about 20 percent of beverage vending machine slots. Choices like yogurt, fresh fruit, trail mix, lower-fat ice cream bars, fruit bars, and bagels with cream cheese replaced the usual food items.[80]

Water, milk, 100 percent juice, smoothies and sport drinks increased to 88 percent of all beverages. Soda sales dropped to 12 percent. All beverages sold for $1.00.

"The arrangement has been rewarding for all parties," says Enid Hohn, director of Child Nutrition Services. "The schools and vending company are making more money, the students are eating and drinking healthier foods, and food service is able to instill healthy eating habits that will last a lifetime."

The first year the school generated $200,000 more in sales than previous years, and received nearly $15,000 in commissions compared with $9,000 under the old contract. The school store went from losing money to a profit of $700 a day with new and healthier options.

Genethia Hudley-Hayes, one of the three co-sponsors of the motion that passed the LA USD school board, said it's important the district not be contributing to the unhealthy lifestyles of children, especially blacks and Latinos.

These children, she said, "Suffer greater childhood obesity, juvenile diabetes, asthma.... Why do we let them get off the bus and have them rush immediately to drink a sugar-caffeinated drink?" Nearly half the students in the district's poorest schools are overweight or at risk of overweight. "It's a health issue," said Rosemary Lee, a teacher at Logan Street Elementary School. "I have kindergartners who are 90 pounds at 4 or 5 years old. I have kids who come to school with a soda for breakfast."

Under the new rules all schools in the Los Angeles district are prohibited from selling carbonated drinks during school hours, starting in January 2004. Allowed are water, milk and drinks of at least 50 percent fruit juice and sports drinks with less than 42 grams of sugar per 20 ounce serving. Most soda companies include some of these items in their offerings.

In drinking soda, either regular or sugar-free, the Minnesota Dental Association recommends drinking as quickly as possible and rinsing off the teeth. In its school posters, the group points out that sugar in soft drinks combines with mouth bacteria to form acid—

and diet soda contains its own acid – that eats away at children's teeth and causes cavities. Acid attacks the teeth for about 20 minutes after taking a sip, and it starts all over again with every sip. Dentists discourage drinking soda from bottles, to deter sipping throughout the day.

The Minnesota group offers these tips to prevent acid damage to tooth enamel:

- ⋆ Drink soda from a can, not a bottle with a replaceable cap.
- ⋆ Drink soda from a straw to reduce sugar-exposure to teeth.
- ⋆ After drinking soda, rinse out your mouth with water.[81]

Increasingly, parents calling for healthy nutrition in schools have been winning their battles—sometimes at the local level, sometimes at district and state. Ultimately, the rebellion goes all the way to Washington. National legislation is being proposed to improve student nutrition and reduce the rates of childhood overweight by restricting sales of competing foods and beverages.

Groups like the Comprehensive School Nutrition Policy Task Force in Philadelphia want to go farther—to making healthy nutrition a school priority. They have set a goal to revolutionize how kids, parents, teachers, administrators and staff think about food.[82] "We're trying to get people back in touch with what they know is right," said Sandy Sherman, the task force's leader and a nutrition educator at the Food Trust in Philadelphia.

All teachers would like to have their classrooms full of students who are fit, healthy and eager to learn. Healthy children have increased attention, creativity, and ability to learn. They score higher on tests and are more likely to achieve their full academic potential.

In the lunchroom, thin girls hover over the salad bar, emerging with only a small plate of lettuce. Across the room, a worker plunges a big basket of French fries and another of chicken nuggets into vats of hot fat, and serves up generous portions, along with sweet sauce and ketchup. A big bottle of Mountain Dew caps the student lunch. For the larger child, however active, whatever he or she eats, the pressure and harassment is all there—between students, teachers, and staff.

Schools have long recognized the problems of hungry children. Many provide both breakfast and lunch for children who are neglected, of low income, or whose parents both work. These measures do not begin to touch the problems of girls and boys who go hungry because they fear weight gain, or who lack energy because they are so inactive. Schools can do far more to address the role they play in children's lives when it comes to eating, weight concerns, socializing and developing self respect—qualities that may not be part of the curriculum but nonetheless are critical to the learning process.

Comprehensive school health programs can prevent future health problems, improve economic productivity, reduce the spiraling costs of health care, and improve educational outcomes. Schools can prevent many health problems, detect others at early stages, and thus avoid the worst effects.

A greater awareness is needed of the opportunity and responsibility facing schools so that educators will recognize the severity of eating and weight problems for youth today, and approach them in a comprehensive way, using Health at Any Size concepts that will benefit all children and harm none. It is a major health crisis, and school administrators, boards and parents need to take effective steps to address the problems.

The Health at Any Size approach is well suited for use in schools. The focus is on positives, not negatives, on adding nutritious foods rather than restricting food, on adding pleasurable movement, and on ensuring a nurturing environment for each child. At the same time, this approach helps to prevent the six major weight and eating problems: overweight, eating disorders, dysfunctional eating, undernutrition, hazardous weight loss, and size prejudice.

Integrating the Approach

Comprehensive school health programs provide unique opportunities throughout the school experience to introduce health principles. They reinforce important changes in the health and lives of the 45 million American school children, and for their families, school staff and community. The Comprehensive School Health Program developed by the Centers for Disease Control and Prevention (CDC) Division of Adolescent School Health, recognizes that education and health are interrelated and that healthy children who feel safe and accepted in their environment can learn better and achieve more academically.

The CDC program encompasses the following eight interdependent components[83]:

* ★ Healthy school environment
* ★ Health education
* ★ Physical education
* ★ Nutrition services
* ★ Health services
* ★ Counseling, psychological, and social services
* ★ Health promotion for staff
* ★ Family and community involvement

Within each of these components, schools address six key risk behaviors:

* ★ Physical inactivity
* ★ Poor eating habits
* ★ Tobacco use
* ★ Behaviors that result in intentional or unintentional injury
* ★ Abuse of alcohol and other drugs
* ★ Sexual behaviors that result in HIV infection, other sexually transmitted diseases, or unwanted pregnancies.

All eight components are important in a comprehensive school program that seeks to address eating and weight issues. The six risky behaviors also cut across the complex issues of body image, weight and eating, in a number of ways. For example, poor eating habits and physical inactivity are associated with a wide range of health problems. Violence, harassment, and suicide are linked to disturbed eating, eating disorders, size prejudice and low self-esteem. Sexual and physical abuse are known risks for eating disorders.[84] Teenage girls smoke to lose weight and refuse to quit for fear of regain. And the risk of unwanted preteen pregnancies increases with early puberty, related to higher levels of body fat and sedentary living.

The challenge is to integrate into the school's health program the components that can prevent these interrelated problems. This can do much to stimulate students' intellectual growth and their ability to learn, as well as their overall health and well-being.

Healthy School Environment

To address health risks related to inactivity, CDC encourages school policies that provide adequate indoor and outdoor facilities, offer extracurricular activities, provide access to facilities outside school hours, prohibit substituting other courses or activities for physical education, and prohibit using activity as punishment (such as making students run laps or do push-ups for inappropriate behavior during PE class).

To improve poor eating habits, CDC asks schools to establish policies that restrict access to foods of low nutritive value, allow adequate time to eat meals (at least 10 minutes for breakfast and 20 minutes for lunch, counting from the time they are seated), prohibit use of low nutritive food as reward or withholding food as punishment, and ensure that fund-raising efforts support healthy eating.

Schools are responsible for supervising conduct and protecting students, and for giving guidance in how to get along in society. Many schools now teach the Character Counts' Six Pillars of Character—respect, caring, fairness, trustworthiness, responsibility, citizenship—at all levels. They have established policies of zero tolerance for harassment, bullying, name-calling and shaming others. Such policies define what this means, create a confidential process of reporting, and specify consequences. Including zero tolerance of size bias helps to reduce the size prejudice that exists in schools.

In-service training for teachers and staff is effective in helping them assess their own attitudes, convey size acceptance concepts, and eliminate weight discrimination from all school activities. Physical, emotional and social surroundings that are safe, secure and accepting of each individual enhance the well being, intellectual development, and productivity of students and staff. Students who feel safe are free to direct energies to learning and to develop in natural, healthful ways.

Health Education

Health education inside and outside the classroom from kindergarten through high school helps youngsters integrate healthy choices into their lives. The Health at Any Size message—using a sequential curriculum that builds on concepts taught in preceding years—is important at every age group: live actively, eat well and feel good about yourself and others.

Life skills training helps students cope assertively with everyday issues: communicating with others, building friendships, active listening, saying "no" to unreasonable requests, resisting pressures, making decisions, media literacy, coping with anger and conflict resolution. Healthy body image curricula begins in kindergarten, and is especially important during puberty when students experience profound body changes. They may go through puberty earlier or later than classmates, and need reassurance that this is normal. Youngsters of all ages can be taught that theirs is a good body and it's important to take care of it.

Developmentally appropriate nutrition concepts are taught at every grade level. Positive, simple, consistent nutrition messages need to be integrated into all areas from classroom teaching to athletics to the cafeteria. With the extent of disturbed eating and dieting going on today, this nutrition education will include activities that help children normalize their eating. What does it mean to be too hungry? Too full? How does the stomach feel when it's just right?

Health education needs to deal appropriately with the level of dysfunctional eating, undernutrition, hazardous weight loss, eating disorders, size prejudice and overweight that are real issues for students today. Required nutrition classes in junior high and high school are more important than ever in coping with today's high rates of obesity and eating disorders. Creating awareness is a first step in helping teachers recognize these problems so they can address prevention at early stages.

Physical Education

Healthy kids need daily opportunities during school hours to exercise, play and learn new skills, to help them maintain strong and healthy bodies. Active children have more energy and learn better.

For elementary students, the CDC recommends that schools require 150 minutes of physical education per week throughout the school year, with students being moderately or vigorously active for at least 50 percent of class time. This is to be spread over at least three days a week, and preferably over five days (30 minutes per day).[85]

The National Association for Sport and Physical Education (NASPE) guidelines advise that this class time be in addition to a daily recess period that promotes active play.

For middle school and high school students, CDC recommends 225 minutes of required PE per week, preferably every day (45 minutes per day), with students being moderately or vigorously active for at least 50 percent of class time.

To reduce inactivity, teachers are advised to avoid practices such as having many students stand in line or on the sidelines watching others or waiting a turn, using games that eliminate students, using activities in which less than half of students have a piece of equipment or an active role, and allowing more skilled students to dominate activities and games. Recommended student to teacher ratio is about the same as other classes (not more than about 25 children) so students can learn well, be safe, and get appropriate instructional feedback and support from teachers.

Nutrition Services

Nutritious and appealing meals that are consistent with what they are learning in health education help students develop good eating habits and strong healthy bodies. To promote positive eating attitudes and habits, it's important that children enjoy eating well and eat sufficient food to fuel their needs for energy and to supply their bodies with essential nutrients.

CDC recommends that schools make both nutritious breakfast and lunch programs accessible to all students, providing one-fourth of the day's nutrition standards at breakfast and one-third at lunch. Meals will meet National School Lunch standards, and offer a variety of healthy food choices and easy selection of foods consistent with healthy weight.[86]

Using local foods whenever possible is advised. These are fresher and more nutritious than foods that have been shipped back and forth across the nation for processing and packaging, and often cost less. Some schools have a policy that the district shall purchase locally grown food as the first priority, and that the district shall work with other local school districts and local farmers to organize cooperative buying and distribution systems, where possible.

Scheduling adequate time for eating is important. It is recommended that children be allowed 20 minutes of actual eating time, after they are seated.[87] Yet, typically after being served, a child has only about eight to 12 minutes remaining in the lunch period. Meals need to be pleasurable, with enough time to eat and socialize. When time is short, studies show it adds to plate waste. And some children don't eat enough food in the brief time allowed.[88]

Timing of school lunch makes a difference, too. It may be helpful to schedule lunch after recess. One study in grades one to three found that when recess comes before lunch, children eat more vegetables and meat or meat alternate and drink more milk. They come to lunch ready to eat and are less rushed or distracted by wanting to go out and play with friends. They experience less stomach discomfort and dizziness, and less food is wasted.[89]

Health Services

The school nurse, public health nurse, and other school resources provide support and a consistent approach with activity, eating and weight issues. They distribute educational materials, and offer individual and group advice. They may be involved in testing, identifying students with special needs, and making referrals to health professionals. Screening for disordered eating in all students, or for students considered at risk, may be advised.

The school nurse may be put in charge of weighing, measuring or testing body fat in students. Whether schools need these measurements is controversial. When they are taken, it is important to avoid shaming and stigmatizing the larger child. Weighing needs to be done in private with no other children present. Comments by the health service provider should be neutral. For example, Joanne Ikeda, California nutrition specialist, suggests that if a child makes a negative comment about his or her body, it is appropriate to ask, "Why do you feel that way?" and to say, "I wish you felt more positive about your body. Your body is a good body. I hope you will take good care of it."

Counseling, Psychological, and Social Services

Counselors work with individual students and parents as needed in disordered eating issues, develop support groups, refer students to specialists when needed, and extend team efforts into the community. Integration of weight and eating issues into the counseling program is important today in helping schools deal effectively with these problems.

A nutrition coordinator or designated point person in each school who understands these issues can be a team leader working with counselors, teachers, coaches and administrators to identify and prevent eating and weight problems.

Health Promotion for Staff

Teachers and staff with healthy lifestyles and attitudes are powerful role models for children. Thus, there is an urgent need for in-service training and attitudes of self-acceptance among teachers and staff.

Retreats, training conferences, and in-service workshops for teachers, staff and community health teams offer opportunities to integrate healthy lifestyle concepts into their own lives. Many states bring health teams together for summer training and program planning. The five-day North Dakota Roughrider Health Conference has the dual focus of building strong coalition teams and strengthening personal wellness skills for each team member. The teams return to their communities with training and renewed motivation to develop meaningful school and community health programs.

Effective school policies will offer staff members annual physical health screenings, and wellness programs, including fitness, healthy eating, and tobacco-use cessation, that are free or low-cost.

Family and Community Involvement

Successful school health programs include parents and other community members in planning and activities, so that school efforts will be supported and reinforced in the home and community.

In-school prevention efforts are strengthened by reaching out to families and communities. Schools can give families many opportunities to learn about healthy lifestyles by sending home information, involving families in school-sponsored activities, and directing them to community-based programs.

Schools can provide much helpful information to parents on family-based healthy weight practices. When parents become concerned about a child's weight, it is helpful to have information and resources available that provide recognized principles for maintaining healthy weight. These may include handouts, adult education classes, or referrals to community agencies on Health at Any Size concepts, how to make healthful changes together so the child does not feel deprived or stigmatized, avoiding dieting, eating at regular meal and snack times, being a role model for active living and healthy eating, and finding ways to give emotional support for children with weight issues. It can include physical activities the whole family will enjoy, such as family fitness programs.

The CDC recommends that schools provide community access to school gymnasiums and outdoor recreational areas when school is not in session, during evenings, weekends, and school vacations.

Physical Activity Programs

Sports Play and Active Recreation for Kids (SPARK) is an ongoing federally-funded program designed to increase the quality and quantity of physical activity by restructuring elementary school PE around lifetime activities. SPARK emphasizes fitness activities that can be enjoyed over a lifetime, and by one or two people, such as swimming, biking, walking and aerobic activities. Children play frisbee games, jump rope, and learn aerobic dances.

Important features are:

★ Training and follow-up for teachers. During the first year, SPARK trainers take a half-day refresher course every four months and are visited weekly by a consultant.

★ A detailed curriculum of four-week units, each centered around a specific sport. Skills transfer from one sport to the next.

In 12 schools on the Navajo reservation near Window Rock, AZ., the SPARK program has helped 1,250 children in third through sixth grade integrate activity with their tribal culture, while spending 30 minutes, three times a week in moderate to vigorous activity. The first 15 minutes is spent on teaching aerobic skills, the second 15 minutes on sports skills. Native dances are taught in the aerobics unit.

Project leaders hope this program will make a difference in the high prevalence of overweight among these children. The aim is to turn children on to movement, so they find activity fun and exciting. Teachers say it works. But while special programs work in school, Sallis says that getting children to continue to be active outside school hours has been more difficult than expected.

In Michigan, the Exemplary Physical Education Curriculum (EPEC), for grades K through 8, was developed by the Michigan Governor's Council on Physical fitness to enable schools to establish a physical education curriculum that provides students with necessary skills, knowledge, and motivation to live a physically active lifestyle now and as adults. Some of the objectives include strength/endurance, flexibility, aerobic fitness, knowledge of benefits of exercise, and RESPECT (responsibility, effort, self-control, perseverance, exemplary leadership, compassion, teamwork).

Michigan is promoting "Brain Breaks," active breaks for the elementary classroom teacher to use between lessons or as a transitional activity. (Available for downloading from the Web site: http://www.emc.cmich.edu/BrainBreaks/TOC.htm)

Curbing Abuses

For sports in which weight is important for peak performance or appearance, it is essential that coaches, parents and athletes keep a healthy perspective. Full nutrition and healthy growth and development for the athlete must not be compromised. Every sport has athletes with eating disorders. Athletes may be asked or encouraged to lose weight quickly—requests that often lead to restrictive dieting and, in some cases, eating disorders. Weight loss may help their performance temporarily, but can lead to serious health problems and even death.

The U.S. Olympic Committee states that the average and healthy range of body fat for young women is 20 to 22 percent. But many female athletes and dancers and their coaches strive for 10 to 14 percent or even lower.

Barbara Bickford, a lawyer and assistant professor of exercise and sport science at the University of North Carolina, says schools could be held liable if they allow students with eating disorders to participate in sports. "What's right for the athlete is often in conflict with what's right for the team or the coach's career advancement," she says.

Media Literacy

The way women and girls are portrayed in the media has long been a subject of concern. There are far fewer females than males throughout the media and they are often shown in stereotypical ways—as sex objects, victims, in domestic roles, and endlessly preoccupied with their appearance. Men and boys are also stereotyped. All this can be seriously damaging to both genders. It affects the way they think about themselves and their bodies, and how they relate to each other.

GO GIRLS! (Giving Our Girls Inspiration and Resources for Lasting Self-esteem) from the National Eating Disorder Association is an action-oriented prevention program that follows through with media literacy, activism and advocacy projects. Teenage girls develop critical thinking skills, learn how to be critical viewers of the media, and use the media to communicate their own messages in their own words with the goal of changing important aspects of their environment in regard to marketers' images of women.

An excellent source of videos, training kits and teacher and parent guides is the Canadian Media Watch Web site (www.mediawatch.ca). Suggestions are given on how to build a media literacy unit around special events, involving a variety of activities that draw on research, analysis and written and verbal communication skills. It includes information on how educators and parents can help shape the media environment into one that celebrates and reflects the diversity of women and girls.

Librarians are the gatekeepers who decide which magazines come into school libraries and resource centers. As such, they face a daunting responsibility with which teachers of media literacy can help. Which of the teen magazines, if any, should be granted subscriber status? What is the impact on girls of anorexic models and a relentless focus on make-up and catching a boyfriend?

Certainly some tend to be less offensively stereotypical than others, but given the commercial nature of such magazines, it is difficult to find any teen or women's magazines that consistently overcome the content focus dictated by their advertisers.

Planning Prevention Programs

Some schools may develop their own program for preventing childhood obesity and eating disorders. Others will be part of state-wide prevention programs that are being implemented in many states. In these programs it is important that eating disorders and obesity be addressed together in an integrated, comprehensive manner. Some obesity specialists have seen a contradiction between trying to prevent eating and weight problems, but the Health at Any Size approach bridges that barrier. With its emphasis on healthy lifestyles, it addresses the needs of all children regardless of weight or eating behavior pattern. It does no harm.

Developing prevention programs is a long-term commitment.

"Prevention is a marathon, not a sprint," says Linda Johnson. "Many prevention programs have fallen short because our approach has been single-pronged and of short duration. Often what is convenient, easy and cheap does not benefit youth."

She says a successful prevention program will:

- ⋆ Develop a needs assessment
- ⋆ Build in measurable goals and objectives

- ★ Use researched, theory based, proven effective programs
- ★ Deal with problems in a comprehensive way
- ★ Work with an active advisory council
- ★ Include ongoing evaluations.

A comprehensive effort that includes school, community and families is most likely to bring about real change, says Johnson, Director of School Health Programs at the North Dakota Department of Public Instruction. Prevention programs also must do no harm to vulnerable individuals. It's clear the wrong kind of prevention is useless and can make matters worse.

"Prevention is neither a luxury nor a fantasy, but a necessity," says Michael Levine, PhD, Professor of psychology, Kenyon College, and president of the board of directors of Eating Disorders Awareness and Prevention (EDAP). He says preventing eating disorders is challenging and controversial, because it promotes change in education, mass media, public health and politics.[90] It is now clear that prevention efforts must start early, focus on changing behavior rather than providing knowledge, and must be a sustained effort.

Prevention Programs

School prevention programs are a logical place to start. An example is the national multi-based Child and Adolescent Trial for Cardiovascular Health study (CATCH). Nearly four thousand fifth graders in four states went through the CATCH program, in which they received health intervention in diet, physical activity, and related health indicators. The CATCH intervention focused on four components:

1) Training food service staff to plan healthier school lunches.
2) Instructing physical education teachers how to increase students' enjoyment of and participation in moderate to vigorous physical activity.
3) Incorporating classroom curricula such as goal setting, role modeling and skill building in teaching healthier behaviors.
4) Improving family support with family fun nights and activities in the home.

Three years later, these students continued to practice much of what they learned. They pursued more vigorous physical activity levels and their diets were lower in total fat and saturated fat than students in the control groups.Over the three years, however, the differences were narrowing, and the authors suggest that the interventions should be continued through the middle and high school years.

Work Out Low Fat (WOLF) is a Minnesota program for Native American youth aimed at reducing the risk factors of type 2 diabetes and overweight. It emphasizes Native traditions and promotes physical activity and low fat eating in grades 1 through 4. Fitness Fever is another Minnesota—based program for elementary school-age children that reaches 700 schools annually during February.

A School Health Index is a tool to evaluate school programs against the centers for Disease Control and Prevention school health guidelines on physical activity and healthy eating. Designed to help schools identify their strenghths and weaknesses, prioritize actions for improvement, and develop a team approach to implement recommendations. (For this index, contact CDC or visit the Web Site www.cdc.gov/nccdphp/dash/SHI/index.htm).

Preventive programs are most promising when they have first assessed the need and timing for prevention and then delivered the program about one year before the age when the behavior starts, experts say. Research-based, theory driven curricula are most effective (such as social learning theory or behavior change theory). Comprehensive programs are integrated throughout the school and involve family and community.

Two major models of primary prevention for eating disorders are identified by Michael Levine and Niva Piran, of the University of Toronto. The first is what they call *Top-Down* or leader driven. Patterned after drug and smoking prevention programs, this model aims to give students the knowledge, skills and encouragement needed to reduce their risks and increase their strengths. It decreases negative body image, dieting and other stresses, and improves communication, problem-solving, decision-making, healthy lifestyle and other competencies.[91]

The second method is the *Feminist-Empowerment-Relational* model, developed by Piran when she was asked to help curb the high rate of disturbed eating and eating disorders at an elite Toronto ballet school. The school was recording nearly two new cases of anorexia or bulimia nervosa every year, or about 10 percent of the girls (age 10 to 18). Piran met with all students from two to six times in small focus groups and used their knowledge and experience to guide action and changes in the system. All staff were included in exploration.

Her method empowers girls and women to change themselves and their environments through group dialogue, similar to that in a consciousness-raising group, fostering respectful discussion about issues that are often silenced or felt to be shameful, and working with the system to bring about favorable changes. It encourages girls and women to work individually and together to change what they as a group identify as unhealthy and unfair influences in their lives. Students were soon strongly demanding safe and respectful treatment of their bodies by school staff and peers.

During Piran's ten-year intervention, no cases of bulimia and only one of anorexia developed at the school. High eating disorder scores dropped from 50 percent of the girls in 1987 to about 15 percent. Surveys revealed similar decreases in body dissatisfaction and the number of students who binged, vomited, used laxatives, went on diets or skipped meals.

Levine and Piran advocate combining these two models into prevention programs that include these components[92]:

* ⋆ Media literacy and ways of analyzing the culture
* ⋆ Student discussion of the impact of culture
* ⋆ Nutrition education that promotes healthy eating and challenges dieting
* ⋆ Techniques for developing personal competencies

Teacher Training Needed

Teachers are requesting training on dysfunctional eating and eating disorders. At every grade level, they are seeing disturbing problems that look like eating disorders. Their students are truly afraid to eat, afraid to gain weight, afraid their bodies are wrong, and they often talk about their bodies and their fears.

Such training will address early detection of warning signs, counseling, parental involvement, appropriate referrals and support for treatment plans. Currently, it can be difficult to get effective help for students in early stages of subclinical eating disorders. Training can help teachers assess their own attitudes and eating behavior. A concern that needs to be addressed is that colleges are sending out young teachers, particularly in the fields of coaching, health and nutrition who have not resolved their own eating issues.

Stanford University offers a class that shows promise of changing behaviors for such young professionals-to-be, called *Body Traps: Perspectives on Body Image.* While the focus is on objectively evaluating the issues, results show significant personal change: improvement in body image, eating attitudes and eating behaviors for class members as compared with a control group. The class includes multimedia presentations and discussions on body image, media and advertising, history of beauty, and disturbed eating. Students are required each week to write a two to three page reaction paper expressing their thoughts, feelings and criticisms from assigned readings.

Issues Strong by Fifth Grade

Evaluation of eating disorder prevention programs in schools show they need to begin early, by fifth or sixth grade. By this time, up to half of girls already "feel too fat" and 20 to 40 percent are dieting. By eighth grade, over half say they have dieted during the past year. These figures do not reflect the intense body dissatisfaction often felt by other girls who are not dieting.

In lower grades these attitudes and behaviors are measurable, but the girls lack dieting commitment, and their beliefs about the importance of thinness have not yet crystallized. Therefore experts say, until about fifth grade, the focus should be on healthy nutrition, positive eating habits and self acceptance, not eating disorders.

But by fifth grade, body shape is much more important. Children who are already dieting at this age may be at increased risk for developing eating disorders because of the effects of calorie restriction and weight loss failures. Yet their susceptibility to thinness messages may be modifiable at this point. This is a time when children's social attitudes and beliefs can be changed, their thinness attitudes are still evolving, and a time when it is likely that parents will prohibit extreme dieting.

Teaching a positive approach toward healthy attitudes and lifestyle is preferable to focusing on the illness. Specialists warn there is risk of promoting eating disorder behaviors and doing more harm than good by drawing undue attention to them. Discussion of eating disorders appropriately begins between fourth and sixth grade when puberty development becomes obvious, says eating disorder specialist Paula Levine. For girls, this is younger than age eleven, and certainly before junior high, "before their self-esteem begins to plummet for other reasons."

While fifth grade may be early enough for discussion of eating disorders in school, it may not be early enough for parents. Paula Levine speaks to new parents in newborn classes about eating disorders, and believes this may have an important impact.

Developing Support Groups

Support groups are needed for young people who struggle with eating, weight and body image issues, or who deprive themselves of food.

Consciousness-raising support groups can be empowering in healing body shame and body dissatisfaction, say Carla Rice and Vanessa Russell, women's studies specialists at the Ontario Institute for Studies in Education in Toronto. Girls in their teenage focus groups were relieved when they realized they were not alone and found the courage to share sexual harassment experiences.[93] As they connected the shame they felt about their bodies to incidents of violence or harassment, the girls grew outraged. Each had endured her humiliation in secret, ashamed because she feared she either deserved the hurtful comments or had provoked them. As they shared their experiences, the girls grew more affirming with each other, and became a force to be reckoned with. Their shame and self-loathing turned to anger as they realized most other girls had the same experiences. This transition from "I deserve to be violated," to "I have been violated," to "I do not deserve and will not tolerate violation," can be a key to empowerment, Rice and Russell suggest.

In organizing support groups for women and girls with severe eating issues, it is important to recognize that without the guiding hand of a professional, distorted thinking about eating, exercise and women's bodies may be perpetuated.

Eating Disorders Screening

During Eating Disorders Awareness and Prevention Week in 1998, 35,897 people were screened at 1,083 sites. They first took the screening test, then attended informational sessions. Those who met the criteria were given referrals for further evaluation. Eating disorder screening is an ongoing program that could be conducted much more widely in health care centers, schools and communities.

The National Eating Disorders Association brings together training teams from around the country for Eating Disorder Awareness and Prevention Week, which is observed in late February in all 50 states and Canada. Every year these teams grow stronger in developing comprehensive programs in their communities. Many continue through the year, highlighted by workshops, seminars, theater events, art and puppet shows and media promotions.

The National Eating Disorders Association came into being in 2001 as a merger of several eating disorders prevention and advocacy organizations, including groups formerly known as EDAP, AABA, NEDO and ANRED. Headquartered in Seattle, it is the source of much helpful educational material on healthy body image and eating disorders, and maintains an active Web site. (www.nationaleatingdisorders.org).

Health providers working with these organizations can help strengthen their own health at any size programs and coordinate efforts to make programs more effective.

Chapter 18

♦ ♦ ❖ ♦ ♦ ❖ ♦ ♦ ❖ ♦ ♦ ❖ ♦ ♦ ❖ ♦ ♦ ❖ ♦ ♦

Shaping a Nurturing Environment

A nurturing environment fosters self-esteem, confidence, and a positive body image, qualities that favor health-promoting behavior. "Feeling good about yourself starts by accepting who you are and how you look," the Canadian *Vitality* program explains. "Think positive thoughts. Laugh a lot. Spend some time with people who have a positive attitude—the type who look at the cup as being half full, not half empty. Positive vibes are contagious. Enjoy eating well and being active. Feel good about yourself. Have fun with family and friends, and you'll feel on top of the world!"[94]

A nurturing environment in the home, school, and community helps children appreciate their strengths, abilities and uniqueness, take pride in themselves and their accomplishments. It enables them to better balance and develop all six wellness dimensions in their lives—physical, social, emotional, occupational, spiritual, and intellectual. It's important for the home to be a safe and comfortable place where children are nurtured, loved and accepted unconditionally. Parents are their children's first teachers and continue as important role models. Moms and dads who feel good about themselves, and who support healthy lifestyles, provide a sound foundation for a lifetime of health and well being.

"Children need to be able to express their ideas so they can go against what others say, without fear. So they can think for themselves. Too many are afraid to express themselves," says long-time elementary schoolteacher Jeannie Thiessen, of Hacienda Heights, Calif. "They are afraid other kids might ridicule their ideas, so they go along with the group."

Young people today need the confidence to combat our culture's extreme focus on appearance, and to accept themselves and others as they are. "The child who has confidence doesn't care if kids laugh at him. He can say, 'No, I don't want a big bottle of soda. It's got 16 tablespoons of sugar in it, and that much sugar is not good for you.'"

In the family, which today takes on many different structures—blended, single-parent, and traditional two-parent—children can learn to make the connection between health and pleasure. Parents nurture when they emphasize the positive, enjoyable aspects of life, as well as teach children to cope with the stresses and disappointments in their lives. Families, teachers and friends can help them find useful roles so they feel needed and important at home and in the community.

Family Communication

Many teens are crying out to their parents for help with their concerns, including body hatred issues. Often their cries are silent, perhaps expressed as a flash of anger or rebellion. They confide that it's hard to talk to parents: *I can't talk to my parents...they're too busy... they won't listen...they don't understand...if I do, they want to take over and run my life...they say it's not that bad and to forget it.*

It's critically important that families talk to each other—beginning with the small everyday talk, praise and reassurances. Working together makes communication easier—cooking a meal, cleaning the yard, painting a bedroom, building a dog house. Perhaps most important is eating together, with the television off. Regular family meals create a special interlude in parents' busy lives when they listen and talk with their children, to tell them in many ways: *I'm proud of you! You're great! Thanks for helping. I trust you. Good work! I love you. You did a nice job. You brighten my day. It's so nice to see you smile!*

Some parents hesitate to talk about feelings because they're ashamed of their own feelings, or don't know how to express them. They may discourage their children from talking about feelings because they don't know how to deal with them. Or they brush them off by urging, *You shouldn't feel that way.* Experts suggest that parents ask, "How do you feel about that?" when a child brings up a problem. Then listen, without offering advice. They advise empowering the child to find his or her solutions. Too often, parents brush past the feelings, and forge ahead to solving problems that should be owned by the child. This can be controlling and destructive, and does not help the child cope in better ways the next time.

Instead, the National Institute of Mental Health advises parents to listen calmly when kids want to talk, giving their undivided attention. Acknowledge their feelings in a noncommittal way, "Oh. . . Hmmm. . .I see. . ." Give the child's feeling a name, such as, "That must be disappointing...that sounds unfair." Gently encourage the child to explore solutions, without taking over. Trust the child and he or she will gain confidence for next time. Use a pleasant tone of voice, and avoid making judgments without hearing it all out.

Acknowledge your teenager's opinions, even if you don't agree. It's a challenge for parents to be clear about important values, yet flexible at the same time. If tough subjects come up on which you disagree, such as drugs, driving behavior, or relationships, keep the door open for later discussion.

An assertive parenting style that is honest and sincere and "speaks the truth in love," helps parents to deal better with these problems, and also models effective problem-solving to children. By contrast, an aggressive style involves hostility, domination, humiliation, put-downs, physical abuse, or nonverbal abuse such as smirking, sneering, profanity, insults, blaming, and sarcasm. On the other hand, the parent with a passive style fears conflict and rejection, manipulates others, and may escape into sleep, forgetfulness, workaholism, drugs or alcohol. Assertiveness can be learned. Parenting help is available through programs and classes, such as at the local school or university, hospital, and WIC programs, and cooperative extension programs.

Nurturing in Child Care

As young children spend more and more of their daytime hours in childcare outside their own homes, or with grandparents or nannies in their own homes, the quality of this care becomes increasingly important. In some states as many as 80 percent of parents of young children are employed outside the home. Thus, many children spend major portions of their waking hours in daytime or after school child care. This care has a profound influence in how they feel about themselves, and on their activity and eating patterns.

With any caretaker, it is important that parents understand and agree with the values being taught to their children. How does the provider address the physical and emotional needs of your child? How does she promote a healthy lifestyle for your child? If needs are not being met, what can you do? Is the provider willing to make changes or get additional training?

Building Assets for Children

A handy tool parents can use in helping their children and teens balance wellness and wholeness aspects is a 40-Assets Checklist, developed by Search Institute of Minneapolis through the *Healthy Communities, Healthy Youth* program. The checklist focuses on 40 assets, or building blocks, that promote the healthy development of children. The Search surveys have shown the more of these assets young people have, the more likely they are to engage in positive behaviors and succeed in school. The fewer assets, the more likely children are to engage in risk-taking behaviors, such as violence, sexual activity, alcohol and drug use.

Parents and communities are urged to find ways of increasing the child's assets. Each is important, and together the benefits are additive. Examples of these 40 assets include:

- ⋆ Family life provides high levels of love and support;
- ⋆ Parents and child communicate positively; child is willing to seek parents' advice and counsel;
- ⋆ Family has clear rules and consequences, and monitors child's whereabouts;

- ⋆ Parents are actively involved in helping child succeed in school,
- ⋆ School provides a caring, encouraging environment;
- ⋆ Both parents and teachers press child to achieve;
- ⋆ Child feels safe in home, school and neighborhood;
- ⋆ Child receives support from three or more non-parent adults;
- ⋆ Child accepts and takes personal responsibility;
- ⋆ Child is optimistic about his/her personal future;

The Search Institute's checklist also sets some benchmark numbers that link with success for young people. The assets call for spending at least:

- ⋆ One hour a day on homework;
- ⋆ One hour a week serving the community;
- ⋆ One hour a week in a religious community;
- ⋆ Three hours a week in lessons or practice in music, theater, or other arts;
- ⋆ Three hours a week in sports, clubs, or organizations in school or community;
- ⋆ Being out with friends "with nothing special to do" two or fewer nights a week.

Support Systems

One of the most valuable resources for young people is having ongoing relationships with caring, principled adults outside the home, the Search Institute research finds. These are people who offer encouragement and guidance, who take time to talk with the child, who give consistent messages about boundaries and values, who care about and trust the child, who call the child by name and count him or her as a friend. They may be neighbors, relatives, teachers, family friends or acquaintances from school, church and community.

Many adults have pulled back from offering support to kids in their communities, because they feel overwhelmed by the frightening problems involving youth that dominate headlines. Often neighbors don't get involved in the lives of children on their block, and may not even know their names. Instead of offering support, they expect schools and professionals to solve problems.

The Search program *Healthy Communities, Healthy Youth* aims to turns this around, by urging people to take action to improve their neighborhoods. Adults are encouraged to initiate simple measures like these: Look at and speak to every child or teen you see. Talk to youngsters about their interests. Send a birthday or congratulatory card, invite a young person to go along to a ballgame. Have an open-door policy so neighborhood kids feel welcome to come in for conversation, refreshments, or just to hang out.[95]

Restore Normal Lifestyles

The best known prevention for weight and eating problems is to restore normal healthy lifestyles. The Canadian *Vitality* program explains what this means: "*Vitality* is a shift in thinking about what healthy living really is. It's a lifestyle for everyone. It's throwing a Frisbee with the kids, having friends over for a potluck dinner, curling up enjoying a good book. It's about healthy eating and active living. It's gardening and cycling, laughing and relaxing. It's good for you—body and soul."[96]

Mothers, fathers and children who feel good about themselves and each other make healthy choices easy—not just for a short period of time but for a lifetime.

Unfortunately, today many parents are so confused and fearful of their own eating, weight and health, that their fears are often multiplied in their children. Parents need to stop dieting, stop talking about hips and stomachs and thighs, and realize that their own attitudes and behaviors may contribute to their own child's eating and weight problems. Restoring normal eating and normal living is a priority for those who have restricted their eating, and also for those who habitually overeat.

Reassurance on Size

It's natural for parents to want their children to be as perfect as possible, but when it comes to weight, "perfect" must be broadly and individually defined, advise Carol Hans and Diane Nelson. In their brochure, *A Parent's Guide to Children's Weight,* they remind parents that children grow at different rates and may have very different body structures from their own brothers and sisters.

They advise parents that a child who is too thin needs the same emotional support as one who is too heavy. "Parents can help the child learn to see food as only one of many possible ways to celebrate a happy event, to ease disappointment, or to erase boredom." And parents can refrain from comments about their children's size or shape, except in a reassuring way. Children who feel supported and secure will be less likely to use food to meet emotional needs and are more resistant to pressures to diet or lose weight in dangerous ways.

Moms and dads need to examine closely their dreams and goals for their children. Are they emphasizing beauty and body shape, especially for daughters? The family is a powerful force in diffusing the anxieties today's youth feel about what they should weigh and how they should look. Parents and other adults can help fearful children restore sound values in their lives, and the sooner, the better.

Yet it is also important not to overreact. Mothers, fathers and significant others in children's lives who are obsessed or worried over their own weight, continually dieting, and often talking about these concerns, can set children up for weight and eating problems at very young ages.

A parent's over-concern about a child's weight further adds to the tension, fear and confusion a child may be feeling. Instead, parents and caring adults can help ease tensions by bringing a flexible, low-key approach to food and weight and focus on supporting the child with love and acceptance. The message is: *You're okay. Your body is okay.* Each child and teen is a special individual, unique, capable and loveable. Each has special talents.

But often parents don't know how to deal with a child who is struggling with dysfunctional eating, an eating disorder, with overweight or size prejudice. The longer children struggle with weight and eating issues, the more likely it is that they develop severe lifelong problems.

A visit to a pediatrician can help put size in perspective and provide scientific basis for reminding a child that individuals grow at different rates. When a child shows a sudden weight drop, medical or emotional problems may be suspected. Professional help from a pediatrician, dietitian or child psychologist may be necessary.

Healing Body Dissatisfaction

Teenagers who struggle with weight, eating, and body image issues often spend a great deal of time and energy trying to improve themselves. They strive for perfection and intensely dislike what they consider their flaws. They invest great amounts of time in thinking about and trying to fix those flaws. Their cries for help may go unrecognized by parents who want to help but don't know how, or are "too busy."

It's unfortunate that young people, even small children, are being made by our culture to feel they have to look a certain way to be loved and accepted. When can we as a nation rediscover the richness of diversity? When can we stop this intense and harmful focus on appearance?

Our children deserve better. It's important to reassure them that they are okay just as they are. Healthy bodies come in all shapes and sizes. Every body is a good body, whether tall, short, heavy or thin. Some kids store fat more easily than others. That's okay. Some mature earlier or later. Some stay small or lean. And that's okay, too. This is the way of the human race, in all its diversity.

The following guidelines from the Iowa paper, *Prevention of Child and Adolescent Obesity in Iowa*, suggest ways that parents can foster a healthy body image:

- Provide praise and positive comments to children that focus on their strengths. Do not refer to body size either as a strength or weakness.
- Openly discuss any concerns children express about their body size.
- Never tease a child about his or her body size.
- Recognize that children may be healthy at a variety of weights.
- Recognize that a child's body shape will change as he or she grows. A short stocky child at age nine may grow to be tall and lanky.

- ★ Parents should avoid talking about their own body faults.
- ★ Discuss how the media uses unrealistically thin models to sell their products.
- ★ In the community, create an environment of acceptance for all children regardless of body size.
- ★ Encourage local media to positively portray children with a variety of body sizes.
- ★ Ensure that resources are available to assist children who are struggling with body image issues.
- ★ Ensure that mental health professionals in the community are familiar with issues of body image disturbance, weight problems, and their relationship to self-esteem.

We can move ahead to helping children appreciate the strengths and abilities of their bodies. We can help them relax about appearance issues and enjoy their own unique characteristics, talents and interests. We can help them accept and recognize that healthy bodies come in a range of weights, sizes and shapes. We can help kids be tolerant of a wide range of body shapes and sizes, and teach them not to stereotype others because of size, but rather to respect and appreciate each individual.

A Healthy Body Image

Fortunately, over the last few years there are encouraging signs that society's narrow ideas about beauty and size may be changing. Even fashion gurus say they are more accepting of a wider range of sizes and shapes. "People want to see a model who inspires strength and self-confidence," explains modeling guru Katie Ford, president of Ford Models.

"Americans are more accepting of their bodies than before. More and more women are saying, 'This is how I am—this is my body, and frankly, I like it,'" says Gunnar Peterson, personal trainer to stars such as Jennifer Lopez, Penelope Cruz and Jennifer Connelly. "Their goals are different. The scale no longer dictates what makes them happy. Now it's more about the way you feel and function than just the way you look."

America Ferrera, 18, who stars as Ana in HBO's *Real Women Have Curves*, explains, "Women are hungry to see larger characters who are strong and confident and aren't ashamed of how they look." The vibrant five-foot star of the Broadway smash-hit *Hairspray,* Marissa Jaret Winokur, agrees. She claims never to have suffered because of her girth. "There may have been girls in high school who said nasty things behind my back, but I was so busy with soccer, theater, and cheerleading that I was oblivious to anyone being mean."

As a nation, we are moving closer to size acceptance. Perhaps we are reaching the tipping point in which the public finally rejects the obsession with the hollow-cheeked female idol, thinness and dieting, and moves on to embrace health and wellness at any size.

Chapter 19

♦ ♦ ❖ ♦ ♦ ❖ ♦ ♦ ❖ ♦ ♦ ❖ ♦ ♦ ❖ ♦ ♦ ❖ ♦ ♦

Healthcare: A New Paradigm

Overweight is increasingly difficult to handle in every pediatric practice. On one hand, physicians are constantly warned about the risks of obesity and admonished in many health directives to motivate the large child to lose weight. They feel responsible for making it happen, and feel pressured to put the child on a diet, knowing he or she will lose weight for a month or two.

On the other hand, they've been down this road many times before. It's quite apparent there's nothing new in the "new" treatment methods. They know that whatever plan they put forward will likely lead to another round of failure for the child—no matter how hard the doctor, child and his or her parents try to make it work.

Moving into the New Paradigm

Moving ahead in the Health at Any Size paradigm (also known as Health at Every Size) frees the doctor from this dilemma. This approach puts the focus squarely on health, not weight. It means the doctor works with the child and parents to establish a healthier, more active lifestyle in an honest, straightforward way. It does no harm. When weight is lost through real habit change—it stays off.

Ellyn Satter, RD, childhood feeding specialist, suggests setting aside weight loss as a goal and focusing instead on achievable goals: improving the attitudes and behaviors that accompany the overweight. "We can help our patients learn to eat and exercise in a healthful and positive way, feel better about themselves, and feel good about their bodies. If we—and they—institute these changes, they might be thinner. But we can't count on it, and we must not promise it."[97]

Paul Ernsberger, PhD, of Case Western Reserve School of Medicine, Cleveland, has developed the diagram *Which Path for the Obese Patient?* to help providers understand differences in goals and the pathways to reach them.

With a health goal, in this model, the treatment moves straight ahead to healthier lifestyle habits, then to improved health, prevention of weight gain, and a positive attitude. On the other hand, a weight goal means calorie restriction. Even when improved lifestyle is a part of this, it leads to a cycle of temporary weight loss, improved health and euphoric attitude that, almost inevitably, is followed by recidivism, weight regain, impaired health and a fatalistic attitude. It's like moving one step forward and two steps back.[98]

Satter charges that our current attitudes and approaches blame children and parents for a child's fatness and promise cures that health professionals can't deliver. "We have led parents to believe that children are too fat because they eat too much and that children can become slim if they eat less. In so doing, we set parents and children up for disappointment and unnecessary self-blame. In encouraging patients to try for weight loss, we find ourselves administering programs we don't totally believe in and accepting outcomes that leave us feeling discouraged and dishonest. It's time to define the problem of juvenile obesity in a way it can be solved."

She says we have overreacted to normal fatness and the growth process—often children will slim down naturally. However, some children are genetically fat. "It is possible that our interventions—restriction of food intake and subsequent struggles and preoccupation with eating—have exacerbated tendencies to fatness and interfered with a child's normal inclination to slim down. Even when obesity does exist, we don't know what causes it. Fat children eat no more, or no differently, than thin children. Nor do we know how to cure it."

The primary aim of treatment for overweight children is for little or no weight gain while growth continues, thus reducing body mass index (BMI). Attaining a reasonable weight and maintaining it, is worthwhile. Instead of struggling against a child's natural weight, parents and health professionals need to recognize and work with it, reassuring children that growth is normal, expecting them to "grow into" their natural size.

Research suggests that 75 to 80 percent of the body fat children carry may have genetic causes. This doesn't mean excessive weight gain is inevitable, but it may mean the child will be always be in the higher weight category. When the physician accepts this reality, it is more easily accepted by child and parent, and they can work together to improve overall health and well being.

Physicians need to be sensitive to the many issues involved in counseling families. Diagnosing a child as obese can label a child unfairly and inaccurately. It can also set up a struggle between parent and child over food and other activities.

What is a Natural, Healthy Weight?

Defining healthy weight as *the natural weight the body adopts, given healthy eating and meaningful levels of physical activity,*[99] makes it reachable for any child maintaining a healthy lifestyle. This contrasts with the more rigid medical definition, which defines a child as at risk at the 85th percentile, and overweight and *needing weight loss* when BMI is at or above the 95th percentile.

The physician can help parents understand that many other factors are involved. For example, many superb athletes fit into the highest category, yet have low body fat and enjoy excellent health. Designating a child as at risk and needing weight loss between 85th and 95th is especially questionable. One-fourth of children will not have elevated body fat levels at this weight, according to USDA studies. BMI alone gives little indication of body fat levels or fitness, both of which may be more closely related to health than is weight. Other factors to consider in whether a child's weight is a concern involves the timing of growth spurts, stage of puberty, and genetic heritage.[100]

Children with a family history of obesity are at higher risk for developing lifelong obesity. However, fatness may be as normal for children at the highest 5 percent, as thinness is for the lowest 5 percent—provided they grow in a consistent and predictable way, and any growth adjustments are gradual and occur over time.[101] If the goal of reducing a child's weight to the 85th percentile is unreachable, then it is destined for failure. It is unfair to ask a child to set such goals. Not only may the medical cutoff point be inaccurate for that individual, but it stigmatizes and can spell permanent failure for the child.

The alternate goal of improving Health at Any Size helps children and adults stabilize at what seems their natural weight, at which they are healthy and well nourished. "We need to realize that we have no real control over a patient's weight and neither does the patient," says Cindy Byfield Dallow, RD, PhD, a registered dietitian who worked many years in a clinical setting with overweight heart patients.[102] She found the Health at Any Size approach effective in working with obese patients who had suffered a heart attack or undergone heart surgery, because the goals to improve lifestyle habits are reachable, while weight loss goals may not be.

An important first step in promoting long-term behavior change is for the large child to feel fully accepted by the health care team. Dallow recommends that health care providers:

1. Start by observing your own thoughts about weight. Do you believe that children can be healthy at their natural size? "If you are just shifting to the new paradigm, it may help to know that it is not unusual to feel some discomfort. After all, we live in this weight-obsessed society and as health professionals, we have been trained to believe that excess fatness equals poor health," says Byfield.
2. Accept the child's weight, as beyond your control. "Our task is to provide accurate and helpful information about lifestyle changes. Our clients' task is to decide which changes they are willing and able to make."
3. Help the child feel accepted right now. Assure patients

they can improve their health, and that this is what is important, regardless of what happens to their weight.

4. Focus on the positive aspects of a healthy lifestyle: pleasure in activity the child chooses; foods to be added to make eating more healthful. Talking about adding foods, such as fruits, vegetables and other missing food groups encourages children to look forward to making positive changes. Emphasizing low-fat or what not to eat feeds into the diet mentality, promotes guilt, keeps children feeling deprived, and is less likely to promote long-term change.

Health providers who are committed to providing quality health care at every size know that children who feel good about themselves, and are supported by the health care system, are more empowered to make healthy changes in their lives. They recognize that much harm has been done by providers who harass and shame large patients, or who prescribe weight loss treatments that are neither safe nor effective.

Improved Health

Marian, age fourteen, was brought into the clinic by her mother, a large woman who has struggled with her own weight all her life. Marian weighs 217 pounds, and she has elevated blood pressure and impaired glucose tolerance, symptoms that often precede type 2 diabetes. Her activity level is low. She rides the school bus, which stops at her door, and avoids physical education and walking outdoors, because she has suffered cruel remarks and is afraid to invite more ridicule. She tries to limit her eating—she skips breakfast and usually lunch—but then begins eating ravenously when she gets home from school and is alone in the house. She usually eats far into the evening as she does her homework. She has little energy and often feels tired.

The traditional approach in treating Marian would be to place her on a low fat, calorie restricted diet, with a weight loss goal of perhaps 50 to 60 pounds. She would be given an exercise plan and asked to keep a food diary. Most likely she would be weighed once a week and praised when weight loss occurs.

Using the new approach, her dietitian discussed Marian's thoughts on dieting, food and exercise. She had lost weight on past diets, but said she "blew the diets" with a big binge every time, just when she was doing well. She blamed herself. The dietitian explained the new approach and together they decided that dieting would not help her achieve her goals and only lead to yo-yoing weight. Rather, eating breakfast and a more substantial lunch would give her the energy she needed and satisfy her appetite for later in the day. Thus, Marian's first goal was to eat breakfast and lunch and to walk in place in front of the television for 5 or 10 minutes when she got home. With her after-school and evening eating, her goal was to eat the evening meal with her family, and otherwise eat as she felt like at the time, without feeling guilt or trying to compensate by skipping meals.

After three weeks, Marian reported feeling more energetic and "proud of herself" for sticking with her goals and the changes she had made. Her weight had not changed, but her walking time had increased from 5 to 9 minutes. She felt better about her body image, and more confident about making other changes.

Three months later, Marian's weight had dropped by only 2 pounds, but she could fit into smaller clothes and felt trimmer. She was walking 20 to 30 minutes five days a week, usually outside, sometimes walking to or from school, something she thought she'd never be able to do. On most days, she ate three meals and two snacks, without the desire to snack in between.

Would Marian have responded better to the traditional treatment plan? Chances are she would have lost more weight, but would have been unable to maintain it. By three or four months she would likely have weighed as much or more than when she began, and given up on her exercise plan. Now her blood pressure and insulin levels are within normal limits, and she's established a physically active lifestyle. What more could we ask?[103] Byfield, who has worked with many patients like this, says health professionals will be most effective by helping their patients believe that health can be achieved now, not just when or if they lose weight. "It is truly in the patient's best interest to use the Health at Any Size approach."[104]

Shifting to the New Paradigm

Healthy lifestyle programs based on nondieting and improving patients' health at every size offer a fresh approach that is flexible, open, accepting, individualized, and family-centered. They focus on the mental and physical well-being of each child in the context of what is appropriate in that child's life. Leaders in the new programs recognize that people are confused and shaken by today's conflicting health messages and need to learn to trust themselves again.

In implementing health-centered programs in the new paradigm, health providers use a variety of approaches. Some begin with a focus on self-esteem and improving body image; others emphasize healthy lifestyle. They make use of individual counseling, group training, or support and consciousness-raising groups. They may conduct programs in schools, community, or health-care settings.

Yet, at the core, the programs will be consistent and comprehensive, shifting emphasis away from weight, and toward self-acceptance, self-trust, empowerment, and the prevention of problems. They will encourage people to eat and move in normal, pleasurable ways, working with their natural regulatory abilities. Physical activity is an integral part of the Health at Any Size approach. When people are comfortably active, they can eat more and be fully nourished. Appetite and hunger are more responsive, and more likely to be synchronized in rhythm with other natural body processes.

In the new programs, participants focus on how they can help themselves be healthier by changing habits in a gradual way, how they can feel better physically and mentally, and learn worthwhile family patterns. The facilitator will ask: What is this individual willing and able to change? Looking at the whole person, what might work in her particular situation? This can help children stabilize at what seems their natural weight, a weight at which they are healthy and well nourished. We can help them understand that keeping a stable weight through adult life is a worthy goal, since most people continue to gain weight as they grow older.

When they gradually change lifestyle habits, some children will lose weight, and if lost this way, it will likely stay off. However, we can't promise weight loss. Some will maintain their weight. Others who are undernourished and have kept their weight unnaturally low may gain weight. We can help them appreciate the mental and emotional benefits of maintaining a more natural weight.

Today we are seeing a shift toward the new paradigm of Health at Any Size, as more experts are advising moving to this approach in treating children. For instance, in its latest *Pediatric Nutrition Handbook*, the American Academy of Pediatrics clearly reveals this shift. It advises physicians that the goal of treatment should be health—to decrease morbidity and risk for morbidity, not culturally-endorsed appearance. It warns about medical problems resulting from diets. The handbook advises regular exercise and nutritionally balanced diets designed to meet growth requirements. For obese infants, reduction in weight should not be attempted, but rather slowing of weight gain.

The American Dietetic Association's Pediatric Manual of Clinical Dietetics advises slow weight loss or weight maintenance for large kids, and notes that it is more important to maintain weight rather than trying to normalize weight. "For obese and overweight children and adolescents who have not experienced their growth spurt, intervention should focus on cessation of weight gain rather than weight loss to allow for growth to an appropriate weight for height."[105]

The American Heart Association calls for primary prevention of obesity in its Scientific Statement *Understanding Obesity in Youth*, because "long-term studies of weight reduction in children have shown that 80 to 90 percent return to their original weight percentile." The paper warns that calorie restriction in children has been associated with many problems. Food restriction should not be attempted in infants, but rather, avoid overfeeding. It reiterates the Pediatric Handbook warning that the risks and difficulties of weight loss may well exceed the benefits.[106]

The Expert Committee Recommendations from the Department of Health and Human Services caution, "An unsuccessful program may diminish the child's self-esteem and impair future efforts to improve weight." It calls for normalized eating: "Establish daily meal and snack times; parents or caregivers should determine what food is offered and when, and the child should decide whether to eat." And it calls for acceptance of large children: "Clinicians who care for families of overweight children must treat them with sensitivity, compassion..."[107] These experts are well aware of the harm that children often suffer from ill-advised weight loss programs.

Overweight children have been treated with low-fat, calorie-restricted diets for more than 50 years without any demonstrable success, charge dietitians Joanne Ikeda and Rita Mitchell, in *Pediatric Clinics of North America.*[108] The Pediatric Nutrition Handbook says as many of 80 percent of kids who go on unsupervised magazine-based diets have medical problems resulting from those diets.

An increasing body of evidence shows that the efforts of physicians and parents often backfire when they try to control children's eating. Instead of helping them slim down, it impedes their ability to self-regulate and puts these children at higher risk for overweight. Limiting calories for growing children has been linked to stunted growth and nutrient deficiencies, especially of iron, zinc, calcium and vitamins A and E. Also linked to dieting and food restriction are disordered eating, low self-esteem, high levels of depression, suicidal ideation, and stress.[109]

However the shift to the new paradigm for some of these authorities is not complete. While they call for healthy lifestyle solutions that do no harm for most kids, they make exceptions for the larger child. The AHA paper encourages "aggressive medical interventions" for the obese child, and suggests that the child as low as the 75th percentile of BMI and body fat should be considered at risk. The Expert Committee of HHS says children with complications may need "rapid weight loss." The ADA manual suggests super-obese patients may benefit from a very-low-calorie protein-sparing modified fast.

While generally discouraging pills and surgery for kids, the AAP handbook offers exceptions. "No evidence supports the role of radical surgery or pharmacologic therapies, *except in extremely obese children in whom all other interventions have failed.*" [Italics added.] Exceptions like this in the hands of some practitioners may be broadly applied to include most larger children, whether or not they have risk factors.

Physicians need to be skeptical about advice that suggests interventions may be suitable for severely overweight children—even though they don't work and are unsafe for others. If a weight loss intervention doesn't work for healthy, moderately-overweight kids and can harm them, why would any responsible physician prescribe it for a severely obese child? And if this child is at high risk, with high blood pressure or blood glucose levels, doesn't this call for even more conservative treatment?

Set Point and Prevention

The big question, which has not been answered, is: How can we lower the set point, so weight is naturally regulated at a lower point? It's quite apparent that the body defends its natural or usual weight, which has been called the set point or settling point. A large body of animal and human research suggests that weight is regulated, just as is body temperature, or salt in the blood stream. After a period of dieting, regulatory mechanisms seem to kick in to bring weight back up to normal. (Or the reverse: after overfeeding and a period of weight gain, weight drops back to normal.) Six months is about the limit of success on any weight loss program before regain begins.[110] Then regain to set point is usually as rapid as was the weight loss, or it may take up to two to five years. Often a ratcheting up of weight and set point seems to occur following a bout of dieting. The person loses 15 pounds, regains 20, then stabilizes at the higher point.

How can this regulatory mechanism be reprogrammed to defend a lower weight? We don't know. A possibility is increased physical activity. Reducing food intake apparently has little effect. This is why prevention is so important. We don't know how to reduce a child's weight to so-called "ideal" in a safe and lasting way. But we can help children maintain a consistent and possibly lower weight through active living and normalized eating while his or her height catches up.

Medical Care in the New Paradigm

The Health at Any size approach usually begins with a traditional examination:

- ★ Routine medical exam including measurement of height and weight and plotting BMI for age on standardized growth charts.
- ★ Testing for any possible medical causes of overweight that require treatment as well as testing for related complications, including elevated serum lipids, hypertension, orthopedic disorders, sleep disorders, gall bladder disease and insulin resistance.
- ★ Review of family history of weight and risk factors for related diseases.
- ★ Nutritional assessment by a dietitian to assess the basic pattern of meals and snacks, frequency of fast food intake, consumption of soft drinks, physical activity, dieting history, and home and cultural environment. When appropriate, an in-depth assessment may be conducted, including eating disorder screening, and psychosocial screening by a psychologist or social worker.[111]

Weight gain pattern may be determined from prior exams, if available, by plotting weight gain and linear growth on the growth charts. Recent or consistent annual increases of 2 or more BMI units may be cause for concern.[112] The standard growth charts are available on the CDC Web site (www.cdc.gov/growthcharts.com) in English, Spanish and French. Included are training modules, a PowerPoint presentation to help health professionals provide expertise, and information on screening, assessing and management.

Physicians dealing with teens will routinely ask lifestyle questions such as the following. "Do you walk to school?...Do you take PE class? Did you eat breakfast today? How much meat did you eat yesterday? Are you dieting? Are you concerned about being fat?"

It is helpful to work with other members of the health care team on a set of questions, and answers that may send up red flags. Responses may suggest referrals to others on the team. If depression is suspected, assessing nutrition should be a first step. It's no coincidence that more girls are depressed today, when one-fourth to half are undernourished. Instead of Prozac, what many depressed teenage girls need is not a drug at all, but food. Eating disorder screening also may be indicated.

When a child shows a sudden weight gain or drop, medical or emotional problems may be suspected. Professional help from a pediatrician, dietitian, or child psychologist may be necessary. Satter advises identifying and correcting any destabilizing influence, which in turn restores the normal regulatory and growth processes. Understanding feeding management may correct the underlying cause of a child's energy imbalance, but it must be focused on parents' feeding practices rather than on what and how much children eat, she says. "Parents may fail to get a meal on the table, then try to control what and how much their child eats."

Parents must respect the division of responsibility, which allows children the freedom to pick and choose from food that the parent has made available. It is when parents intrude on the child's prerogatives that feeding difficulties and disturbances of food regulation occur, she says.[113] Satter finds that some parents are so rigid and controlling they can't trust the child's eating. Other parents are so chaotic, both internally and externally, they can't bring order to feeding. At both extremes, families may need mental health professionals to help them correct the rigidity or chaos.

Unfortunately, such families frequently will not participate in treatment and only want the child put on a diet. They want a quick fix. But Satter says, "It is absolutely unrealistic to expect the child to lose weight when the whole family system is set up to promote the opposite."

Medical Care in the New Paradigm

Recommendations for treatment in the new paradigm include the following:

1. **Assess family readiness for change.** Parents and child need to be fully committed for success in maintaining long-term behavior change, overall change in family dietary patterns, intake and level of physical activity.[114]
2. **Help the child set small, short-term habit change goals that are achievable.** Begin by increasing physical activity. Consider following the Healthy Weight Kids 7-Step program in Chapter 20 Use behavior management principles aimed at permanent change.
3. **Help parents set goals for small, gradual changes preventive of eating and weight problems.** Include family eating patterns, nutrition, physical activity, and stress levels
4. **Do not put the child on a diet or attempt to control eating.** Explain that the child needs to tune in to his or her own inner signals to determine hunger and fullness.
5. **Don't set weight loss goals or promise weight loss.** When weight is lost, encourage the child and parent to regard it as the result of improved habits, rather than an end in itself.
6. **Do no harm.** Don't weight-cycle children. Don't use weight loss methods that have potential for harm.
7. **Do not, through dietary advice, counseling, or other means, contribute to any of the six major eating and weight problems** (eating disorders, dysfunctional eating, undernutrition of teenage girls, hazardous weight loss, overweight or size prejudice). All are interrelated, and trying to fix one area will impact the others, often in negative ways.
8. **Build safeguards into the program, so that whether or not weight is lost or kept off, and even if the program is dropped, the child will have some lasting benefits.** Worthwhile benefits are increased self-esteem, acceptance, self-respect, confidence and sense of well being, as well as improved lifestyle changes in eating, activity and stress management if they are sustained. A follow-

up session can explore this and validate for the child and parents that some success was achieved, if indeed this happened. If it didn't, changes may be needed in the program.

An interdisciplinary team, to include professionals in nutrition, physical therapy, pediatric care, and psychology, is well-suited to providing treatment. Together the team can develop a plan for individualized care addressing the many dimensions of wellness for the child and family in the context of their culture and local community.

It is important that parents be involved in intervention programs. Studies suggest it can be even more beneficial when parents join the child in a program of changing their own activity and eating habits. This has the added benefit of improving family lifestyle, which can be highly preventive of further weight and eating problems for all family members.

Puberty

Puberty is a time of profound physical, emotional, and social changes. Some youngsters will mature early, and others much later: this can be a big concern to them. The physician can reassure them that their rate of development is normal, and help them understand what to expect.

Puberty begins earlier today than in the past, at around ten or earlier for girls, and about age eleven or twelve for boys, and is complete at around age seventeen to nineteen for girls and twenty in boys.[115] During puberty and adolescence, girls tend to gain weight and add body fat, while boys become more muscular. It is a time of higher risk for eating disorders.

Appreciate Ethnic Cultures

Health professionals who educate themselves about the different cultural and ethnic groups are better equipped to relate to adolescents and provide needed services. This is becoming increasingly important. Our youthful population is growing rapidly more racially and ethnically diverse, with 37 percent of adolescents ages ten to nineteen today being Hispanic or members of non-white racial groups, a trend that is projected to increase.[116] A growing number are immigrants, many of them from Latin American countries. Their English skills and educational levels vary. So do their cultural practices and beliefs.

Unfortunately, much of the research that professionals rely on today has studied only white middle-class children and adults.Yet we know that weight, body composition and related health risks differ for these various populations. To be effective, healthy lifestyle programs need to be culturally appropriate and sensitive to these differences.

Each child needs to be understood in the context of his or her own family, neighborhood, school, church, and workplace. Programs in the new paradigm aim to incorporate cultural traditions and values. Parents are assured they can trust their family heritage, that traditional foods and ways of celebrating with food are valuable to pass down through the generations, shaped and expressed in modern ways as they may be, yet honoring the past. Parents learn to trust their own judgment and feel confident that they and their children can make good decisions.

Sensitive Counseling

It's important that physicians treating large children be sensitive to self-esteem and body image issues. Carol Johnson, author of *Self-Esteem Comes in All Sizes,* offers these tips to health professionals who treat large children:

- ★ Assume that an overweight patient knows she is overweight;
- ★ Treat larger patients as individuals;
- ★ Don't assume the large patient is eating excessively;
- ★ Don't blame every health problem on excess weight;
- ★ Provide the same treatment as for a thin patient with the same problem;
- ★ Focus on health, not weight;
- ★ Acknowledge and accept that despite their very best efforts, many patients will not become thin;

- ★ Examine your own attitudes honestly and eliminate the prejudice that arises from cultural messages;
- ★ Measure success by other means than weight loss;
- ★ Emphasize to large patients that their weight has nothing to do with their self-worth;
- ★ Provide armless chairs, and large exam gowns and blood pressure cuffs;
- ★ Don't make large patients afraid to come to you, or they will avoid health care.[117]

Ideally, physicians treat large patients as they do any others, offering the same testing and treatment, when appropriate. A broken finger is treated as a broken finger, not an occasion to blame the patient's weight. They recognize that large children may have special health needs, while not assuming this. They help large kids feel comfortable by treating them with sensitivity, giving them a better understanding of their health and medical conditions, and offering them the best care possible.[118]

Drug Answers: Just Around the Corner?

Many health professionals believe that drug solutions are just around the corner. If so, that corner is still a long way off. We've seen no pill yet that keeps off more than a few pounds, and each has serious drawbacks.

Nonetheless, we can expect aggressive publicity on new anti-obesity drugs and weight loss programs to hit the headlines every few months. It's been going on for at least 30 years. Right now a reported 27 new drugs are in the pipeline. In the meantime, of course, some doctors will continue to prescribe medications that are unproven for long-term health.

The physician should not be fooled. Despite the favorable publicity given to past short-lived miracles, in every case, promises far exceeded results. Ultimately every "miracle cure" was exposed as a failure within a few years. We need only recall the disastrous national experience with the very-low-calorie liquid diets and the Fen-Phen/Redux pills. Both these methods enjoyed years of powerful endorsement by federal health agencies, backed up by hundreds of (short-term) research studies in the medical literature. The industry provided reams of "scientific proof." Who could blame a physician for believing what was presented so convincingly? (See Chapter 9 for more information on these and other weight loss programs).

This game will end only when consumers and their physicians demand long-term proof of safety and effectiveness, and even improved health—over a period of at least three to five years. Children should not be used as guinea pigs for pills that can show only one-year safety and efficacy, just because they are approved by FDA. Let's recognize that at this time we have no safe and effective ways to lose weight long-term, other than lifestyle changes.

Professional Training

Health professionals are requesting more training in medical schools and continuing education courses to address the problem of childhood overweight. A recent national survey found high interest among health professionals in getting more training, especially in behavioral management strategies and parenting techniques. Providers with ten years or more of experience reported the greatest interest in training.[119] In California, a state-wide one-day training program, *Children and Weight: What Health Professionals Can Do About It*, is helping physicians and others shift toward a health-centered perspective in dealing with obesity.[120]

The goal is to help health professionals deal with pediatric overweight in helpful, non-threatening ways, and motivate them to work with parents, schools, and their communities to create environments that promote optimal health for all children.

Medical Clinics

The population of larger people is often under-served in medical clinics, because patients fear staff disapproval and the lectures about weight—almost sure to come. Some medical clinics are moving ahead in this area. They encourage care providers and staff to be accepting, respectful and accommodating of large patients, and ensure that hospital and clinics offer comfortable facilities.

The West River Regional Medical Center, in Hettinger, North Dakota, has been addressing these concerns for the last five years. An advisory group, the Health at Every Size Task Force, brings together health professionals and community leaders from the vast three-state rural area of over 18,000 square miles, which is served by the medical center and its six satellite clinics. The task force offers feedback on public perceptions of attitudes and relationships with patients, participates in training programs, and organizes awareness programs in school and community on such topics as body image, self-esteem, nutrition, and healthy lifestyles. Changes have been made in the physical environment, as well, such as providing sturdy chairs without arms, large-size gowns, blood pressure cuffs and equipment, and improving privacy and weighing issues.

In the Kibbutz

Ideally, a health team will address all eating and weight treatment under one program so that efforts are comprehensive and well coordinated. An example of a comprehensive program that addresses prevention and treatment of both obesity and eating disorders comes to us from a kibbutz in northern Israel. Launched through the community clinic, the program shows two-year success in a population of 680 persons. Targeted for individual attention were all the 38 girls, age twelve to seventeen, and their parents, teachers and significant other adults. Three girls were diagnosed with anorexia nervosa and one at high risk for anorexia, and were referred to a specialist. Twelve were referred with eating problems and received individual counseling in a non-judgmental, supportive, empathetic approach for both teenagers and parents. Six girls with weight problems were assessed and then followed a program of individualized nondiet counseling. In all, 23 girls and women and five boys and men received special help in weight and eating issues. Expenses were kept low, using resources already in place.

Results showed marked improvement after two years in each condition. There was improvement in lifestyle behavior and a greater sense of well-being. Two of the girls with anorexia recovered and the third was much improved. The high-risk girl developed anorexia nervosa, but was diagnosed early and recovered within one year. There was a greater willingness to ask for help for friends.

Moreover, a big change took place in the attitude of clinic team members as the intervention progressed and proved successful. In two years the staff made the paradigm shift from a focus on weight and calories to the broader aspects of body image, eating behavior, internal regulation and coping with social pressures. Through all this, the highly committed team gave strong support to both youth and parents. The team went on to help train teams in other communities.[121]

Eating Disorder Risk

The American Dietetic Association warns against promoting weight loss to individuals who might have binge eating disorder or other eating disorders. When young people come for help with weight loss, ADA recommends counseling on body image issues and how to stop the pursuit of thinness. It may be healthier to suggest they accept themselves at or near their present weight, stop binge eating and learn how to prevent future weight gain, says ADA. This official recognition of the value of normalizing weight is a major step forward in the nutrition field.[122]

Physicians moving into the new paradigm will learn all they can about eating disturbances, eating disorders, the effects of undernutrition and malnutrition, the high-risk periods of early and late adolescence, and how these problems are affecting girls and women today. They will resist oversimplification of these complex issues. And they will seek collaboration between health professionals, teachers and parents in dealing with them.[123]

Eating Disorder Screening

Communities and schools participating in the National Eating Disorders Screening Program have found remarkable success in getting help for individuals with eating disturbances. In 1998, 35,897 people were screened in over a thousand sites during Eating Disorders Awareness and Prevention Week in February. About one-third scored positive for symptoms or concerns consistent with an eating disorder. Ninety percent of these were not in treatment, but nearly half subsequently followed through and saw a clinician. Besides getting young people with eating disorders into treatment, this had the added benefit of reaching many youth at earlier stages of dysfunctional eating and getting help for them.[124]

Training teams from around the country are brought together by the National Eating Disorders Association (NEDA) to prepare for Eating Disorders Awareness and Prevention Week, which is observed in all 50 states and Canada. Health providers working with these teams can coordinate efforts to make their own programs more effective. (For more information visit www.nationaleatingdisorders.org.)

Health Clubs

The large child may be referred to a physical therapist for help in setting up a fitness program. This may include joining a health club. It's important that the health club be a comfortable place for the large youngster. Fitness centers have been criticized for taking the fun out of movement—and adding plenty of anxiety. It can be intimidating when a thin, muscled trainer, in stunning spandex, hustles the youngster through fitness testing and goal setting, throwing out rapid-fire numbers about heart rate, calorie burn, and equipment dials.

The client is expected to get up to speed on a quickly escalating 10-week program of workouts on various machines, maintaining heart rate between 60 and 80 percent for 30 minutes. It can be confusing, and too much may be expected, too soon, for the out-of-shape youngster. These clubs don't have a solid record of success. Dropout rates at fitness centers are high—reportedly half of all clients drop out the first week, and over 70 percent in the first year. For the large kid, it may take a good deal of courage just to begin.

New approaches at some health and fitness centers make them comfortable for larger children and adults. Or there may be opportunities to work out in school or university facilities. Establishing long-term fitness needs to be the goal.

There is a need for workout centers especially for larger kids, similar to the exercise program for large women at the research center in George Washington University Medical Center, Washington, DC. Clients there stick with the 14-week program, and most continue their exercising for months and years after they finish, say Jolie Glass, director, and Wayne Miller, exercise science professor. Their most important reason for staying? They feel safe. "Surprisingly, they don't mean physically safe, they mean emotionally safe. These women love to come to a place where the health club atmosphere and attitude is absent, where they can exercise at their own level without feeling intimidated," says Glass.[125]

The clients also rank the caring atmosphere high on their priority list, and a staff that is knowledgeable and sensitive to issues of body size and acceptance. "Many…need to talk about how their exercise is affecting them emotionally, spiritually, and psychologically, in addition to how it is affecting them physiologically," says Glass. "These factors, along with the social aspects, help them change their attitude from an angry and determined 'I can exercise' to a pleasant and satisfying 'I like to exercise.'"

The first question most people ask in the health club is, "How much weight will I lose and how fast?" Trainers at the University Medical Center work hard to change this attitude. They emphasize that whether weight is lost or not, there are major benefits in aerobic fitness, strength and flexibility, blood pressure and cholesterol profile, as well as lower risk of diabetes, cardiovascular disease, osteoporosis and premature death. They point out that not all overweight people will lose weight in an exercise training program.

For the health or fitness professional, Miller recommends individualizing a physical activity program based on what the person finds enjoyable, is easily accessible, and within his or her capability. Progress should be measured in strength, flexibility and endurance, not weight lost.[126]

Recommendations Miller gives for the health or fitness provider include:

1. **Perform an exercise evaluation.** Testing for strength, flexibility, and endurance provides valuable information that can be used to individualize the exercise prescription (instead of body weight).

2. **Select exercises or activities that are enjoyable, easily accessible, and within the functional capacity of the individual.** This will help ensure safety and adherence to the program.
3. **Set the exercise intensity according to what is most relevant to the individual.** In general, low intensity exercise of long duration will provide the most fat to fuel mix as well as increase total caloric expenditure (40 to 60 percent of maximal aerobic capacity or heart rate range).
4. **Add strength and flexibility training.** Strength training will help maintain lean body mass as well as metabolic rate. Flexibility training will help maintain functional capacity and may prevent injury.
5. **Focus the activity plan on improvement of overall health and quality of life.** If a reduction in body weight occurs, this should be viewed as a side benefit of lifestyle change, not the end product.

"We have been applying these recommendations to hundreds of clients in our clinical exercise programs for over ten years and have witnessed only a few injuries, seen modest weight losses, shown significant decreases in disease risks and symptoms, and have high adherence ratios," says Miller.

Monitor Obsessive Activity

When they promote fitness, trainers need at the same time to monitor young people for signs of overtraining or activity disorder, such as fatigue, injury, loss of emotional vigor, or increased compulsivity. Obsessive exercise can be most harmful when combined with calorie restriction, as it often is in athletic girls.

For girls recovering from eating disorders, exercise should not be recommended until eating behaviors are relatively stable. Then professionals might prescribe low intensity, low duration aerobic exercise as well as strength training to increase strength, muscle mass and possibly prevent bone loss. For patients with a history of eating or activity disorders, Glass recommends:

- ★ Educate the patient concerning the potential health benefits and risks of exercise.
- ★ Create a written agreement with the patient that specifically details the exercise program and eating plan.
- ★ Require the patient to keep exercise records and review these regularly for signs of activity disorder.
- ★ Require the patient to consume a calorie-containing sport drink during the exercise session.
- ★ Monitor body weight and reduce exercise activities if weight begins to drop.[127]

5 Health Care Myths

Myth #1. Healthy weight, as currently defined, depicts the range of lowest health risk (BMI 18.5 to 24.9).
Fact: The point of lowest mortality is a BMI of about 24.5 for Caucasians, 27 for African Americans, and after age 55, 26.5 for Caucasian women and 29.8 for African American women, with only weak association after age 75, according to a review of 236 randomized, controlled studies by the National Institutes of Health, NHLBI (See Chapter 8).

Myth #2. Obesity causes the health risks associated with it.
Fact: We don't know; both may be caused by a third factor. Inactivity is shown as a strong contributing factor that may cause both obesity and related risks (others may be stress and weight cycling). Increased activity dramatically improves most health risks whether weight is lost or not (See Chapter 2).

Myth #3. Current treatments are safe and effective (diet, drugs, surgery).
Fact: All current weight loss methods should be considered experimental, since none are proven long-term safe and effective. They only weight cycle most people or worse, cause injury or even death. (See Chapter 9.)

Myth #4. Health is always improved by weight loss.
Fact: At least 15 large long-term studies show higher death rates with weight loss, including the Framingham Heart Study, Harvard Alumni Study, and NHANES I follow-up. Health risks may be relat-

ed to loss of lean body mass: muscle, bone and organs (See Chapters 2 and 9).

Myth #5. Scare tactics and an emphasis on thinness help people lose weight, prevent obesity, and do no harm.
Fact: Obesity rates rose steeply over the last 30 years, as pressures to be thin increased. Scaring children and adults about the risks of obesity adds to their stress, anxiety, and potential immune suppression leading to higher risks, and fails to help them lose weight. An overemphasis on thinness can lead to body hatred, hazardous weight loss, malnutrition, size discrimination, and eating disorders (See Chapters 5 and 10).

Unfortunately, much current health care for obesity is based on these myths, resulting in weight cycling, physical and emotional damage, and even death. With the Health at Any Size approach, children and adults of every size are empowered to move ahead to improved health and wholeness in body, mind and spirit.

Chapter 20

♦ ♦ ❖ ♦ ♦ ❖ ♦ ♦ ❖ ♦ ♦ ❖ ♦ ♦ ❖ ♦ ♦ ❖ ♦ ♦

Seven Steps to a Healthier Weight

Healthy Weight Kids is a seven-step program for helping children and teens develop and adopt a healthy, confident, diet-free lifestyle in which sound habits come so naturally, they need not think about them. It works for youth of all sizes and ages. With this plan young people on the wrong track can change direction, rediscover active living and normalized eating, and build a strong foundation for a positive health journey through life. As a parent, you can help free them to live in normal, healthy ways, restore life's balance in body, mind and spirit and move on to what's really important in their lives.

The focus is on four major areas of life: living actively, eating well, feeling good about ourselves, and feeling good about others. The goal is for lasting change that makes a real difference, not quick results. So relax and enjoy the journey with your child. The steps are listed below:

1. Normalize activity. Active living is basic to good health. Review your child's school activity and sports programs. Plan a goal of 30 minutes of moderate activity, on most days, for preteens, teens and adults, and at least 1 hour of active play for younger children. At home, establish a regular activity program, preferably for the whole family. Provide access to a variety of sports and activities they'll continue through life so each child can succeed. Find ways to break up long stretches of inactivity. Limit television to 2 hours or less per day. Don't rush this process. If you begin at ground zero, it may take several months before you approach these goals. If you and your children are not regularly active, begin with a 5-minute walk on most days (at least 5 days a week), and keep up that relatively easy level for a full four weeks to establish the habit. The key to developing enjoyable active habits that last a lifetime is to begin to slowly and increase your pace gradually. Have fun together.(See Chapter 14 for more information on living actively).

2. Normalize eating. Establish regular mealtime eating habits, three meals a day and one or two snacks, beginning with breakfast. Stop all dieting and food restriction. Instead, help your children respond to their own internal signals of hunger and fullness, so they eat when hungry and stop when full. Explain they should eat till their stomach feels just right. For a time they may overeat, if they've been restricting. Explain that this is okay, and that it will soon normalize when foods are no longer forbidden. Give up, for now at least, the goal of weight loss. Shift the focus to wellness. Parents are their children's most important role models, and if they eat well children will follow those patterns. Respect Satter's golden rule in feeding children: Parents are responsible for what is presented to eat and the way it is presented; children are responsible for what, how much and even whether they eat. This of itself relieves stress for both children and parents, and provides more energy. Take time to relax while eating and eat family meals together at least once each day, if possible, with the television off. (See Chapter 14 for more on how to eat well). Continue Step 1 activities: If walking at the level of 5 minutes a day, continue this 4 weeks, then begin adding 2 to 3 minutes a week.

3. Balance sound nutrition. In this plan the child first learns to normalize eating patterns and tune in to body signals, as in step 2, then gradually begins to modify food choices, if needed. Balance, variety and moderation are key nutrition principles. Balance means eating at least the recommended amounts from all five food groups in the Food Guide Pyramid: breads and cereals, fruits, vegetables, meat and alternates, and milk and dairy. Begin the day with a healthy breakfast that includes enough protein to keep the child energized till lunch. To ensure variety, help the child choose many different foods from these groups. Be patient if a child dislikes certain foods. Set a good example, continue to offer the food, but don't make an issue of it. Understand that all foods can fit in a healthy diet, but encourage children to avoid extremes: don't overeat of high-fat, high-sugar foods, and don't restrict them severely. Healthy food choices keep children well-nourished and energized to meet the events and challenges of the day. (See Chapter 16 for more on sound nutrition). Continue Steps 1 and 2 activities, making improvements gradually.

4. Feel good about yourself. A nurturing environment in home, school, and community promotes all aspects of growth and development for children, in mind, body and spirit. Evaluate what is going on in your child's environment, how it affects your child, and if there are negative aspects, how they can be improved. Then take steps to move ahead. Your unconditional love and acceptance, as a parent, promotes your child's self-esteem and self-respect. Teach positive thinking and positive self-talk. Daily affirmations help build self-confidence. Celebrate and enjoy each child's special characteristics and talents. Accept and trust the child, and have confidence in his or her ability to make changes. Encourage a healthy body image, and teach that every body is a good body. Help children avoid focusing on weight or shape, or talking about it in a negative way. If anxiety and stress are problems, relaxation techniques can be helpful. Encourage children to become involved in activities and organizations in which they make use of their strengths and unique abilities, and encourage them to take pride in themselves and their accomplishments. For teens, keeping a journal can be helpful. (See Chapters 18 and 21). Continue Steps 1, 2 and 3 activities, moving gradually forward in these areas.

5. Communicate feelings. Promote communication and sharing of feelings from the time children are young. Share your own feelings with them in positive and appropriate ways. Listen attentively, calmly and noncommittally when your child wants to talk about problems, and encourage sharing of feelings by asking, "How do you feel about that?" Instead of solving problems for children, we need to empower them to solve their own problems at their appropriate age level with helpful listening and encouragement. Good communication builds positive relationships and keeps parents in touch with what their children are doing and thinking. (See Chapter 18 for more on enriching communication). Continue Steps 1, 2, 3 and 4 activities, moving gradually ahead. Avoid taking on too many changes at once, or striving for perfection. Work to maintain each new habit for at least four months.

6. Feel good about others. Help your child develop good relationships, not only with their peers, but also with caring neighbors and other adults. Promote acceptance, respect and tolerance of diversity, and set a good example. Insist on zero tolerance for size bias in school. Encourage children to get involved in community and volunteer activities, and to find ways of helping others at their appropriate age level. Continue Steps 1, 2, 3, 4 and 5 activities, making gradual improvements as seems reasonable and positive in the child's life. Avoid taking on too many changes at once. Avoid striving for perfection. Work to maintain each new habit for at least four months. Move on to Step 7 only as seems appropriate, when other changes are being well maintained.

7. Balance the dimensions of wellness. As we consider the whole child in body, mind and spirit, keep in mind that weight and eating are only part of wellness, and need to be kept in perspective. What are the child's broader needs? What are his or her interests? Consider other health and safety issues, such as avoiding substance abuse and violence, getting regular medical check-ups, following up on medical recommendations, and practicing safety in traffic, recreation and work. Consider changes that might be helpful in the intellectual, emotional, social, spiritual, occupational dimensions. Help your child develop interests and skills that lead to success, pleasure and fulfillment, apart from appearance. Would your child benefit from taking piano lessons, joining 4-H or scouts, learning to ride a horse, or getting involved at your church or place of worship? It is rewarding to connect with the wider world out there and find ways that each child can contribute. Since Step 7 moves ahead to these broader components of wellness it is usually preferable to postpone these changes at least four or five months, until weight and eating issues are first normalized. (See Chapter 11 for more on wellness). Meanwhile, continue Steps 1, 2, 3, 4, 5 and 6 activities, making gradual improvements.

Moving Ahead by Fours

Changing lifestyle takes time and involves not only the physical body, but the conscious and subconscious mind as well. This does not happen overnight. You can expect to move ahead by fours. It takes four days to bring the habit-change decision to the attention of the child's subconscious, to get across the message that he or she really means it. In four weeks the child can change the habit, being aware of the risk of relapse. In four months the habit is well established, as long as all else is consistent. In fouar years it belongs to that child forever.

The first four days are critical, so stick carefully to your plan. This is the time to get the attention of the subconscious, to show you really mean it.

How to Change a Habit

Approach habit changes the way you learned your lessons in grade school. In math you first learned to add and later worked fractions through a gradual process of building each skill on the one before, always maintaining those earlier skills. You worked hard, and earned many rewards, reinforcements, stars and smiley faces that kept you going. You never looked back. Even a baby learns to talk this way, cooing and babbling for months, then finally speaking that first word. Moms and dads encourage baby all along the way by smiling, praising, hugging and repeating the sounds over and over, helping shape them into words.

Your child will progress most easily when you break new health habits into small steps, each appropriate to age level and building on the one before. Don't try to go too fast. As the child moves ahead with a new step, it is necessary to consistently keep up the ones before. It's helpful to make a brief weekly contract or plan, to keep easy records and give rewards, just as your teacher did in school. But it's best to avoid making long-term written plans, as they tend to be discouraging and unattainable. Go with practical weekly plans for at least the first four months.

Learning theory tells us people learn by changing three things: knowledge, attitude, and behavior. It may sound counterintuitive, but the best way to learn is often to "just do it"—change the behavior. Often the attitude change and full understanding will follow.

Honor Good Habits

Your child is probably depending on many helpful lifestyle habits right now. Take stock of the four areas. For instance, is the child regularly active in walking to school? Is she eating three meals a day? Does your child manage stress well?

Discover, strengthen and praise these good habits or any others. Pat yourself and your child on the back. Keep what is helpful, and work on changing harmful habits. A word of caution: In evaluating current habits, remember that extremism is not helpful. Continually over exercising or rigidly controlling one's food intake is a perversion of health and well being and your child or teen may need professional help. Remember that the goal is to normalize your children's lives by developing healthy habits that enrich body, mind and spirit, and allow them to get on with what's important in their lives.

Age Appropriate

For a younger child, these will be parental changes for the most part. You can take direct action. As you make changes and alter the environment, the child will naturally adapt, without detailed explanation or discussion. Reassure the child that these are good changes and will continue. If the child does not easily adapt, or if the changes become stressful, you may be moving too quickly. Return to an easier level of change.

For preteens and teenagers, some changes can be made by parents—such as establishing family meals, or making a regular time for physical activity. For older children, encourage their interest in making changes, and enlist their support in developing a plan. It may be necessary to help them work through some of the stages of readiness before beginning.

Teenagers may work with parents on some changes in the home. For the most part, however, they will need to take charge. Be aware of the stages of change. Is the young person ready to move ahead on this? If not, go slowly. Habit change will not happen unless they are ready and interested. You can help to empower the child and be a role model, but cannot take over decision making. As a parent, consider joining your child in your own journey through this seven-step program. Family-based approaches are shown to be most successful, and studies show this has the added benefit of reducing family stress and improving parents' habits.

When Do We Begin?

You as a parent may be ready to begin. But as you need the cooperation of others, consider their readiness to buy into your plan. Especially with older children, you may need to spend time laying the groundwork. This may take several weeks or longer. Repeatedly explain, in a casual, non-threatening way, what you would like to do, or intend to do, and why.

During the first stage of precontemplation, your spouse and children may not be interested in changing any health habits—they are listening, observing and thinking about it. Your encouragement helps them make a commitment. During the preparation stage, the decision to go ahead has been made, and together you can determine best approach, and develop a plan. The action stage comes next, followed by a maintenance period. Be aware that a relapse stage is possible, and needs to be dealt with decisively, or all that is gained may be lost.

Before beginning this Healthy Weight Kids program, you may want to consider your own readiness to see it through. How committed are you to developing a healthy lifestyle for yourself and others? If you feel the need for more personal preparation, reading Part 2 of the book *Women Afraid to Eat: Breaking Free in Today's Weight Obsessed World*, can be helpful.

Contracts, Rewards and Records

It is helpful to make a brief weekly contract or plan, to keep easy records and give rewards—just as your teacher did in school.

However, avoid making long-term written plans, as they tend to be discouraging and unattainable. Go with practical weekly plans for at least the first four months.

Making a simple written contract with yourself or your child is a valuable tool in reinforcing the new program—a visual reminder of your decision, written on paper you can pick up and hold. This helps to enlist your subconscious mind.

Consistency and following through on a contract is important. Yet, at times you may decide to back up, or make changes that better fit the child and the situation. As part of your contract you promise a weekly reward, either to yourself or your child, as seems appropriate. Reward yourself, or have the child give herself or himself a reward. This helps to reinforce the steps being taken. They may be small gifts, places to go, or things to do, such as a movie or a free afternoon reading a novel. Try different types of reinforcement, but don't use a food-related reward. Keep food emotionally neutral as much as possible. Eating for comfort or as a reward confuses a child learning to eat in response to stomach signals.

Teenagers will probably make their own contracts and give their own rewards. Parents can help as seems appropriate, making sure to respect the young person's privacy.

Rewards are paid at the end of each week. They are for following through and completing the week, not necessarily for doing everything perfectly. So if you or the child has slipped a few times, it's okay. Forgive yourselves and go on. Resolve to do better. Or, if

FIGURE 20.1 **Sample Contract**

Sample Contract for the first week

Date ___________

I pledge that this week I will:

__Walk 5 minutes each day (or march/dance in place)

__Eat 3 meals each day

My reward for completing this contract is _______________________

Signed_____________________

a step proves too difficult, break it into smaller steps, or continue at the lower level another week or two before moving on. Providing rewards may seem somewhat frivolous in the face of obvious health benefits, but don't forget there are often unseen rewards for keeping things the way they are. The old pleasures and rewards seem at times more desirable than any new ones.

For example, your family may decide to take a half-hour walk every evening after dinner. All goes well for three days, but on the fourth you're tired. You really don't want to get up off the couch. Or a favorite TV show is on, or it's raining outside. Your spouse and children are finding excuses, too. The perceived benefits of avoiding the walk begin to outweigh the reasons for taking it. So now, instead of having a new and better habit, or even being at peace with old "couch potato" habit, your family is entangled in a web of failed good intentions, guilt, criticism, and grim resolutions to do better. (Beginning with a shorter walk, perhaps only five minutes, planned as flexible for indoors in inclement weather, can be a more successful approach.)

Records are another aid to help you and your child persist and enjoy the journey. Keep them simple and brief, an easy way to mark your progress. Even though the steps you take are in themselves small, requiring only gradual changes, they will add up to big changes over the weeks and months. It is encouraging to review this record of progress. Like rewards, simple records help to reinforce your success.

Avoid The Negatives

While you and your child are making positive changes, don't allow them to be undermined by negatives. Make a conscious effort to get rid of progress-blockers, such as these listed below. Decide to give up, and encourage your child to forego, for at least the next four months:

- ⋆ Dieting and thoughts of dieting;
- ⋆ Striving for weight loss;
- ⋆ Putting life on hold;
- ⋆ Trying to be perfect;
- ⋆ Perusing the pages of typical fashion or women's magazines, or male muscle magazines.

FIGURE 20.2 **Sample Record**

Sample Record for the first week

Date____________

DAILY RECORD	M	Tu	W	Th	F	S	S
Activity – 5 min.							
Ate 3 meals							

Reward paid________________

To improve your teenager's lives, help them give up all these negatives for four months. Just let them go. Perhaps they will make it four years, and then let them go forever.

Additional Help

If you think your child needs additional help, individual guidance, or can benefit from group support, consult a dietitian or other health care provider who uses the nondiet, Health at Any Size approach. Both individual counseling and group programs are available. Specialists who work with eating disorders can be of help, and may recommend other professionals in your local area. You'll want to find a professional with whom you and your child both feel comfortable.

The social support of group programs is especially valuable for teenagers, where your child will share praise and encouragement, and make new friends. Groups bring a wide array of experiences to the table and talking over accomplishments and difficulties helps each to gain new insights and overcome temporary set-backs.

Teens & Diets No Weigh is a highly recommended, licensed program by HUGS International that has many locations throughout the U.S. and Canada, and is also offered online. (For classes in your area visit the Web Site www.hugs.com). Materials include a Teen

Journal, Parent Guide, cookbook, and online chats, video clips, self-directed materials, and follow-up support. The teen program focuses on health, nourishing eating and activity patterns, and self-acceptance rather than dieting and weight loss.

Further reading

In launching the Healthy Weight Kids program with your child, you'll find further help throughout Part 2 of this book on how to incorporate the many facets of healthy living. Two recent books by this author offer additional insights on health at any size and how both children and adults can move ahead in adopting healthy, diet-free lifestyles. For more information, refer to Part 2 of *Children and Teens Afraid to Eat: Helping Youth in Today's Weight-Obsessed World*, and *Women Afraid to Eat: Breaking Free in Today's Weight-Obsessed World.*

Three highly-recommended books that can be enormously helpful in achieving a healthy lifestyle, are *Staying Off the Diet Roller Coaster*, by Linda Omichinski, *Secrets of Feeding a Healthy Family*, by Ellyn Satter, and *Self-Esteem Comes in All Sizes*, by Carol Johnson. (All are available at www.healthyweight.net.) Other helpful books, Web sites and resources are listed in the resources of this book.

With the seven-step Healthy Weight Kids program you can help your child develop a healthy, confident, diet-free lifestyle. As a parent, you can use it to move ahead in a relaxed but consistent way that will be pleasurable for both you and your child.

The Seven Cs of Successful Change

Taking charge of your health and your life:
Many of us want to make changes in our habits. Taking some time to consider these seven "Cs" of change may help you understand how to get from where you are now—to where you want to be.

1. Caring Enough to Treat Your Body Really Well. Caring about yourself is essential for making any behavior change. Self-care is not selfish—it is what we have to do in order to stop doing one thing and start doing another. Taking good care of yourself also helps you be in better shape to take care of those around you.

2. Choice to Take Small Steps in a New Direction. Change is all about making the choice to do one thing (like taking a walk) rather than another (like watching TV). It doesn't mean that you have to give up all television programs—it just means that sometimes you make the choice to be more active.

3. Creativity to Find a Variety of Food and Fitness Options. The world is filled with stressful situations that can get in the way of our plans to eat well or to be active. The key is to stay calm and to brainstorm a variety of possible solutions.

4. Courage for New Adventures and Everyday Challenges. There are many ways to find the courage you need to make a change. You can discuss your struggles with friends or family; read inspiring stories about people who have made difficult changes; or find strength in faith and prayer.

5. Comfort Through Tough times with Relaxation (or even pampering). Change is hard work and can be stressful even when it's positive. When you are trying to do things differently, you need to rest and recharge your internal batteries. Take time to read a book, to take a nap, to play with the kids or just to do nothing for a while.

6. Confidence to Take Risks and to Make Normal Mistakes. Being confident that you can make positive changes is at least half the battle. Sometimes it helps to make a list of all the changes you have already made, however small.

7. Celebration of the Progress Toward a Strong and Healthy you. Give yourself plenty of pats on the back—just for moving a step closer to your goal.

Reprinted with permission from Eat Right Montana, a coalition promoting healthful eating and active lifestyles. Written by Dayle Hayes, MS, RD, for Eat Right Montana Healthy Families campaign, January 2003. Montana Department of Public Health and Human Services (406/947-2344). Montana Dietetic Association, Helena, MT www.montanadieteticassociation.org/promo.html

Chapter 21

♦ ♦ ❖ ♦ ♦ ❖ ♦ ♦ ❖ ♦ ♦ ❖ ♦ ♦ ❖ ♦ ♦ ❖ ♦ ♦

Helping the Overweight Child

The large child needs lots of love and attention. One of the most important things you can do is to let your child know he or she is okay right now. Nurture your child with love, compassion, gratitude, and appreciation. Reassure your daughter of your unconditional love. You love her for who she is—not for her appearance or her success in losing weight. If you accept your son at any weight, he will be more likely to accept and respect himself. Feeling good about himself will make it easier for him to develop healthier lifestyle habits.

How children feel about themselves often is based on their parents' feelings about them. Consider your own biases. How do you feel about fatness—your own and the fatness of other people? Is your concern for yourself or your child? Are you comfortable with the idea of size acceptance and Health at Any Size? Understanding your own feelings, and why you feel this way, can help you move ahead to what is really important in your child's life. Your support, acceptance, and encouragement are essential. Children need reassurance that every body is a good body. They can be healthy at the size they are.

A Nurturing Environment

In the Health at Any Size approach, living actively and eating well are cornerstones, and because they are easy to see and measure, they often get the most attention. But just as important, and perhaps even more critical, are the other two cornerstones: feeling good about oneself and feeling good about others. The child needs to feel good about himself first, so he can be more open to feeling good about others.

Creating a nurturing environment means the child feels loved, accepted, respected and trusted. Stress is kept at easily manageable levels. Concern is for the whole child—body, mind and spirit.

A nurturing environment promotes laughter and fun, not taking yourself too seriously. When the home is a safe and comfortable place children can more easily appreciate their own strengths and abilities and live up to their rich potential. (And don't forget that parents need nurturing, too. Be gentle with yourself, and with your spouse.)

Sometimes parents feel they need to "fix what's wrong" with a child, so that child can have a happy life in the future. But none of us is going to be perfect, now or in the future. Children need these happy feelings right now. They need to feel they belong, that they're right for their world.

Communicate Without Criticism

Talk to your child, allowing him or her to share concerns about appearance and weight with you. It is important to take the time to listen, without brushing off the concerns.

Puberty can be a difficult time for some youngsters. It's a time of profound body changes, and often weight and fat gain. It's a time of increased risk for eating disorders. Your family can be a powerful force in diffusing the anxieties your child feels about weight and appearance. Keep the lines of communication open. (See chapter 18 for more on communicating feelings).

At the same time, avoid focusing on weight as a problem. This is likely to bring shame and guilt, and is not helpful to moving forward with long-term behavior change.

Instead of fighting against the child's natural tendencies, parents need to work with them. How physically active is your child? What are his or her eating habits? Do family activity and eating patterns contribute to overweight? Many families gather around the television set each evening and sit for hours, hardly moving. Other family patterns may relate to using food in emotional ways, such as to ease a hurt, to reward good behavior, or as a cure for boredom. A child who learns to use food this way may "need" to eat for comfort, when depressed or anxious. Kids can get too fat when their emotional needs are not met, when they don't feel safe, when there is family or social stress. In response to these situations, children may demand food as a way of attracting the parents' attention, or stop being active because they are despondent. A child may develop sedentary habits because someone is overprotective, is intolerant of her noise and mess, or because she is depressed and lacks energy.[128]

Ellyn Satter, a dietitian and family therapist specializing in feeding children, warns, "In all cases, rather than attempting to shift calorie balance with diet and exercise, it is essential to identify and resolve underlying causes to restore the child's normal regulatory and growth patterns. Striving for a particular body weight creates distortions with eating and feeding and interferes markedly with nurturing the child." Or perhaps a medical problem may be influencing your child's weight, and needs to be checked out.[129]

Choosing a Care Provider

If you think your child is overweight, it's important to talk with a pediatrician or family physician. The doctor can put weight into perspective, and help your child understand that individuals grow at different rates. A health exam will reveal any possible medical causes or health risks that require treatment. The provider will measure and plot your child's height and weight according to standardized growth charts. Along with this, the doctor who takes a modern view will consider your child's body fatness, weight history, growth patterns, and maturity.

It is time to look at childhood overweight in a different way, and the physician you choose can help you with this. Consider why the child is putting on excess fat. Is it likely your child has a genetic vulnerability to fat storage? Most severely overfat children do. New research suggests that genes may account for 75 to 80 percent of the body fat children carry. This does not mean weight gain is inevitable, and the health provider can help explore these issues. But not all doctors take this broader view, or are willing to spend this much time with a child. You may want to shop around for a doctor who does, and who is a comfortable fit with you and your child.

When a child shows a sudden weight gain or drop, medical or emotional problems may be suspected. Professional help from a pediatrician, dietitian or child psychologist may be necessary.

Health at Any Size programs

The good news is that the Health at Any Size approach of diet-free living is ideally suited to helping the large or overfat child, no matter what the causes may be. Its focus is on wellness and wholeness, on living actively and eating in normal, healthy ways. It's about acceptance, self-respect, and appreciation of diversity. It reaffirms the truth that beauty, health and strength come in all sizes. Every child qualifies.

The Health at Any Size approach helps parents focus on how to help their child in practical and positive ways. Following a structured program such as Healthy Weight Kids may work well in your family. The overall goal of a successful program is to help the whole family make healthy lifestyle habits. Consider joining your child in your own journey through this seven-step program. When parents and children work together to make gradual changes in family and individual patterns that contribute to inactivity and overweight, studies show the outcomes are more successful.

Whether or not you join your child in improving lifestyle habits, it is important that you become involved in changing family patterns that may contribute to overweight. The four areas to focus on are: living actively, eating well, feeling good about oneself, and feeling good about others. These goals allow your child to feel positive about progress made, while getting on with the rest of his or her life.

Regular physical activity is the single most efficient, healthful, and necessary way to manage weight—in weight loss, in stabilizing weight to allow children to grow into that weight, and in prevention of excessive fat gain. Be a role model, but let the child decide what activities he or she prefers. Don't enroll a larger girl in ballet class if she doesn't feel comfortable there. On the other hand, if she wants to twirl a baton, don't discourage her because of her size.

In healthy eating, parents help the child learn to identify and pay attention to feelings of hunger and fullness. This means not forcing a toddler to eat one more bite. It means allowing extra helpings when desired. Planned meals and snacks give the child regular sources of nutritious foods, help the child develop sensible eating patterns, and encourage the child to practice eating behavior in social situations. Studies indicate that overweight children who eat regular meals can control their weight more successfully.[130]

Perhaps what your child really needs is healing: reassurance of acceptance, respect and appreciation. For some youngsters, relieving stress and improving communication can be more important than increasing activity or improving eating habits.

If following a structured program is not your style, consider how you can build more activity into your child's life. Some suggestions include:

- Walk your child to school;
- Plan active family fun days—hike, visit a zoo;
- Enroll child in a school sport, or community recreation program;
- Sign up for private lessons (such as swimming, aerobics, tennis);
- Join a Scout troop that is active outdoors.

Be content to make small changes that can become long-term habits. Don't try to introduce untried activities too quickly.

Small, Consistent Changes Work Best

When Americans think about losing weight or improving their health, they usually think about making big changes in their lifestyle—joining a health club, buying exercise equipment or going on a serious diet. Then they get frustrated or feel like failures when they can't maintain their new habits over the long haul.[131]

"The secret is to keep it simple," says Lynn Paul, EdD, RD, nutrition educator with the Montana State University Extension Service in Bozeman. Small changes are easier to maintain, and they can make a big difference over a lifetime. Simple changes, like eating breakfast or taking a ten-minute walk, can energize your life." According to dietitian Lynn Paul, black and white thinking is often what gets us into trouble. "People think that they have to eat perfectly or spend an hour at the gym in order to get fit," she says. "Health is not an all-or-nothing proposition; it's about maximizing the positive and minimizing the negative."

Moving toward health goals with your child means maximizing the quality time you spend with your child, and minimizing the disappointments and distress the child feels. It means spending more time walking and less time sitting. It means eating more meals together with family, and spending less time prowling the kitchen for snack foods. It means drinking more water and milk—and drinking less soda.

Parents who want their larger child thin at any cost need to think carefully about what this can mean. Ill-advised weight loss affects the body in profound ways—from stunting to lasting injury, to say nothing of long-term weight gain. (See Chapter 9 for more about potential consequences). Even so, these are physical outcomes. In the bigger picture of wellness for the whole child the consequences are emotional, intellectual, social, spiritual, and possibly occupational, as well. They range from body hatred to eating disorders, from depression to suicidal intent. Death is always a possibility.

Instead, parents need to ask: what is the best approach for this child? What are our long-term hopes and goals for this child? If the goals are health and happiness, will embarking on an endless round of dieting and weight cycling achieve this—or more likely the opposite? Are there better paths to health and happiness?

Goals for Your Child

Parents are very aware of the social stigma associated with being fat. Many have experienced size discrimination first hand, and all have witnessed it. They are determined not to let this happen to their children. But the steps they take to prevent obesity may backfire and cause even more stress and failure for their children.

To the extent that it is an abnormal and unnecessary condition for the child, obesity can be prevented, Satter explains. This process starts at birth, with a positive feeding relationship between parent and child. Infants know how much they need to eat. They give cues to guide the feeding process, and to grow properly they must be supported in eating according to their internal regulatory processes of hunger, appetite and satiety.

For parents of the large child, an important part of prevention is to reduce weight gain while height catches up, and to resist pressure to put their child on a diet. Parents feel guilty and responsible. Their guilt is reinforced by health professionals, school, media, family, and friends who think parents have "done something wrong" and expect them to remedy it. Parents need support in pursuing a moderate approach, and help with their feelings. No criticism.

When you define your child's healthy weight as the natural weight the body adopts, given healthy eating and meaningful levels of physical activity, it helps everyone move on from the destructively narrow definition that labels children in terms of numbers. Weight may level off and allow the child to grow into his or her weight. Longitudinal studies show that more children slim down than stay fat. But trying to micromanage this amounts to an attempt at weight loss that distorts the feeding relationship, Satter warns. Instead, parents must measure outcome by the degree to which they have helped their child establish positive eating and exercise behavior and functional social and emotional skills. Then they must let weight find its own level.

Joanne Ikeda conducted weight management programs in the early 1980s for teens using a behavior modification approach.[132]

"Some of the youngsters I worked with lost weight, some maintained, and some gained," she reports. "All needed more love and acceptance. There was the large boned, aristocratic looking girl accompanied by a mother who wore a size four petite. 'I hope you can do something with her, because I can't,' said the mother haughtily. I felt

> *like saying, 'Sure, I'll just touch her with my magic wand and make her look just like you.'*
>
> *"There were two bosom buddies; one looked fatter than the other. The larger girl kept worrying that her friend would lose weight, and thus have no need of their friendship. She made sure they visited the candy machine before and after every meeting.*
>
> *"The only adolescent who appeared to have escaped serious damage to his self-esteem was a big kid whose mother brought him in, saying, 'Everyone in our family is big, so I don't expect him to lose weight. I just want him to learn some healthy habits.' 'Yes, yes, yes!' was my enthusiastic response. She was right, this boy was big. Big enough to intimidate any peers who wanted to make his size an issue. Plus he was good at using humor to help our group 'lighten up,' and even I was vulnerable to his charm.*
>
> *"I stopped working with fat youngsters when I realized that I was contributing to their distress by reinforcing the idea that there was something 'wrong' with their bodies. But their pain remains with me. It sustains me and provides the motivation for my efforts to promote size acceptance in some very concrete ways,"* says Ikeda.

Parents who try to pressure children by making their love conditional on weight loss need to be told that they are harming, not helping, their children, she says. Size discrimination is often practiced under the guise that it will motivate large children to change their eating and exercise habits so their bodies will become "normal."

There are serious flaws in this thinking. Ikeda explains, "Our children did not create this world where an overabundance of appealing, low-cost, high-fat foods is widely available at a moment's notice. A world where machines perform most of the tasks that used to require human energy expenditure. As adults, we must assume the responsibility for this situation and make every effort to change it . . . in ways that help, not punish our children."[133]

"There is no reason your child cannot lead a happy, productive, full life at whatever size she turns out to be," explains Ikeda. In the brochure, *If My Child is Overweight, What Should I Do About It?,* she tells parents, "Being overweight may seem like the worst possible fate. However, it isn't. A worse fate is feeling rejected and unloved because one is overweight. You can make sure this does not happen to your child. Reassure your child she will be loved by you always, whether she is thin or fat. Help your child to feel good about herself so that overweight is not compounded by low self-esteem."

Treat all Children the Same

Parents should not treat the overweight child differently, such as giving one child different meals, desserts, or snacks than the rest of the family, say Carol Hans, RD, and Diane Nelson, of the Iowa State Extension Service.[134]

They affirm that taking a nurturing and supportive approach to your child's concerns is of primary importance. "Since a parent's primary role is to give support, any action that denies support should be avoided. For example, when playmates' teasing upsets a child, the parent who responds with, 'When you get thinner they won't tease you anymore,' only reinforces the child's suspicion that there is indeed something wrong with him or her. A more positive response is to listen to the child express his or her feelings about that teasing, and then perhaps, ask if other children are getting teased and for what reason. This can lead to a discussion of: 'What do you think you can do about this situation?'" This empowers the child to look for viable solutions.

Choose Healthy Lifestyle Programs, Not Diets

If you need help, choose health providers who facilitate healthy, nondiet lifestyle programs. Don't be tempted by caregivers, family or friends who advocate diets, diet pills, or weight loss surgery. Children should not be put on weight loss diets. It is heartening that now nearly all experts agree on this point, with the current national shift toward the Health at Any Size approach.

"Don't place your child on a restrictive diet," advises WIN, the Weight-control Information Network of the National Institutes of Health, in its 2002 brochure, *Helping Your Overweight Child*. "Limiting what children eat may be harmful to their health and interfere with their growth and development."[135]

Diets don't work long-term (usually not more than six months), are unsafe, disrupt normal eating, are likely to cause weight gain, and can set up a lifelong pattern of failure cycles. Putting children on diets is a form of punishment that asks them to ignore feelings of hunger and may lead them to believe there is truly something wrong for wanting to eat more than their parents want to give them.

When parents fear their child is becoming fat, they often restrict food, says dietitian Joanne Ikeda. But recent research shows this only makes things worse. Children whose parents control their food intake are less able to self-regulate their energy intake. Thus, they may be at higher risk of obesity than kids who are allowed to choose how much food they eat.[136]

Therapists often find these children develop a fear of hunger. They may beg, scavenge, and even steal food. Some parents act more like prison guards than nurturers and caregivers, Ikeda observes. She tells health professionals they must assure parents that infants are born with the ability to regulate their energy intake and this ability needs to be fostered throughout childhood, not interfered with.

Putting a child on a weight loss diet or restricting food even in indirect ways—such as specifying free and limited foods—profoundly distorts the developmental needs of both parents and children. Children need to be nurtured. Parents need to nurture them. Children need to be able to trust their internal processes. Parents need to be able to relax and trust their children and those processes—not be police officers.

Neither are diet pills appropriate for children or teens. With the most effective prescription pills, weight loss is no more than 5 or 10 pounds, except for diet effects when combined with a diet (inadvisable for reasons given above). To maintain even that small loss, or even less the longer they are used, they must be taken daily over the years—yet are only approved as safe for one year. As of May 2002, twenty-seven new drugs were in the pipeline undergoing clinical trials for treating obesity. Five were in Phase 3, closest to FDA approval. Even worse are the many quack diet pills on the market, being sold as food supplements.[137]

Neither is weight loss surgery appropriate for children or teens. It's an elective, unnecessary surgery, in which death rates and complications are high. Long-term side effects, such as the effects of nutrient deficiencies and bone deterioration, are unknown. "Doing something in the first 20 years that can affect you for the next 50 years...ethically it's very hard to justify that," says Dr. Timothy Sentongo, a gastrointestinal specialist at Chicago's Children's Memorial Hospital.[138] Yet increasingly, dietitians report that surgeons are performing more and more dangerous gastric bypass surgeries on kids.

Bottom line: diets, diet pills and weight loss surgery are dangerous and inappropriate for children. Don't get talked into any of these for your child, either by a health provider or by your desperate child.

Family Coping with Eating Disorders

Dysfunctional eating and eating disorders are commonly diagnosed in large children and teens. Some studies show larger youngsters are even more likely to suffer eating disorders than those of average size, perhaps because they've been trying so hard and unsuccessfully to lose weight for so long. They may be more likely to suffer anorexia nervosa, bulimia, binge eating disorder, and other related disorders. Parents who are concerned that a child may have an eating disorder or eating problem should see their family doctor, dietitian, or an eating disorder specialist. The longer an eating disorder continues before being treated, the more difficult it becomes, so it is imperative to seek help early.

Raising Positive Kids

Large kids can have a hard time in our thin-obsessed society. Overweight is a stigmatizing condition. Larger children may need help learning to deal with prejudice and social and emotional challenges. They grow up thinking less of themselves only if their parents think less of them. Some parents are unaccepting and insist on changing their children. Others blame themselves and are overprotective. Children grow up to feel good about themselves if their families value them for their considerable worth, expect them to be capable, and see their size as only one of their characteristics.[140]

Carol Johnson, author of *Self-Esteem Comes in All Sizes,* and founder of the Largely Positive support groups, says adults must send them enough positive, loving messages to counteract the negative ones they will hear at school, the beach, at parties, and from the media.[141]

> *"As hard as it is to be a fat adult in America, it's even harder for fat kids. Kids long to fit in and be accepted by their peers. Damage to self-esteem can begin at a very young age. If it's not mended, the scars can last a lifetime.*
>
> *"It's imperative that parents and supportive adults provide larger kids with the tools to realize they're just as good as thinner kids, that weight is not a measure of their self-worth. Large kids should not be led to believe losing weight will make them better people. Despite their best efforts, not all kids will lose weight permanently."*

To sum up, instead of encouraging large kids to lose weight or restrict food, it is better to help them build self-esteem and become more active. Focusing on habit change helps to motivate and get this done. Day by day, this will lead to physical, mental and social benefits regardless of any changes in weight.

The stakes are high—for our nation, and for your child. So are the rewards. Being more active as a nation will mean preventing much illness, disability and premature death, reducing health care costs, and maintaining a high quality of life for Americans from childhood into old age. For your child it means being successful and feeling good about his or her efforts.

Large children and self-esteem

Carol Johnson, MA

Yes, more children than ever are overweight, and, yes, we must take steps to enhance their health and help them manage their weight—but maintaining their self-esteem is equally important. Maintaining a child's self-esteem is not an easy task under the best of circumstances. Overweight children are especially vulnerable to the harmful effects of weight discrimination. This damage can last a lifetime if not nipped in the bud. Here are some tips for parents and caregivers on how to help overweight children maintain their sense of self-worth.

DO:

Do love and accept your child unconditionally—regardless of their weight. This will help them to love and accept themselves. Remember — you love your child not for how they look, but for who they are.

Do treat size and shape as characteristics that contribute to a person's uniqueness. Teach them that diversity is what makes the world so interesting. Nature provides many examples. Flowers, for instance, come in all shapes, colors and sizes — and yet all are beautiful.

Do examine your own biases and ask yourself whether your concern is for yourself or your child. A larger child may make some parents feel embarrassed, and some may feel that having an "overweight" child signifies a family's lack of self-discipline. As with most forms of prejudice, these feelings stem from myths and misinformation.

Do educate yourself about what causes some people to be larger than others so you can separate myths from facts for your children. Books that will help you do this are *Self-Esteem Comes In All Sizes* by Carol Johnson (Gurze Books, 2001 www.gurze.com) and *Big Fat Lies* by Glenn Gaesser (Gurze Books, 2002 www.gurze.com). Then educate your children. Have a discussion about heredity. Explain that body size and shape have hereditary elements, much the same as hair and eye color. Be sure to emphasize that it is not their fault and that they are not to blame if they are above average in weight.

Do emphasize your child's positive attributes and talents and teach them that these are the things that count. Help them to develop the things they're good at.

Do make an extra effort to help them find clothes similar to what their friends are wearing. It's real important at this age to "blend in."

Do arm your children for dealing with the outside world and our culture's obsession with thinness. Tell them that many groups of people have suffered discrimination and prejudice, and that larger people are one of these groups. Help them plan how they would react to negative comments about their weight. Do some role-playing.

Do make your home and family a safe haven for them where they can always count on your support and encouragement. They'll have enough to deal with outside the home in our fat phobic society.

Do be a good role model. Don't criticize your own body. You're the most important person in your child's life. If they see that you like your own body, they'll find it easier to like theirs. Consider reading *Like Mother, Like Daughter* by Deborah Waterhouse (Hyperion, 1997), who writes extensively about the influence mothers have over their daughters with regard to body image.

Do provide examples for them of attractive and successful larger people, both current and historical. Also give them an anthropology lesson and inform them that many other cultures value and desire bodies of ample proportion.

Do help your larger child to unravel the "thin is in" media hype. There are about 400 top fashion models, and less than one percent of the female population has the genetic potential to look like them. Attractive people can come in assorted shapes, sizes and colors.

DON'T:

Don't ever say or imply that your child's weight makes him/her less attractive or less acceptable in any way. This can cause lifelong damage to self-esteem. There is NO connection between weight and self-worth and you are responsible for helping your child realize this. And for heaven's sake, don't tell your child she has "such a pretty face" — if only she'd lose weight. Shaming or teasing a child about their weight or body has the opposite effect and will make them hate their bodies even more.

Don't tell your child that no one will want to date them unless they're thin. First of all, it's not true. Plenty of plus-size teens have boyfriends and girlfriends. Tell your child that lasting affection looks beneath the surface and is not bound by narrow definitions of beauty.

Don't ever put your child on a restrictive diet. Most dietitians now agree that this is not the way to help them manage their weight. Focus on development of a healthy lifestyle. Make physical activity a family affair — go for a family walk, buy family swimming passes to a community pool, have a family "dancing party," go biking together or "go fly a kite!"

Don't become the "food police." Continually nagging your child about what he/she is eating will surely backfire. Children can always find ways of getting "forbidden" foods. In the worst-case scenario, you could be contributing to development of an eating disorder such as anorexia or bulimia. Besides, foods should not be categorized as "good" or "bad." All food has a place in normal eating. This is the view of registered dietitian Ellyn Satter in her book *How To Get Your Kid To Eat, But Not Too Much* (Bull Publishing, 1987).

Despite all your child's best efforts, your child may never be as thin as you think he or she should be. Some heavy children will still become heavy adults — and still live satisfying, fulfilling lives. Researchers will tell you that there is much to learn yet about obesity and what causes it. Teach your child that a rich, rewarding life has just as much to do with development of a healthy attitude and self-image as it does with maintaining a healthy weight.

Developed by LARGELY POSITIVE INC., P.O. Box 170223, Glendale, WI 53217. For more information, visit www.largelypositive.com

Resources

♦ ♦ ❖ ♦ ♦ ❖ ♦ ♦ ❖ ♦ ♦ ❖ ♦ ♦ ❖ ♦ ♦ ❖ ♦ ♦

Books

Andersen, Arnold et al. *Making Weight: Healing Men's Conflicts with Food, Weight, Shape & Appearance.* Carlsbad, CA: Gurze Books.

Benson, Peter. *All Kids are Our Kids: What Communities Must Do to Raise Caring and Responsible Children and Adolescents.* San Francisco: Jossey-Bass Publishers, 1997.

Berg, Frances M. *A New Approach to Dealing with Weight and Eating in Healthier Ways.* Hettinger, ND: Healthy Weight Network.

———. *Children and Teens Afraid to Eat: Helping Youth in Today's Weight-Obsessed World.* Hettinger, ND: Healthy Weight Network, 2000.

———. *Women Afraid to Eat: Breaking Free in Today's Weight-Obsessed World.* Hettinger, ND: Healthy Weight Network, 2001.

Blume, Judy. *Blubber.* Yearling Books, 1976.

Bode, Janet. *Food Fight: A Guide To Eating Disorders For Preteens and Their Parents.* New York: Aladdin Paperbacks.

Cash, Thomas F. *The Body Image Workbook: An 8-Step Program for Learning to Like Your Looks.* Oakland, CA: New Harbinger Publications, 1997.

Cordes, Helen. *Girl Power in the Mirror: A Book about Girls, Their Bodies, and Themselves.* Minneapolis, MN: Lerner Publications Company, 2000.

Costin, Carolyn. *Your Dieting Daughter: Is She Dying for Attention?* New York: Brunner/Mazel Publishers, 1997.

Dee, Catherine. *The Girls' Guide to Life: How to Take Charge of the Issues that Affect You.* New York: Little, Brown and Co, 1997.

Edut, Ophira ed. *Adios, Barbie: Young Women Write About Body Image and Identity.* Seattle: Seal Press, 1998.

Erdman, Cheri. *Live Large!: Ideas, Affirmations & Actions for Sane Living in a Larger Body*. New York: HarperCollins, 1996.

———. *Nothing to Lose—Sane Living in a Larger Body*. New York: HarperCollins, 1995.

Friedman, Sandra S. *When Girls Feel Fat: Helping Girls Through Adolescence.* Buffalo, NY: Firefly Books, 2000.

Gaesser, Glenn and Karen Kratina. *Eating Well, Living Well: When You Can't Diet Anymore.* Parker, CO: Wheat Foods Council.

Gaesser, Glenn. *Big Fat Lies: The Truth about Your Weight and Your Health.* Carlsbad, CA: Gurze Books, 2002.

Ikeda, Joanne and Priscilla Naworski. *Am I Fat? Helping Your Children Accept Differences in Body Size.* Santa Cruz, CA: ETR Associates, 1992.

Institute for Research and Education. *How Did This Happen? A Practical Guide to Understanding Eating Disorders.* Minnesota: HealthSystem, 1999.

Jasper, Karin. *Are You Too Fat, Ginny?* New York: Is Five Press, 1988.

Johnson, Carol. *Self-Esteem Comes in All Sizes; How to Be Happy and Healthy at Your Natural Weight.* Carlsbad, CA: Gurze Books, 2001.

Kilbourne, Jean. *Can't Buy My Love: How Advertising Changes the Way We Think and Feel.* New York: Touchstone, 1999.

Lyons, Pat and Debby Burgard. *Great Shape: The First Fitness Guide for Large Women.* Palo Alto, CA: Bull Publishing, 2000.

MacKoff, Barbara. *Growing a Girl: Seven Strategies for Raising a Strong, Spirited Daughter.* New York: Doubleday, 1996.

Maine, Margo. *Body Wars: Making Peace with Women's Bodies.* Carlsbad, CA: Gurze Books, 1999.

Newman, Leslea. *Belinda's Bouquet.* Boston: Alyson Publications, 1991.

Omichinski, Linda. *Staying Off the Diet Roller Coaster.* Advicezone corp.

———. *You Count, Calories Don't.* Hodder & Stoughton, 1996.

Perry, Cheryl L. *Creating Health Behavior Change: How to Develop Community Wide Programs for Youth.* Minneapolis: University of Minnesota Sage Publications.

Pitman, Teresa and Miriam Kaufman. *All Shapes and Sizes: Parenting Your Overweight Child (Today's Parent Book.)* Toronto: Harper Collins, 1994.

Ryan, Joan. *Little Girls in Pretty Boxes: The Making and Breaking of Elite Gymnasts and Figure Skaters.* New York: Warner Books.

Satter, Ellyn. *Child of Mine—Feeding with Love and Good Sense.* Palo Alto, CA: Bull Publishing, 2000.

———. *How to Get Your Kids to Eat…But Not Too Much—From Birth to Adolescence.* Palo Alto, CA: Bull Publishing, 1987.

———. *Secrets of Feeding a Healthy Family.* Madison, WI: Kelcy Press, 1999.

Smith, Robert K. *Jelly Belly.* Yearling Books, 1982.

Sobal, Jeffery and Donna Maurer. *Interpreting Weight: The Social Management of Fatness and Thinness.* New York: Aldine de Gruyter, 1999.

———. *Weight Issues: Fatness and Thinness as Social Problems.* New York: Aldine de Gruyter, 1999.

Sullivan, Judy. *Size Wise.* New York: Avon Books, 1997.

Thompson, J. et al. *Exacting Beauty: Theory, Assessment, and Treatment of Body Image Disturbance.* Washington, DC: American Psychological Association, 1999.

Vandereycken, Walter and Greta Noordenbos. *Studies in Eating Disorders—An International Series: The Prevention of Eating Disorders.* London: The Athlone Press, 1998.

Waterhouse, Debra. *Like Mother, Like Daughter: How (Girls and) Women are Influenced by their Mother's Relationship with Food and How to Break The Pattern.* New York: Hyperion Publications.

Media Literacy

About Face www.about-face.org

Center for Media Literacy www.medialit.org

GO GIRLS! (Giving Our Girls Inspiration & Resources for Lasting Self-Esteem) www.nationaleatingdisorders.org.

Just Think Foundation www.justthink.org

Media Awareness Network (Health Canada) www.media-awareness.ca.

Media Education Foundation www.igc.org/mef

Media Watch www.mediawatch.org

Mind on The Media www.mindonthemedia.org.

PBS www.pbs.org/mix/imgguide.html

Programs & Training for Parents and Caregivers

Action for Healthy Kids Initiative www.actionforhealthykids.org

Best Start: A Guide for Program Planners www.opc.on.ca/beststart/bodyimg/httoc.html.

Bright Futures in Practice www.brightfutures.org/physicalactivity/

Bullying Prevention Program http://www.colorado.edu/cspv/blueprints/model/programs/BPP.html

Canadian Health Network www.canadian-health-network.ca

Celebrate Healthy Eating. Nutrition education packet for preschool children. dannon.institute@dannon.com or 914-332-1092

Children and Weight: What health professionals can do about it. http://danrcs.ucdavis.edu

Eating Concerns Support Group Curriculum www.nationaleatingdisorders.org.

Feeding with Love and Good Sense. www.ellynsatter.com

Ellyn Satter's Vision training workshops for leaders.

Food Play. www.foodplay.com

Healthy Habits for Healthy Kids www.wellpoint.com

Kid's Project, Packet of size acceptance materials. Kids Come in all Sizes workshops. Council on Size & Weight Discrimination, Miriam Berg, P.O. Box 305, Mt. Marion, NY 12456 (914-679-1209; fax 914-679-1206).

Kids Module—Parents and Children Sharing Food Tasks, by Rita Mitchell. Leaders guide, videotape, handouts for parents. Rita Mitchell, 209 Morgan Hall, U of California, Berkeley, CA 94720 (510-642-3080).

Pyramid Explorer: Nutrition Adventures CD-ROM www.oregondairycouncil.org

Ready Set Go, Ontario Physical Health Educator's Association www.readysetgo.org

SPARK Active Recreation www.foundation.sdsu.edu/projects/spark/index.html

Teens & Diets—No Weigh: Building the road to healthier living, by Linda Omichinski. A Lifestyle Approach to Health & Fitness, by Linda Omichinski and Kathleen Harrison.

Videos

Body Talk: Teens Talk About Their Bodies, Eating Disorders, and Activism www.thebodypositive.org

Breaking Size Prejudice Promotes respect and size acceptance

It's All About You: Make Healthy Choices that Fit Your Lifestyle so You Can Do the Things You Want to Do. Dietary Guidelines Alliance, 233 N Michigan Ave., #1400, Chicago, IL 60601.

Slim Hopes, Jean Kilbourne; How female bodies are depicted in advertising

Health & Wellness

Centers for Disease Control and Prevention www.cdc.gov

Center for Weight and Health www.cnr.berkeley.edu/cwh/

Federal Juvenile Justice/Delinquency Prevention
www.parentingresources.ncjrs.org

Healthfinder www.healthfinder.gov

Healthy Weight Network www.healthyweight.net

Hugs International www.hugs.com

Iowa Health Department
www.idph.state.ia.us/common/pdf/wic/obesity.pdf

Kidpower www.kidpower.org/

Maternal and Child Health
www.mchlibrary.info/KnowledgePaths/kp_obesity.html

MedlinePlus www.medlineplus.gov

Michigan Schools: Promoting Healthy Weight
www.emc.cmich.edu/pdfs/Healthy%20Weight.pdf

Minority Health Resource Center www.omhrc.gov

National Association State Boards of Education
www.nasbe.org/HealthySchools

National Center for Health Statistics www.cdc.gov/nchswww

National Safe Kids Campaign www.safekids.org

National Women's Health Information Center www.4woman.gov

Reuters Health Information Services www.reutershealth.com/

Surgeon General www.surgeongeneral.gov/topics/obesity

Teen Health www.teenshealth.org.

USDA www.usda.gov

Weight Information Network
www.niddk.nih.gov/health/nutrit/win.htm

WIN Wyoming (Wellness in Wyoming) www.uwyo.edu/win-wyoming

Women's Health Information Center www.4woman.org

Women's Health Initiative www.nhlbi.nih.gov/nhlbi/whil

Nutrition & Healthy Eating

5 A Day for Better Health www.5aday.com

American School Food Service Association www.asfsa.org/childnutrition

Beef Nutrition www.beefnutrition.org

Center for Nutrition Policy and Promotion www.cnpp.usda.gov

Center for Weight and Health at U.C. Berkeley www.cnr.berkeley.edu/cwh

Children's Healthcare of Atlanta www.choa.org

Dietitians of Canada www.dietitians.ca

Food Play www.foodplay.com

International Food Information Council www.ific.org

National Dairy Council www.nationaldairycouncil.org

National Network for Childcare Nutrition www.exnet.iastate.edu

Oregon Dairy Council www.oregondairycouncil.org

Wheat Foods Council www.wheatfoods.org

Physical Activity

American Alliance for Health, Physical Education, Recreation and Dance www.aahperd.org

American Hiking Society www.AmericanHiking.org

Canadian Association for the Advancement of Women and Sport and Physical Activity www.caaws.ca

Just Walk It www.justwalkit.com.au

League of American Bicyclists
www.bikeleague.org/educenter/bikemonth.htm

Melpomene: Institute for Women's Health Research
www.melpomene.org

Ontario Physical and Health Education Association
www.ophea.org

Partnership for a Walkable America www.nsc.org/walkable.htm

Physical Education Digest www.pedigest.com

President's Council on Physical Fitness and Sports
www.fitness.gov

Rails-To-Trails www.railtrails.org

Skipping www.iskip.com

Body Image & Self-Esteem

Dads and Daughters www.dadsanddaughters.org

For Girls www.4girls.gov

Girls, Inc. www.girlsinc.org.

Girl Power! www.girlpower.gov

Girl Zone www.girlzone.com.

Eating Problems & Eating Disorders

After the Diet www.afterthediet.com

Association of Anorexia Nervosa and Associated Disorders
www.anad.org

Eating Disorders and Men www.eatingdis.com/men.htm

Harvard Eating Disorders Center www.hedc.com

Mirror Mirror www.mirror-mirror.org

National Eating Disorder Information Centre (Canada)
www.nedic.ca

National Eating Disorders Association (US)
www.nationaleatingdisorders.org

National Eating Disorders Screening Program www.nmisp.org

Something Fishy www.something-fishy.org

Size Acceptance

Amplestuff www.amplestuff.com

Big Beautiful Woman www.bbwmagazine.com

Council on Size and Weight Discrimination www.cswd.org/.

Largesse, the Network for Size Esteem
www.eskimo.com/~largesse

National Association to Advance Fat Acceptance www.naafa.org

Radiance Magazine Online www.radiancemagazine.com

Size Wise www.SizeWise.com

Quackery & Fraud

National Council Against Health Fraud www.ncahf.org

Quackwatch www.quackwatch.com

Notes

♦ ♦ ❖ ♦ ♦ ❖ ♦ ♦ ❖ ♦ ♦ ❖ ♦ ♦ ❖ ♦ ♦ ❖ ♦ ♦

PART I

Chapter 1

[1] Ogden CL et al., "Prevalence and Trends in Overweight Among US Children and Adolescents." *JAMA* 288 (2002): 1728-1732.

[2] Troiano RP and KM Flegal . "Shifts in the Distribution of Body Mass Index of Children in the US Population." *Obestity Res* 4 (1996):S1:68S; Berg F. "Heaviest Children Log Increases." *Healthy Weight J* 11 (1997):1:6.

[3] US Health and Human Services, "Healthy People 2010," Conf edition. Washington, DC, Jan 2000. See www.health.gov/healthypeople.

[4] Troiano RP and KM Flegal . "Shifts in the Distribution of Body Mass Index of Children in the US Population;" Berg F. "Heaviest Children Log Increases."

[5] "USHHS, Healthy People 2010."

[6] Kromeyer-Hauschild K et al., "Prevalence of Overweight and Obesity Among School Children in Jena." *I J Obesity* 23 (1999):1143-1150; Berg F. "Obesity Up for German Kids." *Healthy Weight J* 3 (2000):35.

[7] "Obesity: Prevention and Managing the Global Epidemic: Report of A World Health Organization Consultation On Obesity." World Health Organization/ Nutrition 98.1. Geneva, Switzerland: World Health Organization, 1998.

[8] Morrison J et al., "Mothers in Black and White Households: The NHLBI Growth and Health Study." *An J Pub Health* 84 (1994):1761-1767; Obarzanek E et al., "Energy Intake and Physical Activity in Relation to Indexes of Body Fat." The National Heart, Lung, and Blood Institute, (1994).

[9] Pediatric Nutrition Surveillance System (PedNSS), Division of Nutrition, Centers for Disease Control in Atlanta; Berg F. "High Rates of Childhood Obesity Seen in Assistance Programs;" "Overweight Hits 10-year high." *Healthy Weight J /Obesity & Health* 6 (1992):2:26-27,34.

[10] Berg F. "Prevalences of Obesity Rises For Minorities." *Healthy Weight J /Obesity & Health* 7 (1993):4:72.

[11] Fontvieille AM and E Ravussin. "Metabolic Rate and Body Composition Indian and Caucasian Children." *Critical Rev in Food Sci and Nutr* 33 (1993)4/5:363-368.

[12] Peck EB and HD Ullrich. California position paper "Children and Weight: A Changing Perspective." U of Calif Berkeley, (1986); Heitmann BL et al., "Mortality Associated With Body Fat, Fat-Free Mass and Body Mass Index Among 60-Year-Old Swedish Men." *I J Obesity* 24 (2000):33-37.

[13] "CDC Growth Charts" National Center for Chronic Disease Prevention and Health Promotion, 2000. www.cdc.gov/nccdphp/dnpa/bmi/bmi-for-age.htm.

[14] Centers for Disease Control and Prevention. *News Release,* 2/24/03.

[15] "USHHS, Healthy People 2010."

[16] Heitmann BL et al., "Mortality Associated With Body Fat, Fat-Free Mass and Body Mass Index Among 60-Year-Old Swedish Men."

[17] Ibid.

[18] Federal Update: "BMI Poor Indicator of Body Fat in Individual Kids." *J Am Diet Assoc* 100 (2000):628.

[19] Berg F. *Health Risks of Obesity.* (Hettinger, ND: Obesity and Health,1993) 36-43.

[20] "USHHS, Healthy People 2010."

[21] Bjorntorp P. "Visceral Obesity." *Obesity Res* 1 (1993):3:206-222; Berg F. "Risks Focus On Visceral Obesity, May Be Stress Linked." *Healthy Weight J /Obesity & Health* 7 (1993):5:87-89.

[22] Satter E. *Child of Mine: Feeding With Love and Good Sense* (Palo Alto, CA: Bull Publishing, 2000) 447-448.

[23] "CDC Growth Charts" National Center for Chronic Disease Prevention and Health Promotion, 2000. www.cdc.gov/nccdphp/dnpa/bmi/bmi-for-age.htm.

Chapter 2

[24] Severson K and M May. "Growing Up Too Fat: Kids Suffer Adult Ailments As More Become Dangerously Obese." *San Francisco Chronicle,* 5/13/02.

[25] Ibid.

[26] NIH National Institute of Child Health and Human Development. *News Release,* 3/13/02.

[27] "Major Increase in Diabetes Among Adults Occurred Nationwide Between 1990 and 1998." Centers for Disease Control and Prevention, Atlanta, 8/23/00.

[28] "The Surgeon General's Call to Action to Prevent and Decrease Overweight and Obesity: Overweight in Children and Adolescents," December 2001.

[29] "NIH Strategy Development Workshop for Public Education on Weight and Obesity" (Sponsored by the National Heart, Lung and Blood Institutes, 1992)51.

[30] Duyff R. *The American Dietetic Association's Complete Food & Nutrition Guide.* (Minneapolis: Chronimed Publishers, 1996.)

[31] Ibid.

[32] Gaesser G. *Big Fat Lies: The Truth About Your Weight and Your Health.* (New York: Ballentine Books, 1996)183-201.

[33] Grunstein RR. "Sleep Apnoea—An Unrecognised Complication of Obesity" in *Progress In Obesity Research, eds.* Guy-Grand B and G Ailhoud (London, England: John Libbey, 1999)587-592.

[34] "Obesity: Preventing and Managing The Global Epidemic." Report of a World Health Organization Consultation on Obesity, Geneva, June 3-5, 1997.

[35] Severson K, May M. "Growing Up Too Fat: Kids Suffer Adult Ailments As More Become Dangerously Obese."

[36] Health and Human Services Press Office. *News Release*, 5/1/02; Wang, G, and WH Dietz. "Economic Burden of Obesity in Youths Aged 6-17 Years: 1979-1999." *Pediatrics* 109 (2002)5:E81-1.

[37] Frisch R, ed., *Adipose Tissue and Reproduction (*Basel, Switzerland: Karger, 1990); Berg F. "High Body Fat Brings Early Puberty." *Healthy Weight J /Obesity & Health* 4 (1990):10:73-76; Berg F. "Health Risks of Weight Loss." *Healthy Weight J* 9 (1995):54.

[38] Boodman S. "Girls Beginning Puberty Earlier, Study Finds." *Washington Post,* 4/22/97.

[39] Severson K and M May. "Growing Up Too Fat: Kids Suffer Adult Ailments As More Become Dangerously Obese."

[40] Frisch R, ed., *Adipose Tissue and Reproduction;* Berg F. "High Body Fat Brings Early Puberty;" Berg F. "Health Risks of Weight Loss." *Healthy Weight J* 9 (1995):54.

[41] Thatcher SS. *The Hidden Epidemic.* (Indianapolis: Perspectives Press, 2000.)

[42] Berg F. "Teen Obesity Increases Heart Risk." *Healthy Weight J /Obesity & Health* 7 (1993):2:31.

[43] Berg F. "Obesity in Children and Teens." *Healthy Weight J /International Obesity Newsl* 1 (1986):1-3.

[44] "The Surgeon General's Call to Action to Prevent and Decrease Overweight and Obesity: Health Consequences." Dec 2001.

[45] Fontvieille AM and E Ravussin. "Metabolic Rate and Body Composition Indian and Caucasian Children."

[46] "NIH Strategy Development Workshop for Public Education on Weight and Obesity" (1992)35.

[47] Kotani K et al., "Two Decades of Medical Exams in Japanese Obese Children." *Int J Obes* 21 (1997):912-921.

[48] Conference on the Prevention of Obesity. NIDDK, 1993:64.

[49] Berg F. "Fear of Obesity." *Obesity Newsl* 1 (1986):5-6.

[50] "Bone Mineral Density Reduced in Women With Anorexia Nervosa." *Reuters Health*, Westport, CT (11/20/00); Berg F. "Bone Mass Drops in Anorexia." *Healthy Weight J* 5 (2001):66.

[51] "NHLBI Guidelines: Clinical Guidelines on the Identification, Evaluation, and Treatment of Overweight and Obesity in Adults: The Evidence Report." (Bethesda, MD: National Institutes of Health, National Heart, Lung, and Blood Institute, Preprint June 1998).

[52] Ernsberger P. "Rationale For A Wellness Approach to Obesity." *Healthy Weight J* 14 (2000):20-24, 29.

[53] "Overweight People Progress More Slowly to AIDS." *Healthwatch*, 5/18/2001; Berg F. "Overweight Slows AIDS Progress" *Healthy Weight J* 5 (2001):67.

[54] "NHLBI Guidelines: Clinical Guidelines on the Identification, Evaluation, and Treatment of Overweight and Obesity in Adults: The Evidence Report."

[55] Campos P. "Fat 'Fact' Takes On Life of Its Own." *Rocky Mountain News*, 5/18/02.

[56] McGinnis JM and WH Foege. "Actual Causes of Death in the United States." *JAMA* 270 (1993):18:2207–2212.

[57] "The Surgeon General's Call to Action to Prevent and Decrease Overweight and Obesity: Health Consequences." Dec 2001.

[58] Campos P. "Fat 'Fact' Takes On Life of Its Own."

[59] McGinnis JM and WH Foege. "Actual Causes of Death in The United States."

[60] "Exercise For Older Americans," US Health and Human Services 5/6/02; "HHS Secretary Urges Families to Walk Together On Mother's Day," 5/7/02.

[61] "The Surgeon General's Call to Action to Prevent and Decrease Overweight and Obesity: Measuring Overweight and Obesity," December 2001.

[62] Kassirer JP and M Angell. "Losing Weight—An Ill-Fated New Year's Resolution." *N Engl J Med* 338 (1998):52-54; Berg F. "Medical Journal Questions Obesity Treatment." *Healthy Weight J* 12 (1998):3:36.

[63] Ciliska D et al., "A Review of Weight Loss Interventions For Obese People With Non-Insulin-Dependent Diabetes Mellitus." *Can J Diabetes Care* 19 (1995):2:10-15.

[64] "NHLBI Guidelines: Clinical Guidelines on the Identification, Evaluation, and Treatment of Overweight and Obesity in Adults: The Evidence Report."

[65] Berg F. "Harvard alums risk disease by 'Always' dieting." *Healthy Weight J* 8 (1994):3:52.

[66] Lu H, et al. "Long-term weight cycling in female Wistar rats." *Obes Res* 1995;3:521-530.

[67] Brownell K, and Rodin J. "Medical, metabolic, and psychological effects of weight cycling." *Arch Intern Med 154 (*1994):1325-1330.

[68] Lissner L et al., "Variability of Body Weight and Health Outcomes in the Framingham Population." *New Eng J Med* 324 (1991):1839-44.

Part II

Chapter 3

[1] "Obesity: Preventing and Managing the Global Epidemic." Report of a World Health Organization Consultation on Obesity, Geneva, June 3-5, 1997.

[2] Mayer J. "Genetic Factors in Human Obesity". *Ann NY Acad Sci* 131 (1965):412-421.

[3] Feitosa M et al., "Inheritance of the Waist-to-Hip Ratio In NHLBI-FHS." *Obes Res* 8 (2000):294-301.

[4] Bouchard C et al., "Inheritance of the Amount and Distribution of Human Body Fat." *Int J Obesity* 12 (1988):205-215.

[5] Di Domenico P. "Portion Size: How much is too Much?" *Restaurants USA* 14 (1994):6:18-21; Berg F. "Customers Want Bigger Meals." *Healthy Weight J* 9 (1995):2:26.

[6] "Is Total Fat Consumption Really Decreasing?" *Nutrition Insights 5 (*April 1998), USDA Center for Nutrition Policy and Promotion.

[7] Tataranni PA and E Ravussin. "Energy Metabolism and Obesity," in Stunkard AJ and RI Berkowitz *Handbook of Obesity Treatment* Wadden TA, AJ Stunkard, eds. (New York: Guilford, 2002) 42-71. Stunkard AJ and RI Berkowitz. "The Development of Childhood Obesity," in *Handbook of Obesity Treatment* Wadden TA, AJ Stunkard, eds. (New York: Guilford, 2002) 515-531.

[8] Stock M. "Gluttony and Thermogenesis Tevisited." *I J Obesity* 23 (1999):1105-1117.

[9] Tataranni PA and E Ravussin. "Energy Metabolism and Obesity;" Stunkard AJ and RI Berkowitz. "The Development of Childhood Obesity."

[10] Astrup A et al., "Meta-analysis of Resting Metabolic Rate in Formerly Obese Subjects." *Am J Clin Nutr* 69 (1999): 1117-22.

[11] Wyatt HR et al., "Resting Energy Expenditure in Reduced-obese Subjects in the National Weight Control Registry." *Ibid*: 1189-93.

[12] Astrup A et al., "Meta-analysis of Resting Metabolic Rate in Formerly Obese Subjects."

[13] Ernsberger P. *Personal email communication*, August 6-22, 2002.

[14] Atkin LM and PSW Davies. "Diet Composition and Body Composition in Preschool Children." *Am J Clin Nutr* 72 (2000): 15-21.

[15] Stunkard AJ and RI Berkowitz. "The Development of Childhood Obesity."

[16] Shear CL et al., "Secular Trends of Obesity in Early Life: The Bogalusa Heart Study." *Am J Pub Health* 78 (1988): 75-77.

[17] Berg F. "Fat Intake: Is it Responsible for Rising Obesity Rates. Rethinking Low-fat Advice." *Healthy Weight J* 12 (1998):4:52-58,49,64.

[18] Obarzanek E et al., "Energy Intake and Physical Activity in Relation to Indexes of Body Fat: NHLBI Growth and Health Study" *An J Pub Health* 84 (1994):1761-1767; Morrison J et al., "Mothers in Black and White Households: The NHLBI Growth and Health Study." *An J Pub Health* 84 (1994):1761-1767.

[19] "Is Total Fat Consumption Really Decreasing?"

[20] Miller WC. "Exercise Makes a Difference." *Healthy Weight J* 3 (1988):5; Berg F. "Our Fat Rich, Sugar Rich Diet." *Healthy Weight J* 7 (1987):1-3

[21] Ibid.

[22] Prentice A. "Manipulation of Dietary Fat or Calorie Density?" *Healthy Weight J* 12 (1998):6:87-88.

[23] Willett W. "Is Dietary Fat a Major Determinant of Body Fat?" *Am J Clin Nutr* 67(Suppl) (1998):556-562S.

[24] Williamson D. "School of Public Health Scientists Find US Children Snack More Now." *News Release,* Univeristy of North Carolina at Chapel Hill, 4/6/01.

[25] Schlundt DG et al., "The Role of Breakfast in the Treatment Of Obesity: A Randomized Clinical Trial." *Am J Clin Nutr* 55 (1992):645-51. "Pediatric overweight: Review of the Literature." *Calif Dept of Health Serv.* June 2001:48.

[26] Sutter PM et al., "The Effect of Ethanol on Fat Storage in Healthy Subjects." *N Engl J Med* 326 (1992):983-987.

[27] "Obesity: Preventing And Managing The Global Epidemic." Report of a World Health Organization Consultation on Obesity, Geneva, June 3-5, 1997.

[28] Berg F. "Urging Children to Eat More." *Healthy Weight J/ International Obesity Newsl* 1 (Jan 1987):1-2.

[29] Johnson S and L Birch. "Parents' and Childrens' Adiposity and Eating Style." *Pediatrics* 94 (1994):653-661.

[30] Fisher JO and LL Birch. Parents' Restrictive Feeding Practices are Associated with Young Girls' Negative Self-Evaluation of Eating." *J Am Diet Assoc* 100 (2000):1341-1346.) Berg F. "When Foods are Restricted, Kids Want More." *Healthy Weight J* 15 (2001):4:51-

[31] Berg F. Family Communication. *Healthy Weight J/Obesity & Health* 6 (1992):2:24; Berg F. "Infants and Young Children, Family Tendencies Hold Strong Influence." *Healthy Weight J/Obesity & Health* 3 (1989):12:89,91-92.

[32] Stice E et al., "Naturalistic Weight-Reduction Efforts Prospectively Predict Growth in Relative Weight and Onset of Obesity Among Female Adolescents." *J Consult Clin Psychol.* 67 (1999):967-974.

[33] North American Association for the Study of Obesity, Annual Scientific Meeting. *News Release,* 11/1/00.

[34] Korkeila M et al., "WeightlLoss Attempts and Risk of Major Weight Gain." *Am J Clin Nutr* 70 (1999):965-973.

[35] Rothblum ED. "'I'll Die for the Revolution but Don't Ask Me Not to Diet': Feminism and the Continuing Stigmatization of Obesity," in *Feminist Perspectives on Eating Disorders.* Fallon P, et al., eds. (New York: The Guilford Press, 1994) 64.

[36] Brownell K and J Rodin. "Medical, Metabolic, and Psychological Effects of Weight Cycling." *Arch Intern Med* 154 (1994):1325-1330.

[37] Filer LJ. "Summary of Workshop on Child and Adolescent Obesity." *University Critical Reviews in Food Science and Nutrition* 33 (1993):4/5:287-305.

[38] "Women Have High-Risk Periods for Weight Gain." *MedscapeWire,* 11/6/00.

[39] "Nutrition During Pregnancy." Food and Nutrition Board, National Academy of Sciences Institute of Medicine, 1991; Berg F. "Weight Gain in Pregnancy. *Healthy Weight J/Obesity & Health* 5 (1991):5:72, 75-77.

[40] Ohlin A and S Rossner . et al., "Factors related to body weight changes during and after pregnancy: the Stockholm Pregnancy and Weight Development Study." *Obesity Research* 4 (1996):3:271-276.

[41] "Women Have High-Risk Periods for Weight Gain."

[42] Ravelli ACJ et al., "Obesity at Age 50 in Men and Women Exposed to Famine Prenatally." *Am J Clin Nutr* 70 (1999):811-16.

[43] Phillips DIW and JB Young. "Birth Weight, Climate at Birth and the Risk Of Obesity in Adult Life." *I J Obesity* 24 (2000):281-287.

[44] Filer LJ. "Summary of Workshop on Child and Adolescent Obesity."

[45] Mogan J. *Int J Nurs Stud* 23 (1986):3:255-264.

[46] Stunkard AJ and RI Berkowitz. "The Development of Childhood Obesity."

[47] "Obesity: Preventing and Managing the Global Epidemic." Report of a World Health Organization Consultation on Obesity, Geneva, June 3-5, 1997.

[48] Williamson DF. "Smoking Cessation and Severity of Weight Gain in a National Cohort." *New Engl J Med* 324 (1991):739-745.

[49] Duncan B et al., "Fibrinogen, Other Putative Markers Of Inflammation and Weight Gain in Middle-Aged Adults—The ARIC Study." *Obes Res* 8 (2000):279-286.

[50] Dhurandhar NV et al., "Increased Adiposity in Animals Due to a Human Virus." *I J Obesity* 24 (2000):989-996; Berg F. "Viral Connection to Obesity." *Healthy Weight J* 6 (2000):83.

[51] Stunkard AJ et al., "Direction Of Weight Change In Recurrent Depression. Consistency Across Episodes" *Arch Gen Psychiatry* 47 (1990):857-860.

[52] Berg F. "Prader-Willi: A Defect of Insatiable Appetite." *Healthy Weight J* 10 (1996):6:110-111.

Chapter 4

[53] Booth FW and MV Chakravarthy. "Cost and Consequences of Sedentary Living: New Battleground for an Old Enemy." *President's Council on Physical Fitness and Sports Research Digest* 3 (2002):16:1-8.

[54] Ibid.

[55] Malina RM. "Tracking Physical Activity Across the Lifespan." *President's Council on Physical Fitness and Sports Research Digest* 3 (2001):14:1-8.

[56] Sinha R et al., "Prevalence of Impaired Glucose Tolerance Among Children and Adolescents with Marked Obesity." *N Engl J Med* 346 (2002):802-810; "Nationwide Personal Transportation Survey." *US Dept. Transportation*, Federal Highway Administration, 1997.

[57] Atkin LM and PSW Davies. "Diet Composition and Body Composition in Preschool Children." *Am J Clin Nutr* 72 (2000): 15-21.

[58] "Nationwide Personal Transportation Survey." *US Dept. Transportation*, Federal Highway Administration, 1997.

[59] "Safe Routes to Schools Toolkit," see www.bikeleague.org, also www.bike.cornell.edu/pdf%20files/BicyclingSpokenHereApr2002.pdf.

[60] Tips for implementing CDC school health guidelines: www.eta.aed.org/feature.html

[61] "VSHHS, *Healthy People 2010*."

[62] "Youth Risk Behavior Surveillance—US, 1995." MMWR, CDC, US *Public Health Serv*. 45 (Sep 27,1996):SS-4

[63] Ibid.

[64] NHLBI study. National Heart, Lung, and Blood Institute, NIH, *News Release,* 9/4/02.

[65] Sallis, JF. "Epidemiology of Physical Activity and Fitness and Children and Adolescents." *Crit Rev in Food Sci and Nutr* 33 (1993):4/5:403-408.

[66] NHLBI study. National Heart, Lung, and Blood Institute, NIH, *News Release,* 9/4/02.

[67] Bloomgarden Z. "New Insights in Obesity." *Diabetes Care* 25 (2002):789-795.

[68] Johnson P. "TV Grabs Biggest Share of Kids' Time." *USA Today*, 11/18/99.

[69] "Youth Risk Behavior Surveillance—US, 1995."

[70] "Study Suggests Schools Lacking in Exercise Programs for Children." *News Release,* 2/10/03. National Institutes of Health, NICHD.

[71] Sallis, JF. "Epidemiology of Physical Activity and Fitness and Children and Adolescents." *Crit Rev in Food Sci and Nutr* 33 (1993):4/5:403-408.

[72] President's Council on Physical Fitness and Sports, 1995.

[73] Faith MS et al., "Weight Criticism During Physical Activity, Coping Skills, and Reported Physical Activity in Children." *Pediatrics* 110 (2002):2:e23.

[74] Iverson DC, et al., "The promotion of physical activity in the United States population: the status of programs in medical, worksite, community, and school settings." *Public Health Reports* 100 (1985):2:212.

[75] Petersmarck K. "Shaming Heavy Kids at School." *Healthy Weight J* 13 (1999):45-46.

[76] "Youth Risk Behavior Surveillance—US, 2001. MMWR, CDC, *US Public Health Serv.* 51 (June 28, 2002):SS-4.

[77] Berg F. "Why Teen Girls Drop Out of Sports." *Healthy Weight J/Obesity & Health* 8 (1994):1:13.

[78] Ibid.

[79] Allen JE. "Female Athletes at Risk." *Los Angeles Times*, 6/17/00.

[80] "Why Teen Girls Drop Out of Sports." *Healthy Weight J/Obesity & Health* 8 (1994):1:13; Dwyer E et al., "The Red Flags of Over-Training." *Shape* Apr 1996;122-123.

[81] Costin C. *The Eating Disorder Handbook* (Los Angeles: RGA Publishing Group, 1997)28-44.

[82] Glass J. "Exercise Benefits, Risks, and Precautions for Women." *Healthy Weight J* 13 (1999):4:56.

[83] Berg F. *Health Risks of Weight Loss* (Hettinger, ND: Healthy Weight Network, *1995)* 24-38.

[84] Loosli AR and JS Ruud. "Meatless Diets in Females Athletes: A Red Flag." *The Physician and Sportsmedicine.* 26 (1998):11:45-48,55.

[85] McVoy J. Personal communication, October 1996.

[86] Wright J. *Muscle & Fitness.* (1996):137-138, 221-222.

[87] Dwyer E et al., "The Red Flags of Over-Training." *Shape* Apr 1996;122-123.

[88] *Physical Activity and Health: A report of the Surgeon General* (Atlanta, GA: USHHS, CDC, 1996)72.

[89] "'Obesity Sleuths' Find Chronic Diseases Linked to Behavior Contrary Our DNA." *Science Daily* Bethesda, MD, 7/10/02.

[90] Atkin LM and PSW Davies. "Diet Composition and Body Composition in Preschool Children." *Am J Clin Nutr* 72 (2000): 15-21.

[91] Kelley DE and BH Goodpaster. "Effects Of Physical Activity on Insulin Action and Glucose Tolerance in Obesity." *Medicine and Sci in sports and Exercise* 31 (1999):S619-624.

[92] Whelton SP et al., "Effect of Aerobic Exercise on Blood Pressure." *Ann Internal Med* 136 (2002):493-503.

[93] "NIH Strategy Development Workshop for Public Education on Weight And Obesity." (National Heart, Lung and Blood Institute, 1992)35.

[94] Brodney S et al., "Is it Possible to Be Overweight or Obese and Fit and Healthy?" in *Physical Activity and Obesity*. Bouchard C, ed. (Champaign, IL:

Chapter 5

[95] Fisher JO and LL Birch. "Restricting Access to Palatable Foods Affects Children's Behavioral Response, Food Selection, and Intake." *Am J Clin Nutr* 69 (1999):1264-72.

[96] Ibid. "Restricting Access to Foods and Children's Eating." *Appetite* 32 (1999):405-419.

[97] Ibid. "Parents' Restrictive Feeding Practices are Associated with Young Girls' Negative Self-Evaluation Of Eating." *J Am Diet Assoc* 100 (2000):1341-1346.

[98] Birch LL. "Development of Eating Behaviors Among Children and Adolescents." *Pediatrics Suppl* 101 (1998) 539-549.

[99] *HUGS Club News* (January 1997)6.

[100] Berg F. "Weight-loss Programs for Children and Adolescents." *Healthy Weight J/Obesity & Health* 3 (1989):10:78.

[101] Fabrey W. "Big News" *Radiance*, Fall 1995.

[102] Stice E et al., "Risk Factors for Emergence of Childhood Eating Disturbances." *Int J Eat Disord 25 (1999):375-387.*

[103] Hartung L. "Disordered Eating Patterns in the College Environment." *J Am Diet Assoc* 97 (1997):9:SupplA-60.

[104] Omichinski L. "Teens & Diets: No Weigh." *HUGS International*, www.hugs.com.

[105] McCabe RE et al., "Exploding the Myth: Dieters Eat Less Than Nondieters." *Healthy Weight J* 13 (1999):1:11-13.

[106] Berg F. "Nondiet Movement Gains Strength." *Healthy Weight J/Obesity & Health* 6 (1992):5:85-90.

[107] Young ME. *Diet Breaking: Having it All Without Having to Diet* (London: Hodder and Stoughton, 1995)5-9.

[108] Alexander-Mott L and DB Lumsden. *Understanding Eating Disorders* (Washington, DC: Taylor & Francis, 1994)290.

[109] Levine M. "Prevalence of eating disorders. *Eating Disorders Awareness and Prevention*, Feb 1, 1996. Also, National Association Anorexia Nervosa and Associated Disorders.

[110] "Eating Disorder Awareness Week Kit: Celebrating Our Natural Sizes." National Eating Disorder Information Centre, Toronto ,1996.

[111] "USHHS, *Healthy People 2010.*"

[112] Reiff D and KK Lampson Reiff. *Eating Disorders: Nutrition Therapy in Recovery Process.* (Gaithersburg, MD: Aspen Publishers, 1992)162.

[113] Garner D. "Effects of Starvation on Behavior: Implications For Dieting, Disordered Eating, and Eating Disorders." *Healthy Weight J* 12 (1998):5:68-72.

[114] "Diagnostic Criteria for Eating Disorders." *Diagnostic and Statistical Manual, Fourth Edition* (Washington, DC: American Psychiatric Association, 1994).

[115] Kaplan A and P Garfinkel. *Medical issues and the Eating Disorders* (New York: Brunner/Mazel, 1993).

[116] Ibid.

[117] "Diagnostic Criteria for Eating Disorders."

[118] Friefeld C et al., *The Healthy Weigh.* (Ottawa: Creative Bound, 1993.)

[119] National Eating Disorders Association, 1994. Berg F. *Children and Teens Afraid To Eat* (Hettinger, ND: Healthy Weight Network, 2001.)

[120] Kaplan A and P Garfinkel. *Medical issues and the Eating Disorders.*

[121] "Diagnostic Criteria for Eating Disorders."

[122] Ibid.

Chapter 6

[123] Jacobson MF. "Liquid Candy: How Soft Drinks are Harming America's Health." Washington, DC: *Center for Science in the Public Interest*, 1998.

[124] Byrd-Bredbenner C and D Grasso. "What is Television Trying to Make Children Swallow?" *J Nutr Ed* 32 (2000):187-195.

[125] "New Weapons in the War on Fat." *CBSnews.com,* 6/22/02.

[126] "America's Eating Habits: Changes and Consequences." Washington, DC: USDA, April 1999.

[127] "Dads Action: Tell FDA to Protect Kids from Commercial Exploitation." *Dads and Daughters News Release,* 9/9/02.

[128] "Overexposed: Youth a Target of Alcohol Advertising." *Center on Alcohol Marketing and Youth*, 10/14/02.

[129] *Restaurants USA* 14 (1994):18-21; Berg F. "Customers Want Bigger Meals." *Healthy Weight J* 9 (1995):2:26.

[130] Standard portion sizes may be found at www.nal.usda.gov:8001/py/pmap.htm and are further explained and com-

pared by Ellen Schuster, MS, RD, Oregon State University Extension Specialist, at www.orst.edu/Dept/ehe/nu_n&f_ms.htm

[131] Henneman A. *Sizing Up Food Portion Sizes*. (Lincoln, NE: University of Nebraska Cooperative Extension Service, Oct 2002).

[132] Ibid.

[133] Nestle M. *Food Politics: How the Food Industry Influences Nutrition and Health* (Berkeley and Los Angeles, CA: University of California Press, 2002.)

[134] Rolls B, et al., "Serving Portion Size Influences 5-Year-Old but Not 3-Year-Old Children's Food Intakes." *JADA* 100 (2000):232-234.

[135] Guthrie J et al., "Role of Food Prepared Away from Home in the American Diet: Changes and Consequences." *J Nutr Educ Behav* 34 (2002):140-150.

[136] Zoumas-Morse C et al., "Children's Patterns of Macronutrient Intake and Associations with Restaurant and Home Eating." *J Am Diet Assoc.* 101 (2001):923-925.

[137] "School Health Program Guidelines: Nutrition and the Health of Young People. Public Health Service. The Surgeon General's Report on Nutrition and Health." (Washington, DC: U.S. Department of Health and Human Services, Public Health Service, 1988. DHHS publication no. (PHS) 88-50210)

[138] Williamson D. "School of Public Health Scientists Find US Children Snack More Now." *News Release,* Univeristy of North Carolina at Chapel Hill, 4/6/01.

[139] Ibid.

[140] "Sugar and Sugars." *Food Rap,* 6/7/02. Purdue U School of Consumer and Family Sciences.

[141] "Healthy Eating Index." Center for Nutrition Policy and Promotion, US Department of Agriculture. *1994-96 Continuing Survey of Food Intakes.* July 1998. Update from website accessed January 2003.

[142] Jacobson MF. "Liquid Candy: How Soft Drinks are Harming America's Health."

[143] "What and Where Our Children Eat: 1994 Nationwide Survey Results." *USDA News release,* Apr 18, 1996.

[144] Ibid.

[145] "1994-96 Continuing Survey of Food Intakes for Individuals," *USDA.*

[146] Lino M et al., "The Quality of Young Children's Diets." *Family Economics and Nutrition Review* 14 (2002):52-60.

[147] "Youth Risk Behavior Surveillance—1997." CDC, USDHHS, *Morbidity and Mortality Weekly Report* 8/14/98.

[148] "What and Where Our Children Eat: 1994 Nationwide Survey Results."

[149] Johnson R et al., "The Association Between Noon Beverage Consumption and Diet Quality of School-Age Children." *J Child Nutr & Mngt* 22 (1998):95-100.

[150] Ibid.

[151] Hiza H and S Gerrior. "Using the Interactive Healthy Eating Index to Assess the Quality of College Student's Diets." *Family Economics and Nutrition Review* 14 (2002):3-12.

[152] Lino M et al., "The Quality of Young Children's Diets."

[153] Carlson A et al., "Report Card on the Diet Quality of Children Ages 2 To 9." *Nutrition Insights* 25 (2001).

[154] "America's Eating Habits: Changes and Consequences." (Washington, DC: USDA, April 1999): 104.

[155] Suter P et al., "The Effect of Ethanol on Fat Storage in Healthy Subjects." *N Engl J Med* 326 (1992):983-987.

[156] Kennedy E and J Goldberg. "What are American Children Eating? Implications for Public Policy." *Nutr Rev* 53 (1995):111-126.

[157] Nicklas T. "Dietary Studies of Children: The Bogalusa Heart Study." *JADA* 95 (1995):1127-1133.

[158] "7th European Congress on Obesity, Barcelona, Spain." *I J Obesity* 20 (1996):4:53.

[159] "Healthy Eating Index." Center for Nutrition Policy and Promotion, US Department of Agriculture. *1994-96 Continuing Survey of Food Intakes.*

[160] *Recommended Dietary Allowances,* (Washington, DC: National Academy Press, National Research Center, 1989,)33.

[161] Ibid.

[162] "America's Eating Habits: Changes and Consequences."

[163] Auld G et al., "Perspectives on Intake of Calcium-Rich Foods Among Asian, Hispanic and White Preadoleschent and Adolescent Females." *J Nutr Educ Bhav* 34 (2002):242-251.

[164] Kenyon G. "Dieting May harm Girls' IQ." *Reuters Health*, London, 8/1/00.

[165] Duyff RL. *The American Dietetic Association's Complete Food and Nutrition Guide* (Minneapolis, MN: Chronimed Publishers, 1996)

166 Kretchmer N et al., "The Role of Nutrition in the Development of Normal Cognition." *Am J Clin Nutr* 63 (1996):997S-1001S.

167 Montgomery A. "Cholesterol Tests: How Accurate are They?" *Nutrition Action* (May 1988):4-7.

168 "Youth Risk Behavior Surveillance—US, 1995." MMWR, CDC, US *Public Health Serv.* 45 (Sep 27,1996):SS-4.

169 *Third Report on Nutrition Monitoring In the U.S.* Vol 1 (Sciences Research Office, US Dept of Agriculture, Dec 1995): 135.

170 "USHHS, *Healthy People 2010.*"

171 Kennedy E and J Goldberg. "What Are American Children Eating? Implications for Public Policy." *Nutr Rev* 53 (1995):111-126.

172 Gugliotta G. "Diet Supplement Marketers Target Kids." *Washington Post,* 6/18/00.

173 *Recommended Dietary Allowances,* (Washington, DC: National Academy Press, National Research Center, 1989,)3,32-33.

Chapter 7

174 Jacobson MF. "Liquid Candy: How Soft Drinks are Harming America's Health."

175 "Prevalence and Specifics of District-wide Beverage Contracts in California's Largest School Districts: Findings and Recommendations." Commissioned by the California Endowment, April 2002.

176 "What and Where Our Children Eat: 1994 Nationwide Survey Results." *USDA News release,* Apr 18, 1996.

177 Ibid.

178 Jacobson MF. "Liquid Candy: How Soft Drinks are Harming America's Health."

179 "Public Education: Commercial activities in schools (B-284190)" (Washington, DC: U.S. General Accounting Office, Health, Education, and Human Services Division, September 2000.)

180 Jacobson MF. "Liquid Candy: How Soft Drinks are Harming America's Health."

181 "Prevalence and Specifics of District-wide Beverage Contracts in California's Largest School Districts: Findings and Recommendations."

182 Ludwig DS et al., "Relationship Between Consumption of Sugar-Sweetened Drinks and Childhood Obesity." *The Lancet* 357 (2001):505-508.

[183] "Soft Drinks and School-Age Children." Developed by the North Carolina School Nutrition Action Committee (SNAC), September 2001.

[184] Jacobson MF. "Liquid Candy: How Soft Drinks are Harming America's Health."

[185] "Joint report of the American Dental Association Council on Access, Prevention and Interprofessional Relations and Council on Scientific Affairs to the House of Delegates: Response to Resolution 73H-2000," October 2001.

[186] Jacobson MF. "Liquid Candy: How Soft Drinks are Harming America's Health."

[187] "Joint report of the American Dental Association Council on Access, Prevention and Interprofessional Relations and Council on Scientific Affairs to the House of Delegates: Response to Resolution 73H-2000," October 2001.

[188] "Soft Drinks and Nutrition." Washington, DC: National Soft Drink Association. See http://www.nsda.org/Issues/Partnerships/nutrition.html

[189] Coca-Cola Co. Annual Report, 1997

[190] Thiessen J. *Personal Communication*, 4/2/02.

[191] "Foods Sold in Competition with USDA School Meal Programs: Report to Congress." Washington, DC: Department of Agriculture Food, Nutrition, and Consumer Services, January 12, 2001.

[192] Ibid.

[193] "1994-96 Continuing Survey of Food Intakes for Individuals," *USDA*.

[194] Allensworth D et al., eds. *Schools and Health*. (Washington, DC: Institute of Medicine, National Academy Press, 1997.)

[195] "Prevalence and Specifics of District-wide Beverage Contracts in California's Largest School Districts: Findings and Recommendations."

[196] California State Senate Bill 1520, 5/6/02.

[197] Maryland State Legislature. Senate bill introduced Feb 2001.

[198] "Public Education: Commercial activities in schools (B-284190)"

PART III

Chapter 8

[1] " 'Obesity Sleuths' Find Chronic Diseases Linked to Behavior Contrary Our DNA." *Science Daily* Bethesda, MD, 7/10/02.

[2] Terris M. "Approaches to an Epidemiology of Health." *Am J Pub Health* 65 (1975):1037-1045.

[3] Berg F. "Prevention: The Magic Bullet." *Healthy Weight J* 4 (1990):84.

[4] "Deception and Fraud in The Diet Industry: Hearing Before the Subcommittee on Regulation, Business Opportunities, and Energy of the Committee on Small Business, House Of Representatives." Washington, DC: March 26, 1990.

[5] Ibid.

[6] Vash PD. Testimony at the May 7, 1990, weight loss industry hearings. US House of Representatives Subcommittee on Regulation and Business Opportunities.

[7] Berg F. "FTC Settles Charges Against Weight Loss Companies." *Healthy Weight J* 11 (1997):2:30-31.

[8] Fraser L. *Losing It: America's Obsession with Weight and the Industry that Feeds on It.* (New York: Penguin/Dutton, 1994)103.

[9] "Long-Term Pharmacotherapy in the Management Of Obesity." National Task Force on the Prevention and Treatment of Obesity. *JAMA* 276 (1996):1907-1915; Berg F. "Task Force Advises Against Diet Drugs." *Healthy Weight J* 11 (1997):2:27.

[10] Weintraub M. "Long-Term Weight Control Study." *Clin Pharmacol Ther* 51 (1992):642-646; Weintraub M. "Long-Term Weight Control Study III." Ibid:602-607; Hirsch J. "Comments on Long-Term Weight Loss." *Am J of Clin Nutr* 60 (1994):658-659.

[11] Monson J et al., "The Nurses' Health Study." *New Engl J Med* 333 (1995):677-685; Berg F. "Nurses' Study Garners Headlines." *Healthy Weight J* 10 (1996):1:16-18.

[12] Mundy A. "Weight-Loss Wars: Deaths and a Raft of Lawsuits over Diet Drugs." *U.S. News & World Report*, February 15,1999.

[13] Levitsky D. "Diet Drugs Gain Popularity." *Healthy Weight J* 11 (1997):1:8-12,18.

[14] Berg F. "Diet Pill Controversy Embroils Providers." Ibid:4.

[15] Berg F. What's the Spin?" Ibid:2:24.

[16] Abenhaim L, et al. "Appetite-Suppressant Drugs and the Risk of Primary Pulmonary Hypertension. International Primary Pulmonary Hypertension Study." *N Engl J Med* 335 (1996):609-616.

[17] Manson JE and GA Faich. "Pharmacotheraphy of Obesity—Do the Benefits Outweigh Risks?" *N Engl J Med* 335 (1996):659-660.

[18] Levitsky D. "Diet Drugs Gain Popularity."

[19] Hilts P. "Mix-Up Seen in Backing Obesity Drug.*New York Times* August 29, 1996.

[20] "News Release," FDA, September 15, 1997; Berg F. "Redux, Fen-Phen Withdrawn From Market." *Healthy Weight J* 11 (1997):6:105.

[21] Graham D and L Green. "Further Cases ofValvular Heart Disease Associated with Fenfluramine-Phentermine." *N Engl J Med* 337 (1997):635; Curfman G. "Diet Pills Redux." Ibid:629-630; Berg F. "Heart Valve Damage Implicates Fen-Phen." *Healthy Weight J* 11 (1997):6:107.

[22] Connolly H et al., "Valvular Heart Disease Associated with Fenfluramine-Phentermine." *N Engl J Med* 337 (1997):581-588.

[23] Mundy A. "Weight-Loss Wars: Deaths and a Raft of Lawsuits over Diet Drugs." *U.S. News & World Report,* February 15,1999.

[24] "FDA Approves Sibutramine to Treat Obesity." FDA Talk Paper, November 24, 1997; Berg F. "FDA Approves Meridia." *Healthy Weight J* 12 (1998):2:18.

[25] Thomas PR and JS Stern eds., *Weighing the Options: Criteria for Evaluating Weight-Management Programs* (Washington, DC: National Academy Press, 1995); Berg F. "Review: Weighing the Options." *Healthy Weight J* 9 (1995):3:57-58.

[26] *Choosing a Safe and Successful Weight-Loss Program* (Bethesda, MD: National Institute of Diabetes and Digestive and Kidney Diseases, 1993).

[27] "NHLBI Guidelines: Clinical Guidelines on the Identification, Evaluation, and Treatment of Overweight and Obesity." (Bethesda, MD: National Institutes of Health, National Heart, Lung, and Blood Institute, Preprint June 1998)

[28] Berg F. "NIH Guidelines: An Evaluation." *Healthy Weight J* 13 (1999):2:26-29.

[29] "NHLBI Guidelines: Clinical Guidelines on the Identification, Evaluation, and Treatment of Overweight and Obesity in Adults: The Evidence Report." (Bethesda, MD: National Institutes of Health, National Heart, Lung, and Blood Institute, Preprint June 1998)

[30] Brag G. "In Defense of a Body Mass Index of 25 as the Cut-Off Point for Defining Overweight." *Obesity Res* 6 (1998):6:461-462.

[31] "Obesity: Preventing and Managing The Global Epidemic." Report of a World Health Organization Consultation on Obesity, Geneva, 1998.

[32] Berg F. "American Heart Association Guidelines." *Healthy Weight J* 11 (1997):6:108-110; "American Heart Association Guidelines for Weight Management." *Heart Disease and Stroke* 3 (1994):221-228.

[33] Coulston AM. "Obesity as an Epidemic: Facing the Challenge." *J Am Diet Assoc* 98 (1998):10(S2):16-22.

[34] Hyman FN, Sempos E, et al. "Evidence for Success of Caloric Restriction in Weight Loss and Control." *Ann Int Med* 119 (1993):681-687.

[35] Miller WC. "The History of Dieting and Its Effectiveness." *Healthy Weight J* 11 (1997):2:28-29.

[36] Weiss J. "OHRP Suspends NIH Child Obesity Study." *Washington Post*, 11/7/00.

[37] Hawks SR and JA Gast. "The Ethics of Promoting Weight Loss." *Healthy Weight J* 14 (2000):25-26.

Chapter 9

[38] Carmichael M. "Are We Dying to Be Thin?" *Newsweek*, 3/3/03.

[39] "Methods for Voluntary Weight Loss and Control: Technology Assessment Conference Statement" (Bethesda, MD: National Institutes of Health, March 30-April 1, 1992).

[40] Ibid.

[41] Andres, R., D.C. Muller and J.D. Sorkin. "Long-Term Effects of Change In Body Weight on All-Cause Mortality: A Review." *Ann. Int. Med* 119 (1993):737-743; "Methods for Voluntary Weight Loss and Control: Technology Assessment Conference Statement" (Bethesda, MD: National Institutes of Health, March 30-April 1, 1992)142-146.

[42] Berg F. "Bone Loss with Weight Loss." *Healthy Weight J* 8 (1994):5:85-86; Wardlaw G. "Body Weight Influences Osteoporosis Risk. Ibid 10 (1996):1:8-9, 12.

[43] Allison DB et al., "Weight Loss Increases and Fat Loss Decreases All-Cause Mortality Rate: Results From Two Independent Cohort Studies." *I J Obesity* 23 (1999):603-611.

[44] Garner DM. "Pyschoeducational Principles in the Treatment of Eating Disorders" in *Handbook of Treatment for Eating Disorders*, 2nd edition, eds. Garners DM and PE Garfinkel (New York: Guilford Press, 1997)145-174.

[45] Keys A et al., *The Biology of Human Starvation* (Minneapolis, MN: University of Minnesota Press, 1950).

[46] Kassirer JP and M Angell. "Losing Weight—an Ill-Fated New Year's Resolution." *N Engl J Med* 338 (1998):52-54.

[47] Emmons L. "Dieting and Purging Behavior in High School Students." *J Am Diet Assoc* 92 (1992):3:306-312; "From the Centers for Disease Control. Body-Weight Perceptions and Selected weight-management goals and practices of high school students—United States, 1990." *JAMA* 266 (1991):2811-2812; Berg F. "Harmful Weight loss Practices Widespread Among Adolescents." *HWJ/Obesity & Health* 6 (1992):4:69-72.

[48] Ibid.

[49] Ibid.

[50] Marchessault G. "Weight Perceptions and Practices in American Indian youth." *Healthy Weight J* 13 (1999):71-73, 79.

[51] Emmons L. "Dieting and Purging Behavior in Black and White High School Students;" "From the Centers for Disease Control. Body-Weight Perceptions and Selected weight-management goals and practices of high school students—United States, 1990;" "Harmful Weight loss Practices Widespread Among Adolescents."

[52] Garner D and L Rosen. "Eating Disorders Among Athletes." *J Applied Sport Sci Research* 5 (1991):2:17.

[53] Berg F. "Summer Weight Loss Camps: Not a Quick Fix for Overweight Teens." *Healthy Weight J/Obesity & Health* 4 (1990):3:29.

[54] AP Feb 27, 1991.

[55] Wisconsin Interscholastic Athletic Association, 41 Park Ridge Drive, PO Box 267, Stevens Point, WI 54481; 715-344-8580.

[56] Steen S and S McKinney. "Nutrition Assessment of College Wrestlers." *Phys Sportsmed* 14 (1986):100-116; Berg F. "Weight Cycling: Crash Dieting Drops Metabolism for Wrestlers." *Healthy Weight J/Obesity & Health* 3 (1989):2:1-4; Berg F. *Health Risks of Weight Loss, 52.*

[57] "Hyperthermia and Dehydration-related Deaths in Three Collegiate Wrestlers." *Morbidity and Mortality Weekly Report* 47 (1998):105-108.

[58] Emmons L. "Dieting and Purging Behavior in Black and White High School Students;" "From the Centers for Disease Control. Body-Weight Perceptions and Selected weight-management goals and practices of high school students—United States, 1990;" "Harmful Weight loss Practices Widespread Among Adolescents."

[59] Berg F. "The Case Against PPA." *Healthy Weight J/Obesity & Health* 5 (1991):1:9-12.

[60] "The FDA Issues Warning on Phenylpropanolamine." *Broadcast Media,* 11/6/00.

[61] Berg F. *Weight Loss Quackery and Fads.* (Hettinger, ND: Healthy Weight Network, 1995):16.

[62] Berg F. "Bee Pollen 'Cures' Truckers." *Healthy Weight J/Obesity & Health* 5 (1991):2:30.

[63] Ibid. "Slim Chance Awards." *Healthy Weight J* 11 (1997):1:7.

[64] Baker D and AR Sansone. "Overview of Eating Disorders." NEDO, 1994; Berg F. *Health Risks of Weight Loss.* (Hettinger, ND: Healthy Weight Network, 1995) 90.

[65] Mehler P and K Weiner. "Frequently Asked Medical Questions about Eating Disorder Patients." *Eating Disorders* 2 (1994):1:22-30.

[66] Emmons L. "Dieting and Purging Behavior in Black and White High School Students;" "From the Centers for Disease Control. Body-Weight Perceptions and Selected weight-management goals and practices of high school students—United States, 1990;" "Harmful Weight loss Practices Widespread Among Adolescents."

[67] "Youth Risk Behavior Surveillance—1995."

[68] Kaplan A and P Garfinkel. *Medical Issues and the Eating Disorders* (New York: Brunner/Mazel, 1993)101-122.

[69] Emmons L. "Dieting and Purging Behavior in Black and White High School Students;" "From the Centers for Disease Control. Body-Weight Perceptions and Selected weight-management goals and practices of high school students—United States, 1990;" "Harmful Weight loss Practices Widespread Among Adolescents."

[70] Ibid.

[71] Kaplan A and P Garfinkel. *Medical Issues and the Eating Disorders*, 101-122.

[72] Costin C. *Your Dieting Daughter: Is She Dying for Attention?* (New York: Brunner/Mazel, 1997)63.

[73] "USHHS, *Healthy People 2010*."

[74] Tomeo CA et al., "Weight Concerns, Weight Control Behaviors, and Smoking Initiation." *Pediatrics* 104 (1999):918-924; Berg F. "Youth Smoke to Control Weight. *Healthy Weight J* 5 (2000):67.

[75] NIH National Heart, Lung, and Blood Institute. *News Release*, 5/3/2002.

[76] Berg F. "Smoking Cessation Impacts Weight." *Healthy Weight J*, 10 (1996):2:27-28.

[77] "Quitting Smoking Harder for Women than for Men." *NIH News Release*, 5/1/01.

[78] Berg F. "Smoking Cessation Impacts Weight."

[79] Williamson D et al., "Weight Gain Caused by Cessation of Smoking." *Natl Ctr for Health Statistics* 324 (1993):739-745; Berg F. "Smokers Who Quit Gain to Average." *HWJ/Obesity & Health* 5 (1991):6:92.

[80] Huggins CE. "Girls Who Diet Often May be More Likely to Smoke." *Reuters Health*, New York, 3/1/01.

[81] Berg F. *Weight Loss Quackery and Fads*, 16.

[82] Ibid. See also Questionable features (each issue of *Healthy Weight J*) and Slim Chance Awards (each January).

[83] Thomas PR and JS Stern eds., *Weighing the Options: Criteria for Evaluating Weight-Management Programs* (Washington, DC: National Academy Press, 1995)

[84] "NHLBI Guidelines: Clinical Guidelines on the Identification, Evaluation, and Treatment of Overweight and Obesity." (Bethesda, MD: National Institutes of Health, National Heart, Lung, and Blood Institute, Preprint June 1998)

[85] Berg F. "Linking Gallstones with Weight Loss." *Healthy Weight J/Obesity & Health* 7 (1993):3:45.

[86] Yanovski JA and SZ Yanovski. "Treatment of Pediatric and Adolescent Obesity." *JAMA* 289 (2003):1851-1852.

[87] Wooltorton E. "Obesity Drug Sibutramine: Hypertension and Cardiac Arrhythmias." *Canadian Medical Assoc J* (May 14, 2002):166.

[88] Better than slim chances for orlistat and sibutramine to promote weight loss. Drug & Ther Perspect 2000;15(12):1-6.

[89] FDA discussion paper. "FDA Committee Backs Another Anti-Obesity Drug." FDA, Bethesda, MD 11/24/97; Schwartz J. "FDA Approves new Diet Drug for Obese with Warning about Monitoring." *Washington Post, 11/25/97*: A3.

[90] Berkowitz RI and TA Wadden, et al., "Behavior Therapy and Sibutramine for the Treatment of Adolescent Obesity." *JAMA* 289 (2003):1805-1812.

[91] FDA discussion paper. "FDA Committee Backs Another Anti-Obesity Drug."

[92] Ibid.

[93] Mayer K. *Real Women Don't Diet* (Silver Spring, MD: Bartleby Press, 1993)149.

[94] Hendricks EJ. "New Drugs for Obesity: Drugs in Phase 2 Clinical Trials." *The Bariatrician* (Spring 2002):17-21.

[95] Rand C and A MacGregor. "Adolescents Having Obesity Surgery." *Southern Med J* 87 (1994):12:1208-1213.

[96] Contreras J and D Noonan. "The Diet of Last Resort." *Newsweek,* 5/10/02:46-47.

[97] "Guidance for Treatment of Adult Obesity." *Shape Up America!* 1996.

[98] Berg F. *Women Afraid to Eat.*163-164.

[99] Widemark S. "AMA States that Weight Loss Surgery has Ethical and Scientific Problems in the April 2003 *JAMA*." See www.gastricbypass.netfirms.com.

[100] "Experts Discuss Developments in Bariatric Surgery." *Weight-Control Information Network Notes,* Winter 2002/2003.

[101] Widemark S. "AMA States that Weight Loss Surgery has Ethical and Scientific Problems in the April 2003 JAMA." See www.gastricbypass.netfirms.com.

[102] "NAAFA—Speaks Out Against Weight Loss Surgery for Children." *News Release,* 11/6/02. (Sacramento, CA: National Association to Advance Fat Acceptance.)

[103] Contreras J and D Noonan. "The Diet of Last Resort." *Newsweek,* 6/10/02.

[104] Droze K. "Considering Liposuction?" *eDiets.com online news*, 2/3/00.

[105] Parham E. "Alternative Goals Render Successful Outcomes Likely." *Healthy Weight J/ Obesity & Health* 5 (1991):57-58.

[106] Berg F. *Women Afraid to Eat*, 148.

[107] Berg F. "American Heart Association Guidelines." *Healthy Weight J* 11 (1997):6:108-110; "American Heart Association Guidelines for Weight Management." *Heart Disease and Stroke* 3 (1994):221-228.

[108] Keesey RE. "Physiological Regulation of Body Energy: Implications for Obesity" in *Obesity: Theory and Therapy*, eds. Stunkard AJ and T Wadden (New York: Raven Press, 1993)77-96.

[109] Stunkard AJ. *The Pain of Obesity* (Palo Alto, CA: Bull Publishing, 1976)38-39.

[110] Bennett W and J Gurin. *The Dieter's Dilemma.* (New York: Basic Books, Harper Collins, 1982.)

[111] Keesey RE. "A Set-Point Model of Body Weight Regulation" in *Eating Disorders and Obesity*, eds. Brownell K and C Fairburn C (New York: Guilford Press, 1995)46-50; Garner D. "The Effects of Starvation on Behavior: Implications for Dieting, Disordered Eating, and Eating Disorders." *Healthy Weight J* 12 (1998):5:68-72.

[112] Reiff D. *Personal Communication,* 1996. Reiff D and KK Lampson Reiff. *Eating Disorder: Nutrition Therapy in Recovery Process.* (Gaithersburg, MD: Aspen, 1992)162.

[113] Berg F. "Eating Disorders—Physical and Mental Effects." *Healthy Weight J* 9 (1995):2:27-30.

[114] Estes L et al., "Eating Disorders Prevention." *The Renfrew Perspective* 2 (1996):1:3-5; Fallon P et al., eds. *Feminist Perspectives on Eating Disorders.* (New York: Guilford Press, 1994); Berg F. "Kids Fear Being Fat Early." *HWJ/Obesity & Health* 7 (1993):3:46-47.

[115] Smolak L and M Levine. "Toward an Empirical Basis for Primary Prevention of Eating Problems with Elementary School Children." *Eat Disorders* 2 (1994):4:293-307.

[116] "Position of American Dietetic Association: Nutrition Intervention in Treatment of Anorexia Nervosa, Bulimia Nervosa, Binge Eating." ADA, Chicago.

[117] Berg F. *Women Afraid to Eat,* 148.

[118] Keys A et al. *The Biology of Human Starvation* (Minneapolis, MN: University of Minnesota Press, 1950.)

[119] Berg F. *Women Afraid to Eat,* 136; Reiff D and KK Lampson Reiff. *Eating Disorder: Nutrition Therapy in Recovery Process,* 162.

[120] Turnbull C. *The Mountain People* (New York: Simon & Schuster, 1972.)

[121] Berg F. *Women Afraid to Eat,* 139-140.

[122] Young ME. *Diet Breaking: Having it All Without Having to Diet (*London: Hodder & Stoughton, 1995) 41-42, 56-57.

[123] McCabe RE et al., "Exploding the Myth: Dieting Makes You Happier." *Healthy Weight J* 13 (1999):1:9-10.

Chapter 10

[124] *Parade Magazine,* 11/4/1990.

[125] Davis D. "Fat Phobia and Children: Myth & Reality." *Radiance (Fall 1987)*:29-31.

[126] Berg F. "Weight-Loss Programs for Children and Adolescents." *Healthy Weight J/Obesity & Health* 3 (1989):10:78.

[127] Latner JD and AJ Stunkard. "Getting Worse: The Stigmatization of Obese Children." *Obesity Res* 11 (2003):452-456.

[128] Stunkard AJ and E Stellar eds. *Eating and Its Disorders* (New York: Raven Press, 1984) 175.

[129] Dietz W and NS Scrimshaw. "*Potential Advantages and Disadvantages of Human Obesity*" in *Social Aspects of Obesity*, eds. de Ganne I and NJ Pollock (Luxembourg: Gordon and Breach Publishers, 1995.)

[130] Brownell K and C Fairburn, eds. *Eating Disorders and Obesity* (New York: Guilford Press, 1995) 417-421.

[131] Stunkard A and T Wadden. "Psychopathology and Obesity" in *Human Obesity*, eds. Wurtman RJ and JJ Wurtman (New York: Academy of Sciences, 1987) 57.

[132] "Report on Size Discrimination." Washington DC: NEA, Adopted Oct. 7, 1994.

[133] Johnson CA. *Self-Esteem Comes in All Sizes* (New York: Doubleday, 1995) 8-10.

[134] Erdman CK. *Nothing to Lose: A Guide to Sane Living in a Larger Body* (New York: HarperCollins, 1995.)

[135] McAfee L. "Discrimination in Medical Care." *Healthy Weight J* 11 (1997): 5:84, 96-97.

[136] Cowley G. "Our Bodies, Our Fears." *Newsweek*, 2/24/03.

[137] McAfee L. "Discrimination in Medical Care." *Healthy Weight J* 11 (1997): 5:84, 96-97.

[138] Ibid.

[139] Fontaine K, et al., "Body Weight and Health Care Among Women." *Arch Fam Med* 7 (1998):381-385. Also see editorial: Yanovski S. "Large Patients and Lack of Preventive Health Care."

[140] Winston S. "Children's Cruelty Has an Awful Price." Fort Lauderdale: *Sun Sentinel*, ,Aug 28, 1996, 1E; Sun Sentinel Staff. "Boy Kills Self Over School. Staff Report." *Ibid*, Aug 27, 1996, 3B.

[141] Goodman C. *The Invisible Woman: Confronting Weight Prejudice in America* (Carlsbad, CA: Gurze Books, 1995)ix-xi.

[142] Ibid, 4-6.

[143] Miller W. "Health Promotion Strategies for Obese Patients." *Healthy Weight J* 11 (1997):3:47-51; Barlow CE et al., "Physical Fitness, Mortality and Obesity." *Int J Obesity* 19 (1995):S41-S44.

[144] Burgard D. "Psychological Theory Seeks to Define Obesity." *HWJ/ Obesity & Health* 7 (1993):2:25-27, 37.

PART IV

Chapter 11

[1] "World Health Organization. Basic documents" 39th ed. Geneva: WHO, 1992.

[2] Schaefer T. "Lay Strong Foundation of Faith With Your Children." Wichita, KA: Eagle, 11/5/2002.

[3] Prochaska JO and CC DiClemente. "Towards a Comprehensive Model of Change" in *Treating Addictive Behaviors: Process of Change*. Miller W and N Heather, eds (New York: Plenum, 1986) 3-27.

Chapter 12

[4] Omichinski L. *Personal communication,* 2/25/03.

[5] Satter E. "Feeding with Love and Good Sense: Ellyn Satter's Vision Workshops," Madison, WI: 2003

[6] Omichinski L. "Staying Off the Diet Rollercoaster." (Portage La Prairie, Manitoba: AdviceZone Books, 2000.) See HUGS International

[7] Hawks SR and JA Gast. "The Ethics of Promoting Weight Loss." *Healthy Weight J* 14 (2000):25-26.

[8] Sims EA. "Are there Persons Who are Obese, But Metabolically Healthy?" *Metabolism* 50 (2001):12:1499-1504.

[9] Satter E. *How to Get Your Kid to Eat . . . But Not Too Much* (Palo Alto, CA: Bull Publishing, 1987); see also Satter E. *Child of Mine* (Palo Alto, CA: Bull Publishing, 1983.)

[10] *The Vitality Approach: A guide for leaders. Leader's Kit* (Canada: Health and Welfare, 1994.)

[11] Yanovski SZ et al., "Report of a NIH-CDC Workshop on The Feasibility of Conducting a Clinical Trial on Long Term Health Effects of Weight Loss in Obese Persons." *Am J Clin Nutr* 69 (1999)366-72.

[12] Barlow S ane W Dietz. "Obesity Evaluation and Treatment." 102 *Pediatrics* (1998):1-11.

[13] "USHHS, Healthy People 2010, Conf Edition." See also www.health.gov/healthypeople

[14] Berg F. *Women Afraid to Eat*, 222-223.

[15] Miller W. "Health Promotion Strategies for Obese Patients." *Healthy Weight J* 11 (1997):3:47-51.

PART V

Chapter 13

[1] "Prevention of Child and Adolescent Obesity in Iowa: Iowa Position Paper." (Des Moines, IA: Child and Adolescent Obesity Prevention Task Force, Bureau of Nutrition and WIC, November 2000.)

[2] "The Role of Michigan Schools in Promoting Healthy Weight: A Consensus Paper." (Michigan Dept. of Education, in cooperation with the Michigan Dept. of Community Health, Governor's Council on Physical Fitness, Health & Sports, and the Michigan Fitness Foundation, 2001.)

[3] "Kentucky Children at Risk: The War on Weight, Draft Position Paper." Lt. Governor's Task Force on Childhood Nutrition and Fitness, January 2002.

[4] Slaughter C and D Humphries. Connecticut Obesity Prevention and Control Program (draft). Dept. of Public Health. April 30, 2002.

Chapter 14

[5] Fenton M. "Kids Walk-To-School; A Guide to Promote Walking to School." (Atlanta, GA: Centers for Disease Control and Prevention, Dept Health and Human Services, 2000)3.

[6] Marin County Bicycle Coalition, P.O., Box 35, San Anselmo, Calif. 94979, (415-456-3469)

[7] "Walk Queen Mary." Queen Mary School, 6th Ave and Trimble, Vancouver, British Columbia, Canada. See www.gogreen.com/walk/queenmary.html.

[8] Fenton M. "Kids Walk-To-School; A Guide to Promote Walking to School." See www.cdc.gov/nccdphp/dnpa/kidswalk/pdf/kidswalk.pdf

[9] *Active Start*. National Association for Sport and Physical Education, 2002. www.aahperd.org.

[10] "Physical Activity Surveillance." Division of Nutriton and Physical Activity, Youth Risk Behavior Survey, Centers for Disease Control and Prevention, 2002.

[11] Barker M. "Girls on the Run: Coping with the Crisis of Cultural Pressure." *Healthy Weight J* 12 (1998):89-91.

[12] "Motivating Children In Physical Activity." President's Council on Physical Fitness and Sports *Research Digest* (Sept 2000):1-8.

[13] Johnston G. "New Vision for Exercise." *Healthy Weight J /Obesity & Health* 6 (1992):6:108.

[14] Pivarnik J and K Pfeiffer. "Position Paper: The Importance of Physical Activity for Children and Youth." Michigan Governor's Council on Physical Fitness, Health and Sports, July 2002. See www.michiganfitness.org/reference/youth/PositionPaper.pdf

[15] Take 10! International Life Sciences Institute, Washington DC.

[16] "Project SPARK, Sports Play and Active Recreation for Kids." (Bethesda, MD: National Heart, Lung and Blood Institute, March 1995.)

[17] "Behavioral Risk Factor Surveillance System, 1996 – 1998" Atlanta, CDC. cdc.gov/nccdphp/dnpa/aces.htm; Fenton M. "Kids Walk-To-School; A Guide to Promote Walking to School."

[18] Fenton M. "Kids Walk-To-School; A Guide to Promote Walking to School."

[19] Ibid.

[20] Alvord K. *Divorce Your Car! Ending the Love Affair with the Automobile* (British Columbia, Canada: New Society Publishers, 2000.)

[21] *VERB News*, 5/14/03. See www.verbnow.com and www.cdc.gov/youthcampaign

[22] For more information on CDC Active Community Environments, visit these Web sites: www.iwalktoschool.org; www.walktoschool-usa.org; www.ncrc.nps.gov/rtca/index.htm; www.cdc.gov/nccdphp/dnpa/aces.htm.

[23] Zelasko CJ. "Exercise for Weight Loss: What Are The Facts?" *J Am Diet Assoc* 95 (1995):1414-1417; Berg F. "Avoid Weight Loss Focus." *Healthy Weight J* 10 (1996):4:75.

[24] Tucker M and M Reicks. "Exercise as a Gateway Behavior for Healthful Eating." *J Nutr Educ Behav* 14 (2002):Supl 1:S14-S19.

[25] "Obesity Still on the Rise, New Data Show." *News release*, 10/8/02. Centers for Disease Control and Prevention / National Center for Health Statistics (NCHS) Press

[26] Zelasko CJ. "Exercise for Weight Loss: What Are The Facts?"; Berg F. "Avoid Weight Loss Focus."

[27] Goran M and M Treuth. "Energy Expenditure, Physical Activity, and Obesity in Children." *Pediatric Clinics of North America* 48 (2001):4:931-953.

[28] Miller WC et al., "A Meta-Analysis of the Past 25 Years of Weight Loss Research Using Diet, Exercise Or Diet Plus Exercise Intervention." *Intl J of Obesity* 21 (1997):10:941-947.

[29] "National Heart, Lung, and Blood Institute (NHYLBI). Clinical Guidelines on the Identification, Evaluation, and Treatment of Overweight and Obesity in Adults: The Evidence Report." *Obesity Research* 6 (1998):51S-210S.

[30] Welk GJ and SN Blair. "Physical Activity Protects Against the Health Risks of Obesity." *President's Council on Physical Fitness and Sports Research Digest* 3 (2000):12.

[31] Blair SN and EA Leermakers. "Exercise and Weight Management" in *Handbook of Obesity Treatment* eds. Wadden TA and AJ Stunkard (New York: Guilford Press, 2002) 283-300.

[32] Barlow CE et al., "Physical Fitness, Mortality and Obesity." *Int J Obesity* 19 (1995):Suppl 4:S41-44; Miller W. "Health Promotion Strategies for Obese Patients." *Healthy Weight J* 11 (1997):3:47-51.

[33] Blair SN et al., "Physical Activity, Physical Fitness, and All-Cause Mortality in Women: Do Women Need to Be Active?" *J Am Coll Nutr* 12 (1993):4:368-371.

[34] Tremblay A et al., "Normalization of the Metabolic Profile in Obese Women by Exercise and a Low Fat Diet." *Med Sci Sports Exerc* 23 (1991):1326-1331.

[35] Blair SN and S Bodney. "Effects of Physical Inactivity and Obesity on Morbidity and Mortality: Current Evidence and Research Issues." *Med Sci Sports Exerc* 31 (1999):S646-S662.

[36] Zivanic S et al., "Is There A Direct Connection Between (VO2) Max Increase and Insulin Resistance Decrease after Aerobic Training?" (Brussels, Belgium: Program and abstracts of the 35th Annual Meeting of the European Association for the Study of Diabetes, September 28-October 2, 1999) Abstract 186.

[37] "New Study Proves Physically Fit Children Perform Better Academically." Reston, VA: National Assoc for Sport & Physical Education *News Release*, 12/10/02.

[38] Jaffee L and P Wu. "After-School Activities and Self-Esteem in Adolescent Girls." *Melpomene J* 15 (Summer 1996):2:18-25.

[39] Lower Direct Medical Costs Associated with Physical Activity. See www.cdc.gov/nccdphp/dnpa/press/archive/lower_cost.htm

Chapter 15

[40] Berg F. *Children and Teens Afraid to Eat*, p224.

[41] Kratina K and N King. "Hunger and Satiety: Helping Clients Get In Touch with Body Signals." *Healthy Weight J* 10 (1996):68-71.

[42] Omichiski L. *You Count, Calories Don't* (Portage La Prairie, Manitoba: HUGS International, 1999.)

[43] Siegel K. "Purposeful Eating in the Nondiet Approach." *Healthy Weight J* 11 (1997):52.

[44] Satter E. *How to Get Your Kid to Eat . . . But Not Too Much*, see also Satter. *Child of Mine.*

[45] Buechner J. "Stress-Free Feeding and the Prevention of Obesity Workshops." Atlanta, GA: Children's Healthcare of Atlanta, 2002.

[46] Satter E. "Vision Workshops. Feeding with Love and Good Sense."

[47] Child Nutrition and Health Campaign. *J Am Diet Assoc* (October 1995): entire issue.

[48] Walsh K. "Nutrition for Busy Families I." Fessenden, ND: *Herald-Press*, 3/8/97.

[49] Rolls B. Barnett R. *Volumetrics: Feel Full on Fewer Calories*. (New York: Harper Collins, 2000.)

[50] Fortin S. "Supporting Adolescents with Eating Problems." *National Eating Disorder Information Centre Bulletin* 10 (1995):2:1-4.

[51] Robin AL. *J Am Acadmy of Chi and Adol Psych* (Dec 1999).

[52] Smolak L and MP Levine. "10 Things Parents Can Do to Help Prevent Eating Disorders." Seattle, WA: Eating Disorders Awareness and Prevention, Inc.

[53] Dads and Daughters Inspire, Understand and Support your Daughter, organization. Online www.dadsanddaughters, accessed March 15, 2003.

[54] Steinhausen HS. "The Outcome of Anorexia Nervosa in the 20th Century." *Am J Psychiatry* 159 (2002):1284-1293.

Chapter 16

[55] Byfield C. "The New Paradigm in Action." *Healthy Weight J* 14 (2000):27-28.

[56] Hans C, and D Nelson. "A Parent's Guide to Children's Weight" Iowa State Extension, Iowa State U, Ames, 1994.

[57] Audrey Liddil, State EFNEP Coordinator, Power County, University of Idaho, Bannock County Cooperative Extension System.

[58] Frazao E ed. "America's Eating Habits: Changes and Consequences, 1999. Economic Research Service Report. AIB 750." Washington, DC: US Dept. of Agriculture.

[59] Baron JA et al., "Calcium Supplements for the Prevention of Colorectal Adenomas." *New Engl J of Med* 340 (1998):101-107.

[60] Zemel MBG et al., "Regulation of Adiposity by Dietary Calcium." *Federation of Am. Societies for Experimental Biology (FASEB)* 14 (2000):1132-1138.

[61] Carruth BR, et al. "The Role of Dietary Calcium and Other Nutrients in Moderating Body Fat in Preschool Children." *Int. J Obesity* 25 (2001):559-566.

[62] Layman DK et al., "Reduced Ratio of Dietary Carbohydrate to Protein Improves Body Composition and Blood Lipid Profiles during Weight Loss in Adult Women." *J. Nutr.* 133 (2003):411-417.

[63] Dietary Reference Intakes (Dris) for Energy, Carbohydrate, Fiber, Fat, Fatty Acids, Cholesterol, Protein and Amino Acids, 9/6/2002. Institute of Medicine, National Academies.

[64] Reiner S. "CLA: Does Fat Have a Silver Lining?" *Priorities* 3 (1996):4:42-47.

[65] Belury MA, et al., "Fat That May Benefit Diabetes Reduces Weight, Blood Sugar." *Press Release,* 1/27/03.

[66] Child Nutrition and Health Campaign.

[67] "Breakfast: It Really is the Most Important Meal of the Day." Nutrition News for Health Care Providers. Washington, DC, *Nutrition Realities.* Online at www.enc-online.org, accessed July 12, 2003.

[68] Friesz M. *Food, Fun n' Fitness: Designing Healthy Lifestyles for Our Children* (Boca Raton, FL: Designs for Healthy Lifestyles, 2002.)

[69] Rolls B and R Barnett. *Volumetrics: Feel Full on Fewer Calories.*

[70] Dietary Reference Intakes (Dris) for Energy, Carbohydrate, Fiber, Fat, Fatty Acids, Cholesterol, Protein and Amino Acids.

[71] Rolls B and R Barnett. *Volumetrics: Feel Full on Fewer Calories*, 78.

[72] Fast Food Facts, Lincoln University of Missouri Cooperative Extension, Lincoln, Missouri.

[73] Beck P. "Vegetarian Diets." Fargo, ND: NDSU Extension Service, August 1990.

Chapter 17

[74] Squires S. "Kids Produce in School—Feds Offer Pupils Fruit and Veggie Snacks to Fight Fat, Boost Nutrition." *Washington Post*, 2/17/03.

[75] Moskowitz G. "Candy Man Can't at this Healthy School." *LA Times,*10/9/02.

[76] Kadaba LS. "Some Schools Try To Teach A Better Way To Eat Lunch: Mealtime Seen as Overlooked Side of Education." *Philadelphia Inquirer,* 9/26/02,

[77] "A miracle in Wisconsin Schools." 10/14/02 www.stratiawire.com/article.asp?id=655.

[78] Ibid.

[79] DiMassa CM and E Hayasaki. "LA Schools Set to Can Soda Sales." *LA Times,* 8/25/02; "Schools to End Soda Sales." *LA Times,* 8/28/02.

[80] Hohn E, Director of Child Nutrition Services, Vista Unified School District (760-726-2170 ext. 2217) ehohn@vusd.k12.ca.us; see www.vusd.k12.ca.us.

[81] Minnesota Dental Association. 2236 Marshall Avenue, Suite 200, St. Paul, MN 55104; see www.mndental.org

[82] Uhlman M. "Reading, Writing and 100 Percent Juice." *Philadelphia Inquirer,* 5/18/02.

Chapter 18

[83] *Vitality Leader's Kit,* 1994. Health Services/Promotion, Health and Welfare Canada. Ottawa, Ontario, Canada K1A 1B4 (613-957-8331)

[84] Search Institute, *Healthy Communities, Healthy Youth.* Minneapolis, Minn., www.search-institute.org

[85] *Vitality Leader's Kit.*

Chapter 19

[86] Satter E. "Childhood Obesity Demands New Approaches." *Healthy Weight J / Obesity & Health* 5 (1991):3:42-43.

[87] Ernsberger P. "*Which Path for the Obese Patient?*" From a presentation at Texas Human Nutrition Conference, Feb. 1996, College Station.

[88] Hawks SR and JA Gast. "The Ethics of Promoting Weight Loss." *Healthy Weight J* 14 (2000):25-26.

[89] Sims EA. Are There Persons Who are Obese, but Metabolically Healthy? *Metabolism* 50 (2001):12:1499-1504

[90] Satter E. *How to Get Your Kid to Eat . . . But Not Too Much*; also Satter, *Child of Mine.*

[91] Byfield C. "The New Paradigm in Action." *Healthy Weight J 14* (2000): 27-28.

[92] Ibid.

[93] Ibid.

[94] Cooperman N. "Nutrition Management of Overweight And Obesity" in *Pediatric Manual of Clinical Dietetics* ed. Williams C (Chicago: The American Dietetic Association, 1998.)

[95] Gidding S et al., "Understanding Obesity in Youth, American Heart Association Medical/Scientific Statement." *Circulation* 94 (1996):3383-3387.

[96] Barlow S and W Dietz. "Obesity Evaluation and Treatment: Expert Committee Recommendations." *Pediatrics* 102 (1998):1-11.

[97] Ikeda J and R Mitchell. "Dietary Approaches to the Treatment of the Overweight Pediatric Patient." *Pediatric Clinics of North America* 48 (2001):955-968.

[98] Ibid.

[99] Coulston AM. "Obesity as an Epidemic: Facing The Challenge." *J Am Diet Assoc* 98 (1998):10(S2):16-22.

[100] Recommendations for evaluation are given at the *Pediatrics* website www.pediatrics.org/cgi/content/full/102/3e29.

[101] "Prevention of Child and Adolescent Obesity in Iowa: Iowa Position Paper." (Des Moines, IA: Child and Adolescent Obesity Prevention Task Force, Bureau of Nutrition and WIC, November 2000.)

[102] Satter E. "Childhood Obesity Demands New Approaches."

[103] Barlow S and W Dietz. "Obesity Evaluation and Treatment: Expert Committee Recommendations."

[104] Hofmann AD and DE Greydanus. *Adolescent Medicine* (Stamford, CT: Appleton & Lange, 1997.)

[105] *Developing Adolescents: A Reference for Professionals* (Washington, DC: American Psychological Association, 2002.)

[106] Johnson C. *Self-Esteem Comes in All Sizes: How to be Happy and Healthy at Your Natural Weight.* (Carlsbad, CA: Gurze Books, 2001.)

[107] Berg M et al., "Weight-Related Diseases and Conditions." *Healthy Weight J* 11 (1997):5:89-92.

[108] Story MT et al., "Management of Child and Adolescent Obesity: Attitudes, Barriers, Skills and Training Needs Among Health Care Professionals." *Pediatrics* 110 (2002):210-214.

[109] Ikeda J and L Brainen-Rodriguez. "Physicians Learn to Promote Body Satisfaction." *Healthy Weight J* 13 (1999):3:39-41. The training kit "Children and Weight: What Health Professionals Can Do About It" is available from the Center for Weight and Health, College of Natural Resources, U of California, Berkeley, (510-642-1599) www.cnr.berkeley.edu/cwh)

[110] Latzer Y and S Shatz. "Comprehensive Community Prevention of Disturbed Attitudes to Weight Control: A Three-Level Intervention Program." *Eating Disorders* 7 (1999):3-31.

[111] "Position of American Dietetic Association: Nutrition Intervention in Treatment of Anorexia Nervosa, Bulimia Nervosa, Binge Eating." ADA, Chicago.

[112] Levine MP. "Prevention of Eating Disorders, Eating Problems and Negative Body Image" in *Controlling Eating Disorders with Facts, Advice and Resources,* 2nd edition, ed. Lemberg R (Phoenix, AZ: Oryx Press, 1999) 64-72.

[113] Garner DM et al., "Eating Disorders Screening Program." (San Diego CA: Presentation at the Academy for Eating Disorders 1999 annual meeting, June 11-12, 1999.)

[114] Glass J. "Exercise Benefits, Risks and Precautions For Women." *Healthy Weight J* 13 (1999):58-60.

[115] Miller WC. "Exercise Prescription for the Large Person." Ibid:54-57.

[116] Glass J. "Exercise Benefits, Risks and Precautions For Women."

Chapter 21

[117] Satter E. "Childhood Obesity Demands New Approaches." *Healthy Weight J /Obesity & Health* 5 (1991):3:42-43; Satter E. "Internal Regulation and the Evolution of Normal Growth as the Basis for Prevention of Obesity in Childhood." *J Am Diet Assoc 96* (1996):9: 860-864.

[118] Satter E. "The New Paradigm of Trust." *Healthy Weight J* 6 (1995):110-111.

[119] Hans C, and D Nelson. "A Parent's Guide to Children's Weight" Iowa State Extension, Iowa State U, Ames, 1994.

[120] Fogle C et al., "Eat Right Montana" *Healthy Families 2003*, Montana Department of Public Health and Human Services.

[121] Ikeda J et al., "Two Approaches to Adolescent Weight Reduction." *J Nutr Educ* 14 (1982):90; Ikeda J. *Winning Weight Loss for Teens* (Palo Alto, CA: Bull Publishing, 1989.)

[122] Ikeda J. "Promoting Size Acceptance for Children." *Healthy Weight J* 6 (1995):109.

[123] Hans C, and D Nelson. "A Parent's Guide to Children's Weight" Iowa State Extension, Iowa State U, Ames, 1994.

[124] "Helping Your Overweight Child." Weight-control Information Network, NIDDK.

[125] Johnson S and L Birch. "Parents' Adiposity and Children's Adiposity and Eating Style." *Pediatrics* 94 (1994):653-660.

[126] Hendricks EJ. "New Drugs for Obesity." *Bariatrician* (Summer 2002):16-18.

[127] Tanner L. "Surgery May be a Remedy for Obese Kids." *AP Chicago*, 11/4/02.

[128] Fortin S. "Supporting Adolescents with Eating Problems." *National Eating Disorder Information Centre Bulletin* 10 (1995):2:1-4.

[129] Bruch H. *Eating Disorders: Obesity, Anorexia Nervosa and the Person Within.* (New York: Basic Books, 1973.)

[130] Johnson C. "Self-Esteem Comes in All Sizes." www.largelypositive.com

Tables, Figures, Charts References

Part I

[a] Table 1.1 (p. 7)
All Children by Age (1999–2000 NHANES Study)
Ogden CL et al., "Prevalence and Trends In Overweight Among US Children and Adolescents." *JAMA* 288 (2002): 1728-1732.

[b] Table 2.1 (p. 22)
Tracking Overweight into Adulthood
NIH Strategy Development Workshop for Public Education on Weight and Obesity, National Heart, Lung and Blood Institute, 1992, p. 35.

Part II

[c] Figure 3.1 (p. 47)
Parental Food Prompts
Klesges RC et al., "Parental Influences on Children's Eating Behaviors and Relative Weight." *Journal of Applied Behavior Analysis,* 16 (1983): 371-378; Berg F. "Urging Children to Eat More." *HWJ/International Obesity Newsl* Jan 1987:1:1–2.

[d] **Figure 4.1 (p. 60)**
Decline in Activity with Age
Youth Risk Behavior Surveillance—US, 1995. MMWR, CDC, US Public Health Service 45 (Sep 27,1996):SS-4; US Dept of Health and Human Services. "Physical Activity and Health: A Report of the Surgeon General." Atlanta, GA: USDHHS, CDC, 1996.

[e] **Table 4.2 (p. 73)**
Booth FW and MV Chakravarthy. "Cost and Consequences of Sedentary Living: New Battleground for an Old Enemy." *President's Council on Physical Fitness and Sports Research Digest* 3 (2002):16:1-8.

[f] **Table 5.1 (pp. 82–83)**
Eating Behavior Patterns
Berg F. *Children and Teens Afraid to Eat* (Hettinger, ND: Healthy Weight Network, 2001.)

[g] **Figure 5.2 (p. 86)**
Teens: Find Out What Rules You
Omichinski L. "Teens & Diets: No Weigh." 1995 HUGS International Inc

[h] **Table 6.1 (p. 105)**
Healthy Eating Index
"Healthy Eating Index." Center for Nutrition Policy and Promotion, US Department of Agriculture. *1994–96 Continuing Survey of Food Intakes.* July 1998. Update from Web site accessed January 2003.

[i] **Table 6.2 (p. 106)**
Recommended Calorie Intake
Recommended Dietary Allowances, (Washington, DC: National Academy Press, National Research Center, 1989) 33.

[j] **Figure 6.1 (p. 109)**
Calcium Intake
On chart: "NHANES III, Phase 1, 1988-91"
"Table 129A. Daily Intake of Calcium for Persons 2 Months and Older by Sex and Age, 1988-91." NHANES III, Phase 1, 1988-91. Health/Human Services, US Dept of Agriculture. National Center for Health Statistics, 1997.

[k] **Figure 6.2 (p. 111)**
Iron Intake
"Table 132A. Daily Intake of Iron for Persons 2 Months and Older by Sex and Age, 1988–91." NHANES III, Phase 1, 1988–91. Health/Human Services, US Dept of Agriculture. National Center for Health Statistics, 1997.

[l] **Figure 6.3 (p. 113)**
Calorie Intake
"Table 101A. Daily Intake of Energy in Kilocalories for Females 2 Months and Older, 1988–91." NHANES III, Phase 1, 1988–91. Health/Human Services, US Dept of Agriculture. National Center for Health Statistics, 1997.

[m] **Figure 6.4 (p. 114)**
Median Daily Intake (Girls)
Third Report on Nutrition Monitoring in The US, Vol 1-2, Dec 1995. Life Sciences Research Office, US Health/Human Serv, US Dept of Agriculture. Natl Ctr for Health Statistics, NHANES III. Nov 14, 1994.

[n] **Figure 6.5 (p. 115)**
Median Daily Intake (Boys)
Third Report on Nutrition Monitoring in The US, Vol 1–2, Dec 1995. Life Sciences Research Office, US Health/Human Serv, US Dept of Agriculture. Natl Ctr for Health Statistics, NHANES III. Nov 14, 1994.

Part III

[o] **Figure 9.1 (p. 163)**
Dieting and Purging
"Dieting and Purging Behavior in Black and White High School Students." *J Am Diet Assoc* 92 (1992):3:306-312; "Adolescents Dieting." *JAMA* 266 (1991): 2811-2812; Berg F. "Harmful Weight Loss Practices Widespread among Adolescents." *HWJ/Obesity & Health* 6 (1992):4:69-72.

[p] **Figure 9.2 (p.193)**
Starvation Syndrome
Berg F. *Children and Teens Afraid to Eat* (Hettinger, ND: Healthy Weight Network, 2001.)

Part IV

[q] **Figure 11.1 (p. 211)**
Wellness Wheel
Based on Wellness Wheel model by William Hettler of the National Wellness Institute and the University of Wisconsin at Stevens Point. In Ardell, D.B., *High Level Wellness: An Alternative To Doctors, Drugs, and Disease.* Berkeley, CA: Ten Speed Press, 1986. p. 326. See http://www.gwu.edu/~cade/wellness.htm

[r] **Chart 12.1 (p.225)**
Vitality Chart
The Vitality Approach: A Guide for Leaders. Leader's Kit, 1994. Health Services/Promotion, Health and Welfare Canada. Ottawa, Ontario, Canada K1A 1B4 (613-954-5995) www.hc-sc.gc.ca

[s] **Figure 12.2 (p. 231)**
Health at Any Size Wheel Merged with Wellness Wheel
Berg F. *Children and Teens Afraid To Eat* (Hettinger, ND: Healthy Weight Network, 2001)

Part V

[t] **Table 14.1 (p. 271)**
Iron Sources
Duyff RL, The American Dietetic Association's Complete Food and Nutrition Guide. 1996. P108. Minneapolis: Chronimed Publishing.

[u] **Table 15.1 (p. 293)**
Moving from Weight-Loss Focus to Normalized Eating
Smolak L, Levine MP. 10 Things Parents Can Do. Reprinted with permission from the National Eating Disorders Organization; Tulsa, OK (918-481-4044); Berg F. *Children and Teens Afraid to Eat* (Hettinger, ND: Healthy Weight Network, 2001.)

[v] **Figure 16.1 (p. 298)**
Food Pyramid
Dietary Guidelines for Americans, 1995. US Department of Agriculture and US Department of Health and Human Services.

[w] **Table 16.2 (p. 310)**
Healthy Fast Food Options
Fast Food Facts, Lincoln University of Missouri Cooperative Extension, Lincoln, Missouri.

Index

A

B

C

D

E

F

G

H

I

J

K

L

M

N

O

P

Q

R

S

T

U

V

X

Y